£27.99

Baghelkhand, or the Tigers' Lair

Gurgi *torana* in Rewa Fort.

Baghelkhand, or the Tigers' Lair
Region and Nation in Indian History

D.E.U. Baker

OXFORD
UNIVERSITY PRESS

OXFORD
UNIVERSITY PRESS

YMCA Library Building, Jai Singh Road, New Delhi 110001

Oxford University Press is a department of the University of Oxford. It
furthers the University's objective of excellence in research, scholarship,
and education by publishing worldwide in

Oxford New York
Auckland Cape Town Dar es Salaam Hong Kong Karachi
Kuala Lumpur Madrid Melbourne Mexico City Nairobi
New Delhi Shanghai Taipei Toronto

With offices in
Argentina Austria Brazil Chile Czech Republic France Greece
Guatemala Hungary Italy Japan Poland Portugal Singapore
South Korea Switzerland Thailand Turkey Ukraine Vietnam

Oxford is a registered trade mark of Oxford University Press
in the UK and in certain other countries

Published in India
by Oxford University Press, New Delhi

© Oxford University Press 2007

ISBN-13: 978-0-19-568321-9
ISBN-10: 0-19-568321-8

Typeset in10/12 New Baskerville
by InoSoft Systems, Noida
Printed in India by De-Unique, New Delhi 110 018
Published by Oxford University Press
YMCA Library Building, Jai Singh Road, New Delhi 110001

To
The late Rama Shanker Misra and family, Rewa

Prefatory Note

ॐ

This work is a study of nation-building in India, also described as 'nationalizing' or the process of 'nationalization'. It is not a history of Baghelkhand. The work does indeed study that history over a long period of time to reveal what become clear as the research proceeded, namely a steady encroachment by centralizing states and other external forces on one Indian region and, hence, as I would suggest, on the other regions of the country as well. While this process was not without gaps and regressions, and was certainly not predetermined, it did betoken a movement by a region towards incorporation into a wider entity, the Indian nation state, by 1947.

With nation-building and not a regional history as the focus, readers may find gaps in the sources. To explore the theme of integration I cast as wide a research net as possible. This included a vast range of primary and secondary sources, including references to the geology, geography, archaeology, art, architecture, religion, economics, sociology, and politics of Baghelkhand, sources that are especially to the fore in the first part of the work. In the second part the sources are largely archival, and comprise the records of the Foreign and Political Department, the Political and Home Departments, and Ministry of States; with the associated records of the Central India Agency, the Baghelkhand Agency, and the English files of Rewa State and Vindhya Pradesh to 1956.

The sources used are overwhelmingly in English, as by far the greater part of the archival, library, and research material is in that language. I have used Hindi sources only where these seemed relevant to the type of study being undertaken, and where the services of a translator were readily available. Hindi sources not used include older histories of Rewa that reproduce old-fashioned studies in English; besides recent works by younger scholars on the prehistory and architecture of Baghelkhand published after the research for this work was complete.

Acknowledgements

ᏨᏒᏚᎣ

I researched this book in the following institutions and libraries from 1990, and wish to thank the librarians and staff concerned for their help: in Delhi, the National Archives of India, Nehru Memorial Museum and Library, Central Secretariat Library, Archaeological Survey of India, National Museum, Indian Institute of Agricultural Research, and Jawaharlal Nehru University; in the University of Delhi, Delhi School of Economics, Science Library, and St Stephen's College; in Kolkata, the National Library, National Museum, Anthropological Survey, and Geological Survey of India; in Rewa, the Awadesh Pratap Singh University, Central Library, Maharaja Library, State Archaeology and Museums Department, and Thakur Ranmat Singh College; in Bhopal, the Archives of the Records Section (General Administration Department), Archaeology and Museum Library, Birla Temple Library, and National Archives; in Mumbai, the Bombay Natural History Society; in Nagpur, the Madhya Pradesh Central Record Office and C.P. Club; in Sagar, Sir Hari Singh Gour University; in Jabalpur, Rani Durgawati University and the State Forest Research Institute; and in Indore, Rani Ahilyabai Holkar University and Daly College.

Ravi Singh of New Delhi and G.N. Chaturvedi of Rewa kindly made available their personal libraries. Mrs Sheela Goel helped me to see material in Thakur Ranmat Singh College, Rewa. A.H. Nizami of Rewa gave me his large collection of articles on the history of Baghelkhand.

I also acknowledge with thanks the small grants given by the Indian Council of Historical Research to enable me to begin my research.

All research rests on the support of numerous people, often unknown to the readers, but without whose help research could not proceed. I owe a very deep debt of gratitude to the late Rama Shanker Misra and family of Rewa, who have constantly supported my work, provided information, translated texts, helped me to meet those connected with the research, and arranged trips and visits, besides providing a home base to a historian who did not know Rewa. Others who gave valuable assistance include Probir and Binoo Sen, formerly of Bhopal; Sudhir Ranjan and Nandini Mohanty; and K.M. and Jaya Acharya, both of Bhopal.

Sanjeev Rampallivar, Medical College, Rewa; Devendra Singh, and Ajay Singh of the Department of Ancient History, Awadesh Pratap Singh University, both of Rewa; N. Raghunathan of the Economics Department, St Stephen's College, Delhi, and P.S. Dwivedi, formerly head of the History Department of St Stephen's College, accompanied me on various trips and excursions; and Raghu also took the photographs that adorn this book. Chattarsal Singh of Nagod, Uma Kumari, and Krishna gave generous hospitality and made possible several visits to Bhumara; Gaurav Masaldan of the Excise Department helped with accommodation and transport in Satna; and Gambhir Singhji of Sohagpur and family helped me to see the Kalachuri remains at Singhpur and Antara, and took me to Amarkantak. Brajeshwar Banerjee, an old student, and his family enabled me to stay at and explore Amarkantak.

Academically, Nayanjot Lahiri, Professor, History Department, University of Delhi and an old student, rescued my first chapter from the errors of a non-archaeologist; P.S. Dwivedi made detailed corrections and suggestions for most chapters; and J.N. Tiwari, formerly of Banaras Hindu University, read and commented on the early parts of the book. Upinder Singh, formerly head of the History Department, St Stephen's College, lent books, corrected mistakes, and answered my many queries relating to ancient India.

Contents

CRISO

Abbreviations

ॐ

Journals

AA	*Artibus Asiae*
AI	*Ancient India*
CR	*Calcutta Review*
EI	*Epigraphia Indica*
E&W	*East and West*
GRI	*Geographical Review of India*
IAR	*Indian Archaeology: A Review*
IESHR	*Indian Economic and Social History Review*
IF	*Indian Forester*
IGJ	*Indian Geographical Journal*
IHRC	*Indian Historical Records Commission*
IICQ	*India International Centre Quarterly*
JAS	*Journal of Asian Studies*
JASB	*Journal of the Asiatic Society of Bengal*
JGSI	*Journal of the Geological Society of India*
JIH	*Journal of Indian History*
JMPIP	*Journal of the Madhya Pradesh Itihas Parishad*
JVU	*Journal of Vikram University*
ME	*Man and Environment*
MGSI	*Memoirs of the Geological Survey of India*
MI	*Man in India*
NGJI	*National Geographic Journal of India*
OA	*Oriental Art*
PP	*Prachya Pratibha*

RASB	*Royal Asiatic Society of Bengal*
SA	*South Asia*
SAS	*South Asian Studies*

GOVERNMENT

A/B/C	A/B/C proceedings
ASI	Archaeological Survey of India
B	Bundle
BA	Baghelkhand Agency
BC	Bundle Correspondence
BD	By (order of) Darbar
Bgkd	Baghelkhand
BOB	Bank of Baghelkhand
BOI	Bank of India
Bukd	Bundelkhand
CIA	Central India Agency
CP	Central Provinces
CRO	Commonwealth Reforms Office
D	Deposit (file category)
DG	District Gazetteer
E	Establishment
F	Foreign Department
Fam	Famine
FP	Foreign and Political Department
FR 1/Feb.	Fortnightly Report for the first half of February
FS	Foreign and Secret Department
G	General
GOB	Government of Bengal
GOI	Government of India
HP	Home Political Department
I	Internal
IO	India Office
ISFEC	Indian States Financial Enquiry Committee
KW	Keep With
MP	Madhya Pradesh
MPCC	Mahakoshal Provincial Congress Committee
M/S	Ministry of States
P	Political
P&R	Political and Reforms

PW(D)	Public Works (Department)
RDO	Rewa Darbar Office
Rev	Revenue Department
RS	Rewa State
RSA	*Rewa State Administration Report*
S	Secret
SNT	Sagar and Narmada Territories
Sup	Superintendentcy
Supp	Supplement(ary)
VPR	Vindhya Pradesh Records
VP Admin	*Vindhya Pradesh Administration Reports*

OFFICIALS

AGGCI	Agent for the Governor-General in Central India
CC	Chief Commissioner
CGS	Chief of General Staff
CIO	Central Intelligence Officer
CIT	Commissioner, Income Tax
CM	Chief Minister
CMO	Chief Medical Officer
CR	Crown Representative
CSec	Chief Secretary
DSec	Deputy Secretary
FA	First Assistant
FSec	Foreign Secretary
GG	Governor–General
HSec	Home Secretary
JSec	Joint Secretary
MSec	Military Secretary
O/	Officiating/
PA	Political Agent
PMin	Political Minister
Polad	Political Adviser to Viceroy
PSec	Political Secretary
PrSec/PS	Private Secretary
PSV	Private Secretary to Viceroy
RCN/R	Regional Commissioner, Navgaon/Rewa
Res	Resident
SOS	Secretary of State
SP	Superintendent of Police

TEXTS, DOCUMENTS

AICC P	All India Congress Committee Papers
CII	*Corpus Inscriptionum Indicarum*
CRR	Crown Representative Records
DNB	*Dictionary of National Biography*
IG	*Imperial Gazetteer*
ISC	Indian States Committee
JDR	Jubbulpore Divisional Records
LSI	*Linguistic Survey of India*
NRR	Nagpur Residency Records
RCE	*Rewa Commission of Enquiry*
RMCI	*Representative Men of Central India*
RTC	Round Table Conference
Sleeman P	Papers of W.H. Sleeman

Illustrations

ᆭ

Figures

Maps

Plates

Introduction

CR§O

The nationalization of the regions is one of the epic themes of Indian history. Here, the process is seen as the outcome of a dialogue between the region of Baghelkhand and centralizing states, located mostly in northern India, and other external forces such as migration. Events surrounding this dialogue assumed a complex and even paradoxical shape: on the one hand external states and forces brought new political, social, and economic influences to bear on the region, giving it a distinct identity; on the other, they also created political, economic, and social commonalities with other regions subject to the same influences or from where migration developed. The influence of external states and myriad commonalities advanced the nationalizing process to a point where it led to the region's incorporation in the Indian nation in the twentieth century.

The study traces the above dialogue from prehistory up to 1956. During the prehistoric period the Indian subcontinent achieved a remarkable degree of unity, as a broadly similar chain of human evolution developed more or less simultaneously across India. As part of this evolution humans in a number of nuclear zones throughout the subcontinent transferred from hunting and gathering to the food production and herding of the neolithic culture. In some places, too, their descendants and others used iron, ushering in India's protohistory.

The unity of prehistoric India disappeared with the onset of the historical period. The growing complexities of political, social, and economic life created differing identities in the regions as well as differential rates of development between them. Yet at the same time the similar processes at work in the different regions slowly, even haltingly, set in motion the creation of a national whole that forms the chief interest of this work. It is thus possible to see India as a congeries of regions, to some degree distinct in themselves, yet sewn together over the centuries to form a nation state.

In traversing the continuum between nation and region, the study seeks to define more exactly the notion of region, which is often used so loosely as to have no specific meaning. Here region is discussed as a distinctive space defined by its geology and resulting physiography, a particular social structure, crop patterns, cultural profile, language, and political history. Together these give a region a distinct identity vis-à-vis other regions in the subcontinent.

Region has a slightly different focus in the two parts into which the text is divided. In the first part the region comprises Baghelkhand as a whole. In the second the regional focus is on Rewa state: Baghelkhand's foremost political formation covering most of its area, but shorn of the smaller princely states conquered by the Bundelas and only integrated with the region at Independence.[1]

I am aware that using region when examining, say, prehistoric and early historic events and peoples is to impose an artificial geographical boundary on influences that knew no such boundaries. I do so, however, in order to build up the notion of regional identity that only becomes more explicit over the course of time. Similarly, I use words such as India, Rewa district, Teonthar *tahsil*, or the Parasmania plateau to locate areas throughout the course of the study, regardless of the fact that such places may have had other names in the course of time, or perhaps no name that has come down to us. This has been done to help contemporary readers familiar with these names to locate areas in the text at any time, whether in prehistory or the historical period.

The word 'state' appears freely in the text—as in central or regional states, the Mughal, Kalachuri or Baghel States. In using this word I refer to political formations from the first millennium BC on that brought a degree of power—military, revenue, administrative, cultural, and religious—to bear on the people of a given territory, and were not merely agencies subduing a tract to acquire booty or extract revenue. However, though the regional and central states are the two poles under discussion, the study focuses on integrating the regional state, and the centralizing states remain more of a counterfoil to the main interest of the work.[2]

The use of the phrase 'central' or 'centralizing state' is somewhat akin to the modern usage whereby the national government is also known as the central government, or more familiarly as 'the centre'. Centralizing is thus seen here as an act tending to focus power in a supra-regional state that seeks to control, invade, subject, or utilize in some way the people and resources of a region or regions.

This study seeks to widen the understanding of nationalism and nation beyond the European concept of the nineteenth and twentieth centuries. One may ask what was it that the Congress movement cemented into a political whole? How was it able to do it? I believe that that movement could only succeed by using the components of an integrative process that over hundreds of years criss-crossed the country with myriad social and economic commonalities and centralizing political influences—over and above regional particularities—in the manner discussed here for one region.

I also question the application of certain post-colonial or postmodern theories to Baghelkhand today. While there is a value in analysing the texts produced by British colonizers and the colonized, this is not the only way of studying the influence of the colonial process on a society. As this study shows, Baghelkhand was colonized by prehistoric peoples, the Mauryas, Guptas, Kalachuris, Baghels, Mughals, and others long before British traders and officials arrived in India. Therefore an attempt is made here to assess the social, economic and political impact of various colonialisms, rather than merely that of Britain, whose very different colonialism was part of worldwide capitalism. I explore these other colonalisms using a variety of 'texts': the provenance of prehistory, architecture, sculpture, painting, inscriptions and artefacts, in addition to looking at traditional political, social and economic institutions still current in the region.

While there can be no doubt that British colonialism left an impact on Baghelkhand (though it was not a part of so-called British India), it is my view that social, economic, and political changes resulting from colonialism have not basically altered the outlook and structure of society in Baghelkhand. Brahmans were sufficiently important to receive land grants and religious commissions in the fifth century; Kayasthas and Vaishyas are named in the Kalachuri period; the word Rajput was known from around 1000 AD; and artisans and the lower social communities, including the hill and forest people, were identifiable at various times in the first millennium AD. While not subscribing to the notion of the unchanging peasant or village, I note that this tiered social map with its accompanying ideology and behaviour remains largely in place in Baghelkhand today. It is my observation, too, that there remains an enduring inner life among the rural masses of north-eastern Madhya Pradesh that differs little from that of their forbears of previous centuries.

Notes

1. These included the petty states of Maihar, Jaso, Nagod, Sohawal, and others.
2. The British Government of India receives greater exposure in sections dealing with the nineteenth and twentieth centuries.

PART A

THE REGION: BAGHELKHAND

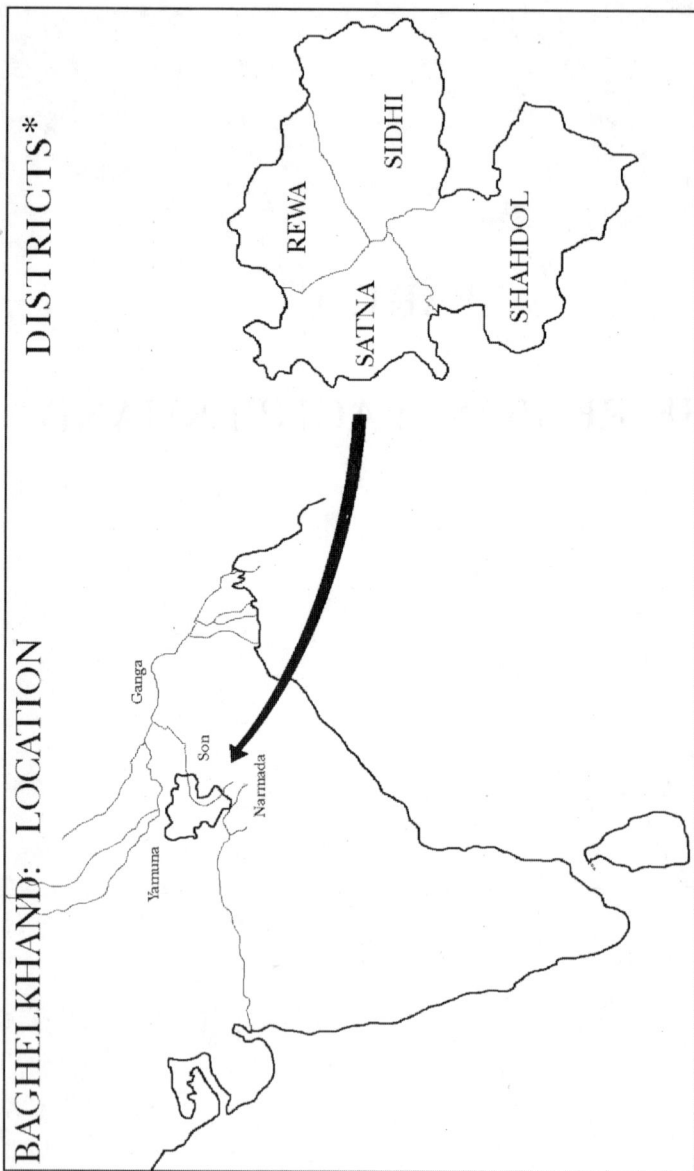

BAGHELKHAND: LOCATION

DISTRICTS*

REWA

SATNA

SIDHI

SHAHDOL

Yamuna

Ganga

Son

Narmada

Map 1

*Since this study was undertaken, Shahdol District has been subdivided. In this text Shahdol refers to the undivided district of that name.

1

The Region and its First Inhabitants to *c.* 800 BC*

⚭

During the prehistoric period what were to become the distinct regions of the Indian subcontinent existed only as physiographic spaces with their respective variations in weather and appropriate fauna and flora. A common process of human evolution beginning about 100,000 BC and continuing till the advent of iron unified these spaces and their inhabitants, as roughly similar phases of human development occurred throughout India. Even the transfer from the hunting and gathering of the upper palaeolithic people to the food gathering and herding of the neolithic dwellers took place in a number of nuclear zones spread over the subcontinent. Let us examine this process of human evolution as it occurred in the region of Baghelkhand—the first of many integrative experiences that united the region with others in the subcontinent subject to broadly similar influences.

*I am very deeply indebted to Nayanjot Lahiri, an old student of the College and now Professor, History Department, University of Delhi, for her advice and the referral of a number of articles on the archaeological sections of this chapter. I am also grateful for the many corrections and suggestions made by P.S. Dwivedi, formerly head of the History Department, St Stephen's College, and by J.N. Tiwari, formerly of Benares Hindu University.

I

DEFINING THE REGION

Like most countries India is a congeries of regions sewn together into a nation state. In the case of some regions the process of integration seems complete; but in others it remains incomplete and even in doubt. Moreover, some Indian provinces or states contain regions that seek to leave these composite entities and establish their own place in the nation. This text aims to describe the dialogue of one Indian region, Baghelkhand, with various centralizing states and influences that concluded with its being incorporated into the Indian nation in 1947, and forming part of the Hindi-speaking State of Madhya Pradesh from 1956.

In this text the word region is used to describe an area that is somewhat distinct from other such areas in the subcontinent, though it also shared important characteristics with them. A region's name frequently conjures up an identity that is peculiar to it. The region of this study, Baghelkhand, comprises north-eastern Madhya Pradesh. Baghelkhand has two meanings: most immediately it is the land of the Baghels, a Rajput clan holding the *jagir* of Vaghela in Gujarat, which established itself in the region from the fourteenth century. However, the word Baghel itself derives from *bagh* or tiger, such that the Baghel kings claimed for themselves the attributes of the tiger, and by the nineteenth century rampant tigers formed part of their state's emblem. Baghelkhand thus also means an abode of tigers.

Though the word Baghelkhand came into regular use as late as the nineteenth century, even now it is known to few outside the region. In earlier times Baghelkhand had other names which have dropped out of use, and now refer only to a particular phase of its history. Thus Kalachuri Rajputs knew it as part of their kingdom of Dahala, while the Mughals described it as Bhatta or Bhatha, or Bhatha Gahora after an early fort of the Baghels. For some time they also knew it as Bandhav after the fort at Bandhavgarh. From the seventeenth century the area seems to have been known as Rewa State, though by 1800 Baghelkhand was no longer a single political entity, but also contained the petty states conquered by Panna, Rewa remaining by far the largest state in the region. The last ruler but one in the colonial period, Maharaja Gulab Singh, frequently used his clan name for the area, and for the sake of simplicity it is this name that is used in this work for the region at any point in its prehistory or history.

A region is also defined physiographically. At base, Baghelkhand forms a catchment area for two major rivers, the Tamasa or Tons and the Son, both flowing into the Ganga. The Son divides the region in half, and is flanked on either side by plateau or hilly areas. These are the Rewa-Satna plateau to the north, and the so-called Baghelkhand plateau to the south. The former's southern limits are defined by the Kaimur hills, a striking escarpment of the Vindhyan range which forms the region's backbone, and follows the line of the Son river. The more complex Baghelkhand plateau[1] below the Son forms one of the eastern plateaus of the Indian peninsula.

Baghelkhand's location emphasises its separateness within the subcontinental landscape. The region occupies a zone of disengagement between the Gangetic plain and the Deccan plateau, marked off from the former by the northern scarp of the Rewa plateau and from the latter by the Amarkantak plateau and the Maikal hills. The valley of the Ken and the Bhanrer plateau define the region's western border, and the Hazari Bagh and Chhota Nagpur plateaus its eastern. This isolation coupled with its often-difficult terrain created an 'escape in space'[2], a catchment area for wandering peoples from which they did not or could not easily emerge. These same factors posed formidable barriers to any large-scale military invasion of the area.

Certain characteristics of culture and society distinguish Baghelkhand from other regions. Over the centuries expanding states or migrating peoples deposited cultural layers that shaped the region's identity. Although a particular layer may have withered or even disappeared, names, sites, artefacts, rock art, cave shelters, inscriptions, *stupas*, styles of sculpture and architecture, or even merely a memory, remain to mark its passage and to provide the region with a unique cultural profile that bears testimony to local as well as external influences.

Despite these particularities, the folk ways of people in Baghelkhand have much in common with those in adjoining parts of central and northern India, illustrative of the integrative process at work. From the first millennium BC rulers and migrants brought the social systems, beliefs, values, and festivals that crystallized into the way of life common amongst Hindus today. Migrating hill and forest people similarly introduced their cultural forms of myth, song, dance, language, and religious observance, which to some degree remain and to some extent have been modified by the dominant culture.

The region also became home to the distinctive dialect of Bagheli. The utterance of prehistory all but disappeared; and even the languages of the hill and forest communities—the Mundari of the Kols and the Dravidian speech of the Gonds—largely gave way to Bagheli, the mix of Awadhi, Kanauji, and Bundeli[3] introduced by migrants which, with its accompanying songs, sayings and, in modern times, its literature, holds a distinctive place in the identity of Baghelkhand.

Though regional society conforms to the caste structure of society at large, immigration has given it a distinctive shape.[4] Brahmans and Rajputs, especially Baghels, together with merchant communities dominate the upper social levels. Typical north and central Indian agricultural communities constitute the middle levels; with artisan and other occupational castes and the hill and forest people forming the lower levels. The distinctive feature of Baghelkhand society is the large place occupied by the scheduled castes and hill and forest communities in relation to the remaining population.

At times centralizing states, mostly in northern India, left a wider than regional impress on Baghelkhand as they sought to turn it to their advantage. Prominent among these were the Mauryan State, the Sunga Kingdom, the Gupta Empire, and the empire of Harshavardhana. Early Muslim states affected the region principally by compelling people from other areas to take refuge there. Mughal governments also pressed the region, though it did not regularly pay tribute or offer troops to their armies. Of all the centralizing states British India wielded the greatest influence in Baghelkhand, incorporating it more closely into a national political economy, a process completed by successive governments of independent India after 1947.

Between these centralizing thrusts and in dialogue with them, local states influenced the region's history and so its identity. The first such state was that of the Kalachuri Rajputs who included much of Baghelkhand in their Kingdom of Dahala. The other was the Rewa State of the Baghels, which succeeded Dahala, rising from the fourteenth century to control large areas in Baghelkhand, Bundelkhand, Mirzapur, and the Gangetic lowlands. Encroachments by the Mughal centre or regional rivals from the late sixteenth century on reduced the state's influence and size, until it stabilized under the centralizing politics of British rule from the nineteenth century.

II

THE REGIONAL ENVIRONMENT

Geology

As Baghelkhand's physiography has shaped its history, it requires some explanation. The region's build has evolved from its geological history–a complex process, there being scarcely a rock formation of the subcontinent that is not found there. At base Baghelkhand is Archaean, a rock formation predominantly igneous and metamorphic more then two and a half billion years old. In places more recent formations have overlaid the Archaean system, but where uplifted by tectonic surges it has risen to the surface as in the Maikal hills. Such rocks contain important minerals and perhaps the earliest traces of biological activity.

The subsequent Vindhyan system is more visible. Millions of years ago the region lay beneath an inland sea, formed when the waters of the Aravallis and other highlands poured their sediments into an ancient syncline. In places about ten metres deep, the sea was fringed by a coastline featuring dunes and sand bars created by tidal currents. Tectonic disturbances with after-pulsations and faulting forced these sediments upwards; then drainage, probably in a north–south direction, denuded the sediments and their scarps retreated, with peneplains forming possibly due to subsidence. This sequence produced the bold profile of the Kaimur escarpment and parts of southern Baghelkhand with its large deposits of silt and sandstone, and sandstone hills. On one such hill stands the ancient fort of Bandhavgarh.

During another round of tectonic disturbances about 350 million years ago faulting occurred in the denuded and subsided Vindhyan system. As a result 'great land masses [sank] ...bodily between parallel fractures, and in the areas thus depressed a series of land or fresh-water deposits have been preserved', comprising the detritus of previous formations.[5] As the area of deposition lay south of the Vindhyas, it is likely that drainage continued to be in that direction. Changes in temperature and pressure subjected the resulting sedimentary material to faulting, folding, and intrusion, after which a period of calm ensued. This rock formation is known as the Gondwana system.

The distribution of Gondwana rocks in Baghelkhand is overwhelming. The basins of the Són and its tributary the Chhoti Mahanadi have a thick sedimentary fill from the late carboniferous period, while continuous outcrops occur from the Son south in sandstones, shales, clay, and extensive coal deposits, the latter deriving from the contemporary development of vegetation that was home to the region's early faunal life.

Further erosion of the Gondwana landscape gave way at the end of the Triassic Age to more volcanic activity, accompanied by successive lava flows which were to form the rock and soil system known as Deccan Trap. As a prelude further marine action deposited the Lameta formation of limestone with its subordinate sandstone and clays, as in Shahdol.[6] However, gigantic outpourings of lava overwhelmed these beds together with some older eroded surfaces as they gushed through fissures such as the dykes in the Gondwanas near Rewa, or flowed across country from distant points. The resulting Trap formation is extensive on the Rewa plateau, where it rests on Gondwana and Archaean rocks. It can also be seen in the laterite of the Rewa hills, in the basins of Singrauli and Sohagpur, and in the basaltic Trap covering the Maikal plateau. As earlier, erosion set in once the lava flows ceased.

Baghelkhand took final shape during the Pleistocene period, which began about 2.5 million years ago and closed with the brief phase of the Holocene. In the temperate zones of the northern hemisphere successive rounds of glaciation and retreat of the ice sheets marked the Pleistocene, resulting in fluctuating levels of the sea and other water bodies. Further south, these events had their counterparts in pluvial and sub-pluvial phases. Thus, as the last ice age retreated, warmer climates set in in central India, bringing higher rainfall and changes in animal and plant life. There, strongly flowing rivers deposited their alluvium of sandstone, silt, boulder conglomerates, and decomposed bedrock in thick layers in river valleys, those in the Tons valley being up to 45 metres thick. Geologists believe that the river flows reversed direction during this period, possibly due to tectonic disturbances.

During the Holocene from about 10,000 years ago a tropical climate developed in Baghelkhand as monsoon rains increased, accompanied by changes in vegetation. The greater run-off cut down into the Pleistocene sediments of the river courses, incising and deepening channels, and even creating gorges. The erosion exposed successive Pleistocene layers, revealing to later investigators evidence of the first human life in Baghelkhand.

Baghelkhand's geological formations weathered to produce distinctive soil regimes that have an important bearing on its economy. North of the Kaimur, soils are mainly sedimentary from the weathering of sandstone and shale mixed with other elements. Rewa and Satna have extensive areas of alluvial soil, that of Teonthar in the Gangetic lowlands being exceptionally fertile. Kaimuri soil is generally gravelly and poor, but the Son valley below contains rich loams and clays. Apart from pockets of Deccan Trap and black loam, Sidhi's soils are generally poor with stretches of sand. Shahdol has two main soil types: red, sandy soil mostly of Archaean origin, and the black soil of west Shahdol and parts of the Maikal hills formed from weathered Deccan Trap.

Physiography and Drainage

As we have seen Baghelkhand comprises two plateau or hilly regions divided by the Son furrow and the accompanying escarpment of the Kaimur. In Rewa district the plateau rises to about 300 metres, and is marked by low hills. A scarp defines the plateau's northern edge, while on the south it slopes upwards to culminate in the Kaimur. In Satna the plateau is studded with hills or denuded ranges that converge into the Panna hills on the north (among which stands the sentinel of Kalinjara); to the west it rises into the rugged Bhanrer ranges, and on the south it forms the Parasmania plateau.

The Kaimur scarp of the Vindhyas crosses Baghelkhand obliquely, terminating at Sasaram in Bihar. From five to six kilometres broad, the average height of the Kaimur is about 380 metres, rising in places to over 500 metres. Uneven everywhere, the scarp's southern face hangs like a great wall over the Son valley, its lower levels 'broken by ravines that...[run] surging' to its base.[7] This formidable terrain makes the scarp passable in only a few places.

The plateau south of the Son river presents an even more dramatic appearance than its northern counterpart. The plateau's

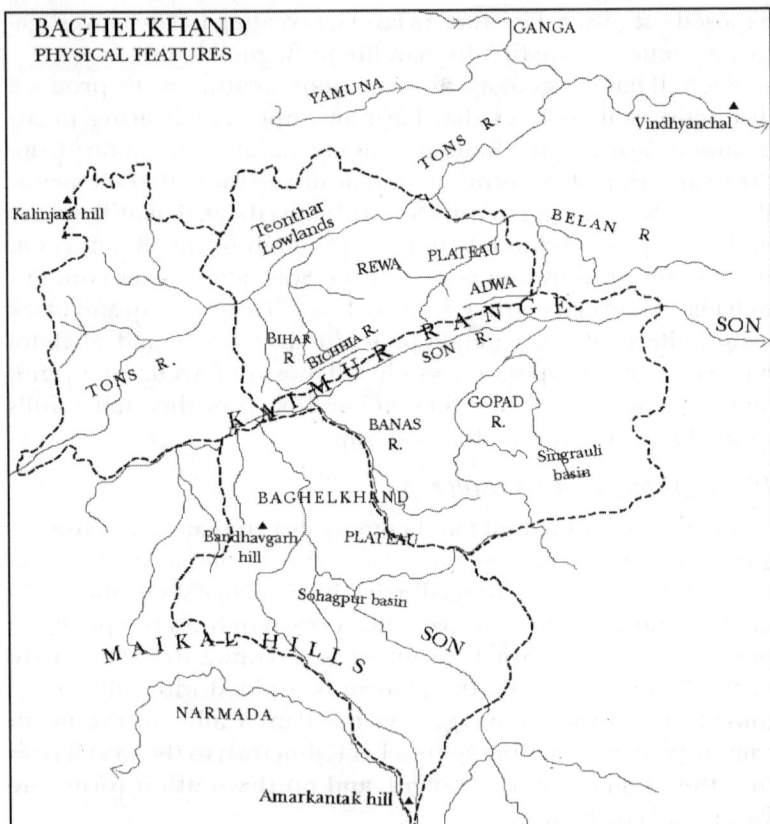

BAGHELKHAND
PHYSICAL FEATURES

GANGA

YAMUNA

TONS R.

Vindhyanchal

Kalinjara hill

Teonthar
Lowlands

BELAN R

REWA

PLATEAU

ADWA

BIHAR R

BICHHIA R.

SON R.

KAIMUR RANGE

SON

TONS R.

BANAS R.

GOPAD R.

Singrauli basin

BAGHELKHAND

Bandhavgarh hill

PLATEAU

Sohagpur basin

SON

MAIKAL HILLS

NARMADA

Amarkantak hill

Map 2

more regular features comprise parallel ranges enclosing the alluvial valleys of Singrauli and Sohagpur. However, between the Son valley and the Maikal hills

the whole country is covered with ... a sea of ... hills, broken up and scattered about in the most indescribable confusion; here, starting from a central nucleus and sprawling over the country in ray-like spurs; there isolated in bold craggy looking citadels which form naturally impregnable fortresses, while in places they trend away in long narrow flat-topped ranges or rise out of the valleys in steep sugar loaf cones. But they have a tendency to group themselves into ill-defined blocks running north and south at right angles to the Kaimurs and the Maikals.[8]

The Maikal hills form the southern part of the Baghelkhand plateau. Extending for 480 kilometres at about 460–500 metres, they comprise a series of flat-topped plateaus, of which the best known is the Maikal plateau. Capped with laterite, the plateau has developed over Deccan Trap with Gondwana and Archaean rocks exposed in places. In the south the plateau culminates in the bluff promontory of Amarkantak at about 1,000 metres, which forms the divide between the Son, Narmada, and Mahanadi rivers.

The major rivers of Baghelkhand discharge their waters into the Ganga. The Tons and its tributaries the Bihar and Bichhia rise in the northern face of the Kaimur; the two latter streams converge at Rewa and join the Tons main stream below the Chachai falls in north Rewa. The Son and its tributaries drain the hilly country south of the Kaimur. The parent stream rises near Pendra and flows north, joined by its tributaries the Johilla and the Chhoti Mahanadi. It turns north-east due to the Khenjua range, and flows through the narrow plain below the Kaimur, whose fault lines mark the divide between the Vindhyan and Gondwana rock systems.[9] Joined by its tributaries in Sidhi, the Son flows on to join the Ganga in Bihar. Baghelkhand's other major river is the Narmada but, though it has reportedly given its other name of Rewa to the former state and its capital, it flows only briefly through Baghelkhand before entering Mandla.

Climate

Baghelkhand's climate today is broadly similar to that of central India and the northern plains. However, its weather in the prehistoric period differed markedly from the present. During the last northern glaciation the middle Son valley was cooler and drier than it is now, though streams and rivers held permanent water. From about 100,000 BC wet and dry periods alternated. In one arid phase stronger winds blew in winter and weaker in summer. Slightly before or during the Holocene, the wind patterns reversed and vigorous summer winds with weaker winter winds developed. A strong south-west monsoon brought heavier rain to central India, increasing the forest cover as well as the run-off. At the same time average temperatures rose and a yearly weather cycle set in, more or less conformable to present conditions.

The region's key season is the monsoon period from June to September. Baghelkhand lies on the path of the south-west and north-east monsoons, though the latter affects mostly the eastern part of the region. Once the rains begin, temperatures fall slowly until September when the monsoon withdraws. Thereafter temperatures fall further and the cold weather sets in, marked by westerly depressions with spells of rain. January is the coldest month, when frost may strike the valleys and the *sal* forests drip with morning dew. By March temperatures begin to rise again and the humidity drops in preparation for the long, dry summer when the loo blows, bringing dust, though occasional storms give relief from the heat before the monsoon sets in once more.

Local factors modify these weather patterns. Monsoon rains lose much of their intensity by the time they reach the region, while the forested hills of the south receive a higher rainfall than the centre and north. The southern hills are also cooler in summer than the Rewa plateau.

The region's weather is marked by extremes. Due to its inland location Baghelkhand may experience drought, when streams and wells dry up and vegetation dies. Sidhi regularly suffers from drought due to uncertain rains coupled with poor soil. Yet heavy rains may bring floods in the Son and Tons systems, sweeping away villages and drowning people and cattle. At one with these extremes are the violent storms of summer, such as that which engulfed the French traveller, Louis Rousselet, in 1867:

During the night...we experienced one of those terrible hurricanes, so common at this season throughout the mountainous regions....The tempest burst upon us with so much suddenness that...the canvas khanats were rent asunder, the stakes flew up in the air, and the wind furiously swelled under our tent. We rushed outside, and at this very moment a typhoon of rain and dust, mingled with pebbles and branches, hurled us to the ground, carrying me to some distance, stifled and bruised .... Thunderbolts constantly ploughed the ground, bursting through the darkness with great violet-coloured flashes .... then suddenly calm succeeded, and...the sky appeared glittering with stars.[10]

The Forests of Baghelkhand

Forests form an important element in the regional environment, covering as they do extensive areas in Satna, Sidhi, and Shahdol. They were even more extensive in prehistoric times, as evidenced by the recovery of Gondwana fossils.[11] T.W. Hughes was the first to find fossils while prospecting for minerals in Sidhi in 1880. More recent discoveries there include spore and pollen assemblage from the Gopad river area. A site near Churhat has yielded a large number of plant-leaf fossils typical of a moist deciduous forest. Archaeologists have also discovered pine and oak pollen from the Baghor III occupational site in Sidhi, and conifer remains comprising leafy twigs with spinally arranged leaves at Bansa in Rewa. Coal seams provide abundant evidence of ancient forests in Shahdol.

Forests continued down through the Pleistocene to the Holocene.[12] For the former, evidence suggests galleria forests and grasslands near swamps and pools, and along the flood plain of the middle Son valley. These were probably deciduous woodlands with stands of *sal*, though one report claimed that dry deciduous forest in loams and clays could contain teak. On poorer soils in the western Son valley acacia was much in evidence, together with other species typical of tropical thorn forests. In some places higher ground supported broad-leaved deciduous trees and climbers, and in others thorn and scrub. In the drier conditions of the last northern glacial grasslands expanded, as is evident from the extensive remains of animals searching for food and water in the valleys. Forests flourished again in the hot, wet conditions of the Holocene.

Information about early historical forests is scanty.[13] In the first millennium sages and others breached the Vindhyan forests to found their ashrams; while Kosambi wrote of the 'endless forest' of the Mauryan period 'where anyone who had the nerve could find refuge'. Sculptures from the Bharhut *stupa* near Satna show a country rich in natural vegetation with abundant fruit. In the seventh century AD Banabhatta sang of the forests in the Son valley:

There rose in his view all sorts of trees, some full of fruit...in blossom...bowed down with fruit, palms...with dark green leaves, Sarala pines and ... lines of Kuruvakas, bristling with their opening buds; every direction was painted with the beauty of the shoots of the red acoka, while a beautiful grey hue was thrown over them by the pollen of the blossoming Kesarus ... assafoetida spread everywhere. Betel nuts abounded on all sides ... everywhere was heard the pleasant murmur of the bees ... while the Tamala trees darker than midnight obscured the sunshine.[14]

Eight centuries later, Sultan Mahmud of Malwa struggled through trackless forests to reach the elephant mart at Bandhavgarh.[15] The Mughals also knew Bhatha as a forested zone harbouring elephants.

Since then the picture has changed dramatically.[16] Today there is little forest cover north of the Kaimur beyond reserved patches in remote valleys. South of the Kaimur forests predominate along the upper Son and its tributaries and in the highlands: dry deciduous open forests supporting mostly teak or *sal*, with bamboo and other shrubs as an understorey. *Sal* forms about 38 per cent of the region's forest cover, flourishing in valleys and lowlands especially in Sidhi and Shahdol. Teak covers about 22 per cent of the forest area, invading south Baghelkhand due to its hardy and vigorous coppicing nature. Mixed forests comprise the remainder and are prominent on hill slopes mostly in the northern part of the region. Thorn and scrub forest occurs on the stony country of the northern scarp and the quartzite ridges of the Kaimur.

The Region's Fauna

Baghelkhand supports a rich animal and bird life. The earliest forms of animal life are to be found in the burrows of small worm-like animals found in Vindhyan sedimentary rocks at Churhat in west Sidhi. As scientists report:

Some intriguing bedding plane features ... observed in the ... Chorhat Sandstone are biological, and can be interpreted as the burrows of worm-like ... infaunal animals that excavated tunnels underneath microbial materials. These are original burrows (and)....can only be explained as the works of macroscopic worm-like animals....branching and tier

keeping....these burrows suggest the existence of fairly large.... triploblastic metazoans as early as 1.1 billion years ago.[17]

Lower Vindhyan sediments at Maihar contain shelly fossils and
brachiopods of lower Cambrian affinity.

Fossils bear witness to the vibrant animal life of the Pleistocene
and Holocene, and again these come mostly from the middle Son
valley and tributaries of the Belan north of the Kaimur.[18] The
Baghor formation in the Son valley has proved a rich source of
provenance, the middle to late Pleistocene sediment there yielding fossils of the horse, wild cattle, elephant, hippopotamus, and
rhinoceros, those of wild cattle being most frequent, their habitat
comprising stretches of grassland and browseland in woodland,
bush, and 'swampy, relatively quiet water environments'.

Sediments of the late Pleistocene and early Holocene contain
a wider fossil assemblage, which includes the *chital*, gazelle, *nilgai*,
sambhar, barahsinga, black buck, mouse deer, pig, *gaur*, tiger, leopard, jackal, hyena, and wild dog, indicating the presence of grassland and forests.[19] These remains, contemporary with the earliest
human population of Baghelkhand, demonstrate the large mam-
mal resources available to early hunters. Fossils of sheep and goat
first appear from 19–22,000 years ago, and may indicate the movement of migrant groups with domestic animals from the north.

Baghelkhand's animal population has declined drastically with
the clearing of the forests.[20] Though visitors observed a wide variety of animals there in the mid-nineteenth century, elephants
could only be found 'in some places'; and 1866 marks the last
authenticated sighting of a lion in the region. More recent reports
claim that the white tiger has vanished from west Sidhi, while
hunters have virtually eliminated antelopes from Shahdol. The
district's black buck, *gaur, chinkara* or gazelle, and wild dog are
rare; *sambhar* is disappearing, and the *barahsinga* has 'not been seen
in recent years.'

Despite the decline in numbers, animals still frequent parts of
Sidhi and Shahdol districts, though they are rarer in Satna and
Rewa.[21] The panther may be found on dry ridges in open forests
or lurking near villages; the *chital* in 'grassy glades and shaded
streams'; the *barahsinga* in damp *sal* forests; *nilgai* in the forests of
the plains. Monkeys are seen in open country or forests; the tiger
in deep ravines or hills in forest areas; the *gaur* in forests in hill

or plain country; and scavenging hyenas in all parts, often near villages. The *chinkara* roams in open forests; antelopes live near cultivated land; the wild boar inhabits forests but penetrates agricultural land; bears live in hilly or rocky areas; jackals inhabit open scrub or valley surrounds, as does the black buck.

Shahdol, too, has a larger bird and fish population than other districts, though its birds are typical of Baghelkhand as a whole.[22] Bulbul, *nilkanth*, parrot, crow pheasant, warbler, oriole, crow, and vulture visit villages; *koels* haunt mango groves; bats frequent fruit gardens; the flying fox eats the fruit of the tamarind and bamboo; scrub near cultivation is home to the shrike, partridge, and crow; quails are common in scrub forests and grassy plains; duck, snipe, and crane visit water bodies in winter; and herons and egrets live near tanks, marshes, and river banks. Birds of the forested hills include the pea fowl; parrots prefer the high forest; while the owl and blue rock-pigeon haunt rocky cliffs; the eagle is also a creature of the hills and jungles. Sidhi, too, is home to many of these birds. Fish need perennial water, and despite the dwindling of its waters by early summer, Shahdol dominates the district reports, the upper Son, Johilla, and numerous tanks containing substantial fish populations.

III

THE HUMAN PRESENCE IN BAGHELKHAND

Plant and animal life long pre-dated the first humans using stone tools who entered Baghelkhand and other parts of India during the late Pleistocene some 100,000 years ago. The culture of these people and that of their prehistoric descendants linked Baghelkhand and other parts of India in a rare form of subcontinental unity.

The origin of these first inhabitants and the source of their stone-craft are unknown. Allchin claims that in the early palaeolithic period central India was 'in contact with comparable [stone] industries in central Asia'; though Clark and Williams believe that the lower palaeolithic was more likely to have 'spread along the southern route via the Iranian plateau and Baluchistan'.[23] Humans moving into and through Baghelkhand probably followed the tracks of animals: pathways used by countless others later, which ultimately formed the basis of the modern road system.

As we now know, palaeolithic people inhabited Baghelkhand continuously up to the early centuries BC (and possibly later), utilizing its resources and creating a chain of cultural evolution across its vast area between the northern river plain and the Maikal hills. In river valleys in central Baghelkhand some even crossed from forage to food cultivation, as in the nearby Belan valley with which they may have had some connection. In so doing they were among the first agriculturists in central India well before the waves of agriculturists that moved into the region in the historic period.[24]

Historians and archaeologists have tried with difficulty to identify the prehistoric inhabitants of Baghelkhand.[25] The names of groups that appear in the ancient texts probably throw little light on the prehistoric people who were probably 'related' to their contemporaries elsewhere in the subcontinent. Immigrants into the region in the early historic period encountered groups whom they called Nishadas and Sabaras. In the second century AD, Ptolemy names the Pulindae. K.D. Bajpai has linked the people mentioned in the epics and early texts with the hill and forest communities and other backward groups. Archaeologists of the middle Son valley see the Baiga forest community as possible descendants of the early hunter–gatherers. A. Roy claims ancient origins for the iron-knowing Agarias. Gordon argues that the people of the caves at Morahana Pahar just outside Baghelkhand were 'aboriginals', traces of whose language survive in the speech of the related forest and hill communities of Hos, Kol, and Korku.

The stone tools of the earliest inhabitants, the early palaeolithic people, occur throughout Baghelkhand, generally in the first aggradational phase of its streams and rivers, especially in the Son valley of Sidhi and Shahdol.[26] These tools are also found in open-air sites on low hillocks jutting from the Kaimur, or on undulating ground in the shadow of the scarp. In Satna sites occur on high-relief weathered rock surrounded by hills, or on low relief sites with access to water.

Tool types are common throughout the region,[27] and comprise hand axes, cleavers, scrapers and crude implements made by splitting pebbles. A site on Sidhi's Mohan river yielded a chopper; and on the *nala*s between the Mohan and Banas archaeologists have

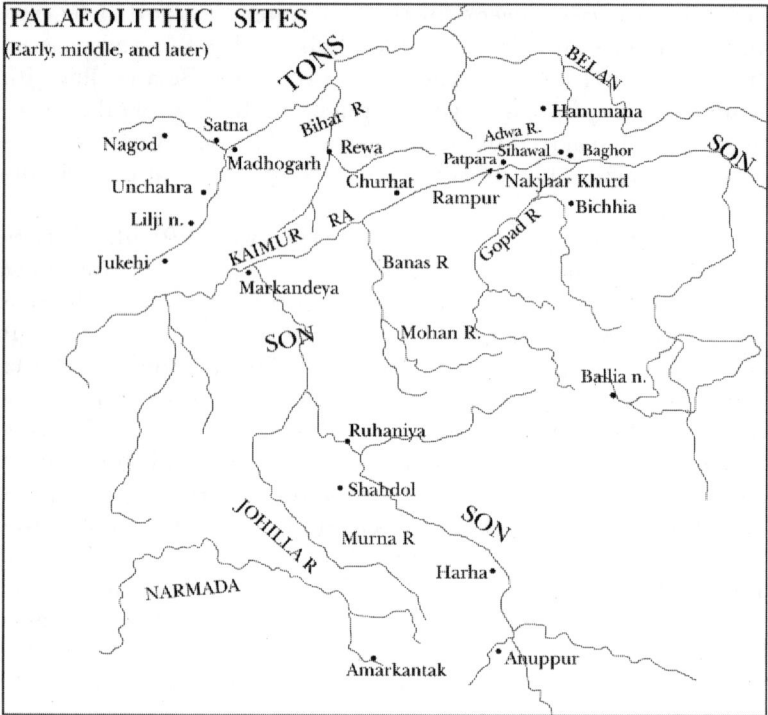

Map 3

found ovate, half-finished tools and flakes. The stone used depended on what was available, and varies from porcellanite near Rewa town to sandstone in parts of Sidhi, or quartzite in Satna. In the middle Son valley tool-makers split pebbles, mostly of quartzite, fine-grained sandstone, or impure chert.

From the find sites we see that early hunters and gatherers were concentrated along the Son and its tributaries.[28] Early palaeolithic remains in Sidhi's middle Son valley are mostly located in an area bounded by Churhat in the west, Bichhia on the east, the Kaimur to the north, and the Son–Gopad confluence on the south. At two sites—Sihawal on the north bank of the Son and Nakjhar Khurd on the south—people continued to make implements for a long period of time, taking material from the river gravels and working it there. Many early palaeolithic sites also occur on the Ballia nadi in Singrauli. In Shahdol early tool–makers inhabited the rivers and *nalas*, especially the upper Son and its tributary the Murna, in addition to sites near Shahdol, Anuppur, Harha, Markandeya, and Ruhaniya. The main find sites in Satna are close to the Lilji *nala* and elsewhere in Maihar, and at Jukehi, Unchahra, and near the Tons at Madhogarh.

A number of early palaeolithic sites occur in Rewa district, including some very ancient locations near Rewa town.[29] Archaeologists have compared the latter provenance with that from Singrauli:

The extreme antiquity of the Rewa implements is shown by the fact that the unaltered stone is quite dark, and the weathering of the older breakage shows in shades of grey of greater paleness according to age. The material of which the Rewa tools is made is in fact black flint, with its laminations appearing even through the heavy patina. A remarkable feature in this context is that the specimen ... of our Singrauli collection betrays the same flinty composition ... and is also patinated in a dirty cream ... colour. This straying of the flinty raw material from the Tamasa basin into the Singrauli basin may represent a close cultural contact that existed between these two areas.[30]

Other sites in Rewa include those near the Bihar river, at Lekhahia hillock, and at many sites in a 92-kilometre belt from Bahera Dubar in the Adwa valley (a tributary of the Belan) across into Mirzapur. As the Adwa runs close to the northern face of the Kaimur, over the scarp from the cluster of early palaeolithic sites in the middle Son valley, it is likely that people of the two valleys were in contact with each other, and possibly also with their contemporaries in the Belan valley.

Between 60,000 and 20,000 BC humans in Baghelkhand evolved further by fashioning smaller tools from fine-grained material in what has been termed the middle palaeolithic culture.[31] Clark and Williams claim that the implements of this period show no resemblance to the middle palaeolithic of the Middle East, Afghanistan, or Uzbekistan, underlining the existence in the subcontinent of areas of human settlement and culture adaptive to the local environment, as in Baghelkhand.

The manufacture of smaller tools took place in a dry phase when forests thinned and game dispersed, making lithic refinements necessary—a utilitarian view that does not rule out the continuous honing of implements by hunter–gatherers.[32] These smaller tools included arrow-heads and spear-heads that could kill animals from a distance, together with scrapers, discoids, borers, and hand axes. Later hunters shaped longer blades, some with faceted striking platforms. In general, the middle palaeolithic people preferred to make their tools from chert or quartzite. Archaeologists have frequently discovered these tools in much the same sites as those of the early palaeolithic people, indicating a continuing process of evolution. Additional sites include those near Satna and Nagod; Ita Pahar and Hanumana in Rewa district; and Amarkantak and places along the Johilla river in Shahdol.

Across the late Pleistocene and Holocene from about 20,000 to 8,000 BC people in Baghelkhand and elsewhere continued to modify their implements, creating what has been termed the upper palaeolithic culture.[33] This refinement took the form of a wide variety of blades together with scrapers, burins, lunates, points, and borers. These more finely-honed tools were made from flakes of chert in the middle Son valley; in Satna and the Adwa valley from chert, chalcedony, agate, and carnelian; and from chalcedonic silica in the Maikal hills.

Archaeologists assert that the more sophisticated tools of the late palaeolithic in the middle Son valley included implements for harvesting wild grasses, indicating not merely a widening diet and an improved standard of living, but also a step towards agriculture. Already in a middle palaeolithic site at Patpara in the same area, archaeologists observed a chert flake bearing a silica gloss on one edge. This could be indicative of a number of activities, including the harvesting of grasses for their grain content, for bedding, or for construction or thatching.[34]

Studies in late palaeolithic Sidhi have confirmed this inference.[35] The site at Baghor I contained a ring-stone; while Sinha found that some tools at the Baghor III site had been used on vegetal materials, suggesting that 'plant processing and a diet of various vegetable foods and fruits was an important part of their subsistence strategy'. Pollen grains in the clay on which the upper palaeolithic assemblage rests at Rampur would support this contention.

Upper palaeolithic implements are again found at or near areas used by early and middle palaeolithic people, especially at sites in Maihar which stone age people 'constantly visited ...from the Lower Palaeolithic to the Mesolithic'.[36] Extensive occupational sites again occurred along the middle Son valley and associated streams; on the medial ridge between the Son and the Kaimur; and riverine locations in the upper Son valley. In Rewa, too, implements were again located at Ita Pahar north of Rewa town, Hanumana, and at many places in the Adwa valley; and in Sidhi along the Ballia *nadi* of Singrauli.

Two remarkable sites in the middle Son valley provide a closer insight into the life of upper palaeolithic people.[37] Baghor I and Baghor III lie within a kilometre of each other near the Kundhera *nala*. Baghor III, the smaller of the two, is the oldest upper palaeolithic site in the valley, dated at ± 11,800 BP. Both give the impression of brief occupancy: either not repeated or possibly inhabited for more than one season. Archaeologists claim that the assemblage at Baghor I was related to 'short term movements from valley to plateau and vice-versa'. The implements found at Baghor III demonstrate the astonishing facility with which its occupants dealt with the animal and vegetable resources of the area. Its

blades/bladelets and shaped tools appear to have been used in a number of activities on various types of material....cutting, whittling, slicing, scraping and piercing, boring and chopping....related to craft activities....food processing and game hunting.[38]

At Baghor I archaeologists also uncovered what they believed to be the first shrine of a goddess to come to light in the subcontinent, dating it to between 10,000 and 8,000 BC.[39]

From about this same time the process of food gathering became more sophisticated on the part of the so-called mesolithic
people. They were more efficient than their forbears, their smaller
and more accurate tools or microliths exploiting the wider range
of animal and food resources available in improving climatic conditions. Using these improved technologies hunters moved further away from their occupational sites into forest interiors. However,
the remains of game fauna and the absence of those of domesticated animals at their sites indicate that the mesolithic people of
Baghelkhand remained nomadic hunters and gatherers.

Mesolithic people gained mastery over the art of flaking, such
that the process of shaping smaller and finer tools reached a
climax.[40] Earlier flakes, thick and asymmetrical, indicated that
tool-makers were unable to control the process of percussion.
However, thin blade practice and possible contact with superior
techniques in the Belan valley taught people how to produce thin,
long, or short symmetrical flakes or blades. Mastery over flaking
also enabled them to make finer and more geometric tools from
hard rocks. These microliths possessed a sharpened edge or parallel blades, and were set in handles of wood or stone to create
javelins, harpoons, knives, and sickles, suitable for spearing and
skinning animals, making baskets, catching and preparing fish,
and harvesting grains. Other mesolithic artefacts included scrapers, lunates, borers, points, triangles, drills, and grinding equipment, the last named underlining the processing of edible grains.

Mesolithic provenance in the region indicates the hunters'
expertise in shaping microliths.[41] Those found at the Lilji *nala* in
Maihar were 'symmetrical in form, with careful retouching'. Tools
at Baghor II in Sidhi included 'bladelets retouched into convex
and ... straight backed microliths, lunates, triangles, trapezes and
truncated forms'. From a site probably near Sohagi *ghat* on the
northern edge of the Rewa plateau the nomadic archaeologist
Carlleyle was much pleased in 1867–8

with a fine crescent shaped object, made of white, creamy chalcedonic
agate, and of the same type-form as the small crescent shaped implements which some years afterwards I found in such number(s) in the
caves and rock shelters on the Vindhyans.[42]

By contrast, the microliths from the Ballia *nadi* in Singrauli re-
minded their finders of a 'degenerate Upper Palaeolithic blade

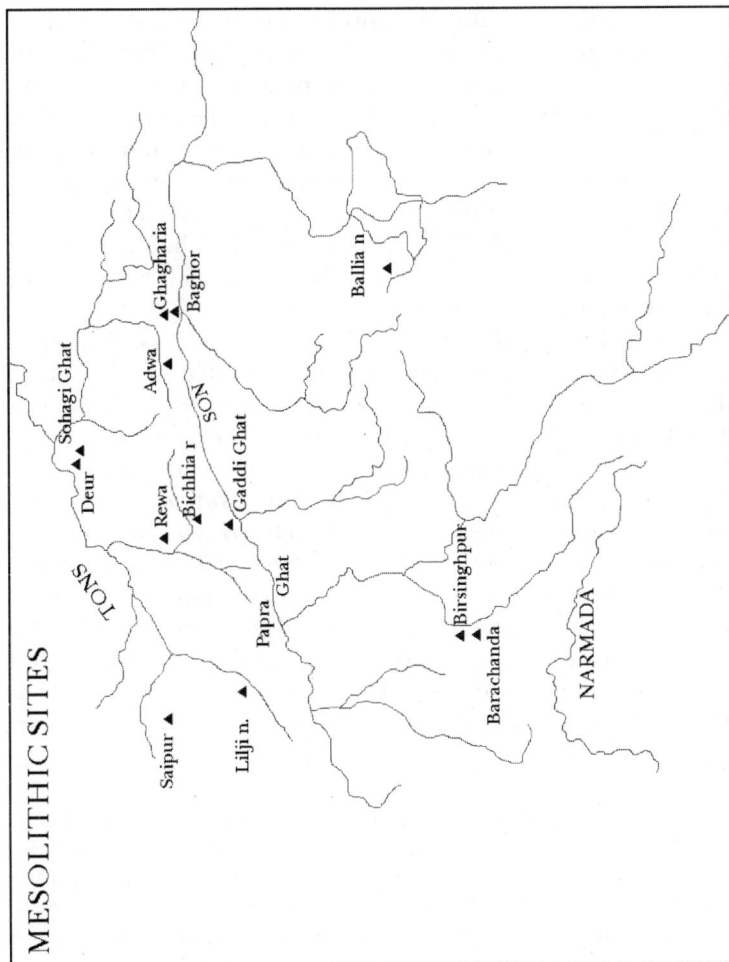

MESOLITHIC SITES

Map 4

tradition'. While this varied quality depended partly on the type
of stone available, there is evidence that tool-makers were seeking
out rocks that suited their newer purposes.[43]

Mesolithic hunter–gatherers occupied a wider variety of sites
than their predecesors, the most prominent being the cave shelters in the sandstone hills of central and northern Baghelkhand
which they used during the rains, camping out in open country
during the remainder of the year.[44] The shelters also served as
factory sites as we see from the tools and waste found near the
shelters at Ghagharia on top of the Kaimur in Sidhi, or those of the
Gaddi group on the Kaimur's northern face in Rewa. However, at
Baghor II and Banki in Sidhi mesolithic people inhabited oblong
or semicircular huts, using post holes to support lean-to structures
of wattle and daub. As these were similar to structures at Chopani
Mando in the Belan valley, it is possible that the middle Son valley
was part of a wider zone in which cultural interchange took place.

Mesolithic people developed their culture over a wide area of
Baghelkhand.[45] There is evidence of some clustering of sites in
the countryside around Rewa town, occurring near passes in the
Kaimur and in the valleys of the Bichhia and other streams.
Mesolithic people also frequented sites in the Adwa valley of Rewa
and the middle Son valley in Sidhi. Here the locations are on river
banks, the hills south of the Son, and on the Kaimur, as in the rock
shelter I at Ghagharia which was intermittently occupied 'up to
the first few centuries B.C.' Mesolithic sites in Satna included
Sagoni on the Rewa road, the Lilji *nala*, and Saipur near Nagod;
with Barachanda and Birsinghpur in Shahdol. As with other phases
of prehistory

there was practically no difference between people living on the banks
of the Kshipra at Ujjain,... at Mandasor on the Shivana,... at Maheshwar
on the Narmada, or those living in the dense forest at Barchanda on the
Johilla. People all over Madhya Pradesh, as in many parts of India, were
living in a Stone Age, when to secure food by hunting, fishing and
collecting ... was the main activity.[46]

Finds at mesolithic sites herald a further shift towards food production.[47] These include pottery for the storage of food and grinding equipment. The Ghagharia I rock shelter contained pottery of
ordinary khaki-ware and cord-impressed ware together with grind
stones. Recent explorations in the Adwa valley have brought to

Figure: 1.1 Kaimur rock-face at Gaddi Ghat, showing the pools
near the Mesolithic shelters there, and the gradual
descent to the Rewa plateau

light similar pottery. It seems likely that those using these sites shaped their own ceramic-ware, but contact with their contemporaries in the Belan valley cannot be ruled out. Baghor II contained 'much grinding equipment', but no pottery. Scattered charcoal there gave a dating of ± 6200 BP for the early mesolithic; whereas occupancy of the Ghagharia shelter continued long after the mesolithic. Sites in Maihar and around Rewa town were devoid of pottery.

IV

The Cave Shelters of the Baghelkhand Mesolithic

As we have seen, cave shelters in Baghelkhand and elsewhere in the country came into focus as camping places mostly used by mesolithic people between 10,000 and 2,000 BC.[48] In Baghelkhand most of these hollows, caves or shelters are located in the Kaimur and northern scarpland, offering sweeping views of the lowlands where game and humans passed to and fro. The striking appearance of these shelters is the result of geological action and the weather:

These shelters were formed when horizontally laid sandy sediments were metamorphosed into a tough orthoquartzite. These level rock shelters were broken or displaced by tectonic upheavals, and weathered by different agents such as the sun, wind and water. This was how cliffs, caves and rock shelters, as well as huge rock structures, which in many cases look like gigantic fortresses, were formed. When man appeared on the scene millions of years later, he found shelter under these rock structures.[49]

Mesolithic people used the temporary shelters for making tools and storing food, and possibly for ceremonial or communal gatherings, though at no time were the numbers large.[50] Varma also found evidence of systematic burials taking place in shelters. The Ghagharia shelters overlooking the Son valley were excellent examples of such sites, set in a zone of ample rainfall and amid forests teeming with wildlife,

Many cave shelters contain paintings that 'recapture the sense of a lost hunting and gathering world'.[51] Such shelters occur where the upper sandstone strata have been fused to hardness; they are not found in porous basalt formations which encourage the growth of moss or fungus. In Baghelkhand's open type of shelters the painted surfaces are easily accessible, and are most certainly the work of the mesolithic hunters who stayed there. The desertion of most shelters after the mesolithic period left a gap in rock art, painting activity only resuming in some shelters with the introduction of iron.

The paintings are the work of people 'who were acutely observant, imaginative, and had complete control of their media'.[52] Animals form the main subject of the earliest paintings, the painters who depended on hunting for their existence painting their quarry again and again, especially those they feared. *Sambhar* and deer are most commonly painted, but the buffalo, tiger, leopard, bear, elephant, rhinoceros, *nilgai*, horned deer, fox, and monkey also appear. Painters depicted their subjects grazing, standing, or running, singly or in groups, and without scenery or background. Sometimes they etched their figures in bold outline; sometimes they painted in their bodies, or partially painted them with crosshatching. The paintings are small, as the shelters were generally

Figure: 1.2 Mesolithic cave paintings at Gaddi Ghat

not large enough for bigger figures. In the Ghagharia rock shelter domestic animals appear as the mesolithic yielded to the neolithic way of life.

Human figures introduced later normally appear as part of hunting or trapping scenes, or are depicted dancing in a group.[53] Males and females are generally attired in the same fashion, and usually appear in groups. When painted with animals, humans are far more stylized than their prey, though the representations are lively enough. In some instances painters expressed the human element with the outline of a hand.

As a medium, painters generally used what appears to be the red oxide of iron that occurs in a pure form in the Vindhyan region.[54] Lumps of it were found in caves also. In addition, painters used yellow ochre, manganese, and the green of moss, and appear to have ground their paints to a fine powder before making a paste, using either blood serum or egg white as a binder. The resulting colours ranged from purple through crimson and vermillion to terra cotta, light orange and brown—the colours that we see today.

Mesolithic rock paintings show a progression of styles that may reflect the 'mental development of the painters', or merely the different way individual painters perceived their subjects.[55] The earliest paintings are bold and life-like, with animals in natural postures. Painters made no effort at composition; and humans are absent. In the next phase artists used red ochre to paint animals in stylized forms: straight lines and sharp angles replaced rounded body contours, while maintaining the shape and identity of the animals concerned. In this phase humans often appear in group scenes with animals. Painters did not paint limbs proportionate to the figures, but they evoked a sense of movement. In a third phase painters reduced figures to symbols, representing them as circles, angles, or dots, before returning to a naturalistic style again with life-like figures. A final phase is marked by a flat white-wash over the ochre, painted on top of other paintings—a phase that marked the end of prehistoric painting in the region.

Archaeologists and historians have long sought to explain why mesolithic people painted their shelters.[56] Kosambi thought that the animal outlines were used for 'ritual target practice'. Others suggest that the figures record the achievements of hunters, art reflecting their occupation; or are a way of propitiating dangerous foes. Alternatively, was it merely a case of simple folk with time to spare during the monsoon decorating their living spaces, as homo sapiens has done ever since?

Mesolithic people occupied the shelters during the rains, and for the remainder of the year moved elsewhere—timings that depended on the movement of their prey.[57] As animals moved to the hills for grazing and water during the monsoon, the semi-nomadic hunters climbed up to their rock shelters, relatively safe from wild animals and the season's rainy winds. After the rains the hunter–gatherers descended to the plains, as animals moved down to be near water and fodder for the summer. The shelters at Deur Kothar, the Gaddi and Papra *ghats*, and elsewhere on the Kaimur are close to the paths used by animals in their seasonal wanderings, that subsequently formed modern lines of communication.

In time these patterns of transhumance acquired further complexity.[58] Mesolithic dwelling sites in Allahabad, Pratapgarh, and elsewhere in Uttar Pradesh have yielded artefacts of grey Belan chert, and Lahiri suggests that mesolithic people ferried stone from the Baghelkhand and other hills nearby for use by the inhabitants of the stoneless plains. Many of the stone factory sites lay on the frontier between the hills and the plains, and those carrying stone thus set up a new kind of relationship between the two zones. Even wider circles of exchange can be seen in the sherds of Malwa-ware found at neolithic Kunjhun; while the neolithic and later pottery found at Ghagharia I suggests a relationship of the cave-dwellers with more advanced people.

Some archaeologists have given these movements to and from the Gangetic plain an even wider significance, claiming that what were once seasonal migrations gradually became a permanent settlement in the more attractive plains.[59] They contend that groups of people moved from the hill regions of Mirzapur and Baghelkhand to colonize the alluvial plains of the Yamuna and Ganga during the terminal Pleistocene, carrying with them their newly evolved techniques of food production:

Sharp changes in climate and growing aridity, [and] the consequent ecological change, on the one hand, and the assured supply of water in the lakes in the Ganges valley, full of fish, tortoise and shell, plentiful supply of grass in the virgin fields of the Ganges, on the other hand, provided stimulation for the movement of both animals and men.[60]

It is more than likely that this change of location hinged on the advances in agri-technology, impelling some people to converge on more fertile regions. Thus, as Sharma and Misra assert that the Vindhyan excavations and material collected from sites in the Ganga valley provide evidence of a shift from the Vindhyas to the lowlands,[61] so it may be argued that the evacuation of the mesolithic cave shelters of Baghelkhand was the prelude to a move to the more fertile Son and Adwa valleys, the epicentre of the Baghelkhand neolithic—though this requires substantiating.

V

THE BAGHELKHAND NEOLITHIC

From about the third millennium BC human beings in the subcontinent began cultivating grains and domesticating animals in a further phase of the evolutionary cycle known as the neolithic. This shift from hunting and gathering to a more settled agrarian economy required the clearing of forests, planting of crops, and provision of equipment to prepare and store the food grown on, or perhaps harvested from, nearby sites. It is thought that these changes went hand in hand with a rise of population in the more genial climate of the Holocene.

Archaeological evidence demonstrates that humans achieved the epic transition from the mesolithic to the neolithic culture in Baghelkhand's middle Son and Adwa valleys.[62] With the Belan valley, these areas formed one of the subcontinent's nuclear zones in which this transition took place. Clark and Williams are clear that the neolithic flaked stone industry in the middle Son valley 'resembles and is derived from the mesolithic tradition', evident in the 'inverse retouching of flakes and blades'. They also believe that this shift from hunting and gathering to food production need not have involved any 'significant ethnic change'; though investigations at Ghagharia I shelter suggest that users, who were contemporary successively with the neolithic–chalcolithic and iron ages developed a 'viable symbiotic relationship with local food producers' and were thus not the producers themselves.

Kunjhun II, occupied from about 4,500 BC, is Baghelkhand's neolithic site par excellence.[63] Situated on a terrace on the right bank of the Son about 36 kilometres north-east of Sidhi, it is the

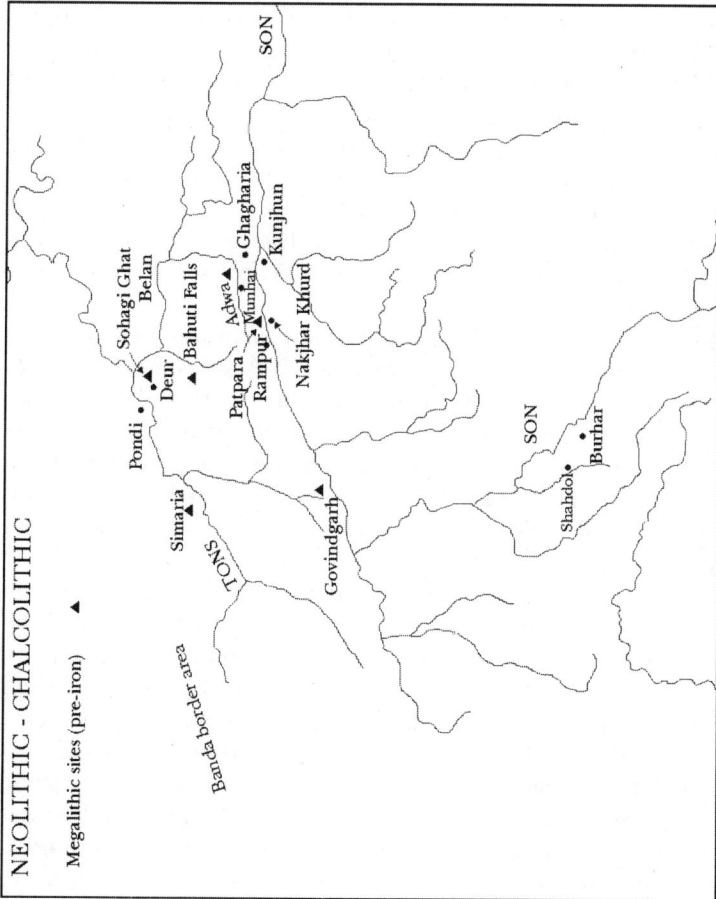

NEOLITHIC - CHALCOLITHIC

▲ Megalithic sites (pre-iron)

SON

Sohagi Ghat
Belan
Ghagharia
•Ghagharia
Kunjhun
Bahuti Falls
Adwa
Munha
Nakjhar Khord
Pondi •
Deur
Patpara
Rampur
Simaria
TONS
Govindgarh
Banda border area

SON
Shahdol
Burhar

Map 5

only site in the region to yield appreciable faunal remains, including those of the domesticated dog. The bones of the slaughtered animals showed the 'typical fracture patterns associated with butchery', and were most commonly those of the *gaur*, medium and small deer, and the antelope.

Other finds at Kunjhun II indicate that people were enlarging on the agricultural practices begun during the mesolithic period.[64] The site contained the remains of wild and domesticated rice, with neolithic ring-stones and grindstone fragments; while the longish bladelets found there were 'inversely retouched and used for cutting plant remains'. Dwellers at Kunjhun continued to fashion microliths, using a sophisticated process whereby they carried cobbles of chalcedony, chert and agate up to the site, and fired them in shallow pits to produce 'flakeable stone of excellent quality'.

The inhabitants of Kunjhun also left an impressive array of neolithic pottery and associated artefacts.[65] Besides sherds of cord-impressed ware, pottery finds included a spouted vessel, basins, platters, a deep bowl and a necked jar 'in fabric, tempering material, surface treatment, firing condition and state of preservation' similar to the pottery of Koldihwa and Mahagara in the Belan valley. Also found at the site were a clay dabber, terra cotta bangles, and lumps of burnt clay 'with reed impression'.

Other neolithic sites,[66] mostly in the middle Son valley, included the Ghagharia rock shelter I which contained cord-impressed ware in its upper layer; Lalanahia yielded basin-shaped querns and cord-impressed rusticated ware; the Kunjhun river face had neolithic sherds, flakes of stone and bone, vessels decorated with the cord-impressed design, together with black burnished and red-slipped ware, two sherds of painted pottery, a small cattle figurine of baked clay, and a ladle; while Rampur and Nakjhar Khurd yielded neolithic celts on basalt. Recently, archaeologists have identified a number of neolithic sites in the adjacent Adwa valley of Rewa district. The only other reported neolithic find comes from a site between Burhar and Shahdol in the south.

These finds give Baghelkhand not merely a place in the Vindhyan neolithic, but also in the subcontinental neolithic.[67] Subbarao claims that the implements found at Kunjhun II are indistinguishable from those at Raichur and Bellary in Karnataka, and generally conform to the south Indian neolithic. Guha, too, sets the Vindhyan neolithic firmly in its subcontinental perspective, while underlining the indigenous nature of the culture:

> Numerous communities throughout India...had successfully domesticated a wide range of plants and animals a thousand or more years before the beginning of PGW at the end of the second millennium BCE; furthermore, many, if not most of these were located, not in what became the core cultural area of the central Gangetic plain, but in hilly peripheral regions such as the Kaimur ranges.[68]

Neolithic people in the middle Son and Adwa valleys also developed the use of copper technology, adding further complexity to their farming and herding culture.[69] They continued to use stone implements, besides developing hand-painted and -thrown pottery that was not always wheel-turned. The use of copper is generally dated from the third millennium, but reached maturity in the first.

Five sites with chalcolithic remains have so far come to light in Baghelkhand, and again the most significant of these are in the middle Son and Adwa valleys, the cradle of the region's prehistory.[70] On the Kaimur above the Son, the Ghagharia rock shelter I contained neolithic and chalcolithic pottery, its inhabitants either developing this themselves or acquiring the pieces by exchange. In the Adwa valley, Munhai yielded bronze and copper pieces. In addition, P.K. Mishra found copper objects and pieces 'in a spatter form' at the cave shelter (and *stupa*) site of Deur Kothar near the Sohagi *ghat*. No chalcolithic sites have so far come to light in the upper Son valley, though what appear to be 'ancient' copper workings exist at Cherka in that area.

The discovery of two chalcolithic sites at entry points to the region would seem to suggest that they were the work of people from outside.[71] Copper-knowing agriculturists were already settled in the river valleys around Baghelkhand and, given the location of our two sites, they could be the work of people moving in from those valleys. Pondi in the Teonthar lowlands south of Allahabad yielded 47 rings and five celts 'apparently of copper'. The other site is at Gobari on the Jhuri *nala* near Satna's border with Banda. Copper-knowing people could have reached this site either from the Ganga–Yamuna valley or from Eran, a colony founded by such people in their drive up the Narmada.

The subsequent appearance of pre-iron megaliths indicates further changes in Baghelkhand's cultural life towards the historical period.[72] However, rather than seeing the megalithic as a funerary culture in its own right, Chakrabarti views it as 'nothing more than a burial style which emerged in the context of the neolithic–chalcolithic'. Dating largely from the mid-second millennium, the megalithic funerary monuments included flattish mounds on barrows, cairn circles, cist burial sites and menhirs, all requiring some effort to construct. Some archaeologists link the Baghelkhand megaliths with those of the adjacent Ganga valley; others suggest that such influences may have percolated through from Vidarbha and further south.

Pre-iron megaliths occur across a vast area of Baghelkhand from Satna's border with Banda to Mirzapur and Bihar in the east, and from Sidhi north to Lapari in Allahabad district.[73] Many of these are located on sites with a previous history of occupation, though Gobari in north Satna is the only example to date of pre-iron megaliths occurring on a chalcolithic site. Other megalith sites with prehistoric antecedents include Patpara, a palaeolithic site in the middle Son valley; Madighat in north Rewa, a locality that boasts rock shelters with paintings and microliths; and the Sohagi *ghat* locality, near an old pathway up from the plains. Palaeolithic Govindgarh near a pass over the Kaimur has cists, barrows and menhirs; and archaeologists have recently reported several pre-iron megaliths on prehistoric sites in the Adwa valley.

Pre-iron megaliths on sites that appear to have had no previous occupation include the flattish mounds and barrows in enclosures at Simaria, 25 km north-west of Rewa; megaliths of the cairn type with cists up to 2.5 m high at Pamariya in the Ramnagar *tahsil* of Satna district; those in the vicinity of the Bahuti falls in north Rewa; and others in the middle Son valley.

Thereafter Baghelkhand crossed the divide between prehistory and the historical period, indicated by the presence of iron remains at megalith sites. These must have been inhabited by local people working iron, and visited by those collecting it; and it is to this aspect of the region's protohistory that we now turn, as well as to those entering the region from outside its borders.

Notes

1. O.P. Misra, 'Comparative study of floristic components of Bundelkhand and Baghelkhand regions', PhD thesis, APS University, Rewa, 1982, p. 38.
2. Ibid., p. 39.
3. P.S. Dwivedi observed that Bagheli is 'a mix of Awadhi, Kanauji and Bundeli, at least superficially in terms of structure and vocabulary'.
4. For convenience, most footnotes document the material contained in the ensuing paragraph. Kols numbered 11 per cent of the population of Rewa state in 1911 (*Central India States Census, 1911,* vol. IV, *Rewa State Census, 1911, Report,* p. 38); 'Jungle tribes' were 29 per cent of the state's population in 1921 (*Rewa State Census, 1921,* pt I, *Report,* p. 55). In 1961 scheduled castes formed 9.6 per cent, and scheduled tribes 33.7 per cent, of the population of Sidhi (*Census of India, 1961, Madhya Pradesh, District Census Handbook, Sidhi District,* p. lvi). In 1961 Gonds formed 24.8 per cent of the population of Shahdol, and 15.4 per cent of that of Sidhi (*Census of India, 1961,* vol. VIII, *Madhya Pradesh,* pt VI, Village survey monograph no. 11, G.N. Tiwari, 'Amwar, a village survey in Madhya Pradesh', Appx B, p. 175). In Rewa 'more than one quarter of the district's population belonged to the scheduled castes and tribes' (*Madhya Pradesh District Gazetteers, Rewa District,* Bhopal, 1980, p. 268). The phrase 'hill and forest people/communities' is used in the text in place of the word 'tribes' or 'tribal'. See S. Guha, 'Lower strata, older races, and aboriginal peoples: racial anthropology and mythical history past and present', *JAS,* vol. 57, no. 2, May 1998, pp. 423–41.
5. *Imperial Gazetteer of India, Central India,* rpt, 1989, p. 10.
6. For the sake of convenience I have used modern place names to indicate location. Here Shahdol refers to the undivided district of that name before the recent excision of Umaria and Anuppur districts.
7. Louis Rousselet, *India and its Native Princes: Travels in Central India and in the Presidencies of Bombay and Bengal,* London, 1878, p. 368.
8. J.M., 'Notes from Rewa', *IF,* vol. IX, 1983, p. 397.
9. Letter by W.D. West, 22 Mar. 1962, *Current Science,* no. 4, vol. XXXI, Apr. 1962, pp. 143–4.
10. Rousselet, *India and its Native Princes,* pp. 377–8.
11. Material in this paragraph is derived from P.P. Satsangi, 'On the occurrence of dicrodium flora in Sidhi district, M.P.', pp. 294–5, in B.S. Venkatachala and H.K. Maheshwari (eds.), *Indian Gondwana,* memoir 21: Sahni volume, Bangalore, 1991; R.K. Varma, *Rewa through the Ages,* Allahabad, 1991, pp. 4–5; Sukh-Dev and M.N. Bose,

'On some conifer remains from Bansa, South Rewa Gondwana basin', *The Palaeobotanist*, vol. 21, no. 1, 1972, abstract 59.

12. G.L. Badam, V.D. Misra, J.N. Pal, and J.N. Pandey, 'A preliminary study of Pleistocene fossils from the middle Son valley, Madhya Pradesh', *ME*, vol. XIII, 1989, p. 43; G.R. Sharma and J.D. Clark (eds.), *Palaeoenvironments and Prehistory in the Middle Son Valley*, Allahabad, 1983, pp. 4–5; R.J. Blumenschine and U.C. Chattopadhyaya, 'A preliminary report on the terminal Pleistocene fauna of the middle Son valley', Sharma and Clark, (eds.) *Palaeoenvironments and Prehistory*, p. 283; J.D. Clark and G.R. Sharma, 'A discussion of preliminary results, and an assessment of future research potential', Sharma and Clark, (eds.) *Palaeoenvironments and Prehistory*, pp. 275–6; J.D. Clark and M.A.J. Williams, 'Palaeoenvironments and prehistory in north Central India: a preliminary report', J. Jacobson (ed.), *Studies in the Archaeology of India and Pakistan*, New Delhi, 1986, p. 37.

13. D.D. Kosambi, *The Culture and Civilisation of Ancient India*, London, 1965, p. 156; S.T. Chacko, 'A cultural study of Bharhut sculptures', PhD thesis, APS University, Rewa, 1985, p. 9.

14. *The Harsa-Carita of Bana*, trans. by E.B. Cowell and F.W. Thomas, Delhi, 1961, pp. 234–5.

15. See A.H. Nizami, 'Elephant-catching expedition of Sultan Mahmud Shah Khilji to Bandhogarh and Sarguja, 1440–1441', *JMPIP*, XII, pp. 9–10.

16. V. Mishra, 'Economic development of forest resources of Baghelkhand region', PhD thesis, HS Gour University, Sagar, 1966, pp. 73, 83, 87.

17. A. Seilacher, P. Bose, and F. Pflüger, 'Triploblastic animals more than one billion years ago: trace fossil evidence from India', *Science*, vol. 282, no. 5386, 2 Oct. 1998, pp. 80–2; R.J. Azmi, 'Discovery of Lower Cambrian small shelly fossils and brachiopods from the Lower Vindhyan of Son valley, Central India', *JGSI*, vol. 52, no. 4, Oct. 1998, p. 381.

18. Clark and Sharma, 'Discussion of preliminary results', pp. 275–6; Blumenschine and Chattopadhyaya, 'Preliminary report' p. 283; Badam et al., 'Preliminary study', pp. 41–2; Sharma and Clark (eds.), *Palaeoenvironments and Prehistory*, p. 5.

19. B. Allchin and F.R. Allchin, *Origins of a Civilisation: The Prehistory and Early Archaeology of South Asia*, New Delhi, 1993, pp. 77–80; B. Allchin, 'Whither South Asian prehistory?' *ME*, vol. XXIII, no. 1, 1998, p. 43.

20. G.F. Pearson, 'Manuscript reports on different parts of India', *CR*, vol. XXXVI, no. LXXII, June 1861, p. 239; W.T. Blandford, 'Zoological notes', *JASB*, vol. XXXVI, pt II, 1867, pp. 189–90; Govt

of Madhya Pradesh, Forest Department, *Working Scheme for the West Sidhi Forest Division, Rewa Circle, M.P., from 1973–74 Onwards*, vol. I, pts I, II, 1973, p. 80; *MPDG, Shahdol District*, Bhopal, 1994, pp. 26–8.

21. *Shahdol Gazetteer*, pp. 25–7, 30; *MPDG, Sidhi*, Bhopal, 1994, p. 17; *Working Scheme for West Sidhi Forest Division*, pp. 84–5; Govt of Madhya Pradesh, Forest Department, *Intensive Forest Management Plan for North Shahdol and Umaria Divisions for 1984/5–1998/9*, pp. 113–14.

22. *Shahdol Gazetteer*, pp. 28–30, 112; *Sidhi Gazetteer*, p. 8; *Report of the Path Enquiry Commission, Appointed to Enquire into the Condition of the Path in Rewa State*, Satna, 1935, p. 177.

23. N. Ahmad, *The Stone Age Cultures of the Upper Son Valley (Madhya Pradesh)*, New Delhi, 1984, p. 102; Clark and Williams, *Paleoenvironments and Prehistory*, p. 38.

24. I am indebted to Nayanjot Lahiri for this observation.

25. K.D. Bajpai, *Cultural History of India*, vol. I, *Madhya Pradesh*, Delhi, 1985, p. 53; Clark and Sharma, 'Discussion of preliminary results', pp. 272–4; A.K. Roy et al., *Planning the Environment: Based on Research Conducted in Shahdol District*, Gandhigram, 1982, p. 3; D.H. Gordon, *The Pre-Historic Background of Indian Culture*, Bombay, 1960, pp. 34–5.

26. Varma, *Rewa*, p. 1; P. Sinha, 'Probability sampling in the context of the stone age of the Satna district, Madhya Pradesh', *ME*, vol. XI, 1987, pp. 85, 89; *IAR, 1961–62*, p. 24.

27. Varma, *Rewa*, p. 1; *IAR 1961–62*, p. 24; R.B. Foote, *The Foote Collection of Indian Prehistoric and Protohistoric Antiquities: Notes on their Ages and Distribution*, Madras, 1916, p. 9; V.D. Krishnaswami and K.V. Soundararajan, 'The lithic tool-industries of the Singrauli basin', *AI*, no. 7, Jan. 1951, p. 62; Sinha, 'Probability sampling', p. 86; V.D. Jha and A.K. Singh, 'Fresh light on the pre-history of Sidhi District', *JMPIP*, no. 11, 1980, p. 61.

28. Sharma and Clark (eds.), *Palaeoenvironments and Prehistory*, pp. 1–2, Clark and Williams, 'Paleoenvironments and prehistory', p. 28; Krishnaswami and Soundararajan, 'Lithic tool-industries', p. 46; A. Ghosh, *An Encyclopaedia of Indian Archaeology*, vol. I, *Subjects*, Delhi, 1989, p. 23; Ahmad, *The Stone Age*, pp. 14–6; *IAR 1962–63*, p. 11; *IAR 1965–66*, pp. 22–3; *IAR 1975–76*, pp. 25–7; *IAR 1991–92*, p. 57; V.D. Misra, J.N. Pandey, and B.B. Misra, 'Lithic industries of Maihar, Satna, Madhya Pradesh: a preliminary study', in V.D. Misra, *Some Aspects of Indian Archaeology*, Allahadbad, 1977, pp. 3–4; Sinha, 'Probability sampling', pp. 82–3, 85. The Ballia *nadi* was under threat of submersion when the above research was undertaken, and has since presumably been inundated.

29. Varma, *Rewa*, pp. 6–7; *IAR 1963–64*, p. 39; Clark and Williams, 'Paleoenvironments and prehistory', p. 28; V.D. Misra, B.B. Misra, and J.N. Pal, 'Recent Explorations in the Adwa Valley in the Districts of Mirzapur (UP) and Sidhi and Rewa (M.P.)', *Pragdhara*, no. 7, 1996–7, p. 60. Some authorities place Lekhahia in Mirzapur district.

30. Krishnaswami and Soundararajan, 'Lithic tool-industries', p. 63.

31. Clark and Williams, 'Paleoenvironments and prehistory', p. 38.

32. For the non-utilitarian view I am indebted to J.N. Tiwari. For tool types, see D.P. Agarwal, 'Dating Indian Archaeology by the radio-carbon clock', *JMPIP*, no. 8, 1970, p. 68; Clark and Williams, 'Paleoenvironments and prehistory', pp. 28–30, 38; Varma, *Rewa*, p. 1; *IAR 1991–92*, p. 57. For site continuity: Ahmad, *The Stone Age*, pp. 14–16; *IAR 1987–88*, p. 80; Misra, Pandey and Misra, 'Lithic industries of Maihar', p. 3; *Shahdol Gazetteer*, p. 33; Sharma and Clark, (eds.), *Palaeoenvironments and Prehistory*, pp. 1–2. For additional sites, Sinha, 'Probability sampling', p. 84; *Shahdol Gazetteer*, p. 33; *IAR 1973–74*, p. 19.

33. Varma, *Rewa*, pp. 1–2; Badam et al., 'Preliminary study', p. 42; *Shahdol Gazetteer*, p. 33; Sinha, 'Probability sampling', p. 83; *IAR 1991–92*, p. 57.

34. R.J. Blumenschine, S.A. Brandt, and J.D. Clark, 'Excavations and analysis of middle palaeolithic artefacts from Patpara, Madhya Pradesh', Sharma and Clark (eds.), *Palaeoenvironments and Prehistory*, p. 67.

35. Clark and Williams, 'Paleoenvironments and prehistory', pp. 30–2; P. Sinha, 'Economic and subsistence activities at Baghor III, India: a microwear study', J.M. Kenoyer (ed.), *Old Problems and New Perspectives in the Archaeology of South Asia*, Wisconsin, 1989, p. 51. Clark and Williams give a dating of ± 11,800 BP for Baghor III.

36. B. Allchin and F.R. Allchin, *The Rise of Civilisation in India and Pakistan*, New Delhi, 1983, p. 58; Ahmad, *The Stone Age*, pp. 14–6; *Rewa Gazetteer*, p. 24; *Sidhi Gazetteer*, p. 21; Sharma and Clark, (eds.), *Palaeoenvironments and Prehistory*, pp. 1–2; Misra, Misra and Pal; 'Recent explorations', pp. 59–60, 62, 64; Badam et al., 'Preliminary study', p. 42; *IAR 1973–74*, p. 19; *IAR 1997–98*, p. 80; Krishnaswami and Soundararajan, 'Lithic tool-industries', pp. 48, 58, 60.

37. Clark and Williams, 'Paleoenvironments and prehistory', pp. 31–2; Sinha, 'Economic and subsistence activities', pp. 47–53; J.D. Clark and M.A.J. Williams, 'Prehistoric ecology, resource strategies and culture change in the Son valley, northern Madhya Pradesh, Central India', *ME*, vol. 15, 1990, p. 23.

38. Sinha, 'Economic and subsistence activities', p. 48.

39. J.N. Pal, 'Upper palaeolithic cultures of the mid-Son valley', *Puratattva*, no. 12, 1980–1, p. 29.

40. H.D. Sankalia, 'The beginning of civilisation in Madhya Pradesh', *JMPIP*, no. 8, 1970, pp. 6–9; *IAR 1975–76*, p. 27; *IAR 1991–92*, pp. 57–9; Clark and Williams, 'Paleoenvironments and prehistory', p. 33; Varma, *Rewa*, pp. 8–9; J.N. Pal, *Archaeology of South Uttar Pradesh: Ceramic Industries of the Northern Vindhyas*, Allahabad, 1986, p. 88; S.A. Brandt, J.D. Clark, J.A. Gutin, and B.B. Misra, 'Rock shelters with paintings on top of the Kaimur escarpment at Ghagharia, and an account of the excavation and analysis of the mesolithic occupation at the Ghagharia I shelter', Sharma and Clark, (eds.), *Palaeoenvironments and Prehistory*, pp. 219–21.

41. Misra, Pandey, and Misra, 'Lithic industries of Maihar', p. 8; *IAR 1986–87*, p. 56; Clark and Williams, 'Paleoenvironments and prehistory', p. 33; Varma, *Rewa*, p. 2; Ahmad, *The Stone Age*, pp. 1–2; Krishnaswami and Soundararajan, 'Lithic tool-industries', p. 60.

42. Ahmad, *The Stone Age*, p. 1.

43. B. Allchin and F.R. Allchin, *Rise of Civilisation*, p. 74; Sankalia, 'Beginning of civilisation', p. 6; Varma, *Rewa*, p. 8; C. Sussman, R. Blumenschine, J.D. Clark, and B.B. Misra, 'Preliminary report on excavations at the mesolithic occupational site at the Baghor II locality', Sharma and Clark, (eds.), *Palaeoenvironments and Prehistory*, p. 172; Krishnaswami and Soundararajan, 'Lithic tool-industries', p. 65.

44. Brandt, Clark, Gutin, and Misra, 'Rock shelters with paintings', p. 219: Sussman et al., 'Preliminary report', p. 187; B. Allchin and F.R. Allchin, *Rise of Civilisation*, p. 72; *IAR 1991–92*, pp. 57–8; Clark and Williams, 'Paleoenvironments and prehistory', p. 33.

45. Ahmad, *The Stone Age*, pp. 1–2; Varma, *Rewa*, pp. 6–9, 12–13; Sharma and Clark, *Palaeoenvironments and Prehistory*, p. 4; Pal, *Archaeology of South U.P.*, p. 31; Clark and Williams, 'Paleoenvironments and prehistory', pp. 33–4; Sinha, 'Probability sampling', pp. 83–4; E. Neumayer, *Prehistoric Indian Rock Paintings*, Delhi, 1983, p. 1; Brandt et al., 'Rock shelters with paintings', p. 219; Misra, Pandey, and Misra, 'Lithic industries of Maihar', pp. 3, 8, 11; Misra, Misra and Pal, 'Recent explorations', pp. 60, 64.

46. Sankalia, 'Beginning of civilisation', p. 1.

47. Clark and Williams, 'Paleoenvironments and prehistory', p. 34; Pal, *Archaeology of South U.P.*, pp. 14, 23–5, 83–7; Clark and Sharma, 'Discussion of preliminary results', p. 272; Gordon, *Prehistoric Background*, pp. 34–5; Misra, Pandey and Misra, 'Lithic industries of Maihar', p. 11; Varma, *Rewa*, p. 6.

48. Ita Pahar, some 36 kilometres from Rewa on the Mauganj road, was a mesolithic shelter site where tools of the middle and upper palaeolithic were found. See *IAR 1961–62*, pp. 22–4.

49. Neumayer, *Prehistoric Indian Rock Paintings*, p. 6.

50. G.R. Sharma and B.B. Misra, *Archaeology of the Vindhyas and the Ganga; Excavations at Chopani-Mando (Belan Valley), 1977–79*, Varanasi, 1980, p. 9; Clark and Sharma, 'Discussion of preliminary results', p. 274; R.K. Varma, 'Rock art of the Vindhyan region', *Fifteenth Congress of Indo-Pacific Pre-History Association*, Thailand, Oct. 1995, p. 7.

51. D.K. Chakrabarti, *India, an Archaeological History: Palaeolithic Beginnings to Early Historic Foundations*, New Delhi, 1999, p. 115; Varma, *Rewa*, p. 7; Neumayer, *Prehistoric Indian Rock Paintings*, p. 6; Varma, 'Rock art of the Vindhyan region', pp. 7, 9, 15; Pal, *Archaeology of South U.P.*, p. 83.

52. B. Allchin and F.R. Allchin, *Origins of a Civilisation*, p. 87; Varma, 'Rock art of the Vindhyan region', pp. 10–11; Clark and Williams, 'Paleoenvironments and prehistory', p. 34; B. Allchin and F.R. Allchin, *Rise of Civilisation*, p. 94.

53. R.K. Varma, 'The rock art of southern Uttar Pradesh with special reference to Mirzapur', K.K. Chakravarty (ed.), *Rock Art of India: Painting and Engraving*, 1984, pp. 207–9; Varma, 'Rock art of the Vindhyan region', p. 11; *Sidhi Gazetteer*, p. 21.

54. Varma, 'Rock art of the Vindhyan region', p. 12; B. Allchin and F.R. Allchin, *Rise of Civilisation*, pp. 94–5.

55. Varma, 'Rock art of the Vindhyan region', pp. 13–15; Varma, *Rewa*, p. 11.

56. Kosambi, *Culture and Civilization*, p. 32; M.D. Khare, *Painted Rock Shelters*, Bhopal, 1981, pp. 14–15.

57. Kosambi, *Culture and Civilization*, p. 39; Pal, *Archaeology of South U.P.*, p. 10; J. Jacobson, 'Static sites and peripatetic peoples: notes on the archaeology of population mobility in eastern Malwa', in L.S. Leshnik and G.D. Sontheimer, *Pastoralists and Nomads in South Asia*, Wiesbaden, 1975, pp. 76–80; Clark and Sharma, 'Discussion of preliminary results', p. 273; Sharma and Clark, (eds.), *Palaeoenvironments and Prehistory*, p. 3; Ghose, *Encyclopaedia*, vol. I, p. 39.

58. Sharma and Misra, *Archaeology of the Vindhyas*, pp. 7–9; N. Lahiri, *The Archaeology of Indian Trade Routes up to 200 BC: Resource Use, Resource Access and Lines of Communication*, Delhi, 1992, pp. 225, 246, 253–4, 317; B. Allchin and F.R. Allchin, *Rise of Civilisation*, p. 74; Clark and Williams, 'Paleoenvironments and prehistory', p. 34.

59. Sharma and Misra, *Archaeology of the Vindhyas*, pp. 7–9.

60. Ibid., p. 7.

61. Sharma and Misra, *Archaeology of the Vindhyas*, p. 8.

62. Clark and Williams, 'Paleoenvironments and prehistory', pp. 38–9; Clark and Williams, 'Prehistoric ecology', p. 23.

63. Pal, *Archaeology of South U.P.*, pp. 43–4; Clark and Williams, 'Paleoenvironments and prehistory', p. 35; Clark and Williams, 'Prehistoric ecology', p. 20.

64. Clark and Williams, 'Paleoenvironments and prehistory', pp. 35, 39; Pal, *Archaeology of South U.P.*, p. 44; Clark and Williams, 'Prehistoric ecology', p. 20.

65. Pal, *Archaeology of South U.P.*, pp. 15, 43–4, 114–15; Clark and Williams, 'Paleoenvironments and prehistory', p. 36, note that a charcoal sample from the Kunjhun river site gave an age of 4, 740 ± 80 BP, which accords with radiocarbon dates from Mahagara in the Belan valley.

66. Sharma and Clark, (eds.) *Palaeoenvironments and Prehistory*, p. 2; Clark and Williams, 'Paleoenvironments and prehistory', pp. 34–6; Sharma and Misra, *Archaeology of the Vindhyas*, p. 25; Pal, *Archaeology of South U.P.*, pp. 9, 17; *IAR 1975–76*, p. 27; D.K. Misra, *Son ka pani ka rang*, Bhopal, 1983, p. 135; Varma, *Rewa*, p. 3; Misra, Misra and Pal, 'Recent explorations', pp. 60, 64.

67. B. Subbarao, *The Personality of India: Pre-and Proto-Historic Foundation of India and Pakistan*, Baroda, 1958, pp. 83, 103.

68. Guha, 'Lower strata, older races', p. 436.

69. Chakrabarti, *India*, p. 238, uses the phrase neolithic–chalcolithic to describe this phase of human evolution.

70. Clark and Williams, 'Paleoenvironments and prehistory', p. 34; *IAR 1980–81*, p. 39; P. Misra, 'Discovering the past', Bhopal, nd, np; Pal, *Archaeology of South U.P.*, p. 71; Misra, Misra and Pal, 'Recent explorations', p. 64; J.N. Pal, 'Chalcolithic Vindhyas', *Pragdhara*, no. 5, 1994–5, p. 13; Ahmad, *The Stone Age*, p. 103; Gordon, *Prehistoric Background*, p. 146. Chalcolithic pottery was found in a few sites in the Adwa valley.

71. B.B. Lal, 'Further copper hoards from the Gangetic basin and a review of the problem', *AI*, no. 7, Jan. 1951, pp. 22–3; Ghosh, *Encyclopaedia*, vol. I, pp. 98, 244; B. Allchin and F.R. Allchin, *Rise of Civilisation*, pp. 269–71.

72. Ghosh, *Encyclopaedia*, vol. I, p. 243; H.P. Ray, 'Bharhut and Sanchi–nodal points in a commercial interchange', B.M. Pande and B.D. Chattopadhyaya (eds), *Archaeology and History: Essays in Memory of Shri A. Ghose*, New Delhi, 1987, pp. 623–4; K.V. Soundararajan, 'Megaliths and black and red ware', A.K. Narain and P. Singh (eds.), *Seminar Papers on the Problem of Megaliths in India*, Varanasi, 1969; Chakrabarti, *India*, pp. 238–9.

73. Ghose, *Encyclopaedia*, vol. I, pp. 243–4; Ray, 'Bharhut and Sanchi', p. 624; *IAR 1975–76*, p. 27; *IAR 1982–83*, p. 40; *IAR 1988–89*, p. 45; Pal, *Archaeology of South U.P.*, p. 12; *Rewa Gazetteer*, p. 24; *Sidhi Gazetteer*, pp. 21–2; Misra, Misra, and Pal, 'Recent explorations', p. 64.

2

Patterns of Migration, Settlement, and Integration: Baghelkhand, *c.* 800 BC to 1300 AD

CRBO

Between *c.* 800 BC and 1300 AD Baghelkhand was constantly in dialogue with nationalizing forces, whether of centralizing states impinging on it or of people migrating there, often under political pressure. This dialogue shaped Baghelkhand's identity, opening it to new political, economic, and social influences; it also forged commonalities with states and peoples beyond the region's borders.*

I

BAGHELKHAND'S PROTOHISTORY

Paradoxically, the earliest evidence of human activity in Baghelkhand in the protohistoric period comes not from migrants from the adjacent river valleys, but from local people developing the use of iron at megalithic and other sites during the first millennium BC. It is likely that iron-knowing people from outside the region arrived later to widen further the social and economic life of Baghelkhand.

Archaeologists strongly affirm the existence of an indigenous iron industry in Baghelkhand.[1] Varma asserts that megalithic people

*This chapter owes much to the criticisms, suggestions and corrections of P.S. Dwivedi and Upinder Singh. My thanks are also due to J.N. Tiwari for his comments.

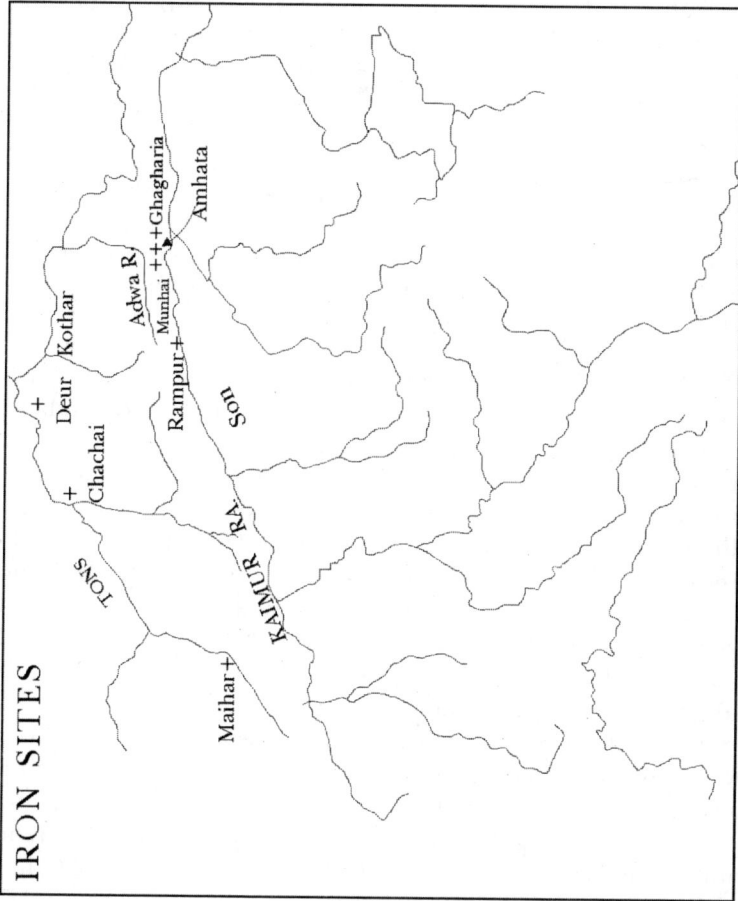

IRON SITES

Chachai +

Deur +

Kothar

Adwa R.

Ghagharia + +

Munhai +

Amhata

Rampur +

Son

TONS

KAIMUR RA

Maihar +

Map 6

in the Adwa valley passed from using copper to iron. Chakrabarti notes that the pre-industrial smelting of local iron ore was 'impressive' in central India—the earliest of all iron sites in the subcontinent, and mentions a pre-modern site in Rewa, probably in the Adwa valley. Guha states that the 'itinerants of the forest'—possibly the Agarias—possessed iron technology. Lahiri believes that the use of iron may even have spread from the Vindhyas to the northern river plains:

The importance of the Vindhyan plateau as a source area for the minerally poor Gangetic plains, going back to the mesolithic period, was greatly enhanced in the early historic period when the urban centres that dotted the plains demanded large supplies of iron, copper, and stone of various kinds.... This region mediated interaction between the Ganges valley and central and peninsular India.[2]

Baghelkhand's indigenous iron industry is spectacularly documented in the megalith sites with iron remains in the Adwa valley.[3] The megaliths here comprise cists, cairn circles, and cists within cairn circles. Several sites also contain upper palaeolithic remains with microliths. While sites are spread along the upper Adwa valley towards the Rewa border with old Mirzapur, two concentrations occur: one at Amhata 93 kilometres east of Rewa, and the other at nearby Munhai, which also contained copper pieces and a rich collection of pottery. Indeed, the sites generally yielded black and red ware, in addition to animal bones, beads and bangles and, in one, a terra cotta muller.

Outside the Adwa valley iron sites are distributed throughout the region.[4] Archaeologists have discovered megaliths and iron slag together with Kotia pottery at a number of sites in the middle Son valley, including Rampur, Kasauli, and Baburi. Above, on the Kaimur, the Ghagharia rock shelter contained iron slag. Other iron finds occur at Chachai in north Rewa and Maihar in Satna. P.K. Misra also found iron objects, slag, and lumps, together with nodules of lime for use in smelting at the cave shelter and *stupa* site of Deur Kothar on the northern scarp.

II

INDIAN AND EUROPEAN WRITING ON THE REGION

Nothing more eloquently affirms Baghelkhand's passage into history than early Indian and European writing about the region. Such writing demonstrates a wider than local awareness of Baghelkhand, extending not only to the subcontinent but to distant Europe as well. This awareness derived from migration into the region from adjacent river valleys, that swelled a local population comprising indigenous iron people, neolithic farmers, and others surviving from the region's prehistory.

Indian writing[5] showing a knowledge of the region includes the *Puranas*, whose oral tradition could be as early as 1000 BC, and the earliest written text around the third or fourth centuries A.D.; the *Ramayana*, from about 800 BC to about 200 AD; and the *Mahabharata*, again from about 800 BC on into the Christian era. European sources include those of Megasthenes, a Greek ambassador at the court of Chandragupta Maurya, 350–290 BC; the Latin authors: Strabo, 64 BC to 23 AD; Pliny, the first century AD; and Arrianus, the second century AD. The other Greek writer was the geographer, Ptolemy, also in the second century AD.

All early Indian writing names the region's rivers.[6] The Tamasa or Tons is the Parnasa of the *Puranas*, issuing from the Rksha mountains, the *Ramayana* noting that it later joins the Ganga. The *Mahabharata*, *Ramayana* and most of the *Puranas* mention the Son as a river of great sanctity such that *sandhya* on its banks ensured that even those who killed Brahmans could attain heaven. The Narmada is the Reva of the *Puranas*, the *Skanda Purana* relating many legends concerning the river's birth.

The early texts also contain information about the country south of the Yamuna and the Ganga, describing it as a forested landscape inhabited by demons and snakes.[7] The *Ramayana* sets the exile of Rama, prince of Ayodhya, in this Vindhyan region. However, Ravana, probably a powerful leader in the Dandaka forest who had extended his sway northwards, kidnapped Sita, impelling Rama to begin an epic journey to secure her release. From the *Valmiki Ramayana* and other works we assume that after leaving Chitrakut Rama passed through western Baghelkhand, crossing the Son and its tributaries on his way to the Dandaka forest.

The *Mahabharata* bespeaks another epic crossing, that of the Vedic advance into central and southern India, symbolized in the legend of Agastya.[8] As the Vindhya mountains had begun to rival the Himalaya, Agastya their guide ordered them to submit, and with their compliance he passed over the ranges on his way south. In the same way, the conflict between Rama and Ravana represents an alliance between those involved in the Vedic advance into the forests of the eastern Deccan and local inhabitants against another ruler (Ravana), who seems to be ruling a society more advanced than that of the local people.

The ashrams of *rishis* and sages south of Chitrakut also reflect the advance of Vedic culture beyond the northern river plains at the hands of migrants and settlers.[9] The epics and *Puranas* all refer to these settlements. The ashrams of Valmiki, Arti, Agastya, and Sarabhanga sought to promote Sanskritic culture among the people of the Vindhyatavi and further south. Valmiki's ashram was on the banks of the Tamasa, contiguous to Dandakaranya, for after leaving the hermitage, Atreyi directly entered the great forest. Early literature names the Mekala *rishi* as doing penance in the Maikal hills. The source of the Satna river is the supposed dwelling site of the hermit Sateekshana, mentioned in the *Ramayana*. Even Kalinjara hill on Baghelkhand's northern border appears in the *Vedas* as a *tapasyasthana*.

The classical writers of Greece and Rome similarly reflected the knowledge of the region spread by early historic contacts with it.[10] The writers obtained their information from Indian sources or from Megasthenes, ambassador of the Seleucid provinces of the Trans-Indus at the Mauryan court in Pataliputra. These writers also described the region's physical features, Megasthenes referring to the Tons as the Prinas. He and Arrianus write of the Son, its name coming from *sona*, red gold or crimson from the colour of the sand the river holds in suspension during the rains. Both writers also refer to the Son as Eranaboas, derived from *hiranyavahu* or golden-armed—a similar epithet. Ptolemy spread his net somewhat wider, including not only the Son and the smaller Tamasa, but also the Narmada and the Cinas or Ken river of Bundelkhand. He refers to the Vindhyas as Ouindion.

III

THE OUTLINES OF A NEW SOCIETY

Migration was an important aspect of the nationalizing process in the region in the early historic period. Mediated by external states and other forces, this inward flow of people created a new type of society in Baghelkhand, as well as linking the region socially and economically with the areas from which the migrants had come.

Pathways such as the *dakshinapatha* not only suggest themselves as migratory passages into Baghelkhand, but also acted as links between the region and the rest of India. If the *patha* is seen not as a specific roadway, but a band of paths passing through central India,[11] then its significance as a line of migration and connectivity is enhanced. However, it was not only migrants who used this many-stranded route. Well before the Christian era travellers, merchants, craftsmen, armies, and Buddhist missionaries travelled to (or through) the region over these paths, their journeyings helping to rescind the 'cultural barrier' perceived by many to exist between the northern plains and central India.[12]

Archaeologists have other ways of looking at the *dakshinapatha* in relation to Baghelkhand.[13] Lahiri writes of the Vindhyan high-lands with their minerals and stone mediating interaction between the Ganga valley and central and southern India. Chakrabarti claims that the iron site at Raja Nala ka Tila near Robertsganj in old Mirzapur lay on an early historic route from the Gangetic plain via Chopan to central India and beyond. Ray proposes the emergence of an inhabited corridor between Andhra and the north through the Vindhyan region.

Some would-be settlers may also have entered Baghelkhand from the west. This would seem to be the case with the Abastanoi or the Ambasthas who moved from the subcontinent's north-west to the Maikal hills in search of security and land in the later first millennium BC:

In Alexander's time the tribe was settled on the ... Asikini....(and) eventually submitted to Alexander.... At the time of the *Aitareya Brahmana* ... they were probably settled in the Punjab.... The Mahabharata mentions the Ambasthas along with...other north-west tribes....settled on the Eastern borders of Punjab. Their country is mentioned in the *Barhaspatya Arthasastra*, where it is associated with Sind.... According to the Jatakas,

the Ambasthas were farmers.... [They] seem to have migrated in later
times to some place near the Mekala hill which is the source of the
Narmada. In the Kurmavibhaga of the *Brhatsamhita*, they are associated
with the Mekalas who dwelt on the Mekala hill.... [which] would seem to
prove that the two were neighbouring tribes. The tribe seems to have
migrated eastwards as well.[14]

Baghelkhand offered considerable promise for migrants. Some
came to exploit the region's mineral resources. Perennial streams
assured settlers of water: the early settlements of Unchahra, Khoh,
Jaso, Rampur, Kothi, Maihar, Nagod, and Sohawal in west
Baghelkhand all took root on the banks of streams. Fertile land was
available in the river valleys of the Rewa plateau, the Son trough,
the basins of Singrauli and Sohagpur, and the lowlands of Teonthar.
Forests offered grazing land for cattle, wood for fuel, implements
and buildings, and edibles to supplement the produce of the
field. In addition, pressure of population and political conflicts in
adjacent areas pushed migrants into the region's comparatively
empty spaces.

There were, however, limits to the region's capacity to absorb
migrants. Extensive hill systems reduced the land available for
cultivation; and soils in these areas as in other parts of Rewa, Sidhi,
and Shahdol were infertile. Apart from the major rivers, no stream
could assure an unfailing supply of water. The profiles of the
waterways, too, with their shallow beds, sandy stretches, gorges, and
waterfalls limited their use as lines of communication. Moreover,
movement across rocky hills and through deep forests remained
difficult until well into the twentieth century.

Brahmans would have been among the foremost colonizers of
Baghelkhand, laying the basis for their later dominance of regional society.[15] They were to be found among the earliest sages
and hermits who meditated and did penance in forest retreats. In
time ashrams developed further, staffed by Brahmans who served
their apprenticeship as teachers, tended their cattle, mastered the
Vedas, and obeyed a senior teacher, to finally emerge as full ini-
tiates. Ashrams may also have housed people seeking a simple life
away from the urban distractions of the north, settling near others
already living in the area as farmers.[16]

Later Brahman migrants carried the process of colonization and
nationalization further, organizing village settlements and building temples. With their monopoly of religious rites and their role

Map 7

in legitimizing the status of migrant groups in the stratified society emerging in Baghelkhand, rulers of early states invited them to their realms, bestowing land on them for their services. Bana's village in the seventh century was inhabited mostly by Brahmans.

Other groups added to what was becoming an increasingly complex society, replicating that in adjacent north India. That traders came to Baghelkhand can be seen from inscriptions at Bharhut near Satna, and from deposits of northern black polished ware, the distinguished pottery of the Mauryan period. Early kingdoms required the protection of warriors; peasants were needed to grow food; craftsmen to build villages and towns; labourers to hew wood and draw water, settling with their patrons on vacant land or among an already existing population. Incoming hill and forest peoples added to the complexity. As elsewhere, many among these diverse groups fused slowly into a hierarchy of communities, ranked in terms of their occupational status and their proximation to the values of the higher *varnas* of the new society.[17] Others remained outside that society.

The early texts provide clues to specific groups making up the new society, among them agricultural peoples who settled in somewhat defined areas and formed elementary administrations.[18] According to the *Puranas*, Karusa in the Singrauli area of Sidhi was the oldest name for the region, where the Karusa people had set up a *janapada*, thought to be part of the Vatsa Kingdom of the Chedis with whom they were connected by marriage. The Mekala *janapada* also finds mention in the *Puranas* but, though named after the plateau, at its greatest extent it appears to have included Dakshina Kosala and the territories of the Dasarna people, of the Chedis, and the Utkalas of the Kalinga country.

Consequent on migration, agriculture made considerable progress in parts of Baghelkhand by the later first millennium BC. After gaining power in Magadha, the Mauryan kings extended their sway over much of India including Baghelkhand, continuing the migration and development that had already taken place, such that

in the early Buddhist era, the Vindhyas must already have had a remarkable agricultural and communications infrastructure.... Everywhere, even in the hill areas which today are covered by dense teak jungles, one runs into the remains of *stupas*, hermitages, dykes for irrigation, or as sources of water supply for the grazing of livestock, and, sometimes, well laid out roads and paths. This infrastructure may have developed in response to the needs of a fairly dense population who occupied the river valleys since Mesolithic times.[19]

The Mauryan state opened Baghelkhand further to outside influences, also placing it more firmly on the subcontinental map, by encouraging Buddhists to establish settlements at Bharhut and Deur Kothar on chords of the *dakshinapatha* passing through the region. Bharhut, fourteen kilometres south of Satna, was located on a major route from Pataliputra through Kausambi. The passage bifurcated at Bharhut, one line turning west for Vidisha, Ujjain, and Pratishthana, the other going south to Tripuri and Amarkantak. Deur Kothar lay on the path from Prayaga into Baghelkhand. Both centres were ideally placed to cater to the religious needs of travellers, traders, and pilgrims, as well as to spread the teachings of the Buddha in the surrounding countryside. In addition, the Mauryan state could use these sites to guard important passages through their domains.

Non-agricultural people also constituted an important segment of regional society and contributed to its economy, as Strabo informs us:

The third caste is that of the shepherds and hunters, who alone are permitted to hunt, to breed cattle and to sell or hire out beasts of burden; and in return for freeing the land from wild beasts and seed-picking birds, they receive proportionate allowances of grain from the king, leading as they do a wandering and tent-dwelling life.[20]

Arrianus added that the third caste lived on the hills and paid tribute in the form of cattle.[21] Pliny identified one such group as the Suari or Sabaras, who with other 'half-wild' people hunted and trapped elephants. Ptolemy is the only author to mention the Phullitae Gondali or Kandaloi, the leaf-clad Gonds; and the Bolingae, who could be the Pulindas or the Balands living east of Sandrabatis (Chandraparbata), a hill in the Maikal area.

We cannot say with any certainty now whether the Sabaras, Nishadas, and others named in the early Indian texts were migrants into the region or in some way connected with its prehistoric inhabitants. As I have suggested, some mesolithic people may have migrated to the Ganga, Son, and other valleys to farm in more conducive surroundings. Others, however, as seems the case at Ghagharia, remained to witness the arrival of food producers. Therefore, whether migrants or those who had absorbed earlier inhabitants, the Sabaras, Nishadas, and others, were certainly present in the region when the early agricultural migrants arrived.

At any rate, with the 'arrival' of the people of the early texts, we leave behind the inchoate prehistoric people and encounter communities with names, living in more defined localities.[22] The Nishadas, Sabaras, and others were hunters and trappers inhabiting the Vindhyatavi and the Dandaka forest, 'ever ready to fall on merchant caravans passing through their territories'. The Nishadas who lived in a Nishada *rashtra* were sometimes also called Bhillas. (Some commentators use the three names interchangeably). As late as the seventh century AD, Banabhatta referred to a Sabara chief as 'lord' of the entire Vindhyan range.

Later Indian writing reflected the economic importance of the forests, which were the non-agriculturists' preserve.[23] By the mid-fourth century AD the forest zone had acquired a name: Mahakantara, the great forest. The available version of Kautilya's *Arthashastra* draws our attention to the use of forests for hunting, capturing elephants, and extracting produce. Though Kautilya contrasted such 'reserved' forests with those inhabited by 'predatory tribes' and used by thieves as hiding places, he proposed that the people dwelling outside the northern plains—hunters, trappers, Sabaras, Pulindas, Candalas, and forest dwellers in general—guard their habitat so that its resources could be tapped.

By the end of the Gupta period the region's interaction with centralizing states and migratory peoples had produced two striking developments. One comprised the breaching of the forests and the related expansion of the agricultural economy. There could be no greater tribute to this achievement than the writings of Banabhatta. Though the evidence is not conclusive, it is likely that Bana's village of Pruthukuta lay in the middle Son valley, not far from the site of the temple at Chandrehe in western Sidhi.[24] Bana's parents died when he was a boy, but as an educated young writer he joined the court of Harshavardhana in Kanauj. Bana knew the Son valley intimately, and may even have been of use to Harsha as he expanded his empire into Baghelkhand. His description of the forests of the Vindhyas, exuberantly and ornately written as it is, cannot fail to impress us about the ready accessibility of the forest to the world around. There are agricultural pockets surrounding the forest, plus agricultural clearings inside, fowlers roam, as do hunters with their intricate traps. We find in it cow pens, as well as iron smelting and charcoal making, as also hermitages. Moreover, the villagers of the region help themselves to its timber, bark, flax, hemp, flowers, peacock feathers, wax and fruit.[25]

Bana's village was on a pathway and provided facilities for travellers.

Urban settlements from the Mauryan period onwards form the other emblem of the region's social and economic advance.[26] Though urbanization came later to Baghelkhand than to the northern river valleys, the growth of population and the presence of streams with lines of communication nearby led to the siting of urban settlements along them. Cunningham conceived of Mauryan Bharhut as a 'considerable city', its surrounding villages forming 'the several Mahallas' of the ancient city. Extensive urban development also took place along the streams and associated paths north of Rewa, both accessible from the northern plains. The archaeologist R.K. Varma discovered 'evidence of large-scale building activity' using locally manufactured bricks in sites there, some of them quite large, and in his view 'urban centres with traces of fortification'.

Itaha, on the Bihar river some 13 kilometres from Rewa city, is thought to be an urban site of the fourth or third century BC.[27] After a preliminary investigation Varma concluded that migrants reached the site between the fifth and fourth centuries, raised the height of the settlement and, using the river as a moat, built a rampart around it. This, with the extensive occurrence of brickbats, Mauryan pottery, terracotta artefacts, punch-marked coins and large storage jars, indicated trade, and supported the probability of Itaha being a buried urban centre of the early historical period.

Finds of northern black polished ware in the region provide further evidence of urban settlement and trade during the Mauryan period.[28] In Baghelkhand this pottery is found at the putative urban sites on the rivers north of Rewa, at the *stupa* site of Deur Kothar, and at Jhar and Madighat in the Teonthar plains. These finds not only reflected the 'increased uniformity of simple material remains' in northern India by 200 BC; they also demonstrated

the growth of a political and cultural system emanating from the
northern plains that enveloped an 'interacting continuum of communities that occupied ... the whole of South Asia.'

Urban development continued on into the first millennium AD.
Arrianus notes the existence of towns in the second century.[29]
About the same time Ptolemy refers to Badaotis, or Bharhut; and
to Balantipurgon, a fort town of the Adeisathroi, which Cunningham
read as the Haihaya *kshetra*—though it could also be construed as
Yadava *kshetra*. Balantipurgaon lay in the upper Son valley adjoining the country of the Bettigoi or Vakatakas, and derived its name
from the Balands, from whom the Chedis took it somewhere before
the fifth century BC.

IV

THE NEWER MIGRANTS AND THE HILL AND FOREST PEOPLE

As we have seen migration was an important nationalizing element
in the dialogue between the region and outside states and forces.
Yet along the *dakshinapatha* and wherever migrants settled, they
encountered an ethnic and cultural element at variance with their
own.[30] These could include remnants of the prehistoric population and the people of the early texts, including the Sabaras,
Nishadas, and others dwelling in specific areas, whom the *Ramayana*
referred to collectively as the Vanaras or forest people. Early literature also refers to the Rakshasas, forest people who were possibly
cannibals in areas south of the Vindhyas. Some commentators
believe the Baigas to be among those surviving from this early
period.

The early texts also noticed the more recently arrived forest
people, as witness Ptolemy's reference to the Phullitae Gondali.
However, long before the Gonds, in the eighth century BC the
related Munda peoples, Kol and Korku, entered Baghelkhand
from the Chhota Nagpur plateau, far from their possible homelands in south-east Asia.[31] This would make them contemporaries
of the early agricultural migrants to the region. They are said to
have established themselves over the pre-existing population in
the areas they occupied, absorbing numbers of them and ingest-
ing elements of their language into their native Mundari.

The Gonds entered the region somewhere after the fifth century BC, moving up the rivers from Karnataka and Andhra to cross the Maikal plateau into Baghelkhand.[32] In far greater numbers than the Kols and Korkus, it is thought that they divided and defeated them. Some commentators claim that the Agarias familiar with iron moved with the Gonds.

Some writers classify the Nagas, another migrant group entering Baghelkhand, as a hill and forest people, though this appears doubtful.[33] Early in the first millennium AD the Nagas entered the region from Malwa, establishing a kingdom there as they had done in other parts of northern and central India. Yet the name Naga appears to have been used for any one of a number of peoples at different levels of cultural evolution. While some are categorized as hill dwellers or residents in caves and forests, others issued inscriptions in Prakrit and Sanskrit, gave donations to the Buddhist Sangha, or even performed Vedic sacrifices. Due to pressure from the Sakas, some claim, the Nagas settled at Nagavadh or Nagod, where they were ultimately slaughtered by the Parihars, as the place name suggests.

The juxtaposition of hill and forest dwellers and increasing numbers of agricultural people may indeed have called forth such retribution. Apart from cultural differences, the former were known to loot caravans; and both sought living space within a common landscape. People in the northern plains, from where many migrants were coming, regarded the Vindhyan territory as a border region and its inhabitants as outcastes and savages; and those returning to the settled plains had to undergo rites of purification.[34]

There is evidence of some tension between the so-called *atavikas* and the Mauryan authorities.[35] Asoka distinguished between *vana* or forests used for elephants, game, and produce, and *atavi*, wild tracts inhabited by hill and forest communities. Scholars believe that one of the emperor's rock edicts displays his anxiety over the latter, nominally subordinate, though enjoying some degree of independence. Other historians go much further. Kosambi claims that Asoka sent *dhamma* missionaries to the forest people, and that Mauryan armies were 'in constant action against forest savages'. Japanese scholars link paintings in some rock shelters portraying 'battle scenes between two races' to the hostility between hill and forest groups and those who invaded their hunting and living space.

Ultimately, however, it was in the interests of the Vindhyan *janapadas*, of Magadha which absorbed them, and other states in the area, to come to terms with the hill and forest people,[36] and this seems to have taken place. In Indian texts Krishna married the daughter of Jambvanta, a forest leader; Rama allied with the Rkshas against the Rakshasas led by Ravana; and Arjun married a Bhil woman. These stories enshrine a political reality. By the fourth century AD Baghelkhand comprised *janapadas* together with some 18 forest chiefdoms, including Dahala based on Tripuri. From the time of Samudragupta AD (330–380), all the *janapadas* and chiefdoms fell under the sway of the Gupta Empire. In the late fifth century Maharaja Hastin of Khoh near Unchahra acknowledged Gupta overlordship, as did the belt of forest principalities which Hastin controlled.

Harshavardhana, too, seems to have included the hill and forest chiefs of the region within his empire—some as feudatories, others apparently independent of rule from Kanauj.[37] Banabhatta's *Harsa-Carita* refers to a powerful Sabara chief who helped Harsha search for his sister who had fled to the Vindhyatavi following her royal husband's death in battle. Bana addresses Harsha thus:

'My lord, there is a general of the Sabaras named Bhukamp, the lord of all this Vindhyan Range, the leader of all the village chiefs—this is his sister's son, Nirghata, who knows every leaf in this Vindhyan forest, and still more its localities'....
Nirghata ... spoke: 'Sire, scarcely the deer can wander here unnoticed by the general, much less then women'....[38]

However, as with the decline of the Guptas, Harsha's death left the Sabaras and other feudatories to their own devices.

Bhukamp's readiness to help Harsha underlines the integration achieved between the rulers, the agriculturalists, and the hill and forest people of Baghelkhand. Guha points to the economic integration that occurred even before the Christian era:

There are suggestions that communities occupying diverse terrains were already intregrated into a common political economy. All the classical reports concur in describing the population as made up of hereditary occupational groups, one of which was nomadic herdsmen and hunters.... It would appear that various lifeways were integrated into a complex political economy in the last centuries BCE, and that communities located in specific environmental niches specialised in particular activities. Some would have paid tribute to kings, others been paid in kind by the villagers....possibly a testing of relationships by raiding and reprisal.[39]

As elsewhere in India, a process of mutual acculturation took place, such that while the food-gatherers adjusted themselves to the language and religious customs of the agriculturists, the latter adopted some of the beliefs and rituals of the forest and hill dwellers, including animal sacrifice to propitiate their divinities. Agriculturists, too, probably brought wild cereals under cultivation in open areas, while some forest people learnt the techniques of cultivation, others forming a rural labour force.[40] The hunter–gatherers also provided their neighbours with raw materials and food from the forests.

Some degree of linguistic accommodation between widely differing communities also seems to have taken place.[41] By the time of the *Natya Shastra* regional variants of Prakrit had evolved, in addition to the languages used by the Sabaras, Vanancharas, and others. H.L. Jain found the distribution of the non-Sanskrit languages according to occupation and region informative: those who traded in elephants, horses, and camels and lived in pastoral settlements used the Sabara language—an example of how 'occupational-cum-ethnic communities were sufficiently distinct ... to have characteristic ways of speaking'. Also, even though speakers of Sanskrit regarded such languages as inferior, Guha notes that communities such as the Sabaras were 'sufficiently integrated for an upper class audience to understand actors using these dialectical variants'.

The process of mutual acculturation was particularly evident with regard to religion.[42] While the worship of female deities was widespread in early societies, including the Vedic, in central India goddess worship was intrinsic to the lives of the hill and forest people. Archaeologists believe that they have found a prehistoric shrine of a female deity in Sidhi district. In our period Vindhyavasini *devi*, the 'primal earth mother...virginal, dark....wide-hipped and fully-breasted' represented for the Sabaras, Pulindas, and others the presiding deity of the Vindhyas. Living in caves, rivers, forests, and even in the wind, her foremost shrine was on Vindhyanchal, beyond Baghelkhand in Mirzapur, where she alighted after escaping her would-be killer Mahisa. Subsidiary shrines of the goddess under different names crowned other Vindhyan summits. Indeed, the entire range was hers, guardian of its hills and people.

Goddess worship was widely prevalent among the agricultural people of ancient Baghelkhand.[43] The representation of a female figure on a lotus at Bharhut, often interpreted as a scene of Buddha's nativity, very strongly resembles a representation of the goddess Lakshmi. The carving of *devi* images gained momentum early in the first millennium AD, the Gupta rulers encouraging the worship of Lakshmi and other female deities. The goddess cult expanded further from about 500 AD, as we can see from numerous images and remains of *devi* temples in the region where devotion to Durga and other female deities was perhaps more intense than elsewhere in the subcontinent. These developments, together with the assimilation of the non-Vedic Parvati and various snake-goddesses into the Hindu pantheon; the establishment of temples with circular *garbha-griha*s at Gurgi, Chandrehe and elsewhere in the tenth century; and the temple of Sarada *devi* near Maihar, all showed how the worship of the hill and forest people merged with and perhaps even transformed the consciousness of the agricultural people.

It is not clear how far the hill and forest communities ingested Vedic religious practices. In *Kadambari*, Bana ascribes 'the most archaic level of Tantric worship' to the still 'wild' Sabaras, whose

one religion is offering human flesh to Candika, and whose chief had shoulders that were rough with scars from keen weapons often used to make an offering of blood to Candika. The incorporation of Hinduised ... forms into the rituals of tribesmen such as these probably amounted to little more than an identification of their tutelary gods and goddesses with Hindu ones such as Bhairava, Kali and Candika.[44]

Vakpati Raja, another seventh century writer, confirmed Bana's observation: the hero in his poem 'Gauda Vaho' saw leaf-clad Sabara men and women offering human sacrifices at the shrine of their goddess at Vindhyanchal.[45]

Alongside these forms of religious assimilation, the cult of Siva developed in Baghelkhand as in other parts of the subcontinent.[46] By the time of the *Puranas* the Vedic deity Rudra, the element of irresistible force, had become Siva the benevolent and husband of Parvati, in addition to other roles, and ranked among the three

principal Vedic deities. Baghelkhand became a centre of the growing devotion to Siva, and even the shrine of Vindhyavasini *devi*
appears to have been a centre of Saivite worship. With the revival
of Brahmanism during the Gupta period, the cult expanded as the
pensive *mukhalingam* at remote Bhumara in Satna district bears
witness. By the seventh century the worship of Siva was popular in
that part of the Son valley familiar to Bana:

Even before Bana was born, Siva was ... the deity par excellence of the
Vindhyan region. The temple of Siva at Chandreh near the village of
Chandreh on [the] Son seems to represent the site of an ancient temple
of Siva which was in existence during the time of Banabhatta. It was
probably built on the spot where the asrama of the celebrated Risi
Cyavan stood.... Bana was a devout Saiva.[47]

In patterns familiar elsewhere, migrants transplanted their religious myths among the hills and rivers of Baghelkhand.[48]
Brahma's tears falling near Amarkantak created the Son and the
Narmada. Legend also associated Amarkantak with the heroes of
the *Mahabharata*, Yudishthara visiting the hermitage of Markandeya
there. Folklore avers, too, that the Pandavas of Delhi visited
Amarkantak in their forest rambles, and five caves reputedly theirs
can be seen at the site. Bandhavgarh is sacred to the memory of
Rama's brother, Lakshmana, hence its name.

V

THE NATIONAL IDEA AND LOCAL STATES IN BAGHELKHAND

Our exploration of the integrative influences of imperial states
and migratory patterns must refer to the relations between regional rulers and the imperial states impinging on Baghelkhand.
While most of these were located in the northern river plains,
southern rulers also developed wider than regional ambitions and
sought to bring Baghelkhand within their orbit of power.

The Vatsa *janapada* demonstrates the tension between the national and the local organization of power.[49] Vatsa, based on
Kausambi, ingested large areas of Baghelkhand between the seventh and fifth centuries BC. However, in adding to its territory Vatsa
came up against the expanding state of Magadha, which annexed
the *janapada* before the Nandas usurped power there. As lords of

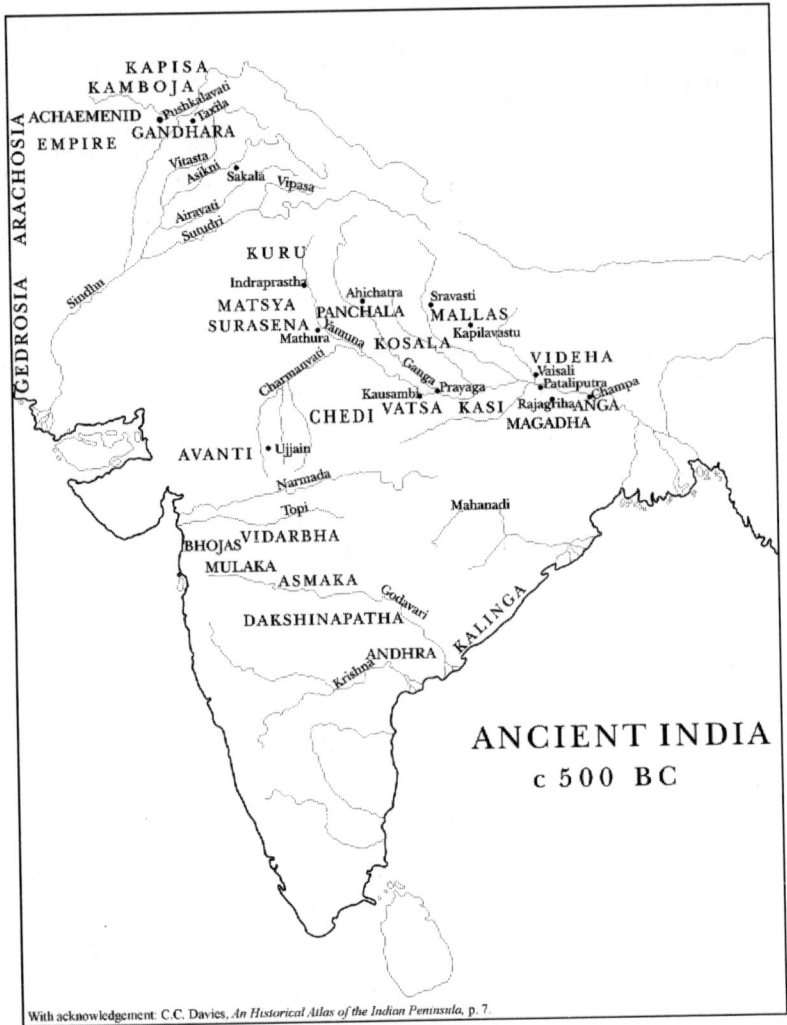

KAPISA
KAMBOJA
ACHAEMENID GANDHARA Pushkalavati
EMPIRE   Taxila
ARACHOSIA
GEDROSIA

Vitasta
Asikni
Sakala Vipasa
Airavati
Sutudri
Sindhu

KURU
Indraprastha
Ahichatra   Sravasti
MATSYA PANCHALA MALLAS
SURASENA Yamuna   Kapilavastu
Mathura   KOSALA
Charmanvati   Ganga   VIDEHA
                 Vaisali
Kausambi Prayaga   Pataliputra
                            Champa
CHEDI VATSA KASI Rajagriha ANGA
                     MAGADHA

AVANTI Ujjain

Narmada
Topi   Mahanadi
BHOJAS VIDARBHA
MULAKA
ASMAKA Godavari
DAKSHINAPATHA   KALINGA
            ANDHRA
Krishna

ANCIENT INDIA
c 500 BC

With acknowledgement: C.C. Davies, *An Historical Atlas of the Indian Peninsula*, p. 7.

Map 8

Aryavarta, the Nandas, too, controlled the region before falling to the superior might of Chandragupta Maurya in 321 BC.

The Mauryas took the national idea enunciated by the Nandas and others much further.[50] Aided by a professional army, the Mauryan rulers expanded from Magadha to much of the subcontinent, including Baghelkhand, where they brought all local rulers under their sway, integrating the various peoples inhabiting their empire into a wider political economy. The Mauryan state also developed administrative structures, defined trade routes, and taxed its citizens, besides encouraging the expansion of Buddhism through the areas under its control.

Despite the demise of the Mauryan state at the hands of the Sungas, the imperial idea did not perish, for the Sungas also encroached on Baghelkhand, part of the *stupa* at Bharhut dating from their reign.[51] The Satavahanas destroyed declining Sunga strength in the peninsula, and their king Satakarni conquered territory north of the Narmada to gain the title Lord of the Vindhya and other Ranges. The Kushanas, too, swept east to Varanasi and south to the Narmada, though a hoard of their coins found in Shahdol may indicate trade rather than domination, as their money enjoyed equal currency with that of other states or rulers.

The periodic weakening of these external powers made possible the rise of local states in Baghelkhand.[52] One such was the Magha kingdom. Sometime tributary to the Kushanas, the Maghas asserted their independence and seized Kausambi in the mid-second century AD, taking their rule from the northern plains south to Bandhavgarh and the Maikal hills. However, the Magha state in turn fell before the imperial Vakatakas of the Deccan who occupied west Baghelkhand to become Vindhyakas and make tutelary the ruler of the Mahakantara. The lords of Mekala similarly treated the commands of the Vakatakas 'with respect'.

Samudragupta's entry into Indian politics in the fourth century AD heralded the most decisive integration of Baghelkhand into an imperial or centralizing state thus far.[53] Samudra conquered northern and central India, seizing Vakataka and other lands in Baghelkhand, defeating Vyaghraraja of Mahakantara, and making all the kings of the Atavika Rajya together with the ruler of Dahala pay their dues and obey his commands. Eran, too, was part of

Samudra's empire. His successors extended these conquests, as Gupta temples in Satna district, a pillar inscription of 460 AD found at Rewa, and inscriptions in Sidhi (485–6 AD) bear witness. Two Gupta feudatories in west Baghelkhand demonstrate the type of integration regional states experienced at the hands of their central overlords.[54] These were the Uchchhakalpas and the Parivrajakas, the former ruling from the Khoh–Bhumara area of Satna district, west to Nachna and north to Jaso and Ajaigarh in Panna; and the latter, probably the more prominent of the two, from Khoh southwards to Dahala and Mekala, and including the forest chiefdoms. Under Gupta rule these kingdoms enjoyed a simple paternal rule with a large measure of autonomy. They encouraged migrants and granted land to Brahmans to endow temples and offer worship in established villages. With the state's approval it is likely that the feudatories expanded their territories, or at least developed them further by allowing people to clear the jungle:

Any group could move out into the jungle on their own, usually organised as a gild (*sreni*) for land clearance with temporary or permanent occupation ... in recognised *rashtra*...areas. Otherwise, they would be—for the time being—beyond the constantly expanding frontiers of any *janapada*, hence beyond the king's jurisdiction. This meant holding out against the forest savages (*atavika*) by force of arms or direct control. Both were possible, for the *sreni* normally indulged in trade and often in manufacture, too.... It was an Arthashastra practice to hire the *atavikas* ... as scouts and army auxiliaries.[55]

The Parivrajakas were still in command when the Hunas reached Eran around 500 AD. Thirty years later the Gupta Empire was finished, and the region once again became a land of small kingdoms.

The national idea revived briefly during the reign of Harshavardhana from Kanauj in the seventh century.[56] Harsha maintained 'firm hold on all the petty states of Baghelkhand' though, possibly through force of circumstances, he conceded a measure of local autonomy to the forest and other chiefs. However, so far as the forest chiefs' representation at court was concerned, they conformed to the 'usual governmental pattern, contributing their share to the state by supplying elephants for the imperial army'.

VI

RAJPUT MIGRATION AND THE BEGINNINGS OF THE REGIONAL STATE

Harsha's death in 674 AD created a vaccum in central India which was filled by waves of Rajput and semi-Rajput clans invading Baghelkhand and other areas and founding local states. In so doing they helped link the region with those parts of the subcontinent where their clan members remained, as well as unifying Baghelkhand by forming states there.

The Rajputs emerged in the mid-first millennium AD, and three or four centuries later the term had become accepted as referring to warrior groups enjoying a kshatriya status recognized by their Brahman priests.[57] In central India, as elsewhere, we can distinguish between two groups of Rajputs. The more prominent of these comprised the Parihar, Chauhan, Chalukya or Solanki, and the Paramara Rajputs. Though all were to claim descent from a mythical figure arising from a fire-pit at Mount Abu, B.D. Chattopadhyaya suggests that they probably evolved gradually within India and were not, as some claimed, migrants from outside. A second group of clans assuming Rajput status included the Chandel, Kalachuri, and Bundela Rajputs who, though claiming descent from the lunar and solar races, were probably warrior groups who intermarried with the forest and hill people in areas through which they passed or in which they settled.[58]

The Rajput and semi-Rajput clans exhibited a remarkable degree of social and geographical mobility. It seems likely that various warrior sub-castes and lineages[59] merged to form distinct clans and, formed or forming, travelled immense distances to different parts of the country, including Baghelkhand, where they contended for territory with local peoples and with each other. Those winning such contests probably began with the Pratihara Rajputs whose kingdom based on Kanauj extended south to the Rashtrakuta border along the Narmada. Among their feudatories were the Chandels, who in time freed themselves of Pratihara control, confining them to the area of Nagod and Unchahra in west Bagelkhand. Once independent, the Chandels built up their Kingdom of Jejakabhukti between the Yamuna, the Narmada, and the Tons. In so doing they wrested Kalinjara from the Kalachuris who contested their bid for territory, and sought to oust them from areas north of the Narmada into which they had infiltrated—a conflict that see-sawed for centuries.

The Sengars were another putative Rajput group entering Baghelkhand.[60] Migrating from Jalaun in the eleventh century, they became Rajas of Mau on some of the most fertile land in Rewa district, seizing the *garhis* of Mangawan, Bichhrata, and Naigarhi from the Bhars, a hill and forest community. Similarly on the move, the Kalachuris took Mau in their drive north in the eleventh century, but as they weakened in the thirteenth century the Sengars regained the initiative in their small but proud principality.

It is difficult to get a clear picture of the forest and hill people in this drawing and redrawing of the 'boundaries' between Rajput and semi-Rajput clans in Baghelkhand.[61] The Gonds, though prominent, were overcome by the Kalachuris as they expanded from Tripuri into Sohagpur. The Khairwars, an offshoot of the Kols, came under pressure from the Chandels in Sidhi. Groups such as the Nishadas, Sabaras, and others were defeated and probably merged with other similar groups. (The Sabaras are thought to have fallen under Gond influence.) The Balands lost much of their territory in Bardi and Aghori to the Chandels and Chauhans, and in the tenth century the Kalachuris seized their stronghold at Bandhavgarh. Deprived of land, they compensated for their loss by settling in Sohagpur and Marwas, in Shahdol. As we have seen, the Bhars lost Mau to the Sengars. However, it may be assumed that with the decline of a particular Rajput clan, the older communities emerged once more, as did the Gonds in Sohagpur with the waning of the Kalachuri state.

The advent of Mahmud of Ghazni in the eleventh century and the formation of the Delhi Sultanate in the thirteenth century transformed political equations in Baghelkhand in startling ways. These pressures compelled Rajput and other groups in northern India to move away, some to Baghelkhand where they settled in new forest clearings or on the lands of those whom they defeated. These shifts were paralleled by movements of agricultural peoples, among them Lodhis and Kurmis, seeking a secure homeland. Indeed, the 'greatest influx of cultivators was stated to have come to Rewa after the fall of Kanauj' to Mahmud in 1019, ending Pratihara rule there.[62]

KASHMIR

EMPIRE Peshwar
of   •Ghazni
MAHMUD of GHAZNI
        R. Jhelum Kangra•
        R. Chenab •Lahore
Multan• R.Ravi
        R.Sutlej •Bhatinda
              Thanesar•
              •Sirsa
              Delhi• TOMARAS
QUSDAR
        R.Indus CHAUHANS Muttra• Kanauj PRATIHARAS R.Brahmaputra
SUMRAS   Sambhar• KACHHWAHAS
                    R.Chambal Prayag •Benares
        •Anhilvara PARAMARAS CHANDELS PALAS
              (PAWARS) KALACHURIS
CHALUKYAS Ujjain
(SOLANKIS) R.Nerbudda
Somnath•   R.Topti R.Mahanadi

        •Deogir
              R.Godavari KALINGA
        CHALUKYAS
              Warangal
              R.Krishna VENGI
        R.Tungabhadra
        CHOLA   INDIA
                            IN
        EMPIRE   1030

              •Gangaikondacholapuram
              R.Kaveri

        CHOLAS

With acknowledgement: C.C. Davies, *An Historical Atlas of the Indian Peninsula*, p. 27

Map 9

The thrusts of Mahmud, the Ghaznavids, and the Delhi Sultanate especially affected the Chauhans. Some members of this clan migrated from land west of Delhi in the face of such pressures, in turn coming up against the Paramaras and Kalachuris. Muhammad Ghori's actions in the late twelfth century pushed some Chauhans further east where they fell upon Chandel Mahoba; but with Prithviraj Chauhan's defeat by Ghori in 1192 and continued Chandel resistance, the Chauhan impulse faltered and their forces dispersed, though others of their clan maintained a presence in Rajasthan.

Moves by Mahmud and the Sultanate also impacted the Chandels. Mahmud defeated them at Kalinjara in 1019, though some seventy years later they repulsed the Lahori Ghaznavids there. Around 1100 Chandel Rajputs took part in a joint effort to defeat these unwelcome intruders, but this action failed, and in 1203 Qutb-ud Din Aibak expelled them from Kalinjara. Iltutmish plundered the area about twenty years later, and Ala-ud Din Khilji finally pushed the Chandels into decline, though they probably still held parts of north Rewa and Sidhi.[63]

VII

A REGIONAL STATE: THE KALACHURI RAJPUT KINGDOM OF DAHALA

Though the Chandel State of Jejakabhukti included parts of Baghelkhand, it was the Kalachuri Rajputs who formed the first substantial state in the region. In so doing they made a major contribution to migration into Baghelkhand, and in linking the region with their extensive territories beyond its borders. The Kalachuris also created a distinctive regional culture, which nonetheless owed much to influences from elsewhere in northern and central India.

The Kalachuris are quite wrongly associated with the Chedis and the Haihayas, a branch of the Yadavas who claimed descent from the mythical Kartavirya Arjuna.[64] It is more than likely, however, that all three were distinct entities. The Chedis, mentioned in the Sanskrit texts, held land in Bundelkhand and west Baghelkhand known as Chedidesa. Though supplanted by the

Haihayas, who in turn succumbed to the Kalachuris, the Chedi name has been unjustifiably attached to those communities. The Haihayas were once located far to the north-west of the subcontinent, but in what was a common pattern they

made their way to the seemingly inhospitable lands of the south and west.... Peasant farmers, and doubtless some Harappans also, displaced by the events of the period..., and dominated by, inspired, and held together in this enterprise by some tough, disgruntled characters of the Aryan Yadavas, provided the pioneering frontier communities.[65]

It is conjectured that the wider Yadava group, including the Haihayas, moved from western India into Malwa with Mahismati as capital, subsequently shifting south into Vidarbha.[66] (We note that Krishna, a Yadava, married a princess of Vidarbha). It is believed that some Haihayas re-crossed the Narmada in the first millennium BC to seize the lands held by the Chedis, hence their wrongful identification with that clan.

The Kalachuris, too, were quite distinct from the Haihaya inheritors of Chedidesa.[67] Reports confirm that they appeared in the first millennium AD. Some claim that their name is derived from Turkish *kulucur*, an officer of the highest rank, and that he or they may have been outsiders who found their way into India, some say with the Hunas or Gurjaras. This lack of clarity apart, it is generally agreed that the Kalachuris moved towards the Narmada in search of land, but Harsha and the Chalukyas of the Deccan pressed them further east towards Chedidesa where they ousted the Haihayas, then in decline. Vamadeva, an early Kalachuri king, married a Haihaya princess, giving grounds for their specious claim that they were descended from that clan, and adding further to the confusion.

Traditionally, the foundation of Kalachuri power[68] dates from their becoming Lords of Kalinjara in the seventh century. However, their expansion was blocked by the Paramaras, as by the Pratiharas and the Rashtrakutas, themselves mutual enemies; but as Rashtrakuta power waned, the Kalachuris were free to combat and defeat their other rivals. Between the ninth and the eleventh centuries, they moved north taking territory in the Tons valley and elsewhere from the Chandels, besides absorbing lands held by the Gonds, Kols, and others.[69] Also, though from the eleventh century on the Chandels recovered lost ground, the Kalachuris continued to hold land north of the Kaimur until the early thirteenth century, and in the south for much longer.

Despite their fluctuating fortunes, the Kalachuri kings laid the foundations of the first major state in Baghelkhand.[70] Their core territory of Dahala comprised Jabalpur district and southern Baghelkhand. Beyond this their lands expanded or contracted depending on their fortunes in war; and beyond this again lay a zone where the Kalachuris raided, adding to the state's wealth. Thus Yuvarajadeva I (915–45) reportedly raided Karnataka, Gujarat, Bengal, Kashmir and Orissa; and Gangeyyadeva (1015–41) occupied Varanasi, lands in the Ganga-Yamuna *doab* and south Malwa, besides winning a victory near the east coast. Karnadeva (1041–63) defeated the Chalukyas and Cholas, and was named 'undisputed Chakavartin of north India'. However, under Yasahkarna (1073–1123) the Kalachuris lost much of their territory, their hold even on the Son valley coming under threat in the reign of Vijayasimha (1192–3). A Yadava invasion followed, and by the mid-thirteenth century the Kalachuri state had ceased to be a force in Baghelkhand.

To govern Dahala the Kalachuris created a simple administrative system in which the monarchy was central:

Some statements in the inscriptions of the Kalachuris indicate...that Kings regarded themselves as men born with divinity.... Kingship was hereditary.... The foremost duty was of a political and administrative nature. His authority was supreme....to provide for security of life and property....enforcing ... the observance of the Arya-dharma (and)....to promote education [and] learning.[71]

The army was a key institution, and after the loss of Kalinjara the Kalachuris relied on Bandhavgarh to safeguard Dahala. The state also issued a coinage, and recorded its achievements in Kalachuri years. Monarchs encouraged migrants, and had forests cleared for cultivation.[72]

Consonant with their view of the monarchy, the Kalachuri kings developed the spiritual life of their people.[73] Their courts sustained writers and other scholars; and kings and queens encouraged religious observance (and political stability) by building Saivite temples and monasteries near lines of communication. Saivism combined with the more indigenous cult of the goddess to weld the dispersed agrarian and hill and forest communities together under their kings. For though the *lingam* remained the focal point of worship in Kalachuri temples, their distinctive circular *garbhagrihas* are thought to represent the *devi*, while the latter's frequent depiction in sculpture was a prominent feature of Kalachuri art.

Notes

1. Varma, *Rewa*, pp. 3, 7–10; D.K. Chakrabarti, *The Early Use of Iron in India*, New Delhi, 1992, pp. 21, 28–9; F.R. Allchin, *The Archaeology of Early Historic South Asia: The Emergence of Cities and States*, Cambridge, 1995, p. 83, notes that the iron finds at Eran of around 1420 BC far predate any of the iron sites in the Ganga valley or the northwest. Guha, 'Lower strata, older races', p. 435.

2. Lahiri, *Archaeology of Indian Trade*, p. 317.

3. Varma, *Rewa*, pp. 7–10; *IAR 1980–81*, pp. 37–9; Pal, *Archaeology of South U.P.*, pp. 70–1, 156.

4. *Ibid.*, pp. 20–1; Clark and Williams, 'Paleoenvironments and prehistory' p. 34; Misra, 'Discovering the past', np.

5. P.S. Dwivedi has suggested these datings.

6. *Rewa Gazetteer*, p. 5; P.K. Bhattacharya, *Historical Geography of Madhya Pradesh from Early Records*, Delhi, 1977, pp. 93–4, 102; J.S. Chauhan, 'Spatial pattern of literacy amongst tribes in the Baghelkhand plateau region', PhD thesis, APS University, Rewa, 1990, p. 18; *Central India Gazetteer*, pp. 98–9; *Shahdol Gazetteer*, p. 10.

7. H.D. Sankalia, *The Ramayana in Historical Perspective*, New Delhi, 1982, p. 165; J. Forsyth, *The Highlands of Central India: Notes on their Forests and Wild Tribes, Natural History and Sports*, New Delhi, rpt, 1975; p. 6; K.D. Bajpai, Presidential address, *JMPIP*, no. 10, 1976, pp. 3–5.

8. *Central India Gazetteer*, pp. 87–8; R. Mukerjee, *A History of Indian Civilisation*, vol. I, *Ancient and Classical Traditions*, Bombay, 1958, pp. 92, 254–5; K.D. Bajpai, *Cultural History of India*, vol. *I, Madhya Pradesh*, Delhi, 1985, p. 139. For the sentence on Rama and Ravana, I am indebted to P.S. Dwivedi.

9. Bajpai, Presidential address, pp. 4–5; P.D. Agnihotri, 'Language and literature in ancient Madhya Pradesh', *JMPIP*, no 8, 1970, p. 31; Chauhan, 'Spatial pattern of literacy', PhD, p. 18; *Central India Gazetteer*, p. 91; *MPDG, Satna*, Bhopal, 1994, p. 9.

10. *Rewa Gazetteer*, p. 5; *Shahdol Gazetteer*, p. 7; *Central India State Gazetteer Series, Rewah State Gazetteer*, vol. IV, *Text and Tables*, rpt, Bhopal, 1997, p. 3; B.N. Zutshi, *Rewa and its Ruler*, Bombay, 1923 p. 14; K.D. Bajpai, 'The Vindhyas, their cultural impact', K.D. Bajpai et al., (eds.), *The Glory that was Bundelkhand*; *Mahendra Kumar 'Manav' Felicitation*

Volume, New Delhi, 1993, p. 198; A. Cunningham, *Reports of a Tour in Baghelkhand and Rewa in 1883–84, and of a Tour in Rewa, Baghelkhand, Malwa and Gwalior in 1884–85,* vol. XXI, pts I, II, rpt, Delhi, 1969, p. 90.

11. I am grateful to Nayanjot Lahiri for this suggestion. See Lahiri, *Archaeology of Indian Trade,* pp. 382–3.
12. Ibid., p. 381.
13. Ibid.; Chakrabarti, *Early Use of Iron,* pp. 280–1; Ray, 'Bharhut and Sanchi', p. 623.
14. B.C. Law, *Indological Studies,* pt. I, Calcutta, 1950, pp. 31–3.
15. Kosambi, *Culture and Civilization,* p. 94; Bajpai, *Cultural History,* vol. I, p. 195.
16. I owe this suggestion to P.S. Dwivedi.
17. V.N. Misra and M. Nagar, 'From tribe to caste: an ethno-archaeological perspective', D. Nathan, *From Tribe to Caste,* Simla, 1997, p. 155.
18. A.H. Nizami, 'Ancient Baghelkhand', unpublished article, p. 1; K.S. George,' Impact of industrialisation on the social conditions of Singrauli, the energy capital of India', PhD thesis, APS University, Rewa, 1992, p. 24; K.D. Bajpai and S.K. Pandey, *Malhar 1975–78,* University of Sagar, 1978, p. 21.
19. Neumayer, *Prehistoric Indian Rock Paintings,* pp. 7–8.
20. Guha, 'Lower strata, older races', p. 437.
21. Ibid., pp. 436–7; G. Oppert, *The Original Inhabitants of Bharatavarsa or India,* Delhi, rpt, 1971, pp. 82 (fn), 113; A Cunningham, vol. XXI, pt. I, *Report of a Tour in the Central Provinces in 1873–74, and 1874–75,* vol. IX, Calcutta, 1879, p. 92. Sandrabatis may be Bandhavgarh or Amarkantak.
22. I. Karve, *Kinship Organisation in India,* Poona, 1953, pp. 278–9; P. Jayakar, *The Earth Mother,* Calcutta, 1989, p. 142; Bajpai, 'The Vindhyas, their cultural impact', p. 198; *Central India Gazetteer,* pp. 15–16.
23. Sankalia, *The Ramayana,* p. 161, Ray, 'Bharhut and Sanchi', p. 626; A.C. Mittal, *An Early History of Orissa,* Varanasi, 1962, pp. 203–4.
24. Bajpai, *Cultural History,* vol. I, pp. 195–6; V. Varadachari, *A History of Samskrta Literature,* Allahabad, 1952, p. 110.
25. S. Ratnagar, 'Hunter gatherer and early agriculturist: archaeological evidence for contact', Nathan, p. 129.
26. A. Cunningham, *The Stupa of Bharhut: A Buddhist Monument Ornamented with Numerous Sculptures Illustrative of Buddhist Legend and History in the Third Century B.C.,* New Delhi, rpt, 1989, p 1; Varma, *Rewa,* pp. 16–17.
27. Ibid., pp. 16, 19–23. I am grateful to Ajay Singh of APS University, Rewa, and Devendra Singh of Rewa for helping me to visit this site.

28. Kosambi, *Culture and Civilization*, p. 133; F.R. Allchin, *Cities and States*, p. 281; Subbarao, *Personality of India*, p. 45; *IAR 1984–85*, p. 48; *IAR 1988–89*, p. 44; P.K. Misra, 'Deorkothar stupa: new light on early Buddhism', *Marg*, vol. 52, no. 1, 2001, pp. 66, 68; Guha, 'Lower strata, older races', p. 436.

29. Ibid., p. 436; J.W. McCrindle, *Ancient India as Described by Ptolemy*, Faridabad, rpt, nd., p. 167; Cunningham, vol. XXI, pt. I, *Reports of a Tour*, p. 92; *Central India Gazetteer*, pp. 416–7.

30. Lahiri, *Archaeology of Indian Trade*, p. 381; Jayakar, *Earth Mother*, p. 48; S.K. Tiwari, 'Riksha, an ancient tribe of Vindhyanchal', P.K. Misra and S.K. Sullerey (eds.), *Heritage of India, Past and Present: Essays in Honour of Professor R.K. Sharma*, Delhi, 1994, vol. II, no. 79, pp. 527–32; *Central India Gazetteer*, pp. 15–16; Bajpai, *Cultural History*, vol. I, p. 52; Sharma and Clark, (eds), Palaeoenvironments and prehistory, p. 4.

31. Karve, *Kinship Organization.*, pp. 271, 273, 175–6, 184.

32. Roy, *Planning the Environment*, p. 2; A.K. Roy, 'Baghelkhand: Some aspects of local history', unpublished paper, nd., p. 4; Karve, *Kinship Organization*, pp. 274–5; *Report of the Path Enquiry Commission*, p. 10.

33. This paragraph owes much to P.S. Dwivedi. See H.L. Shukla, *Language, Ethnicity and History: Dimensions in Anthropological Linguistics*, Delhi, 1985, pp. 94–5; J. Lal, 'Baghelkhand: a study in settlement geography', PhD Thesis, APS University, Rewa, 1982, p. 178; Kosambi, *Culture and Civilization.*, pp. 93–4; *Central India Gazetteer*, p. 425; Bajpai, *Cultural History*, vol. I, p. 27.

34. S. Bhattacharya, 'Central Indian tribes: a historical dimension', K. Suresh Singh (ed.), *The Tribal Situation in India*, Simla, rpt, 1986, pp. 194–5.

35. Mittal, *Early History of Orissa*, pp. 204–5; Kosambi, *Culture and Civilization*, pp. 128, 163; *A Comprehensive Survey of Prehistoric and Tribal Arts in Madhya Pradesh, India: A Preliminary Report*, Faculty of Letters, Osaka University, 1981, p. 12.

36. Mittal, *Early History of Orissa*, p. 205; Tiwari, 'Riksha: an ancient tribe', pp. 531–2; Bajpai, *Cultural History*, vol. I, p. 52; Guha, 'Lower strata, older races', p. 436; B.A. Saletore, *The Wild Tribes in Indian History*, Lahore, 1935, pp. 16, 19; V.V. Mirashi, 'The Pandav dynasty of Mekala', *Indica: The Indian Historical Research Institute*, Silver Jubilee Commemoration Volume, Bombay 1953, p. 270; C.E. Luard, *Chiefs and Leading Families in Central India, 1916*, Calcutta, 1916, p. i; Chauhan, 'Spatial pattern of literacy', pp. 18–19; *Shahdol Gazetteer*, p. 37; D. Devahuti, *Harsha: A Political Study*, Oxford, 1970, p. 161. The *Janapadas* included that of the Kiratas, of eastern Indian origin, in the 'Vindhyan forests'; Vatsa extending south from the

Yamuna; Karusa, continuing in eastern Sidhi; together with a kingdom in the Maikal Hills. A Pali text, *Anguttar Nicaya*, notes that there were 18 forest kingdoms in Chedidesa; Cunningham, *Report of a Tour in the CP*, 1879, p. v; C. Banurji, 'The Kaimur range', *JASB*, vol. XLVI, pt 1, no. I, 1877, p. 25.

37. Devahuti, *Harsha*, pp. 161–2; *Rewa State Gazetteer*, p. 9; Luard, *Chiefs*, *1916*, p. ii.
38. *The Harsa-Carita of Bana*, pp. 232–3.
39. Guha, 'Lower strata, older races', pp. 436–7.
40. See Bajpai, *Cultural History*, vol. I, p. 53.
41. Guha, 'Lower strata, older races', pp. 437–8.
42. J.N. Pal, 'Upper palaeolithic cultures of the mid-Son valley', *Puratattva*, no 12, 1980–1, p. 29; Jayakar, *Earth Mother*, pp. 48–9, 153–4; K.K. Chakravarty, 'Mother goddesses and the classical style in Kalachuri art', K.K. Chakravarty et al. (eds.), *Art of the Kalachuris*, Bhopal, 1991, p. 25, ref. 3; Banurji, 'The Kaimur range', pp 16–17. The fourth-century *Harivamsa* names Durga as Vindhyavasini.
43. O.P. Misra, *Mother Goddess in Central India*, Delhi, 1985, pp. 75, 93; Jayakar, *Earth Mother*, pp. 57–8.
44. D.N. Lorenzen, *The Kapalikas and Kalamukhas: Two Lost Saivite Sects*, Delhi, 1991, p. 16.
45. B.C. Mazumdar, *The Aborigines of the Highlands of Central India*, Calcutta, 1927, p. 10.
46. K.D. Bajpai, 'Impact of saivism on central Indian art', K.K. Chakravarty et al. (eds), *Puratan: Saiva Tradition in Indian Art*, vol. 6, 1989, p. 27; K.D Bajpai, 'The Vindhya region and Banabhatta', *PP.*, vols. IX–X, 1981–2, p. 2; S.N. Misra, *Gupta Art and Architecture with Special Reference to Madhya Pradesh*, Delhi, 1992, pp. 7, 162; Rahman Ali, *Art and Architecture of the Kalachuris*, Delhi, 1980, pp. 17–18; R.N. Nandi, *Religious Institutions and Cults in the Deccan, c.* A.D. *600–A.D. 1000*, Delhi, 1973, pp. 79–80.
47. Bajpai, 'The Vindhya region and Banabhatta', p. 2.
48. *Shahdol Gazetteer*, pp. 7, 321; *Report of the Path Enquiry Commission*, p. 8.
49. S. Kant, *Political and Cultural History of Mid-North India*, New Delhi, 1987, pp. 4–7; *Rewa Gazetteer*, p. 1; *Shahdol Gazetteer*, pp. 33–4. The Nanda kingdom extended as far south as the Godavari.
50. Kosambi, *Culture and Civilization*, pp. 126–7, 131; Luard, *Chiefs 1916*, p. ii; Ray, 'Bharhut and Sanchi', p. 626; Bajpai, *Cultural History*, vol. I, pp. 27, 29.
51. Kant, *Political and Cultural History*, p. 95; *Rewa Gazetteer*, p. 25; Ali, *Kalachuri Art*, p. 3; Bhattacharya, *Historical Geography*, pp. 14–15; N.P. Chakravarti, 'Brahmi inscriptions from Bandhogarh', *EI*, vol. XXXI, no. 23, p. 175: A king, Dhanabhuti, possibly a Sunga

feudatory, was responsible for building the eastern gateway at Bharhut. Kushana coins circulated in the Kausambi area for trade purposes alongside the coins of the Magha kings, who appear to have used Bandhavgarh as a resting place on a trade route to the south.

52. Kant, *Political and Cultural History*, p. 141; *Shahdol Gazetteer*, p. 35; Nizami, 'Ancient Baghelkhand', p. 4; H. Raychaudhuri, *Political History of Ancient India*, Delhi, 1996, pp. 475, 511, 766–7; K.M. Shrimali, *Agrarian Structure in Central India and the Northern Deccan (c. AD 300–500): A Study of Vakataka Inscriptions*, Delhi, 1987, pp. 37, 45, 84, notes Vakataka inscriptions at Nachna and Ganj in the vicinity of Jaso.

53. Bajpai, *Cultural History*, vol. I, p. 29; R.D. Banerji, *The Age of the Imperial Guptas*, Varanasi, 1933, pp. 14, 16; *Rewa Gazetteer*, p. 25; *Shahdol Gazetteer*, pp. 36–7; S.N. Misra, *Gupta Art*, p. 3; Raychaudhuri, *Political History*, p. 786. The Gupta temples in Satna district, especially that at Bhumara, date from a time when the Gupta Empire was weakening, and its writ may even have ceased to run when they were built. The temple at Bhumara, it is thought, dates from the first half of the sixth century.

54. J.G. Williams, *The Art of Gupta India; Empire and Province*, New Delhi, 1983, pp. 103–4; *Rewa Gazetteer*, pp. 25–6; A.H. Nizami, 'Survey of art and archaeology in the Vindhyan region', *Vindhyika Souvenir*, Jabalpur, 1994, p. 1; D.N. Jha, *Revenue System in Post-Maurya and Gupta Times*, Calcutta, 1967, pp. 131–3.

55. Kosambi, *Culture and Civilization*, p. 151.

56. Luard, *Chiefs, 1916*, p. ii; Devahuti, *Harsha*, pp. 161–2.

57. I owe this opening statement to P.S. Dwivedi. B.D. Chattopadhyaya, *The Making of Early Mediaeval India*, New Delhi, 1997, ch. 3. R. Thapar, *A History of India*, vol. I, Penguin, pp. 227–9, suggests that the Rajputs were of foreign origin.

58. Some historians record instances of Rajput nobles settling among Korkus and marrying the daughters of their chiefs; a Chandel princess is said to have married a Kol chief. Oppert declared that the Gond origins of the Chandels was 'an admitted fact'. Some commentators claim that the Kalachuris, too, married into forest families. Bundela Rajputs have been linked with the Bhars.

59. J.F. Richard, 'The Islamic frontier in the east: expansion into south Asia', *South Asia*, no. 4, 1974, p. 107.

60. B.S. Baghel, 'Rewa ke Baghel rajya ka parrashtra sambandh: ek adhyayan' (1360–1859)', PhD Thesis, APS University, Rewa, 1991, p. 100.

61. D.K. Misra, *Son ka pani*, pp. 155, 157; Chauhan, 'Spatial pattern of literacy', p. 98; *M.P. Census, 1961, Sidhi Handbook*, p. lx; B.C. Majumdar,

Aborigines, pp. 34–40; George, 'Impact of industrialization', p. 24; *Rewa State Gazetteer*, p. 80; *Shahdol Gazetteer*, pp. 323–4; Banurji, 'The Kaimur range', p. 24.

62. *Rewa Gazetteer*, p. 81.
63. Cunningham, vol. XXI, pt I, *Reports of a Tour*, p. 118; Ibid., pt II, p. 147; *Sidhi Gazetteer*, p. 27.
64. *Shahdol Gazetteer*, p. 36; *Rewa State Gazetteer*, pp. 8–9; Bhattacharya, *Historical Geography*, pp. 116–17, 123–4, 126–7; F.E. Pargiter, 'Ancient Cedi, Matsya and Karusa', *JASB*, vol. LXIV, pt I, no 3, 1895, pp. 249, 258.
65. Gordon, *Pre-Historic Backgropund*, pp. 133–4.
66. *Rewa State Gazetteer*, pp. 8–9; Pargiter, 'Ancient Cedi', p. 249; Bhattacharya, *Historical Geography*, pp. 126–7; Subbarao, *Personality of India*, p. 167; Jacobson, 'Static sites and peripatetic peoples', p. 72.
67. S. Chhattopadhyaya, *Early History of North India*, Calcutta, 1976, pp. 276–7; Bhattacharya, *Historical Geography*, p. 126; *Satna Gazetteer*, p. 40; *Shahdol Gazetteer*, p. 38; *Rewa State Gazetteer*, p. 9; *Corpus Inscriptionum Indicarum*, vol. IV, V.V. Mirashi (ed.), *Inscriptions from the Kalachuri-Chedi Era*, pt I, Ootacamund, 1955, pp. xliv–li.
68. *Rewa Gazetteer*, p. 27; *CII*, vol. IV, pt. I, pp. lxiv, lxix, lxxii; R.N. Misra, *Sculptures of Dahala and Dakshina Kosala and their Background*, Delhi, 1987, p. 9; H.C. Ray, *The Dynastic History of Northern India (Early Mediaeval Period)*, vol. I, Calcutta, 1931, pp. 589–90.
69. Cunningham, vol. XXI, pt I, *Reports of a Tour*, pp. iii, 103; Roy, *Planning the Environment*, p. 2; M. Mahajan, 'Topographical features of the Kalachuris of Tripuri', *Studies in Indian Place Names*, vol. 17, 1997, p. 17; *CII*, vol. IV, pt I, pp. lxii, cv–cvi; Bose, *History of The Candellas*, p. 86; A.H. Nizami, 'The Baghela dynasty of Rewa: early history', *13th all India Oriental Conference*, Nagpur, 1946, p. 1; Ray, *Dynastic History*, vol. II, p. 728.
70. Misra, *Sculptures of Dahala*, pp. 10, 52–3; *CII*, vol. IV, pt I, pp. lxxxix, xc, xci, cii, cviii; *Rewa Gazetteer*, p. 29; Bose, *History of the Candellas*, p. 102; Ali, *Kalachuri Art* p. 11.
71. Siddhantashastree, *Saivism*, pp. 59–72.
72. Lal, 'Settlement geography', PhD, p. 176.
73. *Rewa Gazetteer*, pp. 28–9; Roy, *Planning the Environment*, p. 2. For a fuller discussion of Kalachuri culture, see Ch. 4.

3

The Making of a Regional State: Rewa to *c*. 1800 AD

CREED

Interaction between the region and centralizing states and other external forces played a key role in shaping Baghelkhand's identity and hastening its integration into a subcontinental polity between 1300 and 1800 AD. The result of that interaction was the creation of Rewa State, the region's main political formation, which now came to play a role in the political life of the subcontinent. This was especially evident in the kingdom's interaction with the Mughal empire; though as Mughal power declined, Rewa faced opposition from its regional rivals.

Migration was the second of the external forces which helped integrate the region with other parts of the subcontinent, shaping its social and economic life along lines similar to that of other regions in central and northern India in the pre-modern period. This was not simply due to migrants transplanting their way of life in the region; but among the migrants were Brahmans and kshatriyas who by the mediaeval period had developed a systematized set of social values incorporating widely differing groups of people into a community, and assigning them particular social and economic roles within that community.[1]

I

BAGHEL BEGINNINGS IN THE REGION

Baghels were the most important of the Rajput clans migrating to Baghelkhand, their kingdom dominating the region for centuries.

The Baghels owed their presence in central India to pressure from Ghaznavid and other Muslim forces who attacked the Solanki kingdom of Saurashtra in the eleventh and twelfth centuries. However, the Baghels first came to notice through local circumstances. At the end of the twelfth century the Solanki king, Tribhuvanapala, died heirless. The Baghels, a Solanki noble family holding the *jagir* of Vaghela, assumed power only to face repeated attacks by the Khilji dynasty of Delhi. In 1298 the forces of Ala-ud Din invaded and annexed Gujarat, where the Baghel ruler lost but subsequently regained his kingdom.[2]

Delhi's invasion of Gujarat again in 1304 led the Baghels to quit Saurashtra and its capital Anhilwara and re-found their kingdom elsewhere, as a nineteenth century historian recounts:

Lieutenants of the Tartar Despot of Delhi let loose the spirit of intolerance and avarice on the rich cities and fertile plains of Gujerat and Saurashtra.... The walls of Anhulwarra were demolished; its foundations excavated and filled up again with the fragments of their ancient temples. The remnants of the Solanki dynasty were scattered over the face of the land.... The most conspicuous of these is the Bagela family, which gave its name to an entire division of Hindusthan.[3]

It is difficult now to trace the passage of the Baghels from Gujarat to the region they later named Baghelkhand. In the welter of legends surrounding their migration, two points emerge with conviction. One is that they came to hold land in Banda district of Uttar Pradesh; and the other, that at an early period they possessed the fort at Bandhavgarh. How they acquired these territories is unclear.

One version—the more credible—has it that the Baghels began moving east in the thirteenth century itself, when Lavana Prasad Baghel reportedly became Governor of Udayapur and Vidisha in Malwa, then under Solanki control.[4] Iltutmish's capture of Vidisha is thought to have led Lavana's son to migrate further east, seizing the fort of Marpha some 26 kilometres north-east of Kalinjara. The presence of two large villages near Marpha—Baghelabari and Baghelan—would seem to confirm the Baghel presence in the area.[5] Marriage to a locally important family with lands on the Paisuni river added to their power in Banda, from where they gradually encroached on nearby Baghelkhand. Some reports claim that the Baghels added Bandhavgarh to their possessions by defeating its Kalachuri occupants, one Karna Deva Baghel receiving the fort in the dowry of a Kalachuri princess.

The Chandels were still strong enough in the fourteenth century to block the expansion of the Baghels.[6] However, though they forced them out of Marpha and surrounding country, the Baghels continued to hold the plateau country of eastern Banda, possibly with the help of the sultans of Jaunpur who were keen to expand their influence south of the Yamuna. It is said also that the Baghels entered the service of the Bhar rajas of Kalinjara, and that some assistance may have come from that quarter.

The Baghel presence in the hill country of eastern Banda gains further credence from their title as chiefs of the *patha*—more usually Bhatha or Bhatta—by about 1400.[7] Baghel power here came to centre on the fort of Gahora, about twenty two kilometres east of Karvi, taken by them from its Lodhi landlords after the loss of Marpha. A sixteenth century genealogy, the *Virabhanudaya Kavyam,* many of whose entries are corroborated by Persian sources, noted that it was Raningadeva Baghel who seized the fort, consolidating the victors' hold over the *patha* by the mid-fourteenth century.

Thereafter, Gahora served as capital of the fledgling state, the Baghel kings gradually improving the town which grew up around the fort.[8] Viramadeva, ruling from the late fourteenth century, dug a lake there. Naraharideva (1425–70) appears to have spent time at Bandhavgarh where the Baghel hold was uncertain. After retaking Bandhavgarh from those who had usurped it, Virasimhadeva (1500–40) returned to Gahora to restore the town and beautify it with 'wide roads and magnificent palaces', though the town mostly comprised quarters for the army and court. When the state's fulcrum shifted south in the sixteenth century, Gahora remained the Baghel capital until the reign of Ramachandra, who shifted to Bandhavgarh to escape Mughal interference.

II

THE REGIONAL STATE OF THE BAGHELS

In time, the Baghel Principality of Bhatha-Gahora evolved into Baghelkhand's predominant state.[9] As early as 1360 the chiefs of Gahora were using the title *maharajadhiraja,* indicating their growing power. Baghel inscriptions from the previous decade document their movement into present-day Satna and Rewa districts. They also came to possess the Son valley and encroached on to the plains of the Yamuna and Ganga the kingdom reaching its furthest limits in the mid-sixteenth century.

Diplomatic marriages, success in war, and even money were among the weapons employed by the Baghels to expand their territory.[10] The marriage of Naraharideva (1425–70) to a queen 'who held a fortress on the banks of the Ganges' gave the Baghels a defensible northern frontier. Salivahan Baghel (1495–1500) is said to have laid out a town on the Jamuna named after him. By force of arms the Baghels subjected the Parihars of west Baghelkhand, and garrisoned volatile Bandhavgarh. Virasimha (1500–40) defeated the Bhar Raja of Sohagpur, besides taking Dahala and Ratanpur, in Chhattisgarh, from the Kalachuris. His successor Virabhanudeva (1540–55) captured Bastar and overran Garha Mandla, though these proved only temporary gains. The great Ramachandra (1555–92) even purchased Kalinjara from the Suri family. As a result, at its height Bhatha extended from Prayaga to Sohagpur and from Kalinjara to Chunar.

Notwithstanding Bhatha's expansion, the state was remarkably vulnerable. In 1440–1 Mahmud, Sultan of Malwa, came to Baghelkhand to buy elephants, but had an unfortunate encounter with Raja Naraharideva, as Mahmud's chronicler noted:

When the king recalled the insincere words and deceitful bragging of Narar Singh, Muqqadam of Gahora, in reply to Saiyad Ahmad, his inherent sense of honour was stirred, the fire of revenge was kindled, and the vein of valour showed its reaction. So he turned to the devastation and extirmination of that territory, and the army came down upon those ignorant people and like an unexpected calamity, sent all those devils devoid of gratefulness, and unbelievers ignorant of god, by the water of the sword to the fire of hell.[11]

Mughal intervention in Bhatha, or Bandhav as they called the state after Ramachandra shifted there, was even more devastating.[12] In 1569 Akbar demanded Kalinjara from Ramachandra and, thirty years later when relations between Bandhav and the Mughal centre worsened, he destroyed the fort at Bandhavgarh after a seige. In the seventeenth century, too, Bandhav, or Rewa as the state came to be known, remained vulnerable to outside interference.

Like other Rajput kingdoms the Baghel state was by and large a family coterie, territorially segmented on the basis of its dominant lineage.[13] As the head of his clan, the Baghel chief ruled his state. His family, their collaterals and connections by marriage, together with the descendants of royal ancestors constituted a second tier forming the core of the state's nobility. These *ilaqadars* or *sardars*, as they were called, held the granted *jagirs*, and in return were obliged to support the raja in war, pay homage, and contribute to state finances. Rulers also confirmed a number of Chauhan, Chandel, and other pre-existing holders in their lands in return for submission to Baghel rule. These lineage and granted lands became dotted with villages, many springing from the parent settlement, to form an interlocking mesh of villages on an estate. At this third level kings and nobles parcelled out villages to Rajputs, Brahmans, and others in return for services rendered. Despite the variety of grants, each alike guaranteed that its peasants recognized not merely the authority of their lord, but also of their lord's lord, the king himself. Peasants on state lands were subject directly to the administration.

However, though the rajas of Rewa were powerful, they were not absolute rulers. Changing conditions modified the original equations, and in time the Rewa *sardars* came to

look upon themselves not simply as vassals of a feudal lord, but as joint occupiers and co-parceners with their Chief in the family lands, and behind the admitted right of the chief to homage, support in war, and obedience, lies the tacit understanding that the control he exercises is limited, and any overstepping of this limit is to be resisted.[14]

The rajas of Rewa were thus 'primus inter pares'. At times Baghel princes or collaterals carved out territory for themselves, and thus did not owe the raja the support and obedience demanded of grantees. Also, many of the pre-Baghel landowners unwillingly supported a raj that had proved too strong for them and sought any opportunity to defy its edicts.[15]

Besides their Baghel base, the kings of Rewa benefited from their alliance with Brahmans, cemented by bestowing them with village lands.[16] Chiefs regarded themselves as the protectors of Brahmans, and Brahmans in turn recognized the Baghels as kshatriyas and the rightful rulers of the realm. The Brahmans of

Mathura also bestowed the rajas with hereditary titles which enhanced their status.

Court functionaries composed flattering genealogies to enhance the prestige of the royal line.[17] The first of these was the *Virabhanudayakavyam*, a Sanskrit poem composed during the reign of Virabhanudeva (1540–55) by one Madhav, and containing details of the family's ancestry—perhaps the only one of its kind in contemporary central India. In 1678 Rupani Sharma, a Sanskrit scholar at the Rewa court, edited a second genealogy dedicated to Bhava Singh (1660–90) based on a manuscript from Kashmir, to which Sharma added 99 colourful *slokas*. However, whereas the *Virabhanudayakavyam* named Bhimadeva as the founding raja, Sharma's genealogy began with Karnadeva of Anhilwara and contained names not in the previous list. A third such composition, the early nineteenth century *Vanshavali*, comprised a highly exaggerated account of the Baghel dynasty.

The rajas of Rewa also bolstered their fortunes by adopting the tiger as their icon.[18] Their name signified the tiger, and genealogists put out the myth of their descent from an eponymous tiger king, Vyaghradeva, a not uncommon device in central India. Despite Akbar's humiliating destruction of Bandhavgarh, later rulers projected the fort in tiger-infested jungles as a symbol of their invincibility, and even named their region Baghelkhand: the land of the Baghels and, by inference, the tigers' lair. In the nineteenth century the state adopted a coat of arms, the chief feature of which comprised rampant tigers above an injunction 'do not make war against tigers'.

As everywhere the monarch's main functions were to defend the state and raise revenue. For the former, the army[19] led by the king and his nobility carved out territory in earlier years, and then defended the lands acquired. The army's core comprised the cavalry. Service grants intended that holders maintained their horses, men, and accoutrements, with irregulars bulking out numbers when required. However, feudal armies were rarely standing armies, and Rewa's was no exception:

It was incorporated on ancient lines.... There were no barracks for soldiers [who]... residing at their own houses,... used to assemble in the Capital on occasions and when called for.... No pay was given to them but instead they were granted *jagirs* for their maintenance. Cavalry constituted the main army in those days,.... Bows, arrows, spears and swords were the main arms.[20]

In time, however, the army's fighting spirit weakened.[21] Morale and fighting prowess went hand in hand, and both suffered when Akbar's forces devastated Bandhavgarh in the late sixteenth century. Lack of training, irregular service, and uncertain prospects of pay also took their toll; and in the seventeenth and eighteenth centuries other armies outfought the Rewa Army, leading to the loss of territory. By Ajit Singh's reign (1755–1809) the army could no longer be relied on to defend the state.

In addition to military power, the Rewa kings used the weapon of marriage to bind their neighbours and former enemies to the state.[22] Thus, Baghel nobles married Chandel or Kalachuri princesses; and the Chalukya kings of Bastar took Baghel princesses in marriage, though Salivahan refused to give Baghel girls to the Lodis of Delhi. By maintaining 'close matrimonial ties' the Baghels also terminated old animosities with the Parihars. However, from at least the seventeenth century Rewa kings looked further afield— to Bundi, Jaipur, Bikaner and Udaipur—for matrimonial alliances for members of the royal family.

The maintenance of internal law and order was also a concern of the Rewa government.[23] The state was a turbulent place, where the most common elements of discord were 'women and land'. *Izzat*, too, was an important factor in an armed Rajput society, where men were more likely to settle quarrels with the sword rather than appeal to arbitration. However, an elementary judicial infrastructure did exist: village *chaukidars* were to report crime and the movement of criminals; local *panchayats* settled petty civil suits; and *chauras*, groups of influential persons at convenient centres, handled more complicated civil and criminal cases. However, there were no fixed procedures and local usage often guided decisions. Tests of guilt by ordeals were not unknown in civil cases. The Shastras and Koran served as guides for deciding cases according to the religion of an individual. In criminal cases, a fine was the main punishment, though in earlier times mutilation was practised. Nineteenth century references to corruption in deciding suits were probably true for preceding centuries also.

Another of the monarch's functions was to raise revenue. In the early years the state obtained revenue through a 'body of adventurers who with the chief at their head periodically sallied forth into the plains and exacted dues from villagers'.[24] Booty captured in battle also contributed to revenues, besides serving as income for the forces themselves. The kings used the revenues for their own as well as state expenses, such that there was no division between the two.

As administration became more settled and warfare declined, revenue from land became an important item of the state's income. This derived from two main sources. One comprised the state or *kothar* villages that paid revenue directly to the government through its appointed agents. Alienated estates were the other source of revenue. On these the *sardars* and other land-holders extracted revenues from their peasants, and passed on an amount equal to one fourth of the revenues to the state. Customs, fines, and other imposts also contributed to Rewa's income.

Mughal models of the seventeenth century may have influenced the administration of the revenue in Rewa as it existed in 1800.[25] Mughal governments sought to introduce a more systematic administration into the Baghel territories, dividing it into *mahal*s which were apportioned to larger *sarkars* within an overarching *suba* such as that of Allahabad. However, though Mughal revenue demands and troop levies from Bhatha or Bandhav appeared in their records, the dues remained on paper, the Baghel territories remaining to all intents and purposes free of any such demands from the central government.

The three-tier revenue administration owed something to Maratha models.[26] These tiers operated on the *khalsa* or *kothar* lands, and comprised officials in the capital, the *parganas*, and the villages. In the capital a *diwan* headed the system, assisted by officials and accountants or *khaskalams*. Where *parganas* existed, they were under officials known as *karindas*, aided by a *tahsildar* and *khaskalams*. *Karinda*s and *khaskalam*s also operated at the village level, generally holding small grants in return for service. At all levels, the role of the accountants was crucial:

From the Court of the chief down to the smallest village, a host of Kayasthas was busy recording receipts and expenditure, and preparing and examining accounts.... The village accountant, during harvest, went round from village to village and recorded the produce ... of each cultivator's harvest, with the share due as State land revenue and other rates and charges. These rough accounts were prepared for all villages and submitted to the pargana officer, who had them examined by the pargana khaskalam.[27]

As the administration developed, the state gave the collection of revenue from *kothar* villages to contractors, whose work dovetailed with that of the state officials.[28] Revenue was mostly paid in kind under a system known as *bhag* rents, in which contractors took a fraction of the produce that varied with the locality. However, the greater the profit taken by the contractors and officials, the less there was for the state.

Kings also found it difficult to realize the state's share of the revenues of their grantees.[29] Over the centuries a complex set of tenures evolved according to the type of grant, and rates were levied accordingly—though, except where rajas could apply force, these increasingly remained unpaid. Moreover, many grants were revenue-free, resulting in further loss to the state. As a result, the large areas alienated together with the uncertainty of their revenues proved financially ruinous for Rewa, such that by 1790 little remained for the raja's expenses apart from dues from customs and lands near the capital. Ajit Singh thus had to rely on loans to run the state, and he himself was 'scarce able to stir for the importunities of his creditors'.

III

A REGIONAL NOBILITY

As to the region's internal power equations, we have already noted that Rewa possessed a powerful nobility, comprising members of the royal family, their relatives, descendants of earlier rajas, and others whom it was in the state's interests to recognize. Among these the *ilaqadars* or *sardars* of the ruling house held many and the largest of the estates, most of which lay south of the Kaimur.[30] Smaller grantees constituted a minor nobility and were known as *pawaidars*, though by the twentieth century that term applied also to the *ilaqadars*. Under specific conditions, the rajas recognized the *ilaqadars* and *pawaidars* in their lands, and appointed the former to civil and military posts in the state.

The descent of individual grants clearly illustrates their royal origins.[31] Among the more prestigious Baghel nobles was the

Pawaidar of Bardadih (later Satna) who was descended from a brother of Raja Amar Singh (1624–40). Chandia in the south was settled on a fourth son of Raja Vikramaditya (1593–1624). The Thakur of Sohagpur was descended from Jamani Bhan, second son of Raja Virabhanu Singh (1540–55). A Raja of Shankergarh, dispossessed by the Mughals, sent the seven sons by his first wife to Churhat, where the eldest held the title of Rao Sahib, and the twelve sons by his second wife to Rampur Naikin. The chief of Lalgaon received his *jagir* from Maharaja Ajit Singh. The Ilaqadar of Itwan was descended from Virasimhadeva's brother; Deora was an off shoot of Itwan. The title to Ghuman estate descended from Janak Deva, also a brother of Virasimhadeva. Indeed, Panasi, Simeria, Baikunthpur, Amarpatan, and Madhogarh were all maintenance grants to brothers of various rajas.

Of the non-Baghel *ilaqadar*s and estate holders,[32] some titles resulted from Baghel marriages with Kalachuri, Parihar, and Gaharwar families, as with Dikshit Brahmans from Banda. Others were held by chiefs from hill and forest communities, such as the Baland Ilaqadar of Marwas, and the Raj-Gond Thakurs of Singhwara and Dharhar—all in Shahdol district. The two latter holdings became tributary to Rewa when Sohagpur passed to the state in 1859, as did the Khairwar *zamindari* of Pendra including Amarkantak.

Prominent among the non-Baghel *ilaqadar*s and holders predating Baghel rule were the Sengar Rajputs of Mau *pargana* in Rewa.[33] The main Sengar foundation comprised the *ilaqa* of Naigarhi (formerly the Mau Raj), whose *thakur* held 107 villages. The 36 *thakur*s of the *ilaqa*s of Gangeo, Pahari, and Jodhpur near Naigarhi were off shoots of the main Sengar clan, and held maintenance grants from the former raja. As late as 1800 the Thakur of Naigarhi claimed sovereignty over his grantees and unsuccessfully asserted his independence from Rewa on the basis of his pre-Baghel origins.

Several important non-Baghel *ilaqadar*s held land in Sidhi district.[34] Chief among these were the Chandels of Bardi, a desolate location at the confluence of the Son and Gopad rivers. In 1819 the Raja of Bardi relinquished his lands in favour of Rewa due to harassment by his kinsmen. Singrauli, a sub-grant of the Bardi Raj held by Khairwars, submitted to Rewa at the same time, though bitterness characterized their subsequent relations. The Chauhans of Sidhi, subjected by the Rewa Raj and strengthened by the migration of clan members from Uttar Pradesh in the nineteenth century, also maintained turbulent relations with the Baghels.

A set of tenures peculiar to Baghelkhand determined the political and revenue relations of the *ilaqadar*s, *pawaidar*s, and other grantees with the Rewa State, though these were not uncontested.[35] The most important of these tenures was the *mamla* grant to younger sons of the royal family and to the holders of estates such as Churhat and Rampur Naikin who were of royal stock. These were maintenance grants, the grantees holding full revenue rights and paying one quarter of the gross revenue to the state. The holders could not sell or transfer their grants. *Jagir* grants, personal and discretionary, also carried no right of alienation. *Jagir*s varied widely in size from large estates to a single village.

A number of less important tenures clustered around this central core.[36] *Nankar* was a maintenance grant for holders of resumed estates, heritable but not transferable; *dewarth* a grant for the support of a temple or indigent persons; *paipakhar* was a grant to Brahmans with all revenue rights, 'but subject to *chauth* from the fourth generation of the grantee'; *murwar* comprised a *muafi* grant for a family whose relatives had died fighting for the state—it was heritable and transferable; *brit* was a temporary revenue-free grant to Rajputs and Brahmans; while *bhaip* gave *brit* rights during a friendship and was thus not hereditary.

The sheer volume of alienated lands created problems for the Baghel state.[37] Grants to the nobility and others comprised a larger area and were more populous than the *khalsa* lands of the state. Rewa thus consisted of a congeries of estates which, though nominally subject to the raja, had no connection with the state lands. As noted above, powerful grantees regarded the king as 'primus inter pares' and, depending on the power the raja could muster, came to see themselves as independent of him except in time of war. The practice whereby the eldest son inherited the estate on his father's death, albeit with the permission of the *darbar*, strengthened the tendency of the larger holders to throw off the raja's authority, and even decline to observe the revenue conditions of their grants.

By 1800 the flaws in the Rewa system had undermined the state's cohesion and threatened its existence, as H.T. Colebrooke, an English traveller, observed in 1801:

Ajeet Singh has neither vigour nor authority to invite or to compel the joint exertions of a tribe of gallant warriors. Having outlived his best faculties, being swayed in all his actions by avarice, and verging rapidly towards the extreme of dotage, he is despised and slighted by his own servants. His authority is openly contemned and defied, even within the limits of his own capital. It is of course wholly disregarded by the numerous feudatories, among whom his nominal dominions are parcelled out. In short, this descendant of an ancient line of Hindu princes exhibits, on a less conspicuous theatre, greater degradation than the Mughal sovereign.[38]

It was the traveller's view that the raja's dominions 'scarcely exceed the bound of his capital'.

It was rather the independent nobility who caught Colebrooke's attention,[39] living simple, 'unpolished' lives in their 'strongholds and fastnesses of mountains and ill-cultivated country'. Although few were literate and some abetted female infanticide, all alike preserved the 'pride, independence and unaltered manners of their predecessors', equally ready to 'shed their blood in any cause which they deemed worthy of respect', whether as independent chiefs, feudatories of the king, or harassing travellers and traders passing through their lands.

IV

THE REGION'S DIALOGUE WITH CENTRALIZING STATES

What of Baghelkhand's dialogue with centralizing states, whether of Delhi or Agra?[40] Even before Baghel rule the Slave dynasty of Delhi threatened the region, then under the Chandels or Kalachuris—Kalinjara, Bandhavgarh, and Dahala alike being objects of imperial aggression. Ala-ud Din Khilji also laid seige to Bandhavgarh, though he failed to take the fort.

Once the Baghels established themselves in the region, they resisted the efforts of the Tughluks to bring them into their orbit. Stories about Gahora's relations with the centralizing Tughluks abound, many of them unreliable.[41] In the fourteenth century Vallaradeva Baghel reportedly aided Muhammad bin Tughluk in the *doab*, the latter confirming him as Raja of Gahora with membership of the Delhi *darbar*. By contrast, Viramadeva (1360–1425?) with lands along the Ganga 'did not think it proper to have relations with Delhi'—then in decline. Viramadeva also combated the Malikzada dynasty of Kalpi with the help of the Sharqis of Jaunpur, who themselves sought to make Kalpi a base in their move towards Delhi.

Bhatha-Gahora continued to defy central initiatives during the reign of the Lodi Afghans in Delhi from 1413 to 1526.[42] Sikander Lodi attacked Bhaidachandra Baghel (1470–95) for allying with Jaunpur, though in 1492 his failure to take Bandhavgarh cast doubts over the centre's military prowess. Bhaidachandra's successor Salivahan (1495–1500) shifted his loyalties to the Lodis when the Sharqi king retreated to Bengal; but when he refused to give a Baghel princess to Sikander Lodi, the Delhi Sultan 'utterly ruined the whole of that territory', compelling Salivahan to move to Bandhavgarh. In 1498 Sikander again failed to capture the fort, but in revenge devastated the country along his line of retreat.

Bowing to the inevitable, Virasimhadeva (1500–40) formed a working relationship with the first Mughal Emperor, Babur (1526–30), following his twin defeat of the Lodis and the Rajput confederacy.[43] In return Babur granted him Bhatha in *nankar jagir*, and with this Baghelkhand entered the centralized orbit of Mughal rule. Virabhanudeva (1540–55) is thought to have initially defied Babur's successor, Humayun. However, when he offered assistance after Humayun's defeat at Chausa in 1539, the Mughal Emperor formally acknowledged him and invited him to 'rule over twelve rajas'. When Sher Shah routed Humayun more decisively at Kanauj, Virabhanu again offered aid; and Rewa legend claims that the Emperor took refuge in Bhatha during the interregnum of the Suris.

The Suris similarly compelled Bhatha to acknowledge their government.[44] To test Vira's loyalty, Sher Shah summoned him to court; but when he joined the Chandel Raja in Kalinjara instead, Sher Shah attacked that fort, installing his son in the rear at Rewa. The emperor died during the siege, but his forces stormed Kalinjara and put its garrison to the sword. Virabhanu appears to have survived and is credited with living until 1555, probably under the suzerainty of Sher Shah's son, Islam Shah, who was crowned Emperor in Kalinjara in 1545.

Once the Mughals restored their rule, first under Humayun and then Akbar (1556–1605), they once again brought an unwilling Bhatha or Bandhav under their control.[45] Raja Ramachandra was thus in no position to refuse Akbar's demand for Tansen, a musician at court, but as he declined to surrender certain Afghan officers in revolt against Akbar, Asaf Khan attacked Bhatha and killed the Afghans. Then, when Ramachandra retired to Bandhavgarh, he besieged that fort—a siege only lifted at the instance of 'Hindusthani chiefs' in Delhi. Thereafter, Ramachandra 'shut himself up in Bandhavgarh', hoping to escape further notice from the centre.

However, the Mughal government kept up its pressure on Ramachandra by encroaching on the region and adjacent territories.[46] In 1569 Akbar's lieutenant Majnun Khan Qaksal attacked Kalinjara, which Ramachandra had purchased from the defunct Suri dynasty, and the Raja surrendered the fort without resistance. In 1580 Akbar tightened the screws further by placing Bandhav in the *suba* of Allahabad together with Jaunpur and Kara-Manikpur, Mughal documents showing the region as owing revenue, elephants, cavalry and infantry forces to the centre. However, Ramachandra still refused to submit personally to the Emperor 'on the grounds of distance', but sent instead his heir Virabhadra with tribute to express his loyalty.

The central government, however, pressed for Ramachandra to submit himself in person to Akbar as a symbol of his region's incorporation in the empire.[47] Fearing that resistance might invite retaliation, Virabhadra arranged for Mughal courtiers to conduct his father to the imperial presence. Ramachandra arrived at Fatehpur Sikri in February 1584, his submission creating a sensation as no chief of Bhatha or Bandhav had previously submitted to any northern ruler. Akbar eased a delicate situation by receiving the old Raja graciously and confirming him as hereditary ruler of Bhatha and Bandhav without tributary obligations.

Akbar forced Bandhav to submit more explicitly following Ramachandra's death in 1592.[48] The Emperor recognized Virabhadra, then at the Mughal court, as Ramachandra's successor; but on the journey to Baghelkhand Virabhadra died in suspicious circumstances; and disturbances at Bandhavgarh indicated that rival factions were struggling for power. The dominant faction sent Vikramaditya, a minor-grandson of Ramachandra, to the Mughal court, but Akbar dismissed the gesture as not sufficiently guaranteeing Baghel submission, and attacked Bandhavgarh to oust Vikramaditya and his supporters. After eight months Mughal forces occupied the fort on 3 July 1597, and a centrally appointed governor took charge there. To complete the humiliation, Akbar had the fort destroyed, captured Gahora, and in 1601 recognized Virabhadra's son Duryodana as ruler.

Though Akbar's government contented itself with the region's humiliation, Jehangir (1605–27) followed a more pragmatic line.[49] Vikramaditya as Raja-in-waiting foolishly attacked Bandhavgarh in 1610, but though Jehangir quelled the revolt, he subsequently bestowed the prince with a *jagir* and in 1616 granted him an audience. At their meeting Vikramaditya apologized and Jehangir pardoned him, recognizing him as Raja of Bandhav—without the Gahora *sarkar*. In a subsequent visit Vikramaditya kissed the royal threshold as the first Raja of Rewa, having abandoned Bandhav in favour of the fort town at the junction of the rivers Bihar and Bichhia.

Vikramaditya's submission opened a new chapter in the region's ties with the Mughal state.[50] Jehangir received Amar Singh (1627–40) in Agra in 1626, and bestowed on him the title of Raja. Amar acknowledged himself as a vassal and joined the Mughal Army in several campaigns: the first Baghel king to enter the imperial service. His son Anup Singh (1640–60) also attended court and brought forces to the Mughal Army, receiving in return Bandhav in *watan jagir*. Bhav Singh (1660–90) similarly accepted a *mansab* from Aurangzeb, who included the Rewa territories in the Kalinjara *sarkar*.

However, the long conflict with the central states of Delhi and Agra had weakened Rewa sufficiently for her to become an easy prey of regional rivals. Between the seventeenth and eighteenth centuries successive Bundela leaders seized state lands in western Baghelkhand, and even sacked and occupied the fort in Rewa.[51]

Under the Maratha banner, Ali Bahadur retrieved Banda from the Bundelas, before turning his attention to Rewa.[52] Stung by a military reversal in 1796, Ali Bahadur launched a revenge attack and compelled the aging Ajit Singh (1755–1809) to pay a crippling indemnity. Although Ali died during an unsuccessful assault on Kalinjara, by the turn of the century Rewa had virtually become a dependency of Banda. The Maratha Bhonslas of Nagpur also attacked Rewa from the late eighteenth century, occupying Sohagpur and Pendra, and later Amarkantak and territory to the north.[53] They had, however, to surrender these gains when the British central government defeated the Maratha confederacy in 1818.

V

REGIONAL SOCIETY TO 1800

As with the nobility, the wider society of Baghelkhand had long since assumed its characteristic shape by 1800, its main configurations being similar to those of adjacent regions of the subcontinent. This commonality was the result of migration and the transplantation of Brahman and kshatriya social values within the context of that migration.

Baghels were the dominant Rajput clan, and their movements up to 1800 mostly comprised internal migration, settling on conquered land, colonizing unsettled areas, or leaving lands overrun by neighbouring states.[54] Baghels dominated the *thakur* community in Rewa district, but they were also prominent below the Kaimur, their villages scattered among the hill and forest people whose lands they had infiltrated. Other Rajput clans mostly remained in the areas of their original holdings: Parihars were found in Rewa district and west Baghelkhand; Rathores almost entirely in Bandhavgarh; Sengars in Mauganj; Chandels in Bardi and Singrauli; and Chauhans mostly in the Gopad-Banas *tahsil* of Sidhi.

As we have seen, other dominant groups settled in Baghelkhand long before the Baghels. Of these the most prestigious were the Brahmans.[55] Owners of land from early times, the Baghels also bestowed land on them; and by 1800 their Kanyakubja and Sarwaria sub-castes were mainly located on the Rewa plateau, and formed an important community in Sidhi. Though strongly connected with land, many Brahmans were involved in rural moneylending and trade. Kayasthas, who occupied important posts in the Kalachuri state, were prominent as accountants under the Baghels. Bania and other traders conducted the business of trade and exchange.

Agriculturists made up the middle rungs of regional society. The formation of the Baghel state opened wide areas to colonization, some of it virgin land, some in areas lightly settled by previous migrants or hill and forest people. The easy availability of land encouraged migration, and it is thought that the main influx of

Hindi-speaking migrants from the north began about 1600[56] as the Mughals deepened their hold on northern India. This movement continued on into the eighteenth century.

The dominant agricultural castes comprised the Kurmis, Lodhis, Kachhis and Ahirs who, though scattered throughout the region, were also concentrated in certain areas:[57] Kurmis or Kunbis and Ahirs were specially prominent on the Rewa plateau; Kurmis were a principal community in east Sidhi, and Ahirs and Yadavas in Shahdol. Of these communities, Kurmis were thought to be the best cultivators, and with Kachhis, Kalars and Ahirs were frequently independent holders or tenants, paying their revenues on time, maintaining their cattle, and keeping their houses and villages clean.

The presence of the lower and untouchable castes in large numbers characterized regional society and underlined its deep divisions.[58] These comprised the artisans and servants of the wider community, and as such their migration must have coincided with that of the middle and upper social groups. Thus service communities such as Kayuts, Kumhars, Telis, Nais, Kahars, and many others were 'ubiquitously settled' in villages through out the region, their lives far more circumscribed than those of the middle and upper castes. Each had its traditional role with prescribed obligations, though it is likely that some among these communities were shedding these roles by 1800.

The large representation of hill and forest people was also a mark of Baghelkhand society.[59] Contrary to earlier opinion, these people were generally not displaced by the upper castes, but frequently lived interspersed among Rajput and Brahman landholders and Hindu peasants in villages on their former homelands, a few as landholders, though most either as small holders or labourers. Their areas of concentration in south Baghelkhand tended to be inaccessible, and marked by difficult terrain, forests, and poor soils which deterred higher caste folk from settling there.

Gonds, Kols, and Baigas were prominent groups within the hill and forest people, together with other smaller communities.[60] Greatest in numbers in south Baghelkhand, they were appreciably strong north of the Kaimur, especially in Rewa district. Gonds were the foremost of these three groups, and were concentrated in south Satna, east Sidhi, and Shahdol, where they were most numerous on the higher areas of the Maikal range in Pushprajgarh and Semri *tahsils*.

Social divisions among the Gonds made it difficult to regard them as a single community. A modern commentator has described them as a 'group of separate ethnic communities, speaking related but independent dialects':

All the sub-sections are different castes; there is no intermarriage, nor inter-commensality, and the members of each sub-section are firmly convinced that ... they are superior to ... other sub-sections.... We can only speak of some sort of solidarity among the Gonds of a certain area, say in a circle of twenty or thirty villages, where people know each other ... eat together ... belong together ... also intermarry and form a social unit.[61]

Gonds also differed widely in economic status. Some were *ilaqadar*s of Rewa State; others were agriculturists, and others again were labourers living in stark poverty in villages of the interior.

Kols were another important component of the hill and forest people.[62] They were the main such group in Rewa district—in fact, the Kols claimed Rewa as their home and Sabari as their mother, possibly linking them with the Sabaras of old. They were also strongly represented in the Gopad-Banas *tahsil* of Sidhi, and in the Beohari, Bandhavgarh, and Sohagpur *tahsils* of Shahdol. While some among them were cultivators, most were labourers who appeared to a British official in the nineteenth century 'completely abject and downtrodden'—a judgement confirmed by Indian census-takers in the mid-twentieth century.

Baigas were another characteristic hill and forest community in Baghelkhand.[63] One of the economically most backward groups, Baigas preferred to live in separate villages in the remoter jungly tracts of Sidhi and Shahdol, where they depended on shifting cultivation and the produce of the forest. Some Baigas were small cultivators in Rewa.

Muslims formed only a tiny minority within regional society, their origins lying in various invasions, the occupation of Bandhavgarh and Rewa from 1598–1603, Rewa's connections with the Mughal government, or in migration. Muslims mostly served as state functionaries, or artisans in villages and towns, as these developed.

VI

PATTERNS OF VILLAGE SETTLEMENT IN BAGHELKHAND

As with regional society, village settlements in Baghelkhand were broadly similar to those in any part of northern and central India by 1800, largely due to migration and to the social structures migrants brought with them. Typical villages of the region comprised a collection of compact or dispersed dwellings grouped according to caste, and housing people engaged in agriculture, labouring, or the crafts and other specialized occupations.

On the Rewa plateau, despite caste segregation the various castes generally lived side by side, though untouchable castes dwelt in a locality separated from the upper caste houses by a street or some distance away.[64] In village Shivpura, Rewa district, the houses of the Chauhan founder–landowners occupied a central position, surrounded by those of Brahmans, Kahars, Telis, Ahirs, Chamars, and Kols in their respective *tola*s. The Brahman *thakur* of Ratangawan village, Mauganj *tahsil,* also lived in a central *garhi,* other castes occupying distinct sites nearby, some in hamlets around the main settlement. The social and economic status of the different groups was clear to any observer: the better built houses of the dominant castes held a central position, while the 'wretched one-room ... huts' of the lowest castes were pushed to the periphery.

Villages south of the Kaimur were more likely to comprise hamlets grouped round a central core than in the north.[65] Sometimes these were well away from the core, as in north Beohari *tahsil* where they were on the edge of the forest and occupied by animal keepers or hunters. Depressed caste hamlets could also be detached from the main settlement.

The location of villages reflected the concerns of their founders.[66] Closeness to streams or rivers was important, especially in north Rewa where the Vindhyan rock system has a low water table. The founders of Rajput and Brahman villages[67] generally sought river lowlands where water was available, cultivation less arduous, and crops more secure. Such lowlands were also more fertile, and were to be found on the Rewa plateau with its belts of alluvial soil; in lowland Teonthar; on the alluvial soils of the Son valley with its ancient *ilaqa*s of Ramnagar, Rampur Naikin, Churhat, Baghaun, and Bardi; the red or brown soils of the Singrauli basin;

and the black cotton soils of Sohagpur. However, where Brahman and Rajput founders held ssuch areas, hard-working agricultural communities settled on higher land where the soil was good and the weather drier.

The defensiveness of a site was another important factor when settling in a region that was subject to raids, invasions, and political volatility.[68] While the village itself with its clustered houses reflected this concern, village founders also built *garhi*s in central or commanding positions to ward off attacks. Baghels built fortified villages on hilltops, river meanders, in the Kaimur foothills, or on elevated sites in the Son valley, cultivation taking place on the land below.

Village names also reflected the concerns of their founders. The diverse people who converged on Baghelkhand brought a variety of toponyms relating to castes, communities, persons, grants, military expeditions, geography, religion, the economy, flora, fauna, directions and structures to the localities where they settled.[69]

Village names themselves may provide clues to the social origins of a settlement.[70] One source claims Dravidian origins for the suffixes *rka, aha, iya, ia, ni, juli* or *jole*: hence Bandraha, Itaha, and Umaria. Dravidian *dol* means a hamlet, and is common in Sidhi and Shahdol where hill and forest people settled in large numbers. The most common Sanskrit suffix is *pur*, as in Mukundpur. Village names ending in *pur* occur predominantly on the Rewa plateau west and in Sohagpur, and were brought by agriculturists coming from the north and west. In forested Bandhavgarh, Manpur tells the story of an old settlement. Dialectical variants may change *pur* to *ur, purwa, war*, or *puri*, as in Kumharwar, Shivpurwar, or Murwar. Agriculturists from the north also named their villages *gram* or *gaon*, as in Ahirgaon, *gawan* being a dialectical alternative. The suffix *garh* normally indicates a fortified Rajput village.

Villages could take the name of their founders, castes and clans, or even one of the gods.[71] Thus Ram Sunder or Kanheri Ram. Brahmapuri or Bamhari occurs in the Gurgi stone inscription of the Kalachuri king Kokalladeva II, which Mirashi identifies with Bahmangaon not far from Gurgi, probably a Brahman settlement. Clans named their villages Rampur Baghelan or Raipur Kalachurian. Forest community names occur in Kolgama, Kolhari, Gondwana, and perhaps Nagavadh. Bharhut could recall a settlement of the Bhars. The names of locally revered deities find a place in Ramvan and Deogarh.

Some villages took their names from their natural surroundings.[72] A place difficult to reach might be called Magraura. Place names with suffixes of *sagar, tal, talab, kund,* and *jhirya* were close to water bodies. Lal Pahar or Pahariya indicates a hill settlement; the suffix *kut* also denotes a hill: thus Amarkut, the old name for Amarkantak. *Khoh* is a ravine or an enclosed space between hills, hence Khoh, Khorar or Sakhkohar. Rundha meaning strangled or blocked refers to a village surrounded on all sides by hills. Villages lying on a route may be Kamariapath or Kohiapath. Other villages have directional names such as Pipri Dakshina or Pipri Uttar. Rewa is thought to be another name for the Narmada, not far away.

Settlers also named their villages from the fauna or flora of the locality.[73] Sarasadollaka with its Kalachuri suffix (from *dol?*) indicated *sarasa,* the Indian crane, identified with Sarsi some 54 kilometres south-west of Chandrehe. *Bagh,* the tiger, old Baghelkhand's most prominent wild animal, gave its name to Baghwar and Baghan. Bagargaon in Sidhi was so named after a tiger was killed there. Other villages with animal names include Bhaiswar (buffalo), Gorsari (pig), Chherhai (bird), Bardadih (bullock), and Gajrahi (elephant). Pipri is named after the pipal tree, and Banwar denotes forest land.

Some village names had a revenue or administrative reference.[74] Parihar kings granted *ubari* villages on the Bhanrer plateau, hence Bhitari Ubari or Itma Ubari. Sengar Rajputs divided land into *dhanwar* and *banwar,* Dhanwar or Dhanwari signifying rice cultivation. Kothar indicates a village paying revenue directly to the state, hence Deur Kothar. The size of a village appears in Bargama, a large village; Majholi is a medium-sized one; and Tukri or Tukia Tola is a small village. Rampur Khurd indicates the small settlement of Rampur village, while Rampur Kalan is the large village of Rampur.

Villages in Baghelkhand exhibited different patterns of layout, often due to their physical setting. More difficult terrain fostered a dispersed type of village where houses were scattered, rather than the more compact pattern of the open plain:

The factors of dispersal are widespread and dominant all over: the valley, basin and plateau surfaces punctuated with ridges and scarps conspire with the irregular distribution of alluvium, general poverty of soil, seasonal river regimes, low watertable, need of terracing for agriculture, large expanses of impenetrable forest, and the presence of tribal people—to provide few spaces except in the open valleys and expansive plateaus, for compact settlement.[75]

Dispersed settlements thus occurred on the medial ranges of the Son valley, the Kaimur and Maikal ranges; the dissected topography of south-west Sidhi with its scattered farmlands; the forested Bhanrer plateau in north Satna; and in rough scrub and woodland where people lived by forestry or pastoralism.[76]

Dispersal could result from other factors besides.[77] Invaders of Baghelkhand generally came from the north or west, so that the more distant eastern Rewa favoured dispersal rather than the compactness necessary for defence. Dispersion could also take place where isolated farms had grown up since the original settlement. Ahirs and Kachhis at times preferred to live separately from the upper castes, as did lower castes and hill and forest people. The higher castes compelled untouchables to live away from the main village due to their association with animal skinning or pig raising.

Compact villages formed the other main type of village layout in Baghelkhand.[78] These occurred where the land was uniform and the soil fertile as on the Rewa plateau, the central river valleys, and the basins of Sohagpur and Singrauli. In the Son valley compact villages developed

typically from Churhat to Sidhi on both sides of the river.... These are connected by cart-tracks, or fair weather roads.... The farmer lives...in the village, setting out daily...to the field. This is a zone embedded with *pahari raman*, deposited yearly during the rainy season when the river is in spate. This bed of alluvium is quickly dissected.... The knots which are free from bad land and out of flood limit offer suitable sites for compact villages.[79]

Other factors[80] encouraging the formation of compact villages included the need for defence; protection against wild animals; or the strong representation of a particular community—whether Brahmans, Rajputs or agricultural castes—as in Satna, west Rewa and mid- and west Shahdol. At Maihar and Amarkantak religion led people to cluster round places of worship. Limestone areas where the water table was low or well construction difficult also fostered compact settlements to enable people to use their water resources economically. Paddy cultivation requiring large numbers of farmers and labourers may give rise to compact settlements, as in Sohagpur, Singrauli, Mauganj, and Maihar. Forest areas often have compact settlements due to the limitation of farming land.

Semi-compact villages with a nucleated site and subordinate hamlets linked by paths to the main settlement occur in east Rewa, the Panna range, the Gopad and Banas basins, and parts of Shahdol.[81] Lower and untouchable castes or hill and forest people occupy such hamlets; though they may also spring up as an outgrowth of an earlier settlement, or due to the immigration of labourers. One can find these semi-compact villages, besides, on slopes or in narrow valleys where agricultural land is scattered.

In some places semi-compact villages comprised a collection of hamlets as in the Son valley where, perched on the foothills and elevated sites, they

offered fortifications against tribal feuds and quarrels between native chiefs.... This hilly and forested valley has remained an abode of robbers, who have kept the inhabitants in a constant state of alarm.... The settlements clustered into hamlets with lines of defence...are often located at the base of the rocky hills of the Kaimur.[82]

Such settlements are commonly found from Sarsi to Deora, on the Kaimur foothills up to Churhat, and in the north of the Deosar and Gopad-Banas *tahsils* along the Son.

Whether dispersed or compact, many villages in Baghelkhand exhibit distinctive shapes.[83] Dispersed settlements may show a linear pattern on high land, in valleys, and along tracks as at Kothi where the village lay between the raja's *kothi* and the fort. Madhogarh is elongated due to its location on a meander of the Satna river. Compact villages may be square or rectangular round crossing paths, an open space, or an old temple, fort, or tank. Circular villages are uncommon, though they may be seen at Bela, or where paths converged on the *garhi* as in Sohagpur or the fort at Unchahra. In Satna villagers built circular settlements to ward off wild animals. Semicircular villages may follow the crescent shape of a meander, a hill range, or a tank. However, by contrast, many villages in the region merely comprise a 'heap of houses huddled together forming an irregular pattern'.

Village density in Baghelkhand largely depended on natural factors, there being fewer villages in difficult terrain.[84] The availability of water also had a bearing on density. Where the water table was low, or soil thin and stony or forest-covered, settlements were few; though in cleared alluvial basins they were denser. In general, north and west Baghelkhand had a higher village density than the east and south.

Village sizes correlated highly with the patterns of density and, though we are using modern estimates, they provide some guide to the position as it developed between 1350 and 1800.[85] Very large villages (with over 2,000 inhabitants) developed on the Rewa plateau and in river valleys. Large villages (2,000–999 inhabitants) were located on the bigger *ilaqa*s in roughly the same areas; medium-sized villages (999–500 inhabitants) were found in all districts—in Sidhi today the highest proportion of the population lives in such villages; in Shahdol these villages house one-third of the district's population. However, the most common type of settlement was the small village (500–200 inhabitants) where hills, forests, poor soil, or insufficient water checked growth. Rewa was predominantly a district of small villages; Satna and Shahdol districts of small and very small villages; and Sidhi of very small villages.

By 1800 Rewa was the principal town in Baghelkhand, its urban status largely due to its being the capital. As we have seen, the Rewa area had been in focus from prehistoric times, and through the Mauryan and Gupta periods. The Kalachuris built Gurgi and its fort of Rehuta nearby, and named the area Rewa *pattala*.[86] It is likely that a settlement emerged at Rewa during the first millennium AD, where the old roads from Allahabad and Mirzapur, after meeting at Mangawan, passed over a rocky ford on the Bihar river after its confluence with the Bicchia.

It is reasonable to assume that the site developed further as the Baghels strengthened their hold on the region. It was sufficiently important in the 1540s for Jalal Khan to build a fort there while his father attacked Kalinjara. Akbar's destruction of Bandhavgarh brought the town further into focus and, when the centre relinquished its hold on the region early in the seventeenth century, Raja Vikramaditya established his rule from there, adding palaces and other buildings which gave it the 'appearance of the chief town'.[87] Despite this Rewa lacked the concentration of industry or trade necessary for urban growth, and thus stagnated over the centuries until 1800.[88]

Other sites gave evidence of urban development. Maihar, where old roads from the north converged at the head of the pass in the upper Tons valley, originated as a fort town with a wall and gates. Remains from the eighth century may provide some clue to its age. Amarpatan, on the road from Rewa to Maihar, probably developed from about the twelfth century. Its old tanks testify to an early settlement, which later decayed and was revived by Maharaja Amar Singh in the seventeenth century.

VII

A REGIONAL ECONOMY

The region's economic life, too, was broadly similar to that of northern and central India due to migration and the common ways of life, modified according to local terrain, soil, and weather. Agriculture was the mainstay of Baghelkhand's economy and hence the principal source of employment, yet it suffered from severe constraints.[89] Crops depended on the rains, and any failure on this front affected all sections of society. For many, hunger and poverty were ever present, but more especially during poor seasons. In a good season, crops produced sufficient food for the population but left cultivators with no incentive to improve their tillage.

Twentieth century figures provide some guide to the social and economic map of Baghelkhand before 1800.[90] The nobility held most and the best land. Cultivators were much larger in number, but many rented their land, and of those holding or renting a significant number would be marginal farmers with uneconomic holdings. Large numbers laboured for owners or tenants and, apart from very small children, an entire family worked to earn their livelihood. Men did the heavier work such as ploughing and levelling, but women also helped with the principal activities of the agricultural year, besides fetching water, weeding, winnowing and milking. Children grazed the cattle. And from this constant round year in and year out there was no escape.

The village was normally self-sufficient, in that it produced the crops and provided the services required by the village community.[91] Chamars were entitled to the skins of dead cattle, but had to make a pair of shoes for every ploughman in the cattle owner's family, and provide leather thongs and twine for their implements. Artisans, together with service communities such as *dhobis* and *nais*, performed their work in return for food. This was especially the case when workers were attached to particular families. Debt bondage was a common practice in Baghelkhand, where it was known as *harwahi*.[92] A *harwaha* was a male labourer, often a Kol or Gond who, having incurred a debt for borrowing money from a Brahman or Rajput landholder, pledged his services and those of his family until he repaid the debt.

Harwahi confirmed the existence of indebtedness at the lower end of rural society.[93] Beyond that there is little evidence of the practice, though it was common in the nineteenth century where every village had its rich folk or moneylender who gave credit. The Maharaja confirmed that it was widespread in 1925; and 25 years later, levels of indebtedness remained high.

Over the centuries landholders and peasants rolled back the region's forests to bring the Rewa plateau and the southern river valleys and basins under cultivation. As clearing proceeded, agriculturists evolved patterns of cropping similar to those of central and northern India, modified by the soils, topography, and climate of Baghelkhand. As in northern India there were generally two harvests in the year: in the *kharif* or autumn season farmers grew rice, maize, *kodon*, *juar*, cotton and pulses with the aid of monsoon rains; and for the *rabi* or spring crop after the winter rains, wheat, gram, barley, sesamum, and oil seeds. In Satna and Rewa the principal crops were rice, *kodon*, wheat, pulses, or *juar*; in Sidhi rice, *kodon*, and barley; and in Shahdol rice, *kodon*, and oil seeds with wheat and maize in some places, though Shahdol was primarily a *kharif* district. Mixed cropping probably also developed from early times as a form of insurance against the failure of a principal crop.

Few fragments of the region's agricultural history from the Baghel occupation to 1800 survive.[94] Immigrant agriculturists such as the Kurmis brought improved farming techniques from the Gangetic plains. Old tanks in Sohagpur *tahsil* bespeak its settlement in the sixteenth century. Between 1790 and 1800 English travellers in Rewa noticed that, though war and plunder had depopulated some villages, land along the great Deccan road from Allahabad was farmed, the stretch between Mangawan and Gurh being 'remarkably well cultivated'; that between Rewa and the

Bhadanpur pass abounded with 'orchards,... ponds and ... temples'; and south to Amarpatan seemed 'fine cultivated country'. Even the country beyond Amarpatan was under cultivation. Centuries old usage marked the passage of the agricultural year in Baghelkhand.[95] The farmer timed his operations by the *nakshatras* or constellations in the path of the moon; and numerous sayings related to the weather falling under their influence and the operations to be performed at the time. Traditional implements included the *hal* or plough, the harrow, a log dragged over a field to smoothen it, the hoe, sickle, and spade. Farmers sowed *kharif* seed broadcast, but may have used a bamboo tube for sowing the *rabi.*[96] Most implements were of wood. Traditional practice also marked the more complex cultivation of rice, which was either sown broadcast as in parts of Shahdol, or transplanted from a nursery to the field as in Beohari and Sohagpur.

Agriculturists did not generally manure their fields, applying cowdung and village sweepings only to crops such as betel and sugar cane.[97] Otherwise they used cowdung as a fuel. Peasants believed that *mair* or wheat soils would raise a crop year after year without manure, irrigation, rotation, or fallow. The non-use of manure was also due to the fact that for centuries fresh land was readily available to replace exhausted fields. However, in some places farmers double-cropped or rotated crops, leaving land unused to regain its fertility. Hill and forest communities in Shahdol practised *dhya* or shifting cultivation on forested hillsides; while in Beohari, villagers burnt *sal* branches to manure the sandy soils before planting—a usage known as *baghor.*

A local way of rejuvenating exhausted land was to shift the village site every few years. At the end of the eighteenth century an Englishman passing through north Rewa reported

frequent traces of villages recently abandoned [and] ... hamlets newly established. The peasants of this district shift their abode at intervals of three or four years, for the sake of changing their lands, and of tilling the ground on which their cottages stood. The soil must doubtless have been enriched by the resort of men and cattle.[98]

This practice did not obtain in fertile Teonthar below the *ghat*; and could only take place where there was vacant land adjacent to a village. On some estates *ilaqadars* shifted their villages with an eye to profit, though tenants had to bear the cost of rebuilding their houses!

The shortage of water in parts of the region ensured that dry farming was the norm, except for rice cultivation.[99] On the Rewa plateau the water table was low, and in many places wells and *nalas* dried up in summer. The tanks common throughout Baghelkhand were generally used for household purposes and for watering cattle, but not for irrigation. *Baharas* or small springs on higher ground provided water for rice cultivation in Beohari, Bandhavgarh, and Sohagpur.

The cultivation of groves and orchards was commonplace in the region.[100] Among these were groves of mango and tamarind, as in the country north of the Kaimur. The *mahua* tree was also an important element in the rural economy, where countryfolk for centuries had used its flower as a food and for distilling liquor. No wonder the peasant was 'as keen on his mahua as he is on his field'.

The pasturing of cattle and other animals was an integral part of the rural economy.[101] Peasants used bullocks to pull their ploughs, and goats and cows to give milk. Lower communities reared goats and pigs also for meat. Livestock was, however, generally nondescript and of poor breed, and thus low in draught ability and milk yield. Pastures, too, were poor, and farmers did not generally provide their animals with cultivated fodder. Reliance on rains to nourish natural pastures meant that livestock lived much below their dietary requirements, wandering at will over uncared-for stretches of open land or forest. Consequently they readily fell prey to disease and death.

The agriculture of the Gonds, Kols, and Baigas (representing the hill and forest people) requires special mention.[102] Possibly before the Baghels came to power, some of these people led by the Gonds took to settled farming. In consequence almost all Gonds came to hold land; some Kols did so also; while the Baigas occupied a midway position. Kols were a major source of agricultural labour; but while they and the Gonds were usually farmers or labourers in more settled areas, the Baigas and Kols practised *dhya*: the 'clean felling and burning in rotation of about eight years of the entire forest cover' to refertilize inferior soils in the south; or its variant *baghor* in Sidhi. Large numbers of people thus subjected the forest country of Sidhi and Shahdol to these processes, thereby destroying the high forests of the state by the

nineteenth century. *Nistar* and grazing in forests further depleted
the region's timber.

VIII

BAGHELKHAND BY 1800: TOWARDS A MARKET ECONOMY?

To assess how far Baghelkhand might be moving towards a market
economy, whether national or regional, by 1800, let us first examine the region's communications. At the turn of the century unob-
structed movement along the major arteries was not possible.[103]
The road north of Gurh in 1790 was sufficiently indistinct for the
British traveller Leckie to make his way 'with difficulty'. Some years
later Colebrooke found the Mirzapur road to Maihar 'infested with
banditti from Bundelcund;' while officials of Maihar State reportedly looted those passing through it. This hindered the trade in
raw cotton from Amravati and Nagpur to Mirzapur, and the returning commodities' trade for Rewa and southern markets.

Communications off the major routes also inhibited trade.[104]
The region's vast countryside lacked effective outlets so that villages existed in conditions that had 'prevailed since time imme-
morial'. The small villages of the Son valley with their low population
and poor communications thus had 'little reason' for contact with
the outside world. Even as late as 1971 formed roads served less
than one quarter of the villages in Sidhi district. Shahdol and
other districts boasted 'rough tracks' that were impassable in the
rains. In the nineteenth century villages were ill-connected with
nearby railway lines: Kothara north of Satna was only six miles from
the nearest station at Jaitwar, but the distance 'could be covered on
foot only'. As a result, getting produce out of villages was difficult
and in many cases impossible.

Means of transport, too, were not conducive to the large-scale
movement of produce.[105] Exceptional were the 'droves of oxen'
seen on the Deccan road from Mirzapur around 1800, though
much of their load was for destinations outside the region. In the
country round Bardi in Sidhi—and this must have been the case
in many out-of-the-way places—even the wheel was unknown, and
pack bullocks carried away produce from villages with a surplus.
In Shahdol, however,

Gonds ... use a small bullock cart with solid wheels of one foot diameter in which they put a bamboo basket for carrying a load of one or two maunds. The driver has to walk by the bullock cart[106]

Beohari *tahsil* reported a similar vehicle. In any case, in the wet season pack bullocks moved more easily than carts. Those able to afford them used horses, elephants, and palanquins carried by servants, the latter moving more readily in the rains than animals. Between villages people moved on foot, as did messengers carrying the post in the countryside.

Despite the poor communications and the constraints of transport, some trade did take place, linking Baghelkhand to the wider economy beyond its borders.[107] As we have seen the Deccan road served more as a conduit for transit traffic, though goods not available locally also entered by this route, and by it Rewa exported *lac*, gum, cotton, and hemp. Timber does not seem to have found its way to a market, being consumed locally for domestic or agricultural use. As noted above pack bullocks moved surplus rural produce, while some villages held fairs and markets near temples and other holy sites on religious festivals.

Banjaras or Lawanas were responsible for moving produce in or through Baghelkhand:

A curious race of nomads ... acting as carriers with herds of pack bullocks. Their name means 'Forest Wanderer'... it has been conjectured ... that they are gypsies.... Each *tanda*, as their camps are called, is commanded by a chief called the *naik*, whom all obey.... Though eminent in the art and practice of highway robbery, the banjaras are ... constantly employed in the interchange of commodities between the open country and the forest territories.[108]

It is likely, too, that Baghelkhand exported some minerals or metals.[109] Much earlier, the argentiferous deposits of Rewa fed the coin industries of north and eastern India. Miners worked the copper at Cherka near Beohari in 'bygone times'. Corundum was quarried in Sidhi at least by the early nineteenth century, and probably much earlier due to the demand for it in Europe where the Hindi *kurand* was named corundum.

Traditional iron mining and smelting for local use and export probably took place on a wide scale in Baghelkhand.[110] Agarias and Lohars effected pre-industrial smelting in many places. Lohars, mentioned in Bana's *Harsa-Carita*, are thought to have grown in numbers during the mediaeval period, and by 1800 were present in large villages, especially in the *tahsils* of northern Rewa. Agarias seem to have been more concentrated in the remoter parts of Sidhi's Beohari and Deosar *tahsils*.

Colebrooke has left a fascinating account of iron smelting in 1801 at Bhadanpur in Maihar on the Rewa road, where merchants could buy or exchange goods for iron:

The furnace is in the shape of half a frustrum of a cone; it is made of clay, and its height is about six feet, two-thirds of which is underground, and the remainder serves as a chimney. The front, being flat, has before it a semi-circular hole, into which the ashes and reduced metal are received, when the door of the gate is opened; through the upper part of that door a double bellows, worked by a single workman, maintains a continual stream of air by means of alternate strokes of his right and left hands. He is relieved by one companion, and their joint labour during twelve hours, suffices to reduce one and a half hundred – weight of iron from eight times its bulk of ore, using two loads ... of charcoal. The iron thus obtained loses a quarter of its weight under the hammer, in preparing it for use but it still contains much scoria, and other impurities.[111]

Gold and silver-smithy, too, were traditional crafts in Rewa State, manufactured by means of hand punches on gold and silver sheets.[112] A caste of metal workers known as Audhias reproduced ornaments of gold and silver for those able to afford them; and in brass, bell– and white-metal for the lower classes. Indeed, the age-old regional craft economy revolved around artisans such as the Audhias and other metal workers, though it is unlikely that their work went outside Baghelkhand.

A traditional textile industry similarly catered to the needs of the court and people of the region.[113] Weavers from the Kori, Julaha, and Panas communities wove the coarse cloth called *gazi*, while Lahangirs manufactured materials of finer quality. The Rangrez and Chhipa castes dyed cloth, different centres special-izing in particular colours for the court and nobility. Here and there dyers catered to the needs of the common folk. It is doubtful how far money was used to purchase cloth: more likely, as with other produce, it was bartered for goods required by the sellers.

Additional crafts contributed to the regional economy.[114] Carpentry was an age-old craft, and Kunderas or carpenters were found in every village, producing agricultural implements, country carts, and furniture. The Basor caste made artefacts from bamboo. The fashioning of pottery and jewellery together with ornaments of *lac* were other traditional crafts common in the region.

Though agriculture and the crafts had their strengths, Baghelkhand's social and economic life was blocked at key points.[115] One was the insecurity of existence represented by abandoned villages, almost every village 'having in it or near it some signs of former habitation' unrelated to shifting village sites. Many villages had been 'erased' through invasion or warfare, a regular feature of region's political life into the nineteenth century. The ravages of tigers could force inhabitants to abandon their village. Floods washed away villages and, as with recurrent bouts of disease, carried off large numbers. These insecurities of life militated against the formation of a stable and prosperous economy.

The low productivity of the region's agriculture itself prevented development. This was especially the case on the Rewa plateau where peasants used poor implements combined with traditional soil management, cultivation, and animal husbandry. The position was even less favourable on the southern plateau with its uneven surfaces and large population of hill and forest people possessing meagre resources. This concentration of people in low-level agriculture led to a low standard of living all round with an accompanying lack of industry and urbanization.

The self-subsistent nature of the economy also posed an insuperable hurdle to economic growth and the development of a market.[116] After satisfying local needs, market potential was mostly taken up with obtaining the necessities of life that could not be produced locally. Even in procuring these or the products of the craft economy, the use of money was probably minimal. Land revenue was traditionally paid in kind; while kings and larger landholders used their agricultural surplus to build forts and temples, further restricting the market and the accumulation of capital. These factors, together with the concentration of the workforce in subsistence agriculture, rendered the economy resistant to growth and unable to develop a commercial and industrial base. As a result the world of the modern economy, whether national or regional, had not begun to impinge on Baghelkhand by 1800.

Notes

1. I owe this sentence to P.S. Dwivedi, who also made many helpful suggestions relating to the chapter.

2. The clan name of Vaghela or Baghel derived from the *jagir* of Vyaghrapalli or Vaghela not far from Anhilwara, given them either by the Chavda or Solanki rulers for services to the state. An inscription of 1304 indicates that the Baghels regained power following the first attack by the Khiljis. E.Z.A. Desai, 'A Persian-Sanskrit inscription of Karna Deva Vaghela of Gujarat', *EI* (Arabic and Persian Supplement), 1975, pp. 16–17, 20.

3. C.T. Metcalfe, *The Rajpoot Tribes,* vol. I, New Delhi, rpt, 1982, pp. 92–3.

4. Bhattacharya, *Historical Geography,* p. 34.

5. *Uttar Pradesh District Gazetteers, Banda,* Allahabad, 1981, p. 229; Cunningham, vol. XXI, pt. I, *Reports of a Tour,* p. 103. An eighteenth century official genealogy inserts an imaginary Vyaghra Deva Baghel into the account of the capture of Marpha.

6. *District Gazetteers of the United Provinces of Agra and Oudh, Banda: A Gazetteer,* vol. XXI, Allahabad, 1929, pp. 163, 165; CIA, P, A, 1902–47, 27–A, 1920, O/PA Rewa to FSec, 8 Mar. 1861; *Shahdol Gazetteer,* p. 41.

7. *Banda Gazetteer,* vol. XXI, p. 169; *Rewa Gazetteer,* p. 30; A.H. Nizami, 'Baghela dynasty of Rewa: genealogical sources', *Proceedings of the Indian History Congress Session,* 1945, p. 1.

8. Nizami, 'Baghela dynasty of Rewa: early history', *Oriental Conference,* Nagpur, 1946, pp. 2–3; Nizami, 'Elephant-catching expedition, A.H. Nizami, 'The Baghela dynasty of Rewa (Virasimhadeva)', *Bharatiya Vidya,* vol. X, 1946, p. 56; H. Shastri, *The Baghela Dynasty of Rewa, Memoirs of the ASI,* no. 21, Calcutta, 1926, p. 6; A.H. Nizami, 'Baghelkhand during the great rebellion of 1857', *M.P. Chronicle,* Jan. 1971, p. 2.

9. Nizami, 'Baghela dynasty', *Oriental Conference,* p. 3; A.H. Nizami, 'The Baghela dynasty of Rewa', *JVU,* vol. II, no. 2, May 1958, p. 1; Cunningham, vol. XXI, pt. II, *Report of a Tour,* p. 156; Roy, 'Baghelkhand', p. 7. Cunningham reports a *sati* pillar of 1350 from Gobari south-west of Rewa, and a stone inscription of 1351 from Kothi north of Satna: 'It is probable that both monuments belong to the Baghel Raja Bhairava Deva, who reigned 1335–55'.

10. Shastri, *Baghela Dynasty,* pp. 6–7, 13; A.H. Nizami, 'The Baghela dynasty of Rewa', *Proceedings, of the Indian History Congress,* 9th Session, Patna, 1946, p. 3; A.H. Nizami, 'Early British relations with Bundelkhand, Baghelkhand, 1802–18', *JMPIP,* 1980–1, p. 21; Nizami,

'Baghela dynasty', *JVU*, p. 1; Nizami, 'Great rebellion', *M.P. Chronicle*, pp. 2–3; *Rewa State Gazetteer*, p. 86; *Shahdol Gazetteer*, pp. 44–5; *Rewa Gazetteer*, p. 35. Naraharideva is sometimes rendered as Naharideva.

11. Nizami, 'Elephant-catching expedition', p. 10.

12. See pp. 94–5.

13. C.E. Luard (ed.), *Chiefs and Leading Families in Central India in 1916, Calcutta, 1916*, p. iii; K. Singh, 'The territorial basis of mediaeval town and village settlement in eastern Uttar Pradesh, India', *Annals of the Association of American Geographers*, vol. 58, no. 2, June 1968, pp. 203, 207–8; D.W.K. Barr, *Administration of the Rewah State*, Allahabad, 1886, p. 70; *Rewa Gazetteer*, p. 181; *Report of the Committee appointed to Enquire into the Nature of the Pawai Tenures in Rewa State*, Allahabad, 1934, pp. 2, 4; J. Lal, 'Baghelkhand: A study in settlement geography', PhD, APS University, Rewa, pp. 43–4.

14. Luard, *Chiefs, 1916*, p. iii; S. Sinha, 'State formation and Rajput myth in tribal Central India', *MI*, vol. 42, no. 1, Jan.–Mar. 1962, pp. 73–4.

15. *Central India Gazetteer*, p. 428; FP, A, Mar. 1862, 457, W.W. Osborne to FSec, 1 Oct. 1860; Barr, *Administration of Rewah*, pp. 8, 33.

16. Lal, 'Settlement geography', PhD, p. 43; FP, S, 33–H, 1929, 1, Encl A in B. Glancy to PSec., 22 Mar. 1929.

17. R. Sharma, *Vaghela Vamsha Varnanam*, with notes and summary by C. Malaviya, pp. 4–5; Shastri, *Baghela Dynasty*, p. 9; Nizami, 'Genealogical sources', pp. 1–2; A.H. Nizami, 'Historiography in Rewa–Vindhya Pradesh: retrospect and prospect', unpublished seminar paper, Shahdol, Feb. 1996, pp. 1–3.

18. W. Crooke, *The Tribes and Castes of the North-Western Provinces and Oudh*, Calcutta, 1896, p. 102; *Rewa State Gazetteer*, np.

19. K.M. Saxena, *Rewa State Directory*, Allahabad, 1947, p. 117; Barr, *Administration of Rewah*, pp. 151, 158–9.

20. *Rewa Directory*, p. 117.

21. See Barr, *Administration of Rewah*, pp. 150–1; and H. Colebrooke, 'A narrative of a journey from Mirzapur to Nagpur', *Early European Travellers in the Nagpur Territories*, Nagpur, 1930, p. 226.

22. Baghel, 'Rewa ke Baghel rajya', PhD, pp. 181–4; H.L. Shukla, *Tribal History: A New Interpretation*, Delhi, 1988, pp. 178–80; 185; Nizami, 'Early British relations', pp. 24–5; *Rewa Gazetteer*, p. 39.

23. Barr, *Administration of Rewah*, pp. 115, 122; *Rewa Gazetteer*, pp. 202, 205, 227; *Rewa State Gazetteer*, p. 53; FP, 22 Apr. 1853, 131, G.A. Bushby to C. Allen, 7 Apr. 1853.

24. *Rewa State Gazetteer*, p. 51. Maharaja Gulab Singh, ruling between 1922 and 1946, also maintained the indivisibility of the Rewa revenues, thereby earning the determined opposition of the central government.

25. Abu'l Fazl, *Ain-i Akbari*, trans. Col. H.S. Jarrett, vol. II, Delhi, rpt, 1978, pp. 169, 172, 177; Nizami, 'Baghela dynasty', *JVU*, p. 4; P.P. Sinha, *Raja Birbal: Life and Times*, Patna, 1989, p. 29; Shastri, *Baghela Dynasty*, p. 13; *Rewa State Gazetteer*, p. 53. See the discussion in chapter V of Maharaja Venkatraman Singh's refusal to join Curzon's Imperial Forces scheme.

26. *Shahdol Gazetteer*, p. 3; *Rewa State Gazetteer*, p. 52–3; *Central India Gazetteer*, p. 412.

27. *Rewa State Gazetteer*, p. 52.

28. *Rewa Gazetteer*, pp. 178, 189; *Sidhi Gazetteer*, p. 141.

29. G.F. Leckie, 'Journal of a route from Nagpore to Benares, by the way of the Souhagee pass, 1790', *European Travellers*, pp. 86–7; Colebrooke, *European Travellers*, p. 227; Baghel, 'Rewa ke Baghel rajya', PhD, p. 117. Between 1881–6 officials noted that there were 6416 populated villages in Rewa. Of these 1432 were *kothar* villages; 2174 were on *ilaqadari* estates; 669 villages paid *chauth*; 167 were rent-free; 138 were in *jagirs* of maharanis and widows; 35 were in possession of the widows of Madhogarh estate; 121 villages supported temples; 269 were held by *jagirdars* in lieu of cash payments; and 1441 were rent-free in perpetuity, mostly held by Brahmans (Barr, *Administration of Rewah*, p. 70).

30. *RSA 1907–8*, p. 4.

31. Luard, *Chiefs, 1916*, pp. 28–9; VP, RDO, 1881–90, 39, Note by J.L. Khare, 15 Feb. 1930; BA, English files, pt, III, 5, 1927, K.S. Fitze to Sec AGGCI, 3 Feb. 1926; RDO, 4, 1925, 26, 100, 1925, Confdl; *Shahdol Gazetteer*, p. 51; Baghel, 'Rewa ke Baghel rajya', PhD, np.

32. Barr, *Administration of Rewah*, p. 8; Luard, *Chiefs, 1916*, p. 30; RDO, Rev, VP Accounts, nos. 1163–1250, 125, 1929–44, Note by J.L. Khare, 29 Dec. 1929; Misra, *Son ka pani*, p. 109.

33. Barr, *Administration of Rewah*, pp. 8, 33; *Rewa State Gazetteer*, p. 78; BA, 10, 1875, Diwan Het Ram's Memo, 18 Aug. 1881; CIA, BA, 430, 1875–83, PA to FA, AGGCI, 15 Apr. 1882; RDO, 1920–?, 26, Indexing section, nd. Rewa's assertions of sovereignty and Naigarhi's of independence made for constant friction, a temporary lull in their bitter relations occurring in 1800 when an illegitimate brother of Raja Ajit Singh subdued Mau and compelled the Sengars to pay tribute.

34. RDO, 1930–44, 34, Rev, J.L. Khare, 20 Feb. 1930; *Sidhi Gazetteer*, p. 30; George, 'Impact of industrialization', PhD, p. 27.

35. *Sidhi Gazetteer*, p. 149; *Rewa Directory*, pp. 150–1.

36. Ibid., *Rewa Gazetteer*, pp. 131–2.

37. See fn. 29; Barr, *Administration of Rewah*, p. 70; *RSA 1907–08*, p. 4; *Rewa State Gazetteer*, p. 57.

38. Colebrooke, *European Travellers*, pp. 226–7.

39. Ibid., pp. 222, 227; Leckie, *European Travellers*, pp. 85–6; Barr, *Administration of Rewah*, pp. 9, 19.

40. Richards, 'The Islamic frontier', p. 98; Nizami, 'Baghela dynasty', Nagpur, p. XXX; A.K. Roy, 'Myth, fable and guile: the art of survival in Shahdol', *India International Centre Quarterly*, vol. 19, nos 1–2, Spring-Summer 1992, p. 12; Cunningham, vol. XXI, pt. I, *Reports of a Tour*, p. 105; *CII*, vol. IV, pt, I, p. cviii; *Ain-i Akbari*, vol. I, Delhi, 1989, p. 396. Despite all this activity, Nizami claims that 'the country … remained *terra incognita* to the Turkish suzerains'. See A.H. Nizami, 'A missing link in the history of Madhya Pradesh: Malikzada dynasty of Kalpi (Bundelkhand)', *JMPIP*, no. 1, 1959, p. 59.

41. A.H. Nizami, 'Biramdeo Baghela; Mukaddam of Gahora', *JIH*, Travancore University, Aug. 1954, p. 1; Baghel, 'Rewa ke Baghel rajya', PhD, pp. 39–44; Nizami, 'Baghela dynasty', *JVU*, p. 1; A.H. Nizami, 'Muhammadan Kalpi and its historical background', *Islamic Culture*, vol. XXVII, no. 3, July 1953, pp. 150–1.

42. Nizami, 'Baghela dynasty (Virasimhadeva)', p. 53; *Rewa State Gazetteer*, p. 13; Cunningham, vol. XXI, pt, 1, *Reports of a Tour*, pp. 107–8; *Rewa Gazetteer*, p. 32; R. Ali, 'The Baghelas-an appraisal', *PP*, vol. XII, nos. 1–2, 1984, p. 95; A. Halim, *History of the Lodhi Sultans of Agra and Delhi*, Delhi, 1974, p. 75; A.A. Khan, *The Glories of Bandhogarh*, nd, p. 6; A. Rashid, *Society and Culture in Mediaeval India*, Calcutta, 1969, p. 75.

43. Nizami, 'Baghela Dynasty (Virasimhadeva)', p. 53; *Rewa Gazetteer*, pp. 33–4; *Representative Men of Central India*, Bombay, nd. p. 3, pt. VIII; Khan, *Glories of Bandhogarh*, p. 6; Shastri, *Baghela Dynasty*, p. 3.

44. Baghel, 'Rewa ke Baghel rajya', PhD, p. 63; *Shahdol Gazetteer*, p. 46; Lal, 'Settlement geography', PhD, p. 176; R. Burn, (ed.), *Cambridge History of India*, vol. IV, *The Mughal Period*, New Delhi, 1963, p. 55; J.M. Walia, *Mughal Empire in India*, New Delhi, nd., pp. 71–2; R.C. Majumdar, *The History and Culture of the Indian People*, vol. VII, *The Mughal Empire*, Bombay, 1974, p. 90.

45. *Ain-i Akbari*, vol. I, pt, III (trans. H. Blochmann), Calcutta, 1939, p. 445; Samsam-ud Daula Shah Nawaz Khan, *Maathir-ul Umara*, vol. I, New Delhi, 1979, p. 37; *Rewa Gazetteer*, p. 35; *Cambridge History of India*, vol. IV, p. 101; *Ain-i Akbari*, vol. I, p. 396.

46. I.H. Qureshi, *Akbar, The Architect of the Mughal Empire*, Delhi, 1987, p. 74; *Shahdol Gazetteer*, pp. 46–7; P. P. Sinha, *Raja Birbal*, p. 27; *Maathir-ul Umara*, p. 582; Bhatha was not one of the *khalsa* provinces of Babur's empire; but Akbar formed it into a *sarkar* of 39 *mahals* within the *suba* of Allahabad.

47. Sinha, *Raja Birbal*, pp. 27–8; *Rewa Gazetteer*, pp. 35–6; Nizami, 'Baghela dynasty', *JVU*, pp. 3–4.

48. *Rewa Gazetteer,* pp. 37–8; *Ain-i Akbari,* vol. I, pt, III, p. 446; *Maathir-ul Umara,* p. 583; Roy, 'Myth, fable and guile', p. 25; Sinha, *Raja Birbal,* pp. 29–31; Misra, *Son ka pani,* p. 157; *Rewa State Gazetteer,* p. 1. Rewa genealogies do not recognize the succession of either Virabhadra or Duryodana, dating Vikramaditiya's accession from the death of Ramachandra in 1592.

49. Sinha, *Raja Birbal,* p. 38; *Rewa Gazetteer,* p. 38; Nizami, 'Historiography', p. 4.

50. *Rewa Gazetteer,* p. 38; R. Ali, 'The Baghelas: an appraisal', *PP,* vol. xii, nos 1–2, 1984, p. 98; *Ain-i Akbari,* vol. I, pt, III, p. 446; Sinha, *Raja Birbal,* pp. 54–5, 75, 115–16; A.H. Nizami, 'Rewa: past and present', *M.P. Medical Conference Souvenir,* Rewa, nd., p. 4. The *Ain-i Akbari* reported that Raja Anup Singh converted to Islam, but no other contemporary source corroborates this. Anup Singh's *mansab* was of 3,000 *zat* and 2,000 *sawars*; and Bhav Singh's 1,000 *zat* and 1,000 *sawars,* indicating the declining prestige of the Baghel chiefs at the Mughal court.

51. *Shahdol Gazetteer,* p. 51; Cunningham, vol. XXI, pt. I, *Reports of a Tour,* p. 112; Nizami, 'Early British relations', p. 41; A.H. Nizami, 'Note on Maihar', *Bharatiya Vidya,* Bombay, 2 Feb. 1945, p. 2; A.H. Nizami, 'Nine gems of the court of Maharaja Bhavasimha of Rewa', *J. Ganganath Jha Oriental Research Institute,* vol. VIII, no. 4, p. 3.

52. *Satna Gazetteer,* pp. 55–6; *Shahdol Gazetteer,* pp. 51–2; Nizami, 'Baghela dynasty', *JVU,* p. 5; Baghel, 'Rewa ke Baghel rajya', PhD, pp. 121–2.

53. Misra, *Son ka pani,* pp. 109–10.

54. FP, A., Aug. 1870, 68, Memo of J.P. Stratton, encl in H. Daly to C.U. Aitchison, 21 June 1870; *Rewa State Census, 1921, Report,* pp. 56–7.

55. R.S. Dube, *Population of Rewa Plateau: A Geographical Analysis,* Kanpur, 1979, p. 6; Zutshi, *Rewa and its Ruler,* p. 13; Govt of M.P., Forest Dept., *Working Plan of the West Sidhi Division, Rewa Circle, for the Years 1988–89 to 1997–98,* vol. I, p. 62; *Satna Gazetteer,* p. 81.

56. R.L. Singh, *A Regional Geography,* Varanasi, 1971, pp. 623–4.

57. Zutshi, *Rewa and its Ruler,* p. 13; *Working Plan for Mada, Waidhan, Jiyawan and Sarai Ranges of the East Sidhi Forest Division, Rewa Circle, M.P., for the years* 1975–76 to 1989–90, vol. 1, p. 62; *Census of India, 1941, Central India,* vol. I, *Rewa State, Report and Tables,* Bombay, 1944, p. 52.

58. The Rewa census of 1941 noted that Domars or sweepers were the only untouchable caste in the state, though this could not have been the case in practice. *Shahdol Gazetteer,* p. 308; *Rewa Gazetteer,* pp. 67, 81; *Rewa State Census, 1941, Report,* pp. 50, 52; *MP Census, 1961, Shahdol Handbook,* p. lxiv; ibid., *Sidhi Handbook,* p. lvii; Lal, 'Settlement geography', PhD, pp. 272–3.

59. FP, A, Aug. 1870, 68, Memo of J.P. Stratton, 21 June 1870; Chauhan, 'Spatial pattern of literacy', PhD, p. 101.
60. *Rewa State Census, 1921, Report*, p. 57; V.P. Gupta, 'Tribal economy in Baghelkhand', PhD thesis, APS University, Rewa, 1974, p. 31; A. Raizada, *Tribal Development in Madhya Pradesh: A Planning Perspective*, Delhi, 1984, p. 31; Chauhan, 'Spatial pattern of literacy', PhD, p. 101.
61. Shukla, *Tribal History*, p. 5; K.D. Bajpai, *Cultural History of India*, vol. I, pp. 56–7; R.S. Baghel, 'Ethno-ecological studies on tribals, with special reference to the Gond system', PhD thesis, APS University, Rewa, 1992, pp. 139–40; *MP Census, 1961*, vol. VIII, Pt VI, 'Amwar village survey', p. 1.
62. *Rewa Gazetteer*, pp. 67–8; *Rewa State Census, 1921, Report*, p. 57: *MP Census, 1961, Rewa Handbook*, p. li; *MP Census. 1961, Satna Handbook*, p. lvii; Barr, *Administration of Rewah*, p. 12.
63. *Shahdol Gazetteer*, p. 75; *Report of the Path Enquiry Commission*, pp. 11, 20; *MP Census, 1961*, vol. VIII, pt VI, 'Amwar village survey', p. 174; *MPCensus, 1961, Sidhi Handbook*, pp. lix–lx; *The Tribes of Madhya Pradesh*, Govt of MP, 1961, pp. 6, 8.
64. *Rewa Gazetteer*, p. 71; Lal, 'Settlement geography', PhD, pp. 138, 141, 165, 169, 170, 274–9.
65. R.L. Singh, *Regional Geography*, p. 637; Lal, 'Settlement geography', PhD, p. 138; A.N. Bhattacharya and L.N. Verma, 'Rural settlement forms in the Son valley', *IG*, vol. 2, no. 2, 1957, pp. 301–2.
66. J. Singh, 'Rural settlement types and patterns in Baghelkhand, M.P.', *NGJI*, vol. XVII, pt 4, Dec. 1971, p. 181; Lal, 'Settlement geography', PhD, pp. 135, 234.
67. Ibid., pp. 132, 135; Bhattacharya and Verma, 'Settlement forms', p. 296; Chauhan, 'Spatial pattern of literacy', PhD, p. 96; Singh, 'Rural settlement types', p. 178.
68. Lal, 'Settlement geography', PhD, pp. 132, 135, 152; Bhattacharya and Verma, 'Settlement forms', p. 301; Singh, *Regional Geography*, p. 635.
69. Lal, 'Settlement geography', PhD, p. 47.
70. Ibid., pp. 32, 34, 36, 38.
71. Ibid., pp. 28, 44–5; R.K. Lal, 'Place-names in the Kalachuri records', *JMPIP*, no. 4, 1962, p. 147; '*ian*' suffixes may reflect a Persian connection.
72. Lal, 'Settlement geography', PhD, pp. 38, 41, 45.
73. Lal, 'Place names', p. 151; Lal, 'Settlement geography', PhD, pp. 42–3, 45–6; Misra, *Son ka pani*, p. 178.
74. Lal, 'Settlement geography', PhD, pp. 43–6.
75. Singh, *Regional Geography*, p. 635.

76. Dube, *Land Use Patterns*, p. 11; Bhattacharya and Verma, 'Settlement forms', pp. 302–3; Lal, 'Settlement geography', PhD, pp. 133, 152, 154.

77. Dube, *Land Use Patterns*, pp. 10, 12; Singh, 'Rural settlement types', pp. 183–4; Bhattacharya and Verma, 'Settlement forms', pp. 302–3.

78. Lal, 'Settlement geography', PhD, p. 133; Singh 'Rural settlement types', pp. 180–1; Bhattacharya and Verma, 'Settlement forms', p. 299.

79. Ibid.

80. Dube, *Land Use Patterns*, p. 10; Lal, 'Settlement geography', PhD, pp. 134, 136; Singh, 'Rural settlement types', pp. 181–2.

81. Lal, 'Settlement geography', PhD, pp. 132, 154; Singh, 'Rural settlement types', pp. 183–4, 188.

82. Bhattacharya and Verma, 'Settlement forms', p. 301.

83. Dube, *Land Use Patterns*, p. 11; Singh, 'Rural settlement types', pp. 184, 186–8; Lal, 'Settlement geography', PhD, pp. 204–10.

84. Singh, *Regional Geography*, p. 637; Lal, 'Settlement geography', PhD, pp. 151, 155. In 1961 south and east Baghelkhand had a density of 16 villages per 100 square kilometres, while north and east parts of Rewa and Satna had a density of 32 villages. Village density in Mauganj *tahsil* was 57 per 100 square kilometres, and in Huzur 41.

85. Lal, 'Settlement geography', PhD, pp. 228–9; *MP Census, 1961, Sidhi Handbook*, pp. xlii–xliv; *MP Census, 1961, Satna Handbook*, p. lxvi; *MP Census, 1961, Shahdol Handbook*, p. xlviii; *Rewa Gazetteer*, p. 61.

86. Bhattacharya, *Historical Geography*, p. 160.

87. *Rewa Gazetteer*, p. 303.

88. Lal, 'Settlement geography', PhD, p. 291; *Satna Gazetteer*, p. 371.

89. *Rewa State Census, 1941, Report*, p. 15; *Rewa Gazetteer*, p. 81; *Report on the Political Administration of the Territories within the Central India Agency for 1883–84*, pp. 179–80.

90. *Census of India, 1971, Madhya Pradesh, Rewa District Census Handbook*, pp. 173–4; *Census of India, 1971, Madhya Pradesh, Sidhi District Census Handbook*, pp. 125–6; *Rewa State Census, 1941, Report*, p. 35; *Rewa Gazetteer*, pp. 81, 271; *Shahdol Gazetteer*, pp. 90–1; *Sidhi Gazetteer, p.* 52; *Working Plan of West Sidhi Forest Division*, pp. 61–2; Gupta, 'Tribal economy', PhD, p. 91. At the 1971 census in Rewa district, 43 per cent of the working population were cultivators, and 40 per cent labourers. At the 1961 census for Rewa district, the majority of scheduled caste and 'tribal' household cultivators 'did not have enough land for bare subsistence'. At the 1971 census in Satna district, 42.3 per cent of workers were agriculturists, and 36.4 per cent agricultural labourers. In Shahdol the comparable figures

were, respectively, 53.8 per cent and 29.96 per cent; and in Sidhi 55.6 per cent and 37.4 per cent, respectively.

91. *Rewa State Census, 1941, Report,* p. 35; *Sidhi Gazetteer,* p. 117; A.K. Dubey, 'A study of the movements for the establishment of democratic political system in the princely states of Vindhya Pradesh', PhD thesis, Rani Durgawati University, Jabalpur, 1991, p. 17; Roy, 'Myth, fable and guile', p. 246.

92. FI, A, July 1890, 293, Note by D. Robertson on the Rewa settlement, 31 Mar. 1890; C. Corfield, *The Princely India I Knew: From Reading to Mountbatten,* Madras, 1975, p. 70; T.C. McCombie Young, 'A field study of lathyrism', *IJMR,* vol. 15, 1927, p. 454; *Report on Intensive Type Studies on Rural Labour in India,* Rewa, 1967–68, pp. 7.2, 7.4. In *harwahi* the lender guaranteed the labourer's food and clothing, and in return the bondsman had to perform any type of domestic or agricultural labour. When the *harwaha* was old enough to marry, his master advanced the money, taking from him a document which 'effaces his freedom for ever'. The practice continued until well into the twentieth century.

93. *Sidhi Gazetteer,* p. 92; D.C. Agarwal, 'Agricultural efficiency in Vindhya Pradesh: A study of the impact of three five-year plans on agricultural industry', PhD thesis, Ahulya Bai Holkar University, Indore, 1968, p. 119; RDO, B no. 3, 1924–5. 1/2C Rev, Cooperative, 1925, Maharaja Gulab Singh, nd. In 1951–2, of cultivators in Satna and Rewa districts 49 per cent and 57 per cent, respectively, were indebted.

94. Roy 'Myth, fable and guile', pp. 13–14; *Shahdol Gazetteer,* p. 96; Colebrooke, *European Travellers,* pp. 225, 229; Leckie, ibid., pp. 86, 88.

95. *Rewa State Census, 1941, Report,* p. 17; *Rewa State Gazetteer,* pp. 25–7; *Shahdol Gazetteer,* p. 100, 103; P.D. Tiwari, 'Agriculture and nutritional level in Rewa plateau', PhD thesis, Hari Singh Gour University, Sagar, 1982, p. 71. Some examples of these sayings are: 'Now as Ardra (15–16 June) has come and the earth must receive the seed; who will welcome me without my husband?' (i.e. the tiller); 'sow only rice in Purva and Punarvasu, and not other food crops'; 'if wheat is sown during Swati and paddy during Ardra, the first will not suffer from the rust nor the latter from sunshine'.

96. For reaping and winnowing practices see M.S. Randhawa, et al., *Farmers of India,* vol. IV, *M.P., Rajasthan, Gujarat, Maharashtra,* New Delhi, 1968, p. 43.

97. Tiwari, 'Agriculture and nutritional level', PhD, p. 69; Lal, 'Settlement geography', PhD, pp. 121–2; *Rewa State Gazetteer,* p. 25; *Shahdol Gazetteer,* p. 105; J.M., 'Notes from Rewa', pp. 399–400; Randhawa, *Farmers of India,* p. 50.

98. Colebrooke, *European Travellers*, p. 228; *Rewa Gazetteer*, p. 97; H. Bomford, *Final Settlement Report of Rewa State*, Lucknow, 1929, pp. 20–1.

99. *Shahdol Gazetteer*, p. 95; *Sidhi Gazetteer*, p. 7; *Rewa Gazetteer*, pp. 83–4; Bomford, *Final Settlement*, p. 12; *Working Plan of the West Sidhi Forest Division*, p. 23; Basic Material relating to Rewa District, Anthropological Survey of India, S.K. Biswas, *District Rewa, M.P., Village Mahari*, (typed copy), 1960; RDO, 44, B 11, W.D. West's Report, 1935; Tiwari, 'Agriculture and nutritional level', PhD, pp. 65, 67. There were centuries' old tanks in Sohagpur, at Intaura in Mauganj, and Ghuman in Teonthar. Huzur *tahsil* had tanks. Small tanks were a feature of the Son valley, and in clearings and villages as far apart as Majhauli and Waidhan in Sidhi, and Marwas in Shahdol.

100. J.M., 'Notes from Rewa', p. 347; Bomford, *Final Settlement*, p. 15; Roy, *Planning the Environment*, p. 8.

101. McCombie Young, 'Lathyrism', p. 454; *Rewa Directory*, p. 152; *Report of the Path Enquiry Commission*, p. 127; *Sidhi Gazetteer*, pp. 74–5.

102. *MP Census, 1961, Satna Handbook*, p. lvii; *MP Census, 1961, Sidhi Handbook*, pp. lix–lx; J.M. 'Notes from Rewa', pp. 398–9; Gupta, 'Tribal economy', PhD, pp. 86–8; *Rewa Gazetteer*, pp. 68, 70; *Shahdol Gazetteer*, pp. 74–5.

103. Leckie, *European Travellers*, pp. 83, 86, 88; Colebrooke, ibid., pp. 175, 221, 224–5.

104. McCombie Young, 'Lathyrism', p. 454; Bhattacharya and Verma, 'Settlement forms', p. 297; *MP Census, 1961, Sidhi Handbook*, pp. 27, 30; *Shahdol Gazetteer*, p. 160; *Satna Gazetteer*, p. 379.

105. Kosambi, *Culture and Civilization*, p. 125, reports 'caravans of 500 or more ox-wagons' on the Deccan route as early as 500 BC; Colebrooke, *European Travellers*, pp. 223, 228; Bomford, *Final Settlement Report*, p. 8; CIA, BA, 345, 1862–3, pt. 1, R. de Bourbel to PWDSec, 7 Aug. 1862; *Rewa State Census, 1941, Report*, p. 18; *Shahdol Gazetteer*, p. 160; *Rewa Gazetteer*, p. 146.

106. *Rewa State Census, 1941, Report*, p. 19.

107. CIA, BA, 345, 1862–3, pt. 1, R.de Bourbel to PWDSec, 7 Aug. 1862; CIA, Fairs 629, 1867–8, PA Nagode to AGGCI, 12 Feb. 1868; *Rewa State Gazetteer*, p. 44; *Sidhi Gazetteer*, p. 101; Colebrooke, *European Travellers*, p. 288; Baghel, 'Rewa ke Baghel rajya', PhD, p. 11.

108. Forsyth, *The Highlands of Central India*, pp. 107–8.

109. U. Thakur, *Mints and Minting in India*, Varanasi, 1972, p. 75; K.P. Sinor, *Mineral Resources of the Rewa State, Central India*, Calcutta, 1923, p. 174; V. Ball, *A Manual of the Geology of India*, pt III, *Economic Geology*, Calcutta, 1881, pp. 421–2; *Sidhi Gazetteer*, p. 83.

110. D.K. Chakrabarti, and N. Lahiri, 'The iron age in India; the beginning and the consequences', *Puratattva*, no. 24, 1993–4, pp. 12, 27;

Roy, 'Myth, fable and guile', p. 14; Sinor, *Mineral Resources*, p. 159; *Rewa Gazetteer*, pp. 112, 119; *Sidhi Gazetteer*, pp. 82–3.

111. Colebrooke, *European Travellers*, p. 225.

112. *Rewa Gazetteer*, p. 112; *Shahdol Gazetteer*, pp. 118–9; *Sidhi Gazetteer*, pp. 83, 87–8.

113. *Rewa State Gazetteer*, pp. 41–2; *Rewa Gazetteer*, pp. 111–2; *Satna Gazetteer*, p. 135; *Sidhi Gazetteer*, p. 82.

114. Lal, 'Settlement geography', PhD, p. 128; *Rewa Gazetteer*, pp. 112, 119; *Shahdol Gazetteer*, p. 118; *Sidhi Gazetteer*, pp. 82–3.

115. RS, Khasgi, 1946, no. 11, Rev, Rev Min's Order, 18 Jan. 1941; *RSA 1924–25*, p. 2; BA, A/6, 1870, Report by Capt. H.L.A. Tottenham, 30 Sept. 1869; *Imperial Gazetteer*, vol. XXI, p. 282; Lal, 'Settlement geography', PhD, pp. 29, 142.

116. *Sidhi Gazetteer*, p. 67; *Shahdol Gazetteer*, p. 192; Roy, *Planning the Environment*, pp. 48–9; Tiwari, 'Agriculture and nutritional level', PhD, pp. 52–4; S.K. Sharma, 'Changing Pattern of resources in the Baghelkhand plateau, M.P.', PhD thesis, H.S. Gour University, Sagar, 1975, pp. 105–6.

4

The Profile of a Regional Culture

CRSO

The outcome of the dialogue between Baghelkhand and central-izing states and forces is nowhere more evident than in the cul-tural profile which the region presents today. Important elements in this profile resulted from the intrusion of external styles or migrating peoples; others represent influences generated within the region itself. The compounding of the two has given Baghelkhand a cultural heritage which, though distinctly its own, also demonstrates its connectivity with other parts of the subcon-tinent subject to similar influences. These connectivities were part of the region's journey into a wider Indian whole by 1947.

I

THE MAURYAN EMPIRE AND BAGHELKHAND

The first major cultural intervention in Baghelkhand by a central-izing state occurred in the closing centuries of the first millen-nium BC when the Mauryan rulers of Pataliputra encouraged Buddhism to spread from the Gangetic heartland into central India. The result of this impulse may be seen at the sites of Bharhut and Deur Kothar, as elsewhere in the region.

The central feature of the Buddhist settlement at Bharhut was a *stupa* set among monastic and other buildings.[1] The original structure dating from about 250 BC comprised a plastered brick tumulus enshrining a relic of the Buddha, topped by a wooden parasol as a mark of dignity. A wooden railing with entrances at cardinal points enclosed the structure, and at one or more of these openings stood *toranas* of wood. Between 175 and 125 BC devotees gave the *stupa* a more dignified appearance by replacing the wooden railings and *toranas* with structures of stone, probably one of the first large-scale experiments in the use of this material at a Buddhist site. They did so during the reign of the Sunga kings who, though patrons of reviving Brahmanism, generally tolerated the Buddhist religion.

The Gupta kings and Harsha also included Bharhut in their domains.[2] Though Brahmanism was then dominant, Buddhism still had a large following, and its shrines remained popular places of pilgrimage. Buddhists thus continued to visit Bharhut up to the eleventh century, after which it was deserted and ultimately obliterated. Over the years people from nearby villages pillaged the settlement for building material; and in the nineteenth century Alexander Cunningham, of the newly founded Archaeological Survey, removed what remained of the structure to museums in Calcutta and Allahabad. Today only the name and a memory survive, together with stone fragments in neighbouring villages.

The main purpose of settlements such as Bharhut was to honour a relic of the Buddha and propagate the Buddhist religion.[3] As Bharhut was located on a chord of the *dakshinapatha*, it was an important destination for pilgrims as well as a staging camp for merchants and travellers, and it was largely their munificence recorded in inscriptions that built the *stupa* and its accompanying settlement. The *stupa* also served as a frontier outpost of the Mauryan empire, reinforcing the state's authority in a region considered to be remote and perilous, and perhaps integrating its diverse population.

The symbolism of the *stupa* could not but impress those who visited it.[4] The Buddha was the enlightened one, and his relics within were believed to reflect knowledge and eternal light. The solid dome represented the 'visible universe', the 'heavenly vault', and in the dark central Indian night the *stupa* became

a huge shining pile, a pillar of fire.... A stupa shone through ... rows of lamps.... Cunningham found on the south-east face ... a series of triangular recesses which were intended for lighting the lamps. The number of recesses in each row is calculated to be six hundred, and there were several such rows.... One can well imagine that [the] network of dia-mond-shaped niches when lit on all sides transformed the monument into a splendid light tower, and it must have been a wonderful view from a distance at night.[5]

Though a funerary monument, the *stupa's* light by night and the portraits and scenes depicted on its railings reflected the joy of living rather than a mood of mourning for the death of a beloved. The inscriptions at Bharhut help to date its construction.[6] Several hundred inscriptions in Sanskrit-influenced Prakrit record the donors and their donations. The inscriptions fall into two groups: those from the railings and those from the gateway. All share common characteristics, except that those on the railings have characters in the Brahmi script of the second century BC, suggesting that they are earlier than those on the gateway. Inscriptions at Ayodhya showing the use of the new pen and the equalization of the verticals help to date the inscriptions on the *torana*, which are somewhat similar. As these inscriptions were not made with the new pen, they may be assigned to a later date in the first millennium, ahead of the time when the Ayodhya records derived the new techniques from the Saka inscriptions at Mathura.

Merchants were prominent among the donors at Bharhut.[7] By the second century BC Bharhut was a key point on the road map of the subcontinent, servicing the trade in shells, diamonds, precious stones, pearls, gold, and other minerals. Traders also brought merchandise from the east coast to Pratisthana via Bharhut. The *dakshinapatha* thus provided the greatest opportunities for profit, as merchants and monks began to stimulate the 'first great development of barter and agriculture on virgin land'. With profits from these ventures and moved by religious devotion, merchants, monks, and others created the 'treasure troves' of Bharhut and Sanchi—the 'two valves of the pulsating heart of Madhyadesa'.

While the hinterland of Bharhut might not have provided donors, it was important for the monastic settlement as for those using the *dakshinapatha*.[8] It is unlikely that the monastic inhabitants would have built their monastery in an economic wilderness, for the area's surplus would have been necessary for the institution's day-to-day existence as for the needs of travellers. Whether the sculptures at Bharhut reflected such a hinterland it is difficult to say, but they depict

a sound and thriving economy.... The country had a rich vegetation....
Animals were domesticated, which improved the financial stability of the
society.... The main occupation on which people depended was agriculture.... Cattle rearing was another occupation.... Smithy was practised
... [from] the ornaments the people are seen wearing.... For transactions
coins were used.... We have the sculpture of a shop where people are
seen bargaining for the sale of bananas.... There were people who were
engaged in different trades ... weavers ... carpenters and masons.[9]

The wider zone around Bharhut held long-term economic promise for merchants.[10] Not far away lay the diamond-bearing conglomerates of Panna; copper deposits existed in Rewa; rich iron ores
were to be found in Baghelkhand as in Hirapur to the west. From
these sources merchants may have contributed to the need for
minerals in the urban centres of the north.

From the inscriptions we see that donors other than merchants
assisted in building Bharhut.[11] Of 216 inscriptions, a few record
gifts by royalty; thirteen are by Buddhist nuns, and nine by monks.
Many donors, possibly pilgrims, came from towns, fifty-two place-
names being mentioned, some more than once. Towns whose
location is known cover a wide area from Pataliputra to Karahakata
(Karhad) in Satara, most of them on the *dakshinapatha*, bearing
eloquent witness to the region's growing subcontinental connections. Many inscriptions name the donors without indicating their
place of residence or occupation. The smaller donations reveal
that less wealthy folk also helped to embellish the *stupa*.

The sculptures belong to the folk art of ancient India.[12] Probably the work of lower grades of craftsmen, the quality of the
carving varies considerably: some pieces show 'crude ingenuous-
ness'; others 'demonstrate the beginning of a fluency in line and
composition'. Yet although

the plastic conception is rudimentary... [and] narration is often extremely abridged....this demotic art impresses by its sincerity ... naivete,
buoyancy and freshness. Not under the restraint of a hieratic coterie,
the simple artisans ... translated on stone ... intense religious aspirations
and fervour.[13]

In the sculptures foreign influences mingle with indigenous
forms and ideas.[14] There is a general consensus among historians
that the Mauryas employed foreign craftsmen, and the evidence at

Bharhut supports this. The Karoshthi letters on sculptures indicate that workmen came from the country of the subcontinent bordering Afghanistan; and the warrior's dress does not seem indigenous. The human-headed bull and winged lion on the railing appear in the monasteries of Archaemenean Iran. Some historians claim, too, that the fluted bell capitals of the Persepolitan order with back-to-back gryphons and the frequently used honey-suckle motif, indicate that workmen were in touch with other west Asian cultures. Commentators also assert that the lotus motif represents the blue lotus growing in the marshes of the Nile and reproduced in the monuments of Egypt and west Asia.

The sculptural art of Bharhut covers a number of subjects, prominent among these being the events and legends connected with the life of the Buddha as told in the *Jatakas*.[15] Snake gods and goddesses, who have a prominent place in Buddhist legend, together with popular deities and other denizens of forest, lake, and river find a place on the railings, evoking a spirituality older than that of Buddhism. Other sculptural remains reflect contemporary society and depict the monarchy, Brahmans, holy men and women, bankers, merchants, housewives, hunters, a honey-setter, needle-smith, wrestlers, and others.

The other main Buddhist settlement was at Deur Kothar on the road from Prayaga into Baghelkhand.[16] This site predated Bharhut's stonework, most of its stone structures having probably been built before the assassination of Brihadratha, the last Mauryan ruler, in 185 BC. The settlement comprised over forty *stupas* spread across a vast scarpland overlooking the Tons as it flows to join the Ganga. A large brick *stupa* dominated the site, approached by a stone pathway through smaller *stupas* of stone or brick.

Deur's artistic achievement falls far behind that of Bharhut.[17] The stone balustrade around the main *stupa* had railings not yet conventionalized; and the pillars of an outer railing vary in design and shape. Different groups of artisans may have produced this result, besides the likelihood that they may have had no prototype to guide them as they struggled to execute in stone what had previously been done in wood. Also, this was probably not art sponsored by the state.

These same factors find expression in the low relief sculptures, simple ornamentation, the paucity of animal and human figures, and the excess stone surfaces not sculpted.[18] None of these feat-

Figure: 4.1 Excavation of the main *stupa* at Deur Kothar; and the site on the edge of the scarp overlooking the Gangetic plain

Figure: 4.2 The reconstructed Mauryan pathway and *stupa*s, Deur Kothar

ures, even the lotus which was a favourite element in the ornamentation at Deur, could match in style or variety the work at Bharhut. Notwithstanding the settlement's early date the Mauryan pillar made its appearance, standing by the western gateway of the balustrade, glistening with characteristic Mauryan polish. An inscription records its dedication by the monks to the memory of the Buddha.

Excavations at Deur Kothar suggest that the site was deliberately destroyed.[19] Those responsible may have been political or other forces hostile to Buddhism, or those who envied the wealth or resented the presence of the settlement among them. These forces or raiders first broke the pillar and smashed the balustrade. Brickbat debris lying on the fragments of the balustrade indicates that they then vandalized the main *stupa*, an event temporarily assigned to the second century BC. The *stupa* was later encased in stone, but this also appears to have been broken causing the bricks to fall out. Subsequent looting of stone and bricks completed the destruction.

Excavations round the main *stupa* have widened our understanding of the site.[20] Among the brick debris archaeologists have found sherds of northern black polished ware, copper objects, iron ore, iron slag and artefacts, terracotta toys and coins—remains that place Deur on the map of the iron industry besides showing that traders visited the site. The rocky scarpland also contained a well-developed water system. The entire area was set within a cave shelter site, several of whose paintings suggest that it was a prehistoric camping place long before the Mauryan period.

Other Buddhist sites also lie in the north of the region, either in the lowlands or in adjacent areas of the Rewa plateau.[21] These include three brick *stupas* with Brahmi inscriptions of the second century BC at Madighat in Teonthar; Bhita on the Rewa road south of Allahabad, and caves near the Kewati falls have Buddhist inscriptions; while punch-marked coins and northern black polished ware occur at Itaha nearer Rewa. A much later inscription of a Kalachuri feudatory Malayasimha, found at Rewa, speaks of the Buddha as Bhagwan; while a five-domed Kalachuri temple at Singhpur has a statute of Tara with *stupas* at the top and a series of statues of the Buddha in different *mudras* nearby.

II

THE GUPTA PRESENCE IN BAGHELKHAND

The Gupta State based on Pataliputra was another imperial power to leave its mark on Baghelkhand and other parts of the country beyond the northern river plains. The art and architecture of the Guptas dominated the period from about 320 AD to the accession of Harsha, with further developments under later Gupta rulers up to 700 AD.[22] During this period the arts revived, and under the patronage of the Gupta kings resurgent Brahmanism fused with regional styles in northern and central India to create a wholly new type of temple consisting of a small flat-roofed shrine with a cella or sanctum containing an image for individual devotion, and a pillared portico open or closed at the sides. It is believed that this style originated near Vidisha and travelled east with migrant artisans in the peaceful conditions created by Gupta rule. Where stone was in short supply, builders used brick; but where stone was plentiful, as in Baghelkhand, they constructed temples accordingly.

In Baghelkhand Gupta temples and inscriptions are mostly centred on Unchahra, Khoh, and Bhumara in Satna district. These lay in areas ruled by the Uchchhakalpa and Parivrajaka feudatories of the Guptas and close to the trade route from Kausambi through Bharhut to Tripuri.[23] The temple at Bhumara lay on a spur of that route across the Parasmania plateau, connecting it with the Gupta temple at Nachna at the foot of the plateau, outside Baghelkhand.

The partly restored temple at Bhumara is by far the most significant of the Gupta remains in the region.[24] Gupta rule may have ceased to be a reality when it was constructed between 485–550, and it probably came up under the aegis of the one-time feudatories then independent of Pataliputra. Artisans of a workshop originating in the eastern Gangetic plain built the temple, which comprises a small windowless sanctuary on a high platform reached by steps on the western side. A suggested circumambulatory passage lit by trellises round the sanctum has disappeared, as have the roof and covered portico. Apart from the sculptures, the other features of note are the chisel marks on a *chaitya* window, which suggest that the artisans cut the stone slabs with pointed tools. Many of these slabs lie on the ground around the temple, as if awaiting their return to the incompletely restored building.

The sculptures at Bhumara demand special mention, for it is here that they became part of architecture.[25] Decoration in Gupta temples was restrained and walls generally remained plain; but Bhumara represents a time when iconographic details were becoming well established, sculptors carving on its walls *ganas* of Siva dancing and playing instruments. In addition,

the temple ... door frames, pillars, beams [and] dado display exquisitely carved scrolls, foliage (and) dwarfs.... The doorway has three bands.... The third band shows the Ganga on the right, and the Yamuna on the left.... On the lintel occurs the bust of Siva.[26]

The Siva *mukhalingam* in the sanctum framed by the elaborate doorway has been described as the 'finest complete work which epitomises the harmony of the mature Gupta style'.

Other Gupta remains[27] include a brick structure near Khoh; the ruins of a large brick temple west of Unchahra; the door frame of a former temple at Piparia south of Bhumara; and a structure at Pithaura north-west of Unchahra. A Gupta structure also exists at Madpha in Rewa district; while Gupta pottery has been found in Teonthar and at other places in that district.

Most of the extant Gupta inscriptions also come from Unchahra, Khoh, and the nearby Parasmania plateau, and similarly date from the time of Parivrajaka and Uchchhakalpa kings.[28] Many of these are copperplate inscriptions recording land grants: eight from Khoh and one of Maharaja Hastin Parivrajaka (510–11) from Majhgawan village near Unchahra. An inscription in Gupta characters referring to a Maharaja Bhimasena was located in a rock shelter on the Ginja hill in north Rewa. Coins from Beldi and Anuppur in Shahdol are ascribed to Chandra Gupta (c. AD 350) There are also several pillar inscriptions—one at Bhumara bearing the names of Parivrajaka and Uchchhakalpa kings; and another at Mada Khara in the Bansagar immersion area of Satna district.

III

THE KALACHURIS OF DAHALA AND THE
FIRST REGIONAL CULTURE

During their period of rule in Dahala between the eighth and thirteenth centuries the Kalachuri kings sponsored and financed a comprehensive culture comprising monastic foundations, temples, sculptures, and minor works.[29] Though this culture represented a blend of local and wider styles, it may be termed the region's first truly regional culture. This venture also drew support from members of the royal family, Saivite monks, courtiers and, in at least one instance, a merchant. While the culture primarily sprang from religious devotion, through it the Kalachuri rulers could also unify a diverse population and stabilize their rule in the countryside.

Inscriptions document the spread of Kalachuri cultural forms from the core area of Dahala into Baghelkhand.[30] The earliest inscriptions of the eighth and ninth centuries from Jabalpur and Sagar are followed by others from the tenth to the twelfth centuries from Gurgi, Rewa, Chandrehe, Bandhavgarh, Maihar, and Mukundpur. Though these generally refer to the rulers and their *acharya*s who founded temples, some document the rulers' provisions for maintaining the institutions.

These inscriptions[31] include the Rewa stone inscription of unknown provenance, recording the fortunes of the Kalachuri State under Gangeyyadeva (1015–41), Karnadeva (1041–72), and others; a later inscription at Rewa refers to the construction of a tank. There is also a large number of copperplate inscriptions from north Baghelkhand, generally recording the grant of villages to Brahmans in the eleventh and twelfth centuries. Others of the thirteenth century from the same area document the power play between the Chandels and Kalachuris.

As for the temples and monasteries Yuvarajadeva I (915–45), a devout Saivite and patron of art and literature, and his queen Nohalla are credited with building many temples, including those at Gurgi and Chandrehe.[32] His successor and fellow Saivite Lakshmanaraja II (945–70) and grandson Yuvarajadeva II (970–90) also had a hand in the work at Gurgi and Chandrehe. Gangeyyadeva (1015–41) installed a Siva *lingam* at Piawan north of Rewa; and Karnadeva (1041–72) was responsible for the temples at Sohagpur, Amarkantak, Baijnath, and Marai. Feudatories of the later Kalachuri Vijayasimha (1188–1210) built temples at Kakredi in north Rewa.

A driving force behind the temple construction was the Kalachuri devotion to Siva, who was central to the Brahmanical revival in Baghelkhand.[33] Saivism thus became the paramount religion of the kingdom; and Buddhism, though tolerated, faded further from the public mind. The rulers also encouraged the *sakti* cult common in the region, important centres emerging at Gurgi and elsewhere in Rewa, Sidhi, and Shahdol.

Monasteries and temples mediated the state's devotion to Siva.[34] The two institutions were generally built side by side, the monasteries to house the monks and the temples to facilitate their and the people's worship of Siva. Besides funding the buildings and endowing them with revenues for their upkeep, the rulers appointed Saivite *acharyas* to found and head the monasteries. Thus Yuvarajadeva I invited Prabhavasiva to found the settlement at Gurgi; while Lakshmanaraja II offered Baijnath to Hridayasiva, who passed on his former charge of the Nolleswara *matha* at Bilheri to his disciple Aghorasiva. Prasantasiva and his disciple Prabodhasiva are credited with building the complex at Chandrehe on behalf of their royal patrons.

The *acharyas* and their monks belonged to the Mattamayura lineage of the Saiva-Siddhanta sect, which originated at Mattamayur in Guna district where Queen Nohalla's family were its earliest known patrons.[35] References to the lineage in inscriptions from Malwa, the Konkan, Orissa and Dahala indicate its widespread following. The *matha* near Tripuri, now called Chaunsath Yogini, was perhaps the earliest of their monasteries, which acted as a centre of learning for centuries, drawing students from Bengal to Kerala. The institutions were systematically organized, and through their worship, doctrine, and philosophy they set the pace of Saivism in central India. As the monasteries proliferated, each developed a spiritual genealogy of its founding ascetic while remaining linked to the mother institution.

Four principles informed the life of the Saiva-Siddhanta sect:[36] *vidya* (right knowledge), *kriya* (building activity), *charya* (daily ritual), and *yoga* (the practice of austerity). In pursuance of these principles

austerities destroyed the darkness of ignorance, and set a person on the path of nirvana which could be obtained by bhaktiyoga;... that salvation came as a downpour of nectar in the form of a bliss that could only be experienced.[37]

For worship ascetics offered the libation of fire; and venerated icons, bathing the icon and offering white garments, sandal and sometimes horses and elephants. On special days it was customary for villagers to bring a wooden bull to the monastery for certain rituals. The ascetics also propagated Saivite *agama*s among the public.

The *acharyas* were influential figures.[38] Their line of successive disciples ran parallel to that of their Kalachuri patrons, and the leading ascetic became the *rajguru* of the reigning monarch. The *acharya* of Gurgi was especially privileged, endowed as he was with the proceeds of many villages and thus a powerful landlord in central Baghelkhand. Besides maintaining the *matha*'s life and worship, an *acharya* was free to spend the revenues in building temples, ashrams and monasteries. Prabodhasiva, the builder of Chandrehe, also 'excavated lakes, dug wells, renovated old temples, and built lanes through mountains, across rivers, streams, forests and thickets'.

In building their monasteries and temples the kings and *acharyas* developed a distinctive architectural style, blending local with national idioms.[39] The turbulent centuries following the decline of the Guptas in the north and the Vakatakas in the Deccan were 'opportune for the transmission of idioms which had already evolved at different centres of artistic activity in the north and in the Deccan'. During this period the classical Gupta–Vakataka idiom was transformed into regional styles of art and architecture, Dahala forming the setting for one such style.

Part of this process concerned the Kalachuris' relations with the Chandels, Paramaras, Pratiharas, and Chalukyas. As the Kalachuris expanded their possessions, they not only encountered opposition from these groups, but also fell under their cultural influence.[40] Some observers claim that the temples at Sohagpur, Marai and Amarkantak were modelled on Chandel forms; others that these and the earlier temples at Bandhavgarh evolved under the influence of the Gurjara–Pratihara *mandapika* shrines, of which possibly the earliest surviving example exists at Mahua in Shivpuri. Queen Nohalla belonged to Ranod and Prabhavasiva to Shivpuri, where the style predominated, and they probably brought with them to Dahala artisans versed in that style. The temple at Indore village in nearby Guna district may also have inspired the artists of Gurgi where Prabhavasiva was *acharya*.

Whatever the source, the result was the distinctive temple style of Dahala, including Baghelkhand.[41] The temples comprised a *garbha-griha* (sanctum), *mandapa* (hall), *antarala* or antechamber between the two, and sometimes an *ardha-mandapa* or portico. These spaces were set in consecutive order on a common platform, and each had a domed roof supported on pillars, with a *shikhara* over the *garbha-griha*. The latter could be circular, square, rectangular, or *tryayatana* in plan as at Amarkantak; but the most common shape in Dahala was *vritta* or circular as at Gurgi and Chandrehe, necessitating a curvilinear *shikhara*. This is believed to be an original contribution of Kalachuri architects to temple styles, and is rarely found beyond their kingdom.

The Kalachuris reproduced this style of temple with variations at their main sites.[42] The style 'evolved through eighth century prototypes' such as the temples at Bandhavgarh, to crystallize on the hill at Gurgi where Yuvarajadeva I built a temple with a circular *shikhara* that 'aspired to be as high as the Sumeru and Kailasa mountains'. Prasantasiva, disciple of Prabodhasiva, built another circular temple in the neighbouring village of Mehsaun. Then, about a century later Karnadeva built the nearby Rehuta fort—the precursor of Rewa as a fortified settlement—indicating the growing prosperity (or perhaps insecurity) of the Kalachuri state.

Gurgi in turn inspired the temple at Chandrehe.[43] The best example of the Kalachuri style in central Baghelkhand, its survival is largely due to its isolated location near the Son's south bank in western Sidhi where the monks could meditate in peace. Begun by Prasantasiva *c.* 950 the temple on its high platform is spectacular with a columned *mandapa* preceding the circular *garbha-griha*, whose *shikhara* is 'covered with vertical bands of the Chaitya window pattern'. The platform provides a *pradakshinapatha* around the shrine.

Prabodhasiva's monastery of 973 AD lies next to the temple.[44] Built of red stone with an open porch and verandah, the monastery has a central courtyard with a narrow verandah supported on pillars, the rooms off the courtyard serving as dormitories and shrine chambers. Part of the building has a first storey, which was either a library or a school for the monks. As the foundation stone tells us, 'in this place ... enemies take leave of their enmity [;] in this forest of austerities ... the minds of all become calm'.

In the eleventh century Kalachuri building activity shifted south to Shahdol, its centres of Sohagpur and Amarkantak secure from the Chandels.[45] The focus of architectural interest here lies in the temples at Amarkantak, source of the Narmada, which are ascribed to Karnadeva (1041–72). His Raja Karna Dahariya (i.e. of Dahala) has a completely different character from the temples at Gurgi and Chandrehe, giving

the appearance of three distinct temples, arranged like a trefoil leaf on a large raised platform and connected with a *maha-mandapa* that was never completed.... [The temple] has three lofty and profusely sculpted towers of graceful outline.... The upper portions of the towers look like a horseshoe.... The spire is similarly of the graceful curvilinear form. The sanctum has an inner roof of intersecting squares within the tower roof, and a gargoyle projects from the outer face of the roof.[46]

Closer to the Narmada *kund* lies a second group of temples, all virtually identical in design. Both groups of temples are built of the local reddish conglomerate which was probably too hard for the sculpture that is conspicuously absent. The other notable Kalachuri remains in Shahdol include the Virateshwar temple in Sohagpur, a rebuilt temple in Singhpur, and others elsewhere.

Under royal patronage Kalachuri artists similarly created a regional style of sculpture.[47] Again the basic component was the 'national' Gupta–Vakataka sculpture which merged with the iconic traditions of the peoples impinging on Baghelkhand. As earlier, art trends travelled due to the 'migration of artisans, conquests, annexation of territory, and through different classes of people who moved from one region to the other'. Some art historians claim that the hill and forest people also influenced Kalachuri art. These varied influences merged with one another to produce a sculpture characteristic of the Vindhyan hills and plateaus between Allahabad and Jabalpur.

Kalachuri artists adorned many of their temples and monasteries with a sculpture whose dominant note was breadth and volume rather than fine configuration.[48] Facial types were squarish with swollen cheeks and big mouth and eyes, set in a 'short-featured body that swells into heavy rounded masses'. This was particularly so of female forms with their full breasts, broad hips, and heavy thighs; the males were tall with broad shoulders.

This sculptural style contained several distinct idioms.[49] Early in the tenth century a minister of Yuvarajadeva I commissioned sculpted *avatars* of Vishnu on Bandhavgarh hill: simple 'lithic primers' that gave little hint of what was to follow. Thereafter figures developed proportion and motion, another idiom emerging at Gurgi where gods and humans alike displayed 'swelling volume and full curves'. Typical of this genre is the bold pair of Siva–Parvati brought from Gurgi to a park in Rewa; and the magnificent *torana* placed by a thoughtful *diwan* in a gateway of the fort at Rewa in the nineteenth century. The *torana* displays the richness of the Gurgi style, the bold reliefs on the pillars conveying something of the sculpture to come at Khajuraho. The lintel depicts Siva's marriage to Parvati.

Tragically, the temple at Gurgi is no more. Rewa's officials and people have systematically destroyed their own cultural heritage, turning it into road metal or village housing, with the sculpture smashed, mutilated, or stolen. Today

the mound is a pathetic scene of destruction, a virtual graveyard of broken sculptures and silhouettes of temple platforms. The quality of the sculptures found here can be judged from broken fragments; a hand, foot or torso which eloquently speak of temples comparable to Khajuraho both in grace and beauty.[50]

Many sculptural pieces are now preserved in the museum at Rewa.

Perhaps the finest examples of tenth century Kalachuri sculpture are to be found in Sohagpur *tahsil* of Shahdol.[51] Memorable are the figure work of the temple doorway at Arjula; the finely cut *kankali devi* at the *devi ka mandir* in Singhpur; and the *matrika* images at Antara, 'vibrant with an arrested, quivering motion'. However, it is the doorway of the restored temple by the tank at Singhpur that marks the zenith of Kalachuri art:

Vishnu seated on Garuda in the centre of the lintel forms the principal focus. At the base of the door ... are representations of the two river deities, Ganga and Yamuna.... Four vertical bands ... arise from above the deities.... Bordering the inner jambs and framing the entire doorway are two separate vertical slabs embellished with a ... floral moulding.... Each vertical register of the doorway projects slightly more than its inner neighbour to impart subtly a sense of depth to one approaching the shrine. The lintel is divided into two parallel horizontal bands containing male and female couples.... Between them is a row of twelve seated females.[52]

From this climax deterioration set in.[53] In the eleventh century Kalachuri sculpture stiffened, and the human form lengthened and expanded laterally. In the succeeding two centuries creativity dried up to produce large, heavy faces, stunted trunks, long life-less legs and huge misshapen hands, with bodies imprisoned by the harness of ornament.

What of the craftsmen who built the Kalachuri temples and shaped their statuary?[54] Kalachuri inscriptions refer to thirty-nine craftsmen, among whom the *sutradharas*—those who designed and completed the buildings—occupied the highest position in the craft hierarchy. The workshops also trained apprentices in differ-ent crafts. The inscriptions name several *sutradharas*, including Sangama, a master craftsman responsible for the Tara image in Sohagpur *tahsil*; and Madhava who worked at Gurgi. Some crafts-men may have been itinerant or, as noted above, come with Nohalla and Prabhavasiva from Shivpuri.

Stadtner, an art historian, also ascribes Krishna pillars at Gurh and Chandrehe to the Kalachuri period.[55] These four-sided and free-standing pillars illustrate scenes from the life of Krishna, and constitute a unique sculptural form in central India. Gurh is only six kilometres from Gurgi, and Stadtner found the figure-work on the pillar there sharing common features with Kalachuri sculp-ture; though he felt that the figures on the pillar at Chandrehe were less 'robust and inventive' than at Gurh. The purpose of these pillars is unclear, but as they did not require a large outlay of money or artists and are generally of a rough quality, they may have been funded by peasants or artisans to show their devotion to the 'cowherd god'.

IV

THE FORT CULTURE OF BAGHELKHAND: BANDHAVGARH

It would be strange indeed if forts did not mark the landscape of Baghelkhand. Over several millennia, centralizing powers sought to include the region in their domains, and immigrant Rajput clans fought each other for its territory. Of these the Baghels triumphed, guarding their land with villages whose names with the suffix *garh* indicated fortified settlements. From these forts the ruling clan defended its hold on Baghelkhand:

the entire region being a tangle of hill and plateau...has also been the promised land sheltering a number of local rulers and patriots, who could defy...foreign domination, and maintain an air of independence for a major part of the historical past. The area is dotted with numerous *garhs* and *garhis*...which....have seen many a battle, controlling as they did large areas under their massive ramparts and benign shadow.[56]

Baghelkhand's more important forts include the ruined Chandel fort at Bardi in eastern Sidhi; the partly ruined *garhi* at Sohagpur, whose oldest parts predate the Baghels; the forts at Unchahra and Nagod, bastions of the Pratiharas; the all but vanished Kalachuri fort at Rehuta near Gurgi; the Baghel fort at Madhogarh by a river crossing; and the fort palace at Rewa whose core dates from the sixteenth century, but which has been substantially overbuilt since then.

Supreme among Baghel forts is that at Bandhavgarh, the pride of the old Rewa State.[57] The hill fort is set in rocky ranges interspersed with grassy swamps and forested valleys in the region's south-west, 25 kilometres north of Umaria. The hill itself is about 800 metres above sea level, and half that height above the surrounding plain. With only one possible approach Bandhavgarh was virtually impregnable, its vertical rock face rising above a steep talus overgrown with jungle. By contrast, the hilltop has a fairly even surface that undulates gently to the north-east. Of equal height to Bandhavgarh is Bandeni, less than a kilometre to the west, one of over thirty hills within the Bandhavgarh national park today.

Bandhavgarh has always evoked a sense of awe among the people of the region.[58] In the nineteenth century the ruler and his *sardars* attached great importance to 'the mystery that hangs about this stronghold'. This derived partly from its natural defensiveness, its location in 'wild and strange' surroundings, and the sight of its dark form looming through the trees. In olden days it served as a refuge for royalty in time of danger, as well as a store for ammunition and treasure. The periodic residence of kings here added to its mystique.

The fort's reputation for invincibility also contributed to the awe in which it was held.[59] Many attempts to capture Bandhavgarh failed: one siege reportedly lasted for twelve years, defenders living off crops grown on the hilltop. This reputation strangely survived Akbar's eight-month siege, for in the nineteenth century those guarding the fort claimed that it was

surrounded on all sides by a morass [*dal dal*] deep enough at the driest season to be impassable by elephants, the only means of crossing which [an artificial causeway of stone always hidden by water] is kept a profound secret; besides which, the approaches to this causeway from the land side, are defended by fortified buildings, which in their turn, as well as the whole of the causeway itself, are commanded by the guns on Bandu. The garrison is asserted to be ... immensely numerous and fully equipped, provisions and ammunition in vast quantities always in store, and the supply of water ... inexhaustible.[60]

Legends contributed to the widespread veneration for the fort.[61] One legend claimed that Rama founded the fort, employing the monkey architects who built the bridge between Lanka and the mainland. When the fort was complete Rama handed it over to his brother Lakshmana who, as Bandhav, was styled Bandhavadisha or Lord of Bandhav. Lakshmana remained the fort's deity and is still worshipped there. A related legend claims that Rama's light on Bandhavgarh could be seen in Lanka, for the hill once stood higher than the Himalaya, until Ravana, Rama's rival, brought his hand down heavily on Bandhavgarh, creating the swampy depression—its 'unfathomable depth' corresponding to the 'vastness of the displacement above'.

The Kols also have a legend, not unconnected with the above, to the effect that Bhagwan (Rama) wanted to build a fort on the hill, and sent Lakshmana to recruit workers. When he failed to find any, Bhagwan

conceived the idea of making all the people poor, for then ... they should be glad to work.... Now ... all were eager for employment and a daily wage. They were put to work, the fort was built as planned.... When the work was finished ... men were still poor ... [and they] began to move out over the face of the earth. They spread thus from Rewa everywhere[62]

The Kols thus conceive of themselves as the builders of Bandhavgarh, possibly because others had seized their land and made them poor, and hence in need of employment.[63]

Legends apart, over the centuries Bandhavgarh acquired a number of historical layers.[64] The Balands, a forest community, made an early claim to the hill, their settlement of Balantipurgon being reported by Ptolemy in the second century AD. In that century, too, the Magha kings of Kausambi, their merchants and artisans carved caves and provided other facilities on Bandhavgarh and nearby hills. As there is no contemporary mention of a fort, the Kol legend would seem to refer to a later date in the first millennium. Art historians ascribe the single-chamber Pratihara-style temples on Bandhavgarh to eighth-century Kalachuri builders. The Kalachuris were still in possession two centuries later, as their inscriptions and the sculpted avatars of Vishnu testify; and though the hill or fort figured in Kalachuri rivalry with the Chandels, the latter were unable to capture it. At an unspecified date, possibly in the fourteenth century, Bandhavgarh fell into Baghel hands.

The caves and inscriptions of the Maghas invite further scrutiny, providing as they do an insight into the nationalizing influences shaping a fort site in Baghelkhand.[65] As noted above, in the second century AD Magha princes from Kausambi, their ministers, merchants, and others excavated over fifty shelters from the soft sandstone rock on the lower slopes of Bandhavgarh and other

Figure: 4.3 Rock-cut caves near the base of Bandhavgarh hill

hills. The caves are of different sizes: some comprise individual cells; some consist of a hall with several doorways; while others contain up to nine cells opening off passages. There are incised forms and decorated pillar designs in several caves, and in some twenty shelters donors left inscriptions after the contemporary practice. However, because the walls are rough, the inscriptions are often difficult to read, while in some the sense is unclear. A few use Sanskrit, but most are in Prakrit, and record the donor and the donation, generally a *lana* or cave shelter; though donations also include a tank, a garden and (surprisingly) a *vyayam shala*.

The inscriptions belong to the reigns of the Magha kings Bhimasena, Pothasiri, Bhattadeva and Chitrasena, and date from 129 to 185 AD, with a gap from 129 to 166.[66] The largest number are from the reign of Pothasiri around 166 AD, and were made in quick succession. Though princes and ministers made donations, merchant donors outnumber all others. Merchant *negamas* or guilds also made donations, one such hailing from Kausambi, a premier city of the Yamuna–Ganga valley. Sons and grandsons of merchants donated shelters as well. However, the *vanijaka* or *negama* donors did not enjoy the wealth of the landed rich who made donations at more prestigious sites. Some artisans grouped in *negamas* of a particular craft are also recorded in the inscriptions.

The inscriptions support the view that the donors constructed the shelters as halting places for merchants, artisans, and others plying between Kausambi and elsewhere.[67] One inscription describes the cave-shelter as *sarthika lana*: one made for traders from a merchant caravan. Perennial streams provided water, and traders or those whom they hired hunted animals for food. One of the shelters on the Ganesh Pahar shows animals in relief, and an inscription terms the cave as a *mrgaya saila*. By their donations the donors also aimed to enhance their social status and earn religious merit. Several scholars claim that the shelters had a specifically religious purpose, but there is only one religious reference in the inscriptions: the proper name Sivabhakta, from which nothing can be inferred. In general the inscriptions are 'silent about any religious leanings or preferences of donors'.

Bandhavgarh's closeness to arterial roads strengthens the view that it served those plying on long distance caravan routes.[68] The area was linked through the Bharhut hub with north and western India. Eastwards from Bandhavgarh a less frequented path went to

Figure: 4.4 Interior of one of the more elaborate rock-cut
caves near the base of Bandhavgarh hill

Sarguja; while old routes west connected it to Tripuri and south
with Chhattisgarh. Indeed, it was due to Bandhavgarh's distant
connections that

the paleography of these ... [inscriptions] shows some correspondence
to the Kusana epigraphs from Mathura, and also bears some affinity with
inscriptions of Western India [under the Kshatrapas] and the Western
Deccan. The dating systems of the Bandhogarh records, giving a
date in the Saka year, season, fortnight and day, are clearly inspired by
the Mathuran system during the Saka period. This ... suggests cultural
penetration and hence cultural contacts from the Ganga–Yamuna Doab,
through the middle Ganga valley into the Rewah area. Such a possibility
will be further strengthened by the arrival of donors from Kausambi to
Bandhogarh. The name of Mathura, too, was not unheard of in the
Bandhogarh records.[69]

Subsequent developments at Bandhavgarh continued to bring
wider as well as local influences to bear on the site.[70] As noted
above, it was probably the Kalachuris who brought 'religion' to
Bandhavgarh in the shape of nine *mandapika* temples, which
Stadtner links to the early Kalachuri structures at Tigawa and

Nand Chand in Jabalpur district. In all these sites the shrine fabric is composed of horizontal slabs with small exterior niches–finely crafted buildings that contrast sharply with the archaic sculptures on the upward path to the summit.

The Baghels, who succeeded the Kalachuris at Bandhavgarh, emphasized the military role of the hill, though a fort there may date from before their occupancy.[71] Although the hill slipped out of their hands at least once between the fourteenth and sixteenth centuries, Baghel chiefs used Bandhavgarh as a refuge when under attack. Raja Ramachandra made it his military capital, taking up residence there after the Mughals occupied Kalinjara and Gahora to become Zamindar-e-Bandhav. After Akbar captured the fort, its importance declined, and more so when Vikramaditya made Rewa his capital.

As the British central state began pressing the Baghels in the nineteenth century, Bandhavgarh became an icon of their regional kingdom. The rajas forbade foreigners to approach, much less enter, the fort, even for the purposes of the central survey.[72] One sceptical British officer debunked the story of the dangerous swamps at the fort's base but, despite his revelations published in British journals, the fort remained closed to foreigners until the death of Maharaja Raghuraj Singh in 1881, when Rewa came under the close supervision of the Government of India.

V

THE CULTURE OF THE BAGHEL COURT

Gahora, Bandhavgarh, and Rewa provided different settings for the court culture of the Baghel kings, the features of which owe much to the high culture of courts in northern and central India.[73] Due to threats from the Chandels and the Delhi Sultanate, court life at Gahora did not develop notably until the reign of Virasimha (1500–40) who beautified his capital and set up court there. The raja was a lover of literature and the arts, and patronized the work of the Sanskrit poet Ramachandra Bhatt. His son Virabhanu was also deeply interested in music and the arts; and poets, musicians, and artists attended the court of his day. However, when Akbar annexed Kalinjara and threatened Gahora, Ramachandra shifted court to 'the King's city' at Bandhavgarh, which a poet described as

Plate 1: Doorway, Gupta temple at Bhumara.

Plate 2: Shiva *mukhalingam*, now restored to the Gupta
temple at Bhumara.

Plate 3: Kalachuri temple, Chandrehe.

Plate 4: The Kalachuri monastery at Chandrehe.

Plate 5: A group of Kalachuri temples near the Narmada *kund*, Amarkantak.

Plate 6: One of three Kalachuri temples at Amarkantak, known as Raja Karna Dahariya.

Plate 7: One of nine *mandapika* temples on Bandhavgarh hill.

Plate 8: Bandhavgarh hill and fort.

Plate 9: The Siva–Parvati grouping from Gurgi in Rewa town.

Plate 10: Doorway of the restored Kalachuri temple, Singhpur, Sohagpur *taksil*, Shahdol district.

glorified by the cultured ladies, inhabited by citizens, cultured, virtuous and content, adorned with crystal-white palaces, studded with moon-like gems ... appearing, as it were, situated on the Himalayan peaks.[74]

Tansen graced Ramachandra's court until summoned by Akbar to Agra.

When Vikramaditya shifted his capital to Rewa, the fort buildings there became the permanent setting for the Baghel court. The raja enlarged Islam Shah's fort and his successors added to the complex, such that by the nineteenth century the fort-palace comprised a bizarre collection of buildings:

The main Darbar hall ... [and] the reception halls were distinguished by ... the stock-in-trade of late Moghul design, and the Darbar Hall was designed to create an atmosphere of Imperial Power.... Even so, this Moghul whimsy is buried deep in a palace, which has all the dark, introverted character of a fortress, and whatever conception of architectural symmetry prescribed the original design, it was soon overwhelmed by a chaos of additions. The palace grew as if it had a life of its own. It acquired temples, courtyards, bathing places, and a bewildering maze of halls, passage ways and dungeons. There ... [is] a vast number of rooms, and it is difficult to conceive that they ever had any real purpose.[75]

Rulers in the nineteenth and twentieth centuries built additional palaces to meet their changing needs.[76] Vishwanath Singh (1834–54) created a lake at Govindgarh, nineteen kilometres south of Rewa, and began a palace nearby. Raghuraj Singh (1854–81) added to the palace which became part fort, part hunting lodge. After the Maharaja died, British officers in charge of the minor Maharaja Venkatraman Singh (1896–1918) condemned the Rewa palace as unhealthy, and built Nai Kothi (opposite the present Venkat Bhavan) where the young boy could 'exercise or breathe fresh air' in the gardens, tennis courts, riding ground, and playing fields which they laid out there. Venkatraman later constructed the grandiose Venkat Bhavan as his official residence. Other royal buildings arose in the vicinity: Pili Kothi for a royal bride who never lived there; and Gulab Singh's (1922–46) two-storey residence, besides a house at Govindgarh.

Learning rather than valour in war characterized the Baghel court, whether in Bandhavgarh or Rewa.[77] Ramachandra and his son Virabhadra (1592–3) were known as patrons of learning. Court culture reached a high point during the reign of Bhava Singh (1660–90), members of his court including the nobility and scholars devoted to literature and logic and 'profound in Vedic erudition'. In the nineteenth century Jai Singh (1809–33) and Vishwanath Singh (1833–54) both patronized learning, and the latter invited Sanskrit scholars from other parts of India to settle in the state.

Noted scholars at the Rewa court (or those patronized by it) included the poet Ramachandra, who wrote the Sanskrit *Radhacarita* at the request of Virasimhadeva; and Govinda Bhatta and Bhushana, Sanskrit and Hindi poets respectively, who enjoyed the patronage of Raja Ramachandra.[78] Virabhadra patronized the Sanskrit scholar Padmanabha Misra of Mithila, whose work was published at Rewa. Writers also produced or embellished with verse the genealogies of their royal masters. Some rulers themselves wrote in Hindi and Sanskrit: Vishwanath Singh composed many works on literature, philosophy, science, and religion in Sanskrit and Hindi under the nom-de-plume of Singh Baghela; while his son Raghuraj composed Hindi poetry and wrote a history of Hanuman and a much admired translation of the *Bhagwata Purana*.

Rewa's rulers were also keen patrons of music.[79] Even the early kings kept musicians at Gahora. Pride of place among musicians belonged to Mian Tansen of Gwalior, the court musician of Raja Ramachandra, whose art led Akbar to carry him off to the Mughal court where his music drew from the Emperor the claim that such a musician had 'not been born for a thousand years'. Much later, Vishwanath Singh had a special place at court for musicians. In general, too, it was said of Rewa's kings that they not only 'contributed immensely to preserve old musical devices, but popularised them with ... innovations':

Music, both Dhrupad and Khayal, found support at their hands.... The Baghela rulers were not carried off their feet by the impact of Turko–Muslim culture, but preserved an individuality of their own.[80]

Bhaktawar of Varanasi sang *dhrupad* and Ustad Muhammad Khan *khayal* at the court of Vishwanath Singh.

Religion played an important part in the life of the Rewa kings.[81] Most early kings were pious men in the Saivite tradition, though later rulers added particular strands to this. Virasimhadeva was a disciple of Kabir, who is said to have blessed the Baghel line at Gahora; and when Kabir died his *chela* was among those who accompanied his remains to Varanasi for cremation. The Kabirpanthi influence was sustained from Ramachandra (who was an intimate of Sant Dharamdas, founder of the Chhattisgarhi Kabirpanthis) through to Vishwanath Singh. From Bhava Singh's time rulers also favoured the Vaishnavite tradition. Vishwanath Singh was a disciple of the Vaishnava philosopher Priya Das, and he and his successors built Vaishnava temples in the Lakshmana Bagh at Rewa, and installed *raj purohits* who exercised a spiritual and temporal influence in the state. Rewa's rulers also had their family deity, worshipped especially at their installation on the *gaddi*.

Other religious observances at court included going on pilgrimage to holy sites, popular with Baghel kings in the nineteenth century when princely warfare ceased and it was easier to move around.[82] Rulers also observed the festival of Dassehra, though this was as much a political as a religious occasion, as they expected all *ilaqadars* and *pawaidars* to attend the capital with their troop levies, mounted and foot.

The Baghel court had its less serious side, which was better reported in the nineteenth century after Rewa was drawn into the orbit of the British central government.[83] Officials complained to rulers against their keeping 'mad' elephants for the 'amusement of fighting', and reported that they ran wild in Rewa town killing 'many people'. One of the rulers' favourite pastimes, especially in the nineteenth and twentieth centuries, was the hunt, and no ruler was more adept at the sport than Raghuraj Singh (1854–81), who

was a good rider, and an expert in all other princely accomplishments. He was a crack shot, and very few can be said to have equalled him in the use of the rifle. During his lifetime, he shot—almost always on foot—more than a hundred tigers, besides a large number of bears, bisons [sic] and other ferocious beasts. He also entrapped some forty two wild elephants. He generally shot animals ... on foot, or from an elephant, but very seldom climbed into the *machans* on a tree. His ponderous rifle was always with him, but it was so heavy that a man of ordinary strength could hardly lift it, to say nothing of shooting with it.[84]

In the twentieth century, Gulab Singh was also an avid hunter, and by his reign the practice of entertaining official guests at tiger shoots was well established.

In and through courtly life ran the thread of protocol and pageantry, producing spectacles that probably changed little over the centuries. A senior British officer visiting Raghuraj Singh after the 1857 revolt described his reception as follows:

> I was always received by the Maharaja with a display of barbaric splendour hardly to be seen in any other state in ... Central India. His Highness' Darbar represented a scene of brocade, *kinkhab*, gold, and jewels, which would require the flowery language of Persia and a Persian pen to describe....no less than two hundred feudatory barons of Rewa were gathered round their Chief, each clothed in a costly costume, or in ancient armour with breast-plate and buckler, and all adorned with jewels, and gold and silver ornaments. The whole scene was one of ... magnificent Eastern splendour;—[but] the town of Rewa, in the midst of which the palace stands ... is a miserable collection of hovels.[85]

The court of Gulab Singh (1922–46) contrasted radically with that of his predecessors. The ruler reserved the term *darbar* for himself, and transformed the court by excluding the nobility and surrounding himself with young and ambitious ADCs drawn mostly from the lower sections of society.[86] These newcomers added jealousy and rivalry for precedence to the traditional intrigues of the court; while the nobles resented their exclusion and grew more determined to maintain the privileges of their status.

However, by then life at court—hidden for centuries under a veil of silence or perhaps complicity—was subject to public comment and official action. Nineteenth century officers of the central government were aware of the 'naked and unashamed immorality' of the Rewa court, where even the parentage of rulers was suspect, though the centre's policy precluded interference.[87] However, against a background of nationalist agitation and the Second World War the central government decisively intervened in princely matters where it considered its interests were at stake.

The activities of Maharaja Gulab Singh and his court especially invited such action.[88] Rumour had it that the Maharaja had hired assassins to kill one, possibly two, of his ADCs. Officials believed that even the *yuvraj*, Martand Singh, was at risk from the 'hard drinking and undesirable thakurs who surround the Maharani'. The Maharrao of Kachchh, too, whose daughter Pravinba married the prince in 1943, was concerned for her happiness in the 'Rewa influence' being created round her husband. As official action commenced, relations within the royal family became tense, Gulab Singh forbidding his wife to meet their son. In 1945, in a dramatic gesture, the senior Maharani appeared on the *deorhi* roof opposite her husband's residence with a pistol and threatened to kill him unless he allowed her access to Martand Singh. This and other facets of life at the late Rewa court came to an abrupt end with the ruler's deposition and banishment from Rewa by the central government in 1946.

VI

THE POPULAR CULTURE OF BAGHELKHAND

Remote from the court, the mass of people in the state lived a life akin to that of rural folk in the adjacent regions of north and central India, indicating the integrative role played by migration. The setting for this culture comprised the region's villages where housing was determined by the materials locally available, Baghelkhand's sandy soil providing the mud that formed the main component of rural housing.[89] Peasants plastered mud on straw or wattle to create walls that would protect them from harsh sunlight or heavy rain. In more backward parts people made dwellings of grass, leaves and bamboo. Most mud-built houses had a tile roof over a supporting thatch of *arhar* or bamboo.

At its simplest the mud house comprised a single room, though the houses of more prosperous folk had several rooms and a courtyard.[90] Roofs were low with a gentle slope, but in heavier rainfall areas steep roofs were not uncommon. Ventilation was poor, windows being 'characteristically absent'. There was no latrine or bathroom. The ordinary person possessed only a cot and occasionally a wooden *chowki* to sit on; better off peasants had some furniture. Interior decoration of houses was unknown, but at marriages or on festivals such as Diwali people whitewashed their houses and often decorated them with painted designs.

The clothing of most people did not alter for centuries.[91] The common dress of males was the *dhoti* to the knees with an upper covering of cotton and a *pagri*. Muslim men wore the pajama and an upper garment. If men had shoes they wore the raised-back leather *juti*, tight to the foot but with open sides. Women in Rewa wore the cotton *dhoti* and *chholi*, though lower caste women dressed in the *gaghra* or *lehanga*. Village women also wore ornaments as an aid to beauty.

In food habits, too, Baghelkhand was an extension of northern India.[92] In the old Rewa ordinary folk ate twice a day, morning and evening. Most were vegetarians, but lower communities ate meat and fish. Males took precedence over females in order of eating. Poorer people ate barley, gram, *kodon* or *matra*, a pea grain known for its energy-giving value; rice and wheat were the staples of the better-off in town and country. The diet of those with land would have been adequate at the least, but the remainder were undernourished. Of the better-off castes Rajputs were 'first with respect to the consumption of nutrients', followed by Jains and Brahmans.

Baghelkhand also shared with northern India the customs relating to marriage and death.[93] In traditional Rewa child marriage was common even among the higher castes. Boys and girls began marrying from about ten years of age, the frequency being higher in the case of girls. Due to the prevalence of dowry, people regarded

girls as a possible future burden; while boys are looked on as a means of support in later life, ... and a means of the spiritual salvation of the father. This attitude is reflected in the neglect of girls, and consequently early marriages.[94]

The less well-off naturally suffered more from the financial burden of dowry. Weddings themselves were costly affairs, often beyond the financial capacity of the parents. Divorce and remarriage were taboo at middle and upper social levels, but common at the lower rungs of society. The joint family system was widespread at all social levels. Females, especially of the upper castes, observed *parda*; and all except Muslims and untouchables cremated their dead.

The health of the ordinary folk of Baghelkhand was precarious.[95] Malnutrition was common. Good drinking water was scarce in all seasons, villagers being innocent of what later ages regarded as elementary hygiene. Contaminated water spread disease, while malnutrition weakened resistance to it. British observers believed that large numbers of people moving to and from pilgrimages and weddings contributed to the spread of disease:

Travellers ... [were] wearied by much journeying, and with health impaired by alternate fast and feast. The growing heat of the sun is beginning to try them by day, while the night air still retains much of its keenness; and the water of the sacred tanks at which they love to drink has grown scanty, and the filth in it ... proportionately contaminated. They are [thus] ... in a fit state to take ... any epidemic that may meet them. The same remarks apply to the members of the numerous *barats*, whom daily journeying and nightly revels soon reduce to a very low standard of health.[96]

The treatment of disease was mostly of a traditional kind.[97] Mendicants, pandits, and others attributed it to a god or an evil spirit, and prescribed the procedure to avert illness or effect a cure. More formal traditional health systems like *unani* and *ayurveda* existed; and places such as Amarkantak were known for their medicinal plants. Modern medical services date from the latter nineteenth century, but these reached only a fraction of the population.

Religious festivals, fairs, and other social occasions provided relief from the hazards and difficulties of daily life.[98] Festivals marking the passage of the seasons were important occasions involving the entire village community. Dassehra and Durga Puja indicated the beginning of the dry weather after the monsoon; Diwali heralded the onset of cooler weather, besides marking the opening of the financial year for traders. Basant Panchami celebrated the beginning of spring. Holi with its colour play and drinking was another spring festival, but it also indicated that summer was at hand. In addition, people kept festivals in honour of Siva, Rama, Krishna, and Ganesh. Muslims too, observed their holy days, generally with the support of local people. Fairs were common in larger villages throughout Baghelkhand, mostly occurring at the time of religious festivals. Devotion to Hanuman made wrestling popular; and there were other traditional sports besides. Drinking and the taking of intoxicants were an accepted part of village life.

People marked the seasons, festivals, or happy events with dance, drama, and song.[99] Though dance did not occupy the place among Hindu castes that it did among the hill and forest communities, people generally celebrated births, marriages, and other festivities with dancing. *Dandiya nritya* was known all over central India, especially on the eve of Holi. Prostitutes and others sang and danced at weddings and at the birth of male children; Ahir women also danced when a son was born. Local or itinerant groups danced or sang, and recited forms of the *Mahabharata* or *Ramayana*, and performed Ram Lila, Ras Lila and Nautanki on festivals. In villages at evening people participated in *bhajan–kirtan*.

People's exuberance similarly found an outlet in Baghelkhand's store of folk songs.[100] A frequent theme was the desire for a male child: the childless wife rued her barrenness or being called a witch, and bemoaned the fact that her husband had turned her out of the house, Other songs included those common at marriages. At village *chaupal*s in the evening Alhats sang with gusto the *Alha*, an account of the fifty-two battles fought by the folk heroes, Alha and Udal, against Prithviraj Chauhan of Delhi.

A largely illiterate population also knew by heart many proverbs, sayings, stories and legends handed down from previous generations.[101] Proverbs often concerned the seasons and the practice of agriculture. Stories and songs from villages subdued by the Baghels related a theme of oppression. Other stories depicted the behaviour of barbers, oil-pressers, *mochi*s, and *kumhar*s, members of the castes concerned considering the sentiments expressed to be their 'characteristic speciality'. Age-old legends told how the Son river 'ran' from the Narmada to marry Johilla, perhaps recollecting some geological event which reversed the Son's flow to its present south–north direction.

The songs, sayings, and tales were generally in Bagheli, the regional dialect whose predominance demonstrated the weak influence of Persian in central India, except in revenue terms.[102] Even the Baghel kings and *thakurs* preferred the region's dialect to the language of the Mughal centre.

Religion was intrinsic to the life of the people of Baghelkhand as of other regions.[103] They visited holy sites commemorating a divine event or person. Chitrakut, a hundred and twenty three kilometres north of Satna, where Rama, Sita and Lakshmana reportedly stayed for some time during their exile from Ayodhya, was a popular pilgrim site. Another famous shrine was that of Sharada *devi* in Maihar, where large numbers went for *darshan* of the goddess. Shrines in smaller places drew people from surrounding areas, often at the time of an annual fair, which was itself primarily a religious occasion dedicated to the local deity.

Pilgrims also visited pools and rivers whose waters they considered sacred.[104] Amarkantak, source of the Narmada, was a centuries-old holy site with its many *tirthas* and shrines, *rishis* and *munis*. A Prakrit inscription marked Kevati *kund* near the fall of the Chhoti Mahanadi over the northern scarp as another ancient religious site. Pilgrims performed *sandhya* on the banks of the Son to receive absolution and attain heaven. The Johilla, a tributary of the Son, was also a sacred stream: the Jawaleswar Siva *lingam* stood at its source; a Kalachuri sculpture at Amarkantak represented Johilla *devi*; and the river's confluence with the Son at Kelhari was sacred to Siva, an annual fair taking place there at Sivaratri.

Religious beliefs, practices and superstitions handed down from generation to generation permeated people's lives in other ways besides. Even in remote areas people followed with 'inherent faith and intensity' auspicious days, and believed in the evil eye, in spirits, and in good and bad omens.[105] In addition,

to believe in miracles and superstitions, ... to be devotees of saints, to marry plants [and] tanks, to offer *pind-daan* in *pitra-paksha* are some of the customs and manners prevalent.... Dargahs of some Sufi saints are important places of reverence for all.... To have *darshan* of [a] snake, neelkanth, *nevia* ... and to worship [a] banyan tree, *neem, tulsi, peepal,* [and] *anwala* ... on certain festivals is considered auspicious for a religious Hindu.[106]

In the same way age-old social customs maintained their hold on the people of the region.[107] Observance of various of the sixteen *samskaras* or tenets governed the manners and customs of society. Name-giving and the thread ceremony were the main initiatory rituals at the middle and upper levels of society. Centuries of caste consciousness determined social status and perpetuated the notion of untouchability. Probably until well into the nineteenth century most people followed their hereditary profession. Middle- and upper-class folk were shy of soiling their hands by manual labour, while Brahmans and Rajputs refused to touch the plough.

The Culture of the Hill and Forest People

Any discussion of Baghelkhand's popular culture would be incomplete without reference to the hill and forest people, whose ways also had much in common with those of similar groups elsewhere in central and northern India.[108] The existence of forty-two such groups in the region—each of them endogamous, each bearing a common name, some speaking their own language and responsive in some degree to folkways not observed by the wider community—reflects the high degree of heterogeneity in hill and forest society. Until fairly recently, some practised shifting cultivation; others took to settled cultivation centuries ago. The hill and forest groups also showed different levels of acculturation to the wider Hindu community. Gonds, Pradhans and others with land generally identified more with middle-or upper-class Hindu ways, while labouring Kols were more akin to the lower and untouchable Hindu castes. In remote areas some groups feared the privileged classes, especially the moneylender or contractor.

It is thus difficult to discern any single cultural pattern among hill and forest people.[109] Some merged gradually into the wider village community, and in the twentieth century most of these groups began describing themselves as Hindus at the census. While not abandoning their worship of nature, many adopted Hindu deities and observed festivals such as Holi. Better off communities like the Gonds began wearing the sacred thread, observing child marriage, and taking the help of priests and astrologers in marriage matters.

Many among the hill and forest people also adopted the regional dialect, Bagheli.[110] Traditionally three main language groups were represented in Baghelkhand: these were Mundari, the language of the Kols and others, whom some linguists claim were descended from the region's earliest inhabitants; the Dravidian languages, the main one being Gondi; and the Indo–European group represented by Bagheli. Over the centuries, speakers of non-Indo–European languages tended to adopt Bagheli, which has thus become the 'lingua franca' of the region, however 'corrupt' or 'broken' the version may be. The use of languages not derived from Sanskrit has declined concomitantly. As a result,

Gondi ... is spoken only in those isolated places of the southern part of Sidhi and Shahdol districts, where the means of transportation and communications are scanty, and the inhabitants are not in touch with the outer world.... In Satna district, even the Gonds speak pure Bagheli dialect. Baigas of Sidhi and Shahdol speak a language which is a mixture of Bagheli, Chhattisgarhi, and Gondwani.... The Kols do not remember that at any time they had a language of their own.[111]

The hill and forest people also built houses with a wood or bamboo frame and thatched or tiled roofs, women plastering the walls with mud, which they then whitewashed.[112] People finished their work by daylight or moonlight, needing light only for eating or securing animals at night. Only a few households had lanterns, and even for dancing at night by the beat of drums lights were unnecessary. Hill and forest people also kept furniture to a minimum, decorating their houses with paintings of animals, humans, or geometrical designs etched in chalk or clay of different colours.

Gonds generally built more substantial houses than those of other communities, using mud bricks or home-made mud, with wooden pillars supporting a tiled roof.[113] The front and back walls had overhanging eaves to protect them from rain. Gond houses also had rooms for cooking and eating, and were generally neat and clean with a fence of bamboo or timber to protect them from wild animals or cattle thieves. Many had verandahs with bamboo or wooden pillars, and a low door into the house causing people to bend. Due to lack of windows interiors were dark and ventilation poor, and there were no sanitary arrangements. An open space for sitting, a vegetable plot, and cattle shelter adjoined the house.

As for Kols and Baigas, the former's housing was simpler and less expensive than that of the Gonds.[114] Kols mostly lived in small single-roomed huts of mud and wattle with a roof of tiles or thatch, keeping their cattle in an adjoining enclosure. Baigas had the nomad's view of housing, their huts being merely camps on life's journey. Walls were again of bamboo or wood supporting a thatched roof, with one door and little or no ventilation. Most houses comprised a single room, so that a family lived, cooked, ate, and slept in the same place. In consequence their houses smelt of wood-smoke and food, and observers found them unattractive and 'never neat and clean'.

Contrary to popular belief the hill and forest peoples of Baghelkhand had a developed technological sense.[115] Gonds were adept house builders, assembling the wooden frame around which their houses took shape. Baigas wielded the axe to clear the forest for shifting cultivation; Gonds used the plough for settled agriculture. Both communities hunted with bow and arrow, the stave and arrow being made of flexible bamboo with bamboo strips for strings. The Baigas used nets and traps for fishing, and wooden tools for household tasks. They also used the digging stick. For centuries Agarias practised the art of making iron.

Male dress among the hill and forest people varied according to social and economic status.[116] The common dress of Kol and Baiga males comprised a *langoti* or *dhoti* as a lower garment and a sheet or rag to cover the upper body. A *chaddar* may have protected them in winter, though the typical Baiga was not affected by the seasons. Baigas began adopting the *dhoti* and stitched *kurta* in the twentieth century, but their traditional rule was to 'wear rough and eat millet', for they could afford nothing better. Gond dress was more substantial as they considered themselves superior among the hill and forest people and wished to display it. They thus wore more and better clothes than Kols or Baigas, dressing in *dhoti* and *chaddar* and, when going out, with a *rumal* and *pagri*. Gond men also wore coats on special occasions.

Women similarly differed in dress according to status.[117] The usual dress of Gond females consisted of a long cloth round the waist with a fold in front. One end went over the head or shoulder like the *sari*; the other they drew between uncovered legs and tucked it up behind. Women traditionally wore no upper garment, covering themselves with one end of the *dhoti*. A blouse for hill and forest women is a very recent invention. Traditionally, garments were made of country cloth; but today some women buy mill cloth at *melas* or from shops in town and village.

Regardless of variations in clothing, men and women of the hill and forest communities adorned themselves with ornaments.[118] Men wore bangles, rings, ear-drops or earrings, and necklets—sometimes of 'precious stones, sometimes a gold or silver coin'. Their women wore bangles of silver, glass, or *lac*, finger rings, anklets, necklaces of beads or metal, and earrings. Some women, especially Gonds, wore *sindur*, toe-rings and other ornaments as a sign of their married status. The quality of these ornaments varied widely, depending on the wealth of the wearer: gold was rare, silver less so; more commonly, ornaments were made of brass, bronze, or other metals. Tatooing of arms, legs, forehead, and chin was also common among women either before or after marriage.

The food habits of the hill and forest people were more standardized than their dress.[119] Most ate twice a day, their staples being *kodon, kutki, juar* or *makka*, depending on what was grown locally. Many preferred rice, but some could not afford it, or their land may have been too poor for rice cultivation. Millet or rice in water, *chapatis* of *juar* or *makka*, and some vegetables were staple

items of diet. Hill and forest people also craved meat, and if close
to forests hunted the boar or deer. However, as game became less
easily available, many kept pigs, goats or fowls for food. Eggs and
fish were other non-vegetarian dishes, besides the flesh of field
rats and tortoises when available. *Gur* had an important place in
their diet. In addition, the jungle provided a store of leafy vegetables, roots, fruits, tubers, and herbs, which were taken with
cereals. *Mahua* was a key item of food. Public feasting also occupied an important place in the food habits of these people.

Hill and forest people drew on the usage of the majority community for some marriage practices.[120] As noted above, some began to adopt child marriage as a sign of claims to a higher social
status; others still regard adult marriage as the norm. Some have
adopted the marriage rituals of their fellow-villagers; marriage
expenditure similarly formed the most important single item of
the budget, and disclosed the economic status of the contracting
families. Gond bride-grooms lived in the bride's house for some
years before settling separately in the girl's village. Among these
groups the joint family existed in a looser form, though many held
it in esteem.

There, however, the similarities between the marriage practices
of the hill and forest people and of the wider community ended.[121]
Gond marriages were simpler than Hindu rites. Many men asked
for the hand of the bride, though family heads might arrange
marriages. The custom of pairing, too, has continued for centuries
among Gonds and others:

Young people in the villages at the occasion of the Full-moon in spring
or summer dance the Karma dances in which all women and men of the
village take part, make friendships, and disappear on the night of the
dance, and after staying for two or three days in the jungle, return, and
they are received in the village as a married couple.[122]

Some Baigas arranged marriages of the yet unborn. People often
did not employ a pandit. As distinct from the practice of dowry, hill
and forest people observed bride-price, so to them the birth of a
daughter was an asset. Unlike Hindus, Gonds preferred cross-
cousin marriages; and divorce and widow remarriage were common. Some permitted married women to remarry, and even allowed
a man to keep a number of wives.

Death customs among the hill and forest people also gradually assimilated to Hindu practice.[123] Previously a medicine man presided over Gond funerals in return for a bottle of *mahua* wine. However, Brahman priests gradually replaced these *ojha*s, requiring gifts in cash or kind. Many came to observe cremation and, like Hindus, collected the ashes on the third day following. In Satna Hindu *nai*s shaved Kol corpses before cremation; and family members paid Brahmans presiding on the banks of the river from where the dead remains were cast. Hill and forest people did not practise *sati*.

No ceremonial occasion among forest and hill people passed without music and dance.[124] Kol women danced; their menfolk never. Women performed the sun dance in September–October, going from door to door with barley sprouting over their heads. Forest and hill folk danced at marriage ceremonies and on Janamashtami and other festivals. The Baiga

dance whenever the season or their lover invites them. Give them a bright moon and a little liquor and their feet begin to move unbidden, and their hands stray towards the drums. The Baigas take ... dancing seriously, and dress well for it.

Gonds also enjoyed dancing.[125] Most of their dances were group affairs in which men and women took part, all moving to the beat of hand-sticks and drum. The two main Gond dances were Karma and Saila, the latter a stick dance of males, largely performed from the end of the rains and through the cold weather. Villages competed with one another to develop their own variations. The Karma dance, popular with Gonds, Baigas, and others was connected with the fertility cult. Elwin notes

that the dance symbolizes the bringing of green branches of the forest in Spring. Sometimes a tree is actually set up ... and people dance around it. The dance is filled with the breath of trees. The men leap forward to a rapid roll of drums—a gust of wind which blows back the swaying forms of the women. Then bending low to the ground, the women dance, their feet moving in perfect rhythm to and fro until the group of singers advances towards them, like the steady surge of the wind coming and going among the tree tops. The Karma seems to have been the oldest dance-form of the Adivasis.[126]

Intoxicants were central to the way of life of hill and forest people:

In the mountainous region [i.e. Shahdol], a visit to the market, ceremonial occasions, dancing, observance of rituals, death, marriage or sickness, harvesting, all begin and end with *mahua* liquor ... a dire necessity in sickness, a comfort in distress, and a luxury in dance and marriage.[127]

Liquor was distilled in shops or obtained through contractors. More commonly, members of these groups brewed *mahua* liquor themselves. Males, even children, were fond of chewing tobacco or smoking its raw leaves in pipes. By report, addiction to intoxicants was high among Kols and Gonds especially, and all members of a family partook on occasions. Drink was thus a major item of expenditure and, where purchased on credit, pushed many families into debt.

Drink had other ramifications besides.[128] Drink and gambling were connected, as people hoped by winning large amounts of money at gambling to pay off those who supplied them with drink. Drink and magic were intertwined, members of these groups offering their priest–magicians drink when curing disease or warding off evil spirits. Religious or social occasions, too, called for a drink. Kols began their drinking bouts ten days before Diwali and nine days before Ramnavami.

Belief in magic was strong, especially among Baigas.[129] The power of their magician priests derived from Nanga Baiga, the Baigas' original *guru*, and it was through such priests that the cosmic forces flowed. As Nanga Baiga bound the mouths of tigers to prevent them from devouring the Baiga people, so the Baiga priest–magician called on his ancestor as he drove nails into trees to guard a village from maneaters. Gonds also believed in magic and practised magic rites. The occasion of Laru Kaj in the old Rewa was associated with pig sacrifice for prosperity, health, and happiness. This took place once in nine to twelve years, the host family inviting their relatives and others of the village for the occasion. In recent times Gonds have replaced the pig with a goat, and the sacrifice only obtains in remote villages.

Myth and legend were integral to the everyday life of the hill and forest people.[130] Gonds and Baigas especially had a treasury of myths to integrate past and present, and to explain the natural world. We have already noted the Kol myth linking them with Bhagwan's call to build a fort on Bandhavgarh. Bhagwan also taught the Baigas not to tear the breast of *dhartia mata* with the plough like the Gonds, but to cultivate *bewar or baghor*, sowing seed in the ashes of burnt trees.

Living close to nature, hill and forest people forged a bond with their plant environment, for

the tribal community makes use of many plants for medicinal purposes. Common ailments ... are treated and cured with the help of herbs of the surrounding vegetation system. Snake bite ... and bone fractures are also treated with plant medicines. Over twenty plants constitute the common package of herbal medicine.[131]

As a result, Baigas and Gonds with their deep knowledge of herbs and roots enjoyed a high reputation as medicine men among the wider hill and forest communities. The source of their remedies lay in the medicinal herbs of the Maikal hills and the forests of Sidhi.

Notes

1. *CII*, vol. II, pt II, H. Lüders (ed.), *Bharhut Inscriptions*, pp. XXXI–iii; S.T. Chacko, 'A cultural study of bharhut sculptures', PhD, A.P.S. University, Rewa, 1985, pp. 17–18; Brown, *Indian Architecture*, vol.1. pp. 13–18; R.C. Sharma, *Bharhut Sculptures*, New Delhi, 1994, p. 9.
2. BA, 513, 1924–30, Pamphlet entitled 'Maha-Bodhi'; Brown, *Indian Architecture*, p. 13; A. Cunningham, *Report of a Tour in the CP*, pp. 2–3; D. Mitra, *Buddhist Monuments*, Calcutta, 1971, p. 96; A. Ghosh, *Remains of the Bharhut Stupa in the Indian Museum, Calcutta*, Calcutta, 1978, p. vii.
3. Sharma, *Bharhut Sculptures*, pp. 13–14; R. Chakravarti, 'Merchants and other donors', at ancient Bandhogarh,' *SAS*, vol. II, 1995, pp. 33–4; Lahiri, *The Archaeology of Indian Trade*, p. 404; H.P. Ray 'Bharhut and Sanchi', pp. 621, 627.
4. Sharma, *Bharhut Sculptures*, pp. 11–2; Chacko, 'Bharhut sculptures', PhD, p. 25; E.B. Havell, *The History of Aryan Rule in India, from the Earliest Times to the Death of Akbar*, London, nd., p. 110.
5. Sharma, *Bharhut Sculptures*, p. 11.
6. K.D. Bajpai, *Cultural History of India*, vol. I, pp. 136–7; A.H. Dani, *Prehistory and Proto-History of Eastern India*, Calcutta, 1960, p. 57; D.C. Sircar, 'Bharhut inscriptions in the Allahabad museum', *EI*, vol. XXXIII, pt. I, Jan. 1959, pp. 57–9.
7. Ray, 'Bharhut and Sanchi', pp. 625–7; V.S. Agrawala, *Studies in Indian Art*, Varanasi, 1965, p. 77; Kosambi, *Culture and Civilization*, p. 140; Sharma, *Buddhist Sculptures*, p. 12.

8. K.D. Bajpai, *Indian Numismatic Studies*, New Delhi, 1976, p. 16; Neumayer, *Prehistoric Indian Rock Paintings*, Delhi, 1983, p. 7; Ray, 'Bharhut and Sanchi', p. 622.

9. Chacko, 'Bharhut sculptures', PhD, pp. 73, 76–7, 81–2.

10. Ray, 'Bharhut and Sanchi', pp. 626–6; Lahiri, *Archaeology of Indian Trade*, p. 404.

11. Ray, 'Bharhut and Sanchi', pp. 626–7. For donations by monastics, see U. Singh, 'Sanchi: The history of the patronage of an ancient Buddhist establishment', *IESHR*, vol. 33, no. 1, 1996, pp. 15–18; *CII*, vol. II, pt. II, pp. 2–10, 16–57; Lahiri, *Archaeology of Indian Trade*, pp. 384–5.

12. Havell, *History of Aryan Rule*, p. 107; Brown, *Indian Architecture*, p. 14.

13. Mitra, *Buddhist Monuments*, p. 96.

14. F.R. Allchin, *Emergence of Cities and States*, pp. 252, 273; Sharma, *Bharhut Sculptures*, p. 14; Ghosh, *Remains of the Bharhut Stupa*, pp. 33–4; Brown, *Indian Architecture*, p. 15.

15. V.S. Agrawala, *Evolution of the Hindu Temple and Other Essays*, Varanasi, 1965, pp. 21–2; Havell, *History of Aryan Rule*, p. 118; Sharma, *Bharhut Sculptures*, pp. 13–4; Brown, *Indian Architecture*, p. 3; Bajpai, *Cultural History*, vol. I, p. 28; Chacko, 'Bharhut sculptures', PhD, pp. 49, 63–71.

16. P.K. Misra, 'Discovering the past', nd., np; P.K. Misra, 'Deorkothar stupa', pp. 52, 66, 71, 73; Varma, *Rewa*, p. 32.

17. Misra, 'Discovering the past', np; Misra, 'Deorkothar stupa', pp. 67–9, 73

18. Ibid., pp. 68–9

19. Ibid., pp. 68, 72–4; Varma *Rewa*, p. 34. Attackers or raiders also visited Buddhist sites elsewhere in the country.

20. Misra, 'Discovering the past', np; Misra, 'Deorkothar stupa', pp. 63, 65–6, 72; Varma, *Rewa*, pp. 32–3.

21. *IAR 1966–67*, p. 20; *IAR 1982–83*, p. ?; W. Garrick, *Report: Tour through Behar, Central India, Peshawar, and Yusufzai, 1881–82*, vol. XIX, Delhi, rpt, 1969, p. 61; Cunningham, vol. XXI, pt I, *Reports of Tours*, p. iv; Varma, *Rewa*, p. 25; R.D. Banerji, 'The Rewah inscription of Malayasimha, the Year 994', *EI*, vol. XIX, pt 8, Oct. 1928, p. 295; D.M. Stadtner, 'Kalachuri art at Singhpur', *OA*, vol. XXVIII, no. 3, Autumn 1982, p. 270.

22. J.G. Williams, The *Art of Gupta India; Empire and Province*, New Delhi, 1983 p. 105; K.V. Soundararajan, *Glimpses of Indian Culture-Architecture, Art and Religion*, Delhi, 1981, pp. 10–13; S.N. Misra, *Gupta Art and Architecture with Special Reference to Madhya Pradesh*, Delhi, 1992, p. 127; R.N. Misra, 'Gupta temple architecture in Madhya Pradesh', *PP*, vol. XIII, nos. 1–2, 1985–7, pp. 85–7.

23. Misra, *Gupta Art*, pp. 11–12, 18.

24. Williams, *Art of Gupta India*, pp. 114, 121–2; Soundararajan, *Glimpses of Indian Culture*, p. 13; Misra, *Gupta Art*, pp. 34, 234–5; see also R.D. Banerji, *The Temple of Siva at Bhumara*: Memoirs of the ASI, no. 16, Calcutta, 1924.

25. Misra, *Gupta Art*, pp. 34, 140; Bajpai, *Cultural History*, vol. I, p. 108; Bajpai, 'Impact of Saivism', p. 29; Williams, *Art of Gupta India*, p. 114.

26. S.N. Misra, *Gupta Art*, pp. 34, 101

27. Ibid., pp. 16, 34; *IAR 1967–68*, p. 67; *IAR 1982–83*, p. 135; *IAR 1983–84*, p. 55; *IAR 1985–86*, p. 55.

28. H. Pathak, *Cultural History of the Gupta Period*, Delhi, 1978, p. 35; *CII*, vol. III, J.F. Fleet, *Inscriptions of the Early Gupta Kings and their Successors*, pp. 106–7, 110–14, 121, 125–30; *Rewa Gazetteer*, p. 298; *IAR 1968–69*, p. 60; *IAR 1982–83*, p. 135; D.C. Sircar, 'Note on Bhumara pillar inscription of Hastin', *EI*, vol. XXXIII, no. 32, 1959–60, pp. 167–71; Kant, *Political and Cultural History*, pp. 238, 357.

29. Misra, *Sculptures of Dahala*, p. 39; R.N. Misra, 'Kalachuri art: determinant factors', Chakravarty, *Art of the Kalachuris*, p. 46. The *shreshthin* Damodara is thought to have built a Vishnu temple at Mukundpur.

30. R.N. Misra, *Sculptures of Dahala and Dakshin Kosala and their Background*, Delhi, 1987, pp. 23–4, 69; S. Punja, *Divine Ecstasy: The Story of Khajuraho*, New Delhi, 1992, p. 208.

31. V.V. Mirashi, 'Rewah stone inscription of the time of Karna: The (Chedi) Year 800', *EI*, vol. XXIV, no. 13, 1937–8, pp. 101–9; H.C. Ray, *The Dynastic History of Northern India* (Early Mediaeval Period) vol. 1, Calcutta, 1931, vol. II, pp. 789, 794, 798–9; Rahman Ali, *Art and Architecture of the Kalachuris*, Delhi, 1980, ', p. 180; R.K. Dikshit, *The Candellas of Jejakabhukti*, Delhi, 1977, pp. 160–1; B. Misra, *Polity in the Agni Purana*, Calcutta, 1965, p. 170; P.K. Bhattacharya, *Historical Geography*, pp. 159–60, 208, 233; *RSA 1910–11*, p. 20; *IAR 1978–79*, p. 82.

32. Ali, *Kalachuri Art*, pp. 4–6; R.D. Banerji, *Haihayas of Tripuri*, Memoir of the ASI, no. 23, Poona, 1922, p. 31; R.N. Misra, *Sculptures of Dahala*, pp. 47, 52.

33. Ibid., p. 27; *Sidhi Gazetteer*, p. 24; *CII*, V.V. Mirashi (ed.), *Inscriptions of the Kalachuri-Chedi Era*, vol. IV, pt. I, p. xxxiv; O.P. Misra, 'Sakti cult and the art of the Kalachuris', K.K Chakravarty, ed., *Art of the Kalachuris*, Bhopal, 1991, p. 105.

34. R.N. Misra, 'Saivite ascetics and their organisation in madhya Pradesh', *Puratan: Saiva Tradition in Indian Art*, vol. 6, 1989, pp. 53–4; R. Ali, 'Saiva Mathas in ancient India', *JMPIP*, no. 11, 1980, p. 67; *Sidhi Gazetteer*, p. 24; CIA, Census, 169, 1920, R.D. Banerji to C.E. Luard, 30 Aug. 1922.

35. S. Huntington, *The Art of Ancient India: Buddhist, Hindu, Jain*, New York, 1999, p. 462; Misra, 'Saivite ascetics', p. 53; P.D. Agnihotri, 'Language and literature in ancient Madhya Pradesh', *JMPIP* no.8, 1990, p. 70; Misra, *Sculptures of Dahala*, pp. 21–3; see also V.S. Pathak, *Saiva Cults in Northern India*, Varanasi, 1960, p. 37,

36. *CII*, vol. IV, pt. 1, p. clix; Misra, 'Saivite ascetics', p. 54.

37. Ibid.

38. Ibid., p. 53–4; Misra, *Sculptures of Dahala*, pp. 23–4, 45; A.H. Nizami, 'Rewa: past and present', *M.P. Medical Conference* Souvenir, Rewa, n.d. pp. 1–2.

39. Misra, *Sculptures of Dahala*, pp. 1–3.

40. Ali, *Kalachuri Art*, pp. 79, 188; Chakravarty, *Art of the Kalachuris*, p. 3; D.M. Stadtner, 'Nand Chand and a central Indian regional style', *AA*, vol. XLIII, no. 1, 1981, pp. 134–5; Misra, *Sculptures of Dahala*, p. 41; R. Ali, 'Vritta samsthanaka temples of Central India', *JMPIP*, 1980–1, p. 123; M.W. Meister, 'Construction and conception: mandapika shrines of Central India', *E&W*, vol. 26, nos. 3–4 (Sept.– Dec.), 1976, p. 409, writes: 'the simplest conception governing stone temples in central India ... is that of a pillared pavilion, the space between the pillars filled by decorated slabs of stone, ... its form as structure growing initially out of wooden prototypes.... Perhaps the earliest surviving example of this type, the Siva temple no. 1 at Mahua ... has an inscription which calls the temple a *sila mandapika* or stone ... pavilion.... It is not surprising to see the Nagara shikhara at times imposed upon it.... Conceptually and structurally, they form a Central Indian type.'

41. B.N. Luniya, *Life and Culture in Mediaeval India*, Indore, 1978, pp. 502–3; Ali, *Kalachuri Art*, pp. 77–8; R.K. Sharma, *The Kalachuris and Their Times*, Delhi, 1980, pp. 257–8; Chakravarty, *Art of the Kalachuris*, p. 26, reports circular temples from Kanpur and Fatehpur districts in UP, and from Raipur and Bilaspur districts in Chhattisgarh. The latter could have come through the Kalachuri rulers of Ratanpur.

42. Chakravarty, *Art of the Kalachuris*, p. 3; A.H. Nizami, 'Ancient Baghelkhand', unpublished article, p. 6; Varma, *Rewa*, p. 45; Garrick, vol. XIX, *Report*, pp. 85–6; Cunningham, vol. XXI, pt 2, *Report of a Tour*, pp. 149–50; Misra, *Sculptures of Dahala*, p. 79; *Rewa Gazetteer*, pp. 296–7. Cunningham could easily trace the remains of the fort walls.

43. Misra, *Sculptures of Dahala*, p. 79; Sharma, *Kalachuris and Their Times*, pp. 260–2; R. Ali, 'Kalachuri art and other contemporary art of central India', Chakravarty, *Art of the Kalachuris*, p. 71

44. Sharma, *Kalachuris and their Times*, p. 262; Banerji, *Haihayas of Tripuri*, pp. 117, 121.

45. Misra, *Sculptures of Dahala*, pp. 31, 49, 84; Sharma, *Kalachuris and*

Their Times, pp. 263–4; R. Sharan, 'The geographical background of the Kalachuri art', *JMPIP*, no. 5, 1967, pp. 49–50; *Shahdol Gazetteer*, pp. 326, 330; Ali, *Kalachuri Art*, p. 68.

46. *Shahdol Gazetteer*, p. 322.

47. Stadtner, 'Singhpur', p. 270; R.N. Misra, 'Kalachuri art: determinant factors', Chakravarty, *Art of the Kalachuris*, p. 45; Chakravarty, 'Mother goddesses, pp. 17, 23; R.C. Majumdar, *History and Culture of the Indian People*, vol. V, *The Struggle for Empire*, Bombay, 1979, p. 659.

48. Misra, *Sculptures of Dahala*, pp. 70, 78; Chakravarty, *Art of the Kalachuris*, p. 3.

49. Misra, *Sculptures of Dahala*, pp. 41, 79–80, 93; Punja, *Divine Ecstasy*, pp. 212–4. See the plate of the Gurgi *torana*.

50. Ibid., p. 211; CIA, PWBranch, 72–S, 1939, Note on the archaeology of Rewa state, 11 May 1940.

51. Chakravarty, *Art of the Kalachuris*, p 3; Misra, *Sculptures of Dahala*, p. 49; *Shahdol Gazetteer*, p. 330; Stadtner, 'Singhpur', p. 270.

52. Ibid.

53. Chakravarty, *Art of the Kalachuris*, pp. 3–4.

54. Misra, *Sculptures of Dahala*, pp. 41, 83, 129–30, 132–3; Punja, *Divine Ecstasy*, pp. 207–8; Misra, 'Determinant factors', Chakravarty, *Art of the Kalachuris*, pp. 43–4.

55. D.M. Stadtner, 'The tradition of Krsna pillars in north India', *AA*, vol. XL, 1987, pp. 60–1, 66.

56. Singh, *Regional Geography*, pp. 624–5. See J. Lal, 'Settlement geography', PhD, p. 40.

57. J.M., 'Notes from Rewa', *IF*, vol. IX, 1883, p. 436. The park's area today is some 44,844 ha. For vegetation in the park see M.N. Buch, *The Forests of Madhya Pradesh*, Bhopal, 1991, p. 125; and for wild life, K.K. Gurung and R. Singh, *Mammals of the Indian Sub-Continent, and Where to Watch Them*, Oxford, 1996, p. 90.

58. BA, 6, 1865–68, C.R. Coles to J.P. Stratton, 25 Aug. 1865; CIA, BA, 346, 1862–6, J.P. Stratton to R.J. Meade, 30 Oct. 1863; BA, 32, 1871, pt I, P.W. Bannerman to AGGCI, 1 Jan. 1873; Nizami, 'Nine gems', p. 2.

59. Ibid., p. 2; R. Sharma, *Vaghela Vamsha Varnanam*, p. 7; G.F. Pearson, 'Manuscript reports on different parts of *India*', *CR*. vol. XXXVI, no. LXXII Jan. 1861. p. 246.

60. Ibid., pp. 2, 45–6. Rewa maintained a garrison there until well into the twentieth century, and had to furnish annual details of arms kept in the fort until 1914. Bandhavgarh served as a prison for local nationalists in the 1930s, and was retained as 'State' property after Rewa joined Vindhya Pradesh in 1948. This is still the legal position, though tourists are freely permitted there these days.

61. *Indian Wildlife* (Insight Guides), Singapore, 1963, p. 261; Pearson, 'Manuscript reports', p. 246.

62. W.G. Griffiths, *The Kol Tribe of Central India* (RASB Monograph Series), vol. II, Calcutta, 1946, p. 209.

63. I am indebted for this observation to P.S. Dwivedi.

64. Chakravarty, *Art of the Kalachuris*, p. 3; Ali, *Kalachuri Art*, p. 6; *Wildlife*, pp. 262–3; Sharma, *Kalachuris and Their Times*, p. 219; *Avataras* of Vishnu include the Sheshasaya Vishnu, Matsya, Kachchhapa, Balaram, and others. These date from 915 AD and are ascribed to the Kayastha minister, Gollaka.

65. N.P. Chakravarti, 'Brahmi inscriptions on Bandhogarh', *EI*, vol. XXXI, no. 23, 1955–56, pp. 167–9, 173; R. Chakravarti, 'Merchants and other donors', pp. 11, 35–9.

66. N.P. Chakravarti, 'Brahmi inscriptions', pp. 169, 171–2; R. Chakravarti, 'Merchants and other donors', pp. 35–8.

67. Ibid., pp. 35, 38–9; N.P. Chakravarti, 'Brahmi inscriptions', pp. 169, 172. The latter author is a prominent supporter of the religious purposes of the donors and their caves.

68. K.D. Bajpai and S.K. Pandey, *Malhar 1975–78*, University of Sagar, p. 22; R. Chakravarti, 'Merchants and other donors', pp. 39–40; J.D. Beglar, *Report of Tours in the South-Eastern Provinces in 1874–75 and 1875–76*, vol. XIII, ASI, Calcutta, 1882, p. 13.

69. R. Chakravarti, 'Merchants and other donors', p. 39.

70. Stadtner, 'Nandchand', p. 134; Stadtner, 'Singhpur', p. 272.

71. See p. 112 above.

72. See Pearson, 'Manuscript reports', pp. 236–74.

73. *Rewa Gazetteer*, pp 32–3; R. Ali, 'The Baghelas: an appraisal', pp, vol. XII, nos 1–2, 1984 pp. 97–8.

74. Sharma, *Vaghela Vamsha Varnanam*, p. 14.

75. Lal, 'Settlement geography', PhD, p. 298; F.P. Gaekwad, *The Palaces of India*, London, 1980, pp. 104–5.

76. *Rewa Gazetteer*, pp. 300, 304; Gaekwad, *Palaces of India*, p. 106; Barr, *Administration of Rewah*, pp. 54–5; *RSA 1926–27*, p. 53; R.S. Misra to author.

77. Misra, *Son ka pani*, p. 158; Sinha, *Raja Birbal*, p. 29; *Rewa Gazetteer*, pp. 37, 39, 42; Sharma, *Vaghela Vamsha Varnanam*, pp. 2, 4, 8–9, 19–20; *Shahdol Gazetteer*, p. 253; Nizami, 'Rewa, past and present', pp. 5–6.

78. RS, Pr Sec Office, 1940–1, 4A/V, 1936–7, Admin, H.D. Sharma 'Some Vaghela rulers and the Sanskrit poets patronised by them'; CIA, Census, 169, 1920, K. Lele to C.E. Luard, 8 July 1920; Bajpai, *Cultural History*, vol. I, p. 145; *Rewa Gazetteer*, pp. 37, 42; R.C. Majumdar (ed.), *History and Culture of the Indian People*, vol. X, pt. II, *British*

Paramountcy and Indian Renaissance, Bombay, 1981, p. 164; Nizami, 'Rewa, past and present', pp. 5–6; *RMCI*, p. 5, pt VIII; G. Grierson (ed.), *The Linguistic Survey of India*, vol. VI, p. 20.

79. Ali, 'The Baghelas', p. 97; Gaekwad, *Palaces of India*, p. 104; Nizami, 'Rewa, past and present', pp. 5–6; Nizami, 'Baghela Dynasty', *JVU*, p. 1; Bajpai, *Cultural History*, vol. I, p. 109.

80. Nizami, 'Baghela Dynasty', *JVU*, p. 1.

81. Nizami, 'Rewa, past and present'; 4; Sharma, *Vaghela Vamsha Varnanam*, p. 6; *IG*, vol. XXI, p. 289. The royal family deity was Shri Ramachandraji.

82. FP, 11 Feb. 1813, 32, J. Wauchope to J. Adam, 17 Jan. 1813; FP, 8, 30 Apr. 1830, 112, GG's office to Commr Cuttack, 23 Apr. 1830. Maharaja Gulab Singh, 1922–46, made the Dassehra celebrations in Rewa one of the highlights of his reign.

83. *JDR*, P, 1818–59, BC 11, 1847, J.H. Sleeman to H.M. Elliott, 20 May 1847.

84. *RMCI*, p. 5, pt VIII.

85. H. Daly, *Memoirs of General Sir Henry Dermot Daly, GCB, CIE*, London, 1905, p. 301.

86. S.R. Ashton, *British Policy Towards the Indian States, 1905–1939*, London, p. 101. For a fuller discussion of the material of this and the following paragraphs see chapter VII.

87. FI, A, July 1887, 186–190, KW2, L. Griffin to FSec, 18 Apr. 1887. Griffin claimed that Venkatraman Singh was the son of his guardian!

88. P, P, 56–P(S)/45, Report, IGP Rewa, 15 Dec. 1945; CRR, CI, P, P, 18(4)–P(S)/42, G.T. Fisher to K. Fitze, 15 Aug. 1942 and 17 Aug. 1942; ibid., Maharrao of Cutch to K. Fitze, 23 Nov. 1943.

89. Lal, 'Settlement geography', PhD, pp. 236–7, 244–5; *MP Census, 1961, Rewa Handbook*, p. xliv; *MP Census, 1961, Satna Handbook*, p. xlviii; *Shahdol Gazetteer*, p. 84.

90. Lal, 'Settlement geography', PhD, pp. 237–8, 241, 247; I. Banerjee, 'A preliminary study of the Maikal plateau of Madhya Pradesh', *GRI*, vol. XXII, Dec. 1960, no. 4, p. 48; *Sidhi Gazetteer*, p. 54; *Satna Gazetteer*, p. 97; *Shahdol Gazetteer*, p. 85; Bhattacharya and Verma, 'Rural settlement forms', p. 297.

91. *Sidhi Gazetteer*, p. 55; *Satna Gazetteer*, p. 98; *Shahdol Gazetteer*, p. 85; *Rewa State Gazetteer*, p. 20.

92. Ibid.; S.K. Jain, 'Environment and nutritional deficiency diseases of Baghelkhand Plateau', PhD Sagar, 1992, pp. 52, 99–100; Biswas, 'Village Mahari', p. 6; McCombie Young, 'Lathyrism', pp. 445–8.

93. *Census of India, 1911*, vol. XVII, *CIA Report and Tables*, Calcutta, 1913, p. 62; *Rewa State Census, 1941, Report*, pp. 31–3; *MP Census, 1961*,

Sidhi Handbook, p. lii; *MP Census, 1961, Satna Handbook*, p. liii; *MP Census, 1961, Shahdol Handbook*, pp. liv–lv; *Sidhi Gazetteer*, pp. 49–50; *Shahdol Gazetteer*, pp. 79–80; R.S. Dube, 'Land use pattern and population in the Lohandwar village, district Rewa, Madhya Pradesh, India', *IJG*, vol. XLIV. July–Dec. 1969, nos 3–4, p. 28; Biswas, 'Village Mahari', p. 13.

94. *Shahdol Gazetteer*, p. 79. Regarding *parda,* the Maharani of Rewa only abandoned the practice during the Sino–Indian war of the 1960s.

95. Tiwari, 'Agriculture and nutritional level', PhD, 1982, p. 170; Kosambi, *Culture and Civilization*, pp. 16–7; Barr, *Administration of Rewah*, p. 209. To Barr it seemed as if the Rewa country was permeated with a 'habitual defiance of all sanitary laws'.

96. Barr, *Administration of Rewah*, p. 210.

97. BA, Witch, 64, 1883; Buch, *Forests of Madhya Pradesh*, p. 28. For the development of modern medical services see ch. V.

98. M.S. Randhawa et al., *Farmers of India*, vol. IV, *Madhya Pradesh, Rajasthan, Gujarat, Maharashtra*, New Delhi 1968 pp. 74–6; *Satna Gazetteer*, pp. 101–2; 104, 347; *Shahdol Gazetteer*, p. 87; *Sidhi Gazetteer*, p. 56; S. Parmar, *Folklore of Madhya Pradesh*, New Delhi, 1992, pp. 47–9; *Rewa State Gazetteer*, p. 21.

99. *Shahdol Gazetteer*, pp. 877–8; *Satna Gazetteer*, p. 95, 102–3; *Rewa Gazetteer*, p. 79; *Sidhi Gazetteer*, pp. 50, 56, 58.

100. *Sidhi Gazetteer*, pp. 48, 50, 58; Parmar, *Folklore of Madhya Pradesh*, p. 124.

101. *Rewa State Gazetteer*, p. 24; *Shahdol Gazetteer*, p. 100; *Sidhi Gazetteer*, p. 68. One such proverb notes': 'He thrives best who drives his plough himself: but average success attends the man who only supervises; while, he who is content with mere reports, soon loses both his cattle and his seed'. See chapter 3, fn. 95. Misra, *Son ka pani*, pp. 101–14, 193; *Satna Gazetteer*, p. 88.

102. *Rewa State Census Report, 1911*, p. 32.

103. *Satna Gazetteer*, pp. 87, 371, 375–6, 380; Misra, Pandey and Misra, 'Lithic industries of Maihar', p. 1; I am grateful to P.S. Dwivedi for the final sentence of the paragraph.

104. *Shahdol Gazetteer*, pp. 9, 322, *Report of the Path Enquiry Commission*, pp. 8, 159; Bhattacharya, *Historical Geography*, p. 271; S.D. Misra, 'Geographical regions of Vindhya Pradesh', *DG*, July 1966, vol. IV, no. 2, p. 70. The *Puranas* describe Amarkantak as a *tirth ratna.*

105. *Sidhi Gazetteer*, pp. 47–8.

106. *Satna Gazetteer*, p. 87.

107. *Shahdol Gazetteer*, p. 77; *Sidhi Gazetteer*, p. 48.

108. Chauhan, 'Spatial pattern of literacy', PhD, 1990 pp. 5–6; R.S.

Baghel, 'Ethno-ecological studies of tribals, with special reference
to the Gond ethnic system', PhD, APS University, Rewa, 1992, p. 1;
Gupta, 'Tribal economy, Baghelkhand', PhD, 1974 p. iv.
109. Chauhan, 'Spatial pattern of literacy', PhD, pp. 5–6; *Rewa Gazetteer*,
p. 69; *Rewa State Census, 1921, Report*, p. 26; *Rewa State Census, 1941,
Report*, p. 50.
110. Shukla, *Language, Ethnicity and History*, pp. 48–51, 78; Lal, 'Settlement geography', PhD, p. 11; *Sidhi Gazetteer*', pp. 38, 46; Parmar,
Folklore of Madhya Pradesh, p. 80; *Report of the Path Enquiry Commission*, p. 24; Grierson, *Linguistic Survey*, vol. VI, p. 122. P.S. Dwivedi
notes that 'some linguists ... recognise the borrowings from the
Mundari into the Sanskrit (including early Vedic) lexicon'.
111. Gupta, 'Tribal Economy', PhD, pp. 51–2.
112. *Rewa State Census, 1911, Report*, p. 3; *Report of the Path Enquiry
Commission*, p. 14; Gupta, 'Tribal economy', PhD, p. 182; *Shahdol
Gazetteer*, p. 85; *Sidhi Gazetteer*, p. 54.
113. Gupta, 'Tribal economy', PhD, pp. 61–2; Baghel, 'Ethno-ecological studies', PhD, p. 43; Jain, 'Environment and nutritional deficiency', PhD, pp. 46–7.
114. Gupta, 'Tribal Economy', PhD, pp. 59–61, 183; S.C. Misra,
'Ethnobiology of tribals in Sidhi district' PhD, APS University,
Rewa, 1986, p. 40; *Rewa State Census, 1911, Report*, p. 3.
115. *Sidhi Gazetteer*, p. 54; V. Elwin, *The Baiga*, London, 1939, p. 107;
Baghel, 'Ethno-ecological studies', PhD, p. 45; Gupta, 'Tribal
economy', PhD, pp. 141–4; Roy, *Planning the Environment*, p. 13.
116. *Report of the Path Enquiry Commission*, p. 12; *Shahdol Gazetteer*, p. 85;
Satna Gazetteer, p. 97; Gupta, 'Tribal economy', PhD, pp. 184–6;
Misra, 'Ethnobiology of tribals', PhD, p. 40.
117. *Shahdol Gazetteer*, p. 85; *Satna Gazetteer*, p. 98; Misra, 'Ethnobiology
of tribals', PhD, p. 40. I am grateful to P.S. Dwivedi for help with
this paragraph.
118. *Sidhi Gazetteer*, pp. 55–6; *Shahdol Gazetteer*, pp. 85–6; *Report of the Path
Enquiry Commission*, p. 13; *Satna Gazetteer*, p. 99.
119. *Report of the Path Enquiry Commission*, p. 13; *Sidhi Gazetteer*, p. 56;
McCombie Young, 'Lathyrism', p. 455; Gupta, 'Tribal economy',
PhD, pp. 187–8; Baghel, 'Ethno-ecological studies', PhD, pp. 43–4.
120. *Sidhi Gazetteer*, pp. 49–50; *Shahdol Gazetteer*, p. 79; *Rewa State Census,
1921, Report*, p. 32; *Rewa State Census, 1941, Report*, p. 31; Gupta,
'Tribal economy', PhD, p. 179.
121. *Shahdol Gazetteer*, pp. 79–80; *Sidhi Gazetteer*, pp. 48–9; Misra,
'Ethnobiology of tribals', PhD, p. 40.
122. *Rewa State Census, 1941, Report*, p. 31.
123. *Rewa Gazetteer*, p. 71; Roy, *Planning the Environment*, p. 24; Griffith,
Kol Tribes, p. 125.

124. *Satna Gazetteer*, p. 103; *Shahdol Gazetteer*, p. 88. The Baiga quotation is from *Sidhi Gazetteer*, p. 58.
125. *Shahdol Gazetteer*, p. 88; V. Elwin and S. Hivale, *Folk Songs of the Maikal Hills*, Madras, 1944, p. 61; Parmar, *Folklore of Madhya Pradesh*, pp. 133–4; Misra, 'Ethnobiology of tribals', PhD, p. 44.
126. Parmar, *Folklore of Madhya Pradesh*, p. 134.
127. *Shahdol Gazetteer*, p. 83; *Report of the Path Enquriy Commission*, p. 14; Barr, *Administration of Rewa*, p. 89; Gupta, 'Tribal economy', PhD, p. 176.
128. *Shahdol Gazetteer*, pp. 83–4; Gupta, 'Tribal economy', PhD, pp. 176–7.
129. Jayakar, *Earth Mother*, pp. 58, 71; Parmar, *Folklore of Madhya Pradesh*, pp. 73–4.
130. V. Elwin, *Myths of Middle India*, np, nd, pp. 71–481 passim; V. Elwin, *Folk Tales of Mahakoshal*, Oxford, 1944, pp. 34, 253, 399, 463, 473.
131. Misra, 'Ethnobiology of tribals', PhD, pp. 1, 19, 89; Gupta, 'Tribal economy, PhD, p. 140.

PART B

THE REGION: REWA STATE

5

Centre and Region in Dialogue: The Government of India and Rewa State, 1803–1922

CR80

While the dialogue between centre and region from 1803 to 1922 was remarkable for its even balance, nationalizing forces gathered pace in Rewa during the period. Initially, the central government's interest in the region stemmed from the need to secure its position as Mughal power weakened and hostile regional forces expanded. Subsequently, too, events in Rewa increased central interference there, the state undergoing three periods of direct rule between 1870 and 1922. Apart from bringing Rewa within its orbit, the central government introduced reforms in its administration that approximated to those in the provinces under direct British control. This ensured that nationalizing political, social, and economic trends affected the state to a far greater extent than at any time in its previous history.

I

CENTRE AND REGION TO 1854

Baghelkhand only gradually impinged on the British political consciousness. The central government was immediately concerned with the possessions of the East India Company and adjoining territories where its interests were at stake. Thus, in the eighteenth century the government signed treaties with Awadh and Varanasi in an attempt to prevent the Marathas from expanding north through Bundelkhand.[1] Not only did the treaties fail to hold, but Chet Singh of Varanasi rebelled and took refuge in Rewa in 1781; and tensions developed between Awadh and Rewa a few years later, alerting the British government to the need to develop relations with Rewa as well.

The Marathas posed the greatest single threat to British interests in central and northern India.[2] In the late eighteenth century Ali Bahadur developed an independent centre of power in the proxy Maratha state of Banda, and across the turn of the century he extended his aggression against Rewa and Bundelkhand to besiege Teonthar, defeat Maihar, and humble the chiefs of Baraundha, Jaso, and Kothi. Though Ali's actions embarrassed his Maratha patrons, when he died in 1802 the Peshwa claimed Banda and even Baghelkhand itself—a claim neutralized by the British victory over Maratha forces in the same year.

Maratha Nagpur remained to threaten Rewa and destabilize Baghelkhand.[3] Sohagpur proved a flashpoint in relations between the two states but, as neither could bend the *tahsil* to its will, in 1807 Rewa invited Nagpur to help dislodge the independent-minded *thakur*. Nagpur promptly occupied Sohagpur and Chandia and, despite strenuous opposition from Rewa, held the territories until 1818. With the Maratha defeat that year the central government annexed Sohagpur and returned Chandia to Rewa, though some years later it awarded Sohagpur and Amarkantak to Nagpur, and this remained the position till 1854 when Nagpur itself escheated to the British crown.

Rewa, too, threatened the interests of the central government.[4] In 1777 Raja Ajit Singh (1755–1809) caused alarm when he conducted the first of several raids beyond his state. Central pressure temporarily halted these activities, but their renewal drew a British force which defeated Baghel and Bundela troops at the 'Battle of the Fords of the Tons' in 1779 before crossing into Rewa territory. This warning notwithstanding, Ajit Singh resumed his raiding; and nobles of Rewa under Raja Jai Singh (1809–34) sheltered persons wanted for crimes in British Awadh. As a result, central forces entered Rewa several times to punish raiders and those who protected them.

Continued disturbances from, or with the connivance of, Rewa compelled the central government to press for a treaty with the state.[5] Although nothing came of this initially, the government claimed a hegemony of sorts over Rewa under the Treaty of Vasai 1802, which signalled the defeat of Pune as successor to the management of Banda following the earlier death of Ali Bahadur. Under this claim the central government garrisoned Mukundpur (south-west of Rewa) and posted a Political Agent to Bundelkhand in 1804. The centre's failure to persuade Rewa to accept a treaty contrasted with the alliances forged with the princes of Bundelkhand which, it claimed, stabilized that region as against the 'fluid and precarious' condition of Baghelkhand.

The raids of Pindaris in or through Baghelkhand further strained relations between centre and region, and made a treaty of some kind inevitable.[6] From the early nineteenth century these horseborne raiders began looting merchant caravans moving along the great Deccan road, in some cases passing unchecked through Rewa. In 1812 Ramzan Pindari of Vidisha plundered Maihar, then swept across Rewa into Mirzapur district, looting villages and factories of the East India Company. The raiders reached to within six and a half kilometres of Mirzapur town, taking the British administration there completely by surprise. Rumours, which the central government discounted, linked the Raja of Rewa with the Pindari raiders.

Nevertheless, the raids themselves combined with the tension between Rewa and Nagpur led the central government to draw the region into its net.[7] On 5 October 1812 British officers signed a treaty with Rewa which acknowledged Jai Singh as its ruler under British protection, but bound Rewa to refer all disputes with its neighbours to the central government. In pursuance of these clauses, Rewa was to permit British troops to be stationed in the state. The treaty also subjected Rewa to a degree of central control far greater than any demands made by the Mughals:

The Rajah of Rewa, being admitted among the number of the allies of the British Government, engages at all times to comply with any just and reasonable requisition connected with the interests and prosperity of that Government, to conform to its advice, and to the utmost of his power to fulfil the obligations of friendship and attachment towards the British power.[8]

The Government of India further compelled Rewa to yield up Kalinjara which had once more come under its control.

However, Rewa was not prepared to submit so suddenly to central authority.[9] The Pindaris continued to use the region as a passage for their raids; but more notably the Raja and his nobility broke the terms of the treaty. The prestigious Rao Sahib of Churhat refused to allow the central government to lay a *dak* line through his *ilaqa*, and denied supplies to British forces there. On 7 May 1813 Sengar landholders attacked British troops near Sattini Itar on the Mirzapur road, killing several of them. For his part, the Raja refused to allow a British news writer into Rewa, and as a snub withdrew his *vakil* from the central government's offices in Calcutta. The government thus accused Jai Singh of being hostile to its 'views and objects', and of being unable to compel his nobility and other subjects to obey the treaty.

After a show of military force and supported by dissident nobles and some citizens of Rewa, the central government imposed a more stringent treaty on Rewa.[10] On 2 June 1813 in the royal camp outside Rewa town the Raja expressed his 'contrition' before the British military commander, and promised to return to 'a proper sense of his relations with the British government'. By this second treaty Jai Singh vowed to observe the earlier agreement; admitted a news writer; and agreed to compel his nobility to permit *dak* lines; to allow British troops from neighbouring territories to pursue 'robbers' into Rewa; and to pay the cost of the British military expedition. The treaty also deprived Churhat and the Sengar landholders of their property rights.

Nine months later, on 11 March 1814, the central government imposed a third treaty on Rewa sealing its further subjection.[11] The government believed that the Raja was instigating the Pindaris to extricate him from the earlier agreements, and in December 1813 sent a force down the Allahabad road, storming the Sengar stronghold of Entauri on the way. To avoid military action the Rewa authorities submitted; Vishwanath Singh, the Raja's eldest son who virtually ruled the state signing on behalf of Rewa, though his father also approved the treaty.

The third treaty marked a distinct shift in the central government's policy towards Rewa.[12] While maintaining its dominance, the government now sought to strengthen the Raja, whose lack of control over his nobility was the 'great obstacle to his becoming an efficient ally'. The agreement thus encouraged the Raja to support a central government which guaranteed Rewa's borders, while upholding previous treaties. Under the treaty the government also transferred the property rights of some Sengar lands to the Raja, while pardoning Churhat. To seal the accord the centre withdrew its troops from Rewa in June, and the Raja declared that his kingdom belonged to the British government.

In keeping with Rewa's submission and the new shift in central policy, the government inserted Rewa into its wider network in central India.[13] In 1822 it placed the state under the oversight of the Agent for the Sagar and Narmada Territories in Jabalpur who was to handle correspondence between Rewa and the central government. This continued at least until 1842, when the government sought to supervise princely states in central India more closely following the Bundela revolt. The Agent continued to look after Rewa together with Bundelkhand, Gwalior, and Jhansi; but in addition the government appointed a Political Assistant for Bundelkhand without separate office, charge, or station until 1853–4, when the post became substantive. These somewhat fluid arrangements stabilized in 1854 when the government formed the Central India Agency comprising the princely states of central India, including Rewa, Sir Richard Hamilton becoming the first Agent to the Governor-General with headquarters in Indore. The Agency thus constituted a band of territory across central India subject to the authority of the central government.

However, despite the treaties and networks Rewa resisted any easy relationship with the centre.[14] Vishwanath Singh, de facto ruler until his father died in 1834, remained at best an uncertain ally with an independent stance towards the centre, secure in his Rajput status and his family's intermarriage with the great families of Rajasthan. Officials complained that he was uncooperative:

During the construction of the road through the Rewa territories [,] objections were constantly started and petty hindrances thrown in the way: the same conduct was adopted towards [erecting] ... a staging bungalow at Rewah, and ... in the Raja's refusal to allow us to establish ferries over certain streams in his territories, ... [or] to forward the Dak.... Officers marching through the Rewa State constantly complain of petty annoyances and impertinences received from the Raja's officers.[15]

The centre also expressed alarm at Vishwanath's Singh's creation of a large army, his warlike postures towards Nagpur, and his going on pilgrimage accompanied by numbers of armed men. However, officers consoled themselves with the belief that he lacked popular support, opposed his nobility, 'screwed' taxes from the peasants, and constructed nothing 'useful' for his people.

Bureaucratic murmurings notwithstanding, Governors-General maintained good relations with the region.[16] Governor-General Bentinck met the ruler when passing through Rewa in 1833; and two years later Vishwanath Singh 'appeared before Lord Auckland' touring in Awadh's Fatehpur district. In 1834 the centre formally recognized Vishwanath Singh's succession to the throne of Rewa on the death of Jai Singh, and invested him with the usual *khillat*. Raja and Governors-General also carried on a cordial, if formal, correspondence.

Several years later the Governor-General proclaimed a policy of non-interference in Rewa, and silenced official tittle tattle by challenging officers to prove Rewa's disloyalty to the government. No less a figure than W.H. Sleeman, sometime Agent with oversight of Rewa, confirmed the state's place in the British arena:

The Rewah Chief first got the title of Rajah about 1760 on the occasion of the Emperor Shah Alam seeking an asylum at Mukundpur in Rewah in his flight before our troops. Before this I do not think the chiefs were styled or considered anything more than Zumeendars. The Rewah Rajah is now received with more honour than any chief in Bundelcund, except Maharaja Benaika Row [of Sagar], inasmuch as he received a salute of 15 guns under instructions conveyed in your letter of 24 August 1842. He had earlier been entitled to a salute under authority of the Governor General's letter to him of 1838, but the number of guns was not before specified.[17]

Though the policy of non-interference in Rewa's internal affairs held, the central government certainly pressed the ruler on matters allied to its interests.[18] Sleeman and others bluntly adverted to the presence in Rewa of bad characters who molested and robbed travellers in the state or in adjacent British districts. To officials, frequent instances of cattle theft were an additional menace, especially when heads of villages or estates in Rewa helped the thieves. Officials loudly touted the case of Guman: under trial for dacoity and murder in Banda, who escaped into Rewa, and was only killed by Banda police intruding into the state at the instance of Sleeman. Sleeman also reported instances of *thagi* in Rewa.

The central government in its moves towards economic integration of the subcontinent also claimed that duties on trade into or through Rewa harmed British commerce.[19] To facilitate the transit trade, in the 1830s the government rebuilt the great Deccan road between Jabalpur and Mirzapur and the branch between Mangawan and Allahabad. However, regional imposts slowed down traffic and threatened to make the north-bound coal trade uneconomical. Central pressure on Vishwanath Singh forced him to abolish transit duties on coal in 1847 while retaining those on other goods, though the centre was unlikely to remain content with a partial response to its demands.

From 1847 central pressures also sought to modify Rewa's social life. The centre began pressing Rewa to act against the age-old practices of *sati* and female infanticide. Official displeasure regarding *sati* peaked that year when British officers witnessed a *sati* from the bungalow on the Deccan road in Rewa town:

We were compelled to withdraw ... having been threatened by the lawless armed retainers of the Rajah, that the consequences would be on our heads.... The suttee was then perpetrated. The woman was ... about forty years of age and seemed to be not in her senses, as if labouring under the effects of stimulants. This has been the third suttee ... enacted at this place in the last six months.... Suttee is said to be openly encouraged by the Rajah and being publicly performed before crowds ... of people.... The smell of the consuming bodies was most offensive....in the bungalow compound. In the Rewah state suttee seems to flourish here in all its pristine vigour.... The Rajah ... had sent a person to stop the business. His messenger never arrived.[20]

Vishwanath Singh abolished *sati* in 1847, but the practice persisted inviting further central ire. Much the same result attended British complaints and royal action against female infanticide.

Brahmanae similarly affronted the sensibilities of the central government.[21] This was the practice whereby Brahmans wounded themselves or murdered their wives, children, and relatives in the presence of the ruler or a judicial officer to protest an unfavourable judgement, thereby placing the victims' blood on the head of the authorities. Vishwanath Singh himself unwillingly witnessed these acts of violence on several occasions and, as in the case of *sati* and female infanticide, tried but failed to stem them.

Integrative influences apart, the policies of the central government strengthened the Rewa monarchy and helped it deal with internal dissension.[22] Safe behind the centre's protective shield,

Vishwanath Singh used every opportunity to entrench himself and unify the state by targeting his nobility and other important land-owners, many of whom had long since abandoned their allegiance to the Raja and usurped the state's revenues. The ruler thus demanded that his *ilaqadars* pay their dues and attend Rewa with troops when required.

To enforce compliance Vishwanath Singh maintained a stand-ing army and (so his detractors claimed), after allowing revenue arrears to accumulate to a point where the landholder could not pay, marched in with his troops, dismantled the fort, and seized the estate or part thereof in payment.[23] Before 1832 when not fully installed as Raja, he reportedly resumed lands worth two lakhs of rent in this way; and though many feudatories sought to protect their independence, Vishwanath Singh proved more than a match for them before, as after, 1834. As a result, once truculent *ilaqadars* and *jagirdars* fell like ninepins before the ruler's strategies.

While the central government could not intervene in Rewa's internal politics, officials realized that the Raja's strong-arm tactics against recalcitrant nobles stabilized the region, and they thus applauded Vishwanath Singh's policies from the sidelines:

The general peace of the country is much more in danger of being disturbed by these petty feudatory chiefs, who occupy small forts in the Jungles, and keep up more troops than they can afford to pay, and commonly infest the roads and set the authority of their own superior Chief at nought. The Rajah's plan, which he has followed systematically ever since his last collision with our Government in 1814, has been of use to the ... tranquillity of the country, and to the security of the roads throughout the Rewah State.[24]

II

REGION AND CENTRE AT BALANCE: THE REVOLT OF 1857–8

By the time the great revolt broke out, Maharaja Raghuraj Singh had been on the Rewa *gaddi* for three years, if effective ruler for a longer period. By skilful manoeuvering, the Maharaja kept Rewa from revolt and maintained connections with the central govern-ment, thereby securing valuable territories for Rewa and somewhat restoring the place the state had yielded in its treaties with the government.

Figure: 5.1 Maharaja Raghuraj Singh, 1854–1880

Born in 1823 and privately tutored, in 1851 Raghuraj Singh married a princess of Udaipur. A son, Venkatraman, was born in 1859. While heir apparent, Raghuraj Singh had tried to unseat his father Vishwanath Singh, as the latter had done to his father many years earlier:

He gathered a large body of troops, intending to seize the Treasury and the Fort. The Fort gates were closed, and the father ... sent an invitation through the High Priest for dinner, i.e. an invitation from the God.... He told his son he would have all if only he waited.... There is now a good understanding between father and son.[25]

From then on Raghuraj Singh aided his father in running the state, formally acceding when Vishwanath Singh died in 1854. The central government recognized his succession, and the Agent for Central India installed the Maharaja in the *darbar* hall of the Rewa palace. A 21-gun salute followed, and the formalities concluded with 'evident harmony and good feeling'.

Despite this initial cordiality, dacoities, *sati*, and an uncertain administration clouded the new ruler's relations with the centre, though the raja's preoccupations gave no hint of these tensions.[26] Of 'unbounded charity' he distributed gold *mohur*s on his frequent travels and pilgrimages; while his 'knowledge and power in discussion' won him respect, as did his becoming an orthodox Vaishnava and disciple of the sage Mukund Acharya whom he appointed *swami* of Lakshmana Bagh. Raghuraj Singh was also noted for his 'genteel manners, handsome personality (and) love of ornaments', besides being devoted to soldiering and the hunt.

In June 1857 the Government of India tightened central control over Baghelkhand by declaring Rewa a Political Agency.[27] Some months earlier the Governor-General had appointed Lieutenant Willoughby Osborne of the Madras Army to attend Maharaja Raghuraj Singh on his pilgrimage to Puri. *Chapatis* (interpreted by some as a portent of an impending agitation) were already circulating in northern India when the party left Rewa, and by the time they reached Puri in March the revolt had broken out in Barrackpore. When the Maharaja arrived in Calcutta on the return journey, ill-health prevented him from meeting the Governor-General, and he returned home as quickly as possible, reaching Rewa in May. Raghuraj Singh requested the centre to accredit

Osborne to his court to strengthen his position at what threatened to be a difficult time. On 17 June the government named Osborne as temporary Political Agent in Rewa, his brief being to handle the political situation in the state and to report to the Governor-General.

A shrewd politico, Osborne understood how crucial Rewa was to the British position in India. The capital commanded highways from Kanpur, Allahabad, Mirzapur, and Varanasi to Jabalpur and Nagpur, besides being on roads to western, southern, and eastern India. The state also adjoined a number of princely states, which would come to the revolt if Rewa gave the signal. As Osborne said: 'all depends upon Rewa'.[28] So began a duet between region and centre that gave a new shape to the government's relations with Rewa and Baghelkhand.

Meanwhile, the revolt began to impinge on Rewa.[29] From June 1857 some districts surrounding the state joined the revolt, and opponents of British rule tried to persuade Raghuraj Singh to support them. Disturbances broke out in the infantry lines in Rewa at the end of July, and in August Osborne reported 'bad feeling' among the *sardars*. In August, too, rebellious troops under Kunwar Singh, Taluqdar of Arrah in Bihar and a relative of Raghuraj Singh, entered the state and massed at the Sohagi *ghat* before beginning their march on Rewa.

Tension mounted in Rewa town.[30] Asserting that he had lost control over his nobles, a panicky Raghuraj Singh accompanied by the *zenana* fled to Bandhavgarh in early September, only to return several weeks later when he learned that the *tahsildar* of Mauganj had blocked Kunwar Singh's passage to Rewa and compelled him to take the Banda road instead. By then, with followers deserting him for not marching on Rewa, Kunwar Singh moved towards Kalpi to aid the assault on Kanpur. Although this relieved the position in Rewa, the *kunwar's* passage across northern Rewa prompted soldiers at Nagod to join the revolt; and reports reaching Rewa indicated that the rulers of Vijayaraghogarh, Maihar, and Sohagpur would follow suit.

The tempo of revolt in Baghelkhand gathered momentum in the remaining months of 1857.[31] The country south of Maihar was particularly disturbed as the Nagpur 52nd Native Infantry passed through it bound for Banda. In early November the Raja of Vijayaraghogarh came to the revolt, killing the *tahsildar* and other

officials. Events began to move in Sohagpur, too. Following contact
with rebels in Rewa, in December revolutionaries there invited
like-minded people in Raipur to join them. At the same time, the
Rewa Army was reportedly divided in its loyalties, and refused to
move beyond Mangawan in pursuit of rebels. At this critical point
British forces en route to Rewa were recalled to defend Kanpur,
while news of the fall of Delhi buoyed the rebel cause everywhere.

Disturbances in Baghelkhand continued on into 1858.[32] In May
an *ubaridar* of Nagod garrisoned the fort there; by July Rewa rebels
rallied in Panna, aided by the chiefs of Jaso and Kothi. Surju
Prasad of Vijayaraghogarh massed troops in the hills bordering
Maihar in September, and in November rebels from Jagdishpur in
Bihar entered Bardi. Rumour also had it that the Sohagpur rebels
were planning to attack Sambalpur. By November, too, rebels south
of the Narmada were preparing to march for Maihar and the north.

However, these disparate moves failed to coalesce into a unified
attack on the British presence in central India.[33] In Rewa town
Osborne and the Maharaja may have known this and, though
Raghuraj Singh was in touch with nobles who favoured revolt, he
did not openly join them, possibly under Osborne's influence.
Chiefs in Bundelkhand, too, remained 'friendly' to the central
government. Under these conditions, efforts from outside to bring
matters to a head failed; and even Nana Sahib Peshwa could not
win over Raghuraj Singh or form a rallying point for the rebels later
in 1858.

In the face of royal inaction, several Baghel *sardars* tried to unify
the agitation in Baghelkhand.[34] These included Dhir Singh,
Lochan Singh, and their leader Thakur Ranmat Singh of Mankhari
in Kothi, whose family also held *jagirs* in Bundelkhand and Rewa.
In February 1858, on behalf of the Baghel clan the *sardars* offered
their services 'for the cause of religion' to the Maratha general
Tatya Tope. The following month Ranmat Singh joined Bundela
rebels in action, but was wounded in an encounter involving the
Diwan of Ajaigarh. Thereafter he and his cohorts took to guerilla
warfare in Baghelkhand, living off the land and taking money from
villages along the way. In August 1858 the group, joined by men
from Banda and Allahabad, camped at Chaukhandi in northern
Rewa under the protection of the Kothi Raja, only to be pushed by
Osborne with a Rewa force towards Kewati. Eluding a search party,
the *thakurs* moved here and there—to Khamariya, Gurh, Marwas,

Changbakhar, Sleemanabad, and even Rewa town. But this very mobility prevented them from organizing any coherent opposition to British influence in the region.

However, the key factor in deflecting the revolt in Rewa and in neighbouring central India was the role played by Osborne and Maharaja Raghuraj Singh.[35] Playing a balancing game amidst central and regional pressures, the Maharaja openly supported Osborne while secretly encouraging the rebels. He reportedly hid Thakur Ranmat Singh within a mile of the Agency bungalow on the great Deccan road in Rewa; and knew that many other rebels were in the capital fomenting revolt. Relatives and old confidants of the Raja who raided Awadh from Rewa similarly stayed in the town. The Maharaja also encouraged kinsmen in Sohagpur to revolt, his letters promising help and informing them of the movement of British troops:

From these letters, it is obvious that in the Mutiny of Sohagpur the Maharaja of Rewa was the guiding hand, though outwardly he desisted from professing any alliance with the rebels. With the shrewdness of a diplomat, he tried to put pressure on the British by creating disturbances from within, while obliging them with military help.[36]

In 1857, however, the Maharaja also came to an understanding with Osborne to provide troops in return for a subsidy: an agreement that outpaced that with the rebels.

Raghuraj Singh cleverly turned his support for Osborne to regional advantage.[37] Earlier in 1857 he had asked Kunwar Singh to leave Rewa, and appointed the illiterate Deenabandhu Pande as Diwan to handle matters on his behalf. Pande was undoubtedly among officials who demanded territorial compensation from Osborne in return for any centrist stance by Rewa. The outcome of these negotiations was a victory for both centre and region. In November 1857 the Maharaja began an offensive against the rebels when Osborne promised him Sohagpur—a strategy that held until the revolt in Rewa died down. Thus, though Raghuraj Singh attended the central *darbar* in Kanpur in November 1858 in fear of detention, he returned to Rewa with Sohagpur and Amarkantak in his pocket, together with the blessings of Lord Canning.

If Maharaja Raghuraj Singh was the protagonist for Baghelkhand and Rewa, Lieutenant Willoughby Osborne was the defender of central interests.[38] Sensing his key role, hostiles tried to finish him

off with a 'stray bullet' as he stood outside his bungalow one
evening in September 1857. About a month later Rewa sepoys and
a town mob surrounded the house. Osborne re-organized his eighty-
strong guard, disarming thirty. He had previously despatched one
of these to the lock-up, but

on careful enquiry I found that the man was not implicated in the
mutiny, and I determined to send him off to his corps. This was not what
they wanted, so a report was spread that the sepoy was to be hung. The
people [were] now excited ... the Sirdars with a lot of their men,
Budmashes etc assembled. I believe the object ... was merely to frighten
me away, but they never calculated ... the effect of excitement on
Budmashes, who resolved to massacre or loot. A more fiendish mob I
never witnessed.... The mob only yelled the more furiously that they
cared not about the Sepoy, but merely to kill my officers and myself,
burn the bungalow and loot. The next day when the Rajah came down
I told him that the British Government would hold him ... responsible
for the action of his people.[39]

Thereafter the mob dispersed, deterred not only by Osborne's
defences, but also by the news that a British force had ascended
the northern *ghats* on the road to Rewa.

The promise of compensation aside, Osborne kept the ruler
and many *sardars* within the centre's orbit.[40] His presence in Rewa
helped calm the *darbar* as well as events in the town. In June 1857
Osborne funnelled the central grant through to Rewa, by which
state troops were sent to protect the northern borders under the
command of Colonel Hinde. Osborne could thus rely to some
extent on these local troops, a factor that persuaded some *sardars*
to support the central cause. A noble, Bisheshwar Singh, helped
protect the Agency bungalow in October and, when Osborne promised to pardon wavering nobles, others 'threw themselves at the
mercy of the ... government'. Osborne claimed, too, that the banias
supported him, and that even the Maharaja 'expressed his deep
regret for all that has occurred'.

Osborne went on to clear the great Deccan road of rebels.[41]
That he did so in tandem with the Maharaja and his Diwan indicates the fine balance achieved between centre and region. In
mid-November 1857 Osborne and Raghuraj Singh joined the armed
force in Amarpatan, and proceeded to open further stretches of
the highway. Following resistance at Maihar, Osborne sent Pande

with troops to encircle the town, which fell in January 1858 together with other forts which the Maharaja hoped to acquire. In the meantime Osborne and Hinde went on ahead, and by early February had dismantled the fort at Vijayaraghogarh, ruling out any further threat from the south. Central forces mopped up pockets of resistance elsewhere in the latter part of 1858.

With Ranmat Singh still eluding capture in November 1858, the centre threatened to invoke its treaties to compel the Maharaja to yield up the rebel.[42] The Diwan thus effected the *thakur's* submission, though the latter had reportedly decided to surrender in the interests of his state. In a poignant moment Ranmat Singh presented himself to Osborne at the *devi ka mandir* outside the Rewa fort to be tried and executed for killing a European in Bundelkhand—a martyr for a cause that was no match for the opposing players. Thereafter, Rewa no longer threatened British influence in eastern central India, and it must have been with some satisfaction that Lord Canning created Maharaja Raghuraj Singh a Grand Commander of the Star of India at Varanasi in 1864.

The Maharaja seized his moment of triumph to strike a further blow for the region by urging the central government to abolish the Political Agency.[43] Canning agreed that such an 'anomalous' and expensive measure should not continue against the ruler's wishes; and in October 1862 the government withdrew the Agency, appointing Osborne to the higher status but lower-profile post of Political Agent in Bhopal. Osborne's assistant C.R. Coles, the Political Agent at Nagod, became Assistant to the Political Agent in Bundelkhand with oversight of Rewa and the petty states of Baghelkhand.

The leading players in these political stakes showed contrasting reactions:

It was not easy for Lt. Osborne to divest himself in peace of the authority he had exercised in turbulence, and the Chief felt that in his presence he was no longer at the head of his State. This was the origin of his application for abolition of the Agency.[44]

But while the Maharaja breathed the Rewa air more freely, Osborne took his transfer badly, even proposing that Rewa become a permanent Agency of the centre—which Canning vetoed.[45] Osborne's detractors within the establishment were overjoyed at his demotion. They had long resented his lone command in Rewa with its direct line to the Governor-General; and had been furious when Osborne announced at a *darbar* in Govindgarh that the centre would recognize a royal adoption failing a direct heir to Raghuraj Singh. Officials in the North-Western Provinces also condemned Osborne for offering the Maharaja Sohagpur and Amarkantak, thereby side-lining their all-powerful Sadar Board of Revenue whose responsibility those areas were. It must therefore have mollified Osborne's critics that Bhopal was at a remove from Rewa, and that the centre had anchored him firmly within the Central India Agency.

III

THE BREAKDOWN OF REGIONAL GOVERNMENT AND THE ESTABLISHMENT OF CENTRAL CONTROL

Though Rewa had rid itself of the Political Agency, it remained within the central orbit, and was shortly to find itself under direct rule by the central government, reversing the regional advantages gained by Raghuraj Singh. There was no hint of this at first, however, as the Maharaja corresponded and sought interviews with the Viceroy; unsuccessfully urged additions to his (now) 17-gun salute; attended central *darbars*; and received central bureaucrats visiting the state to discuss its problems and make suggestions, some even speaking 'seriously' to the ruler when he failed to keep his promises.[46]

Outwardly, at least, Raghuraj Singh remained very much the ruler, entertaining visitors such as the French traveller, Rousselet, whom he received in formal *darbar* at Govindgarh in 1868:

He received us in the audience chamber. Etiquette was scrupulously observed, with nobles ranged on each side of the throne, and the King radiant with jewels and decorations. Everyone rose on our entrance and the King emphatically bade us welcome to Govindgarh. We retired and were conducted into a small saloon, where the King joined us.... He warmly pressed our hands, and frankly declared the pleasure our visit had afforded him.[47]

The Maharaja subsequently paid a return visit to Rousselet, whom he impressed with his 'superb stature ... height of six feet and ...

proud contenance'—here was a 'real Rajpoot, fully sensible of all the importance of his rank and power'.

Yet behind the scenes all was not well in Rewa.[48] After Vishwanath Singh's death the nobility regained their lost independence and reasserted their claims to revenues and dues which Raghuraj Singh's powerful father had restored to the state treasury. Within the *darbar* nobles opposed central interference in Rewa, blocking changes they knew would weaken their power. In the background, if British sources are to be believed, their uneducated sons without outlets for their energies turned to plunder and dacoity. Before such the Maharaja and Diwan were helpless.

The fall in state revenues from 20 to 10 lakhs between 1856–75 was directly related to the nobles' resurgence.[49] Apart from diverting monies within the administration, *ilaqadars* baulked the state of dues, for their incomes had risen since they were first calculated, and there was no way of estimating the amount due many decades later. Many of them had also illegally occupied land which was not assessed to revenue. Non-Baghel nobles, smarting under Baghel subjugation, similarly seized the moment to settle old scores by withholding payments. In addition, the Maharaja freely bestowed land in return for favours and services, further eroding the state's revenue base, while a growing army of contractors took their cut from the revenues they garnered.

Raghuraj Singh was unable to control the situation.[50] Observers saw that the Maharaja was only too aware that Rewa had fallen behind other states, but was too 'vacillating' to do anything, blaming the state's ills on his officials, the new railway to Jabalpur, or the recent abolition of transit dues. Moreover, the ruler had his own problems. All his sons had died in infancy, tormenting him with the prospect of dying without an heir. Indeed not only was the ruler's 'house ... in mismanagement and confusion', his large body was 'soaked with leprosy', and he passed 'sleepless nights', 'demented by anxiety' and at the 'mercy of intriguers'. Central officials were aghast at the results:

The state gradually fell into disorder. The more powerful of the nobles assumed full jurisdiction within their estates.... This was soon followed by others, until the Maharaja lived on sufferance, a mere name, the shadow of a power that had departed. Rewa had become a congeries of small estates, the owners of which had separate interests, mutual hatreds and jealousies.[51]

Though unable to interfere, central officers used their influence in what they saw as the cause of good government and social
reform.[52] They continued to push aggressively against *sati* and
Brahmanae, and used a notable highway robbery in 1867 to compel
the Maharaja to institute high road patrols besides paying for the
goods looted. The central government also acted in several highly
publicised cases of dacoity. It was, however powerless to reform the
Rewa Army and police, accepting that their state was partly due to
low and irregularly paid salaries.

Raghuraj Singh responded in some measure to central pressure.[53] Officials pushed for the clearing and planning of the Rewa
townsite, and by 1869 had made limited progress in levelling the
area and clearing ruins. However, the Maharaja was distinctly cool
to the Agent's educational proposals on the grounds that his
people did not want education. Thus schools begun by R.J. Meade,
Agent, in 1868 and Dinkur Rao, Diwan of Rewa, failed to survive,
though Raghuraj Singh supported a Rewa scholarship at Queen's
College, Varanasi, and contributed to the building of Muir College
in Allahabad.

The Maharaja could take a more positive view of central initiatives on health, as these mostly concerned Europeans in his state.[54]
Osborne had pressed him to open a dispensary with a European
doctor in 1858, medicines being supplied by the central Medical
Department. When the government abolished the Agency, the
department withdrew the doctor and Raghuraj Singh wanted to
close the dispensary. However, Coles at Nagod and the Agent at
Indore persuaded him to continue it under an Indian doctor
despite the ruler's opposition to vaccination. However, the dispensary, reconstructed after the floods of 1867–8, was no match for the
diseases ravaging the region. In 1869, for instance, cholera was
rampant, especially in Satna

among the starving poor. The bodies are thrown into a Nallah to the
west of the Bazar ... [and] very many skulls are to be found lying about
in the jungle, carried there at night apparently by jackals.... Strict and
harsh measures should be enforced on the Rewah authorities in the
Bazar here.[55]

Where the Maharaja saw a benefit to the region, as in famine relief
in 1868–9, he endorsed central proposals and spent vast sums

feeding the poor in Rewa and Satna, thereby earning the 'kindly notice of the viceroy'.

The central government had greater success in pressuring Rewa to accept its economic proposals, bringing Rewa further into line with its country-wide plans.[56] Officials relentlessly pushed road projects, though Raghuraj Singh blew hot and cold over the construction of a road between Rewa and Satna, and was cool to projects further away from the capital, especially as the state had to pay the costs. Defensive regional attitudes also influenced the alignment of the railway between Jabalpur and Allahabad (completed in 1867), such that the line intruded only peripherally into the state through Satna instead of taking the more direct route through Rewa.

It was with a heavy heart, too, that Raghuraj Singh responded to central demands that he abolish duties on goods passing through Rewa State.[57] Despite Rewa's hostility to outside interference, in 1856 the *darbar* abolished dues on thirty-three articles and reduced them on others at central insistence, taxing goods only at the frontiers and Rewa town. When the centre, unhappy with half measures, accused local agencies of levying imposts, Rewa removed duties on cotton in 1861. Under further pressure the Maharaja ordered revenue farmers not to tax railway materials in transit, and abolished all transit duties between Satna and Nagod, matching a similar decision by Nagod for goods going towards Sagar. Finally, faced with the diversion of road traffic to the new railway and urged by the Diwan, Raghuraj Singh abolished transit dues on all goods passing through the state in 1868, except for grazing dues on buffaloes along the Deccan road and an *octroi* on goods for consumption in the state itself.

There was, however, a limit to which the centre or the Maharaja could alter the basic realities of Rewa's social and economic life.[58] Underlying these realities was a self-subsistent economy and largely undeveloped resources. Economic backwardness was in turn related to the lack of communications and Rewa's consequent isolation from the world outside, as a later report from Shahdol suggested:

Backwardness is largely due to [the] invert[ed] tendencies of the population and inaccessibility of a large part of the region. [The] tribal population would not come out of its jungle cocoon of food-gathering

economy. Because of little contact from outside, the non-tribal population also has neither the technology nor consciousness, nor much
need to improve agriculture or to embark on new modes of life.[58]

IV

THE REGION UNDER CENTRAL CONTROL: DIRECT RULE AND THE SUPERINTENDENTCY, 1875–96

It was a measure of Rewa's problems that between 1867 and 1870
Maharaja Raghuraj Singh sought central help in administering his
state. This, together with his death a decade later, led to a central
intrusion into Rewa that brought nationalizing forces to bear even
more forcefully on the region. As a result, by 1896 the administration of Rewa closely resembled that of the adjoining districts of
British India.

At first, however, the Government of India declined to intervene, merely shifting C.R. Coles, the Political Assistant in
Bundelkhand, from Nagod to Satna so that he might visit Rewa
more frequently. The move achieved little.[59] Coles found it unpleasant to prod the Maharaja into action from which he later
retreated, yielding 'to the counsels of those around ... him'. As a
result, officials complained that the state grew 'more and more out
of harmony with the British system' in force in territories on three
sides of Baghelkhand.

Still unwilling to intervene directly, in 1868 the central government persuaded Raghuraj Singh to appoint Sir Dinkur Rao, formerly Chief Minister in Gwalior, as Diwan of Rewa to work under
a newly appointed *mukhtiyar-i-riyasat*, Thakur Randaman Singh, a
distant relative of the ruler.[60] Probably at the Diwan's suggestion,
the new administration instituted courts and offices, began an
English school, replaced revenue contractors with local inter-
mediaries in *khalsa* villages, and induced the Maharaja to abolish
transit duties and aid people suffering in the famine of 1868–9.

However, by 1869 the centrally approved appointment of Dinkur
Rao had failed.[61] Rao had earlier declined appointment as Diwan
unless there was an English officer in Rewa. As the Viceroy refused
to sanction this, Rao lived at Allahabad and visited Rewa as and
when required, besides communicating his views to the ruler from
time to time. As a result, most of the reforms collapsed, though

Raghuraj Singh continued to seek Rao's advice. The experience embittered Rao, who later complained that the state had never reimbursed him for his services, not even to the extent of paying his travel allowance. In central eyes Rao's withdrawal left the confusion in Rewa worse confounded.

In 1870 the Maharaja played his last card, requesting the centre to restore the Political Agency to Rewa and lend money to his bankrupt state.[62] Personal profligacy aside, the ruler had remitted revenues during the famine and spent heavily on relief. The abolition of transit dues also cut into Rewa's income; and in any case state accounting was irregular and much of the revenue did not get as far as the treasury. Establishment pay thus fell into arrears, compelling Raghuraj Singh to borrow from *mahajans* to cover basic expenditure.

The central government, now holding the initiative, set its terms for acceptance:[63] the state was to bear the cost of the Agency to be known as the Baghelkhand Agency, as it included the petty states; and it fixed the loan at ten lakhs repayable at 5 per cent interest in six years. The Maharaja perforce accepted the conditions, and despite an animated debate among officials on the location of the Agent, the Maharaja pre-empted matters by beginning the Agency buildings in Satna in 1871.

The Baghelkhand Agency began with several notable handicaps.[64] The Maharaja found it difficult to repay the loan, and it was some years before officials could effect reforms in the revenue system to enable him to do so. Moreover, the first Political Agent G.R. Goodfellow, true to his name, handed over the first instalment of the loan to the *darbar* to 'do as they liked', the money disappearing quickly without any record of its whereabouts! In 1872 the centre appointed the more worldly-wise P.W. Bannerman as Agent, with instructions not to disburse the loan further until the *darbar* had accounted for the money. The centre also insisted that Bannerman sign every bill, while pressing him to wring repayment from its royal debtor.

Even so, events compelled the central government to assume direct administration of the state in 1875.[65] The Maharaja confessed that he was unable to rule and wished to hand over the administration to British officers while refraining from interference. In addition, despite the loan and the advice of the Political Agent, Rewa made no progress towards financial and other reforms. Henry Daly, the Agent in Indore, argued that though the central government did not seek direct rule, the Rewa debt and the lack of orderly administration was forcing the government's hand. As a result, in 1875 the central government instituted direct rule in the state, placing Rewa even more firmly within its national orbit.

For three years Bannerman struggled with his additional charge, while Raghuraj Singh twitted by his brother chiefs regretted the step he had taken and constantly interfered with the administration, despite his undertaking.[66] In 1877 the Agent's right-hand man Randaman Singh died. Finances continued to be in a confused state. The Agent in Indore could only see 'darkness over all' in Rewa; for J.C. Berkeley, Bannerman's successor, Rewa remained 'a century or two behind' any other princely state where he had served. However, the Agent's control of current finances gave him an edge; and by 1878 Raghuraj Singh had repaid the loan, if from private funds. With this, the centre permitted its Agent to associate the ruler with the management of the state, ushering in a period of comparative stability. Though when the Maharaja died in 1880, officials discovered that he had over twenty lakhs in coins and jewels secreted in the palace: the central loan had not really been necessary at all!

The ruler's death from an apoplectic seizure in February 1880 propelled Rewa more deeply into the central orbit.[67] Before he died Raghuraj Singh placed his four-year-old and only son Venkatraman Singh in the arms of the Political Agent; and though the central Agent, Sir Henry Daly, installed the child ruler on the *gaddi* in October 1880, the delay in doing so masked a debate in the central government on what course to take. By March 1881 the outcome of the debate issued in the Government of India assuming control of Rewa as its 'natural guardian' until Venkatraman came of age, and designating its Political Agent there as Superintendent of Rewa. He was to be assisted by a council of nobles; and an official of the United Provinces, Het Ram, was to be president of the council and Diwan of Rewa.

Colonel David Barr was perhaps the most notable of the Superintendents of Rewa. Gargantuan and genial, but a martinet as regards discipline, Barr left his imprint on Rewa through sheer political flair, never letting the initiative slip from his hands. To gain the support of the people of Rewa, he had to win over the Baghels. Here,

Figure: 5.2 Colonel David Barr, Superintendent of
Rewa, 1882–1886

I had the pleasure between 1882–86 of making the acquaintance of every Rajput thakur in Rewah. Whatever the private jealousies and bickering between different families, I look upon the Sardars and Thakurs of Rewah as a body of well-bred and courteous gentlemen, extremely simple in their tastes, with no pretension to culture or civilisation, innocent of worldly wisdom, but honest and upright, and thoroughly trustworthy.[68]

As a result, Barr enjoyed the confidence of both nobility and council, enabling him to carry out an extensive programme of reforms.

Barr found the Maharanis of Rewa far more difficult to deal with than the Baghel *sardars*.[69] Led by the Chandelin and Ranawat Maharanis, the ladies believed that Barr had usurped their power, and that one of them should have been Regent. They thus subjected the Superintendent to constant villification over the appointment of Het Ram, items of expenditure, and the actions of the council. At one point the Ranawat Maharani took the law into her own hands by sending armed men to compel a debtor to repay her loan, and later retained them in the palace. Barr summoned the 45th Bengal Cavalry from Satna and gave the Maharani twenty-four hours to surrender the sepoys or he would force an entry to the palace. The Ranawat Maharani complied within the given time.

A more serious clash between Superintendent and Maharanis developed over the government's plans for the upbringing of Venkatraman Singh.[70] In 1883 the centre issued rules on the boy's education under an English tutor, and on his residence in new quarters outside the *zenana*, permitting the Chandelin Maharani, the boy's mother, to live with him. Under the rules the other Maharanis could merely visit. The new orders stirred up a hornet's nest, the Chandelin Maharani promptly going into self-imposed exile near Panna, from where she showered Barr with abuse. Though agreeing to return some years later, the Maharani first memorialized the Viceroy and then released details of her treatment at Barr's hands to the press. Despite this embarrassment the centre held firm, and the eccentric but caustic Chandelin Maharani returned to the capital to remain a disturbing element in Rewa's polity.

Central rule also encompassed the areas of finance and the economy, linking Rewa more firmly to the Indian economy. Stabilizing the state's finances was perhaps the Superintendentcy's toughest assignment, for on this depended the state's restoration as a viable unit.[71] Barr's aims were simple, their implementation difficult: to review the entire range of land grants and the revenue rights of all parties including the state, and to deal with those who had illegally acquired property and usurped state revenues. To this end Barr and his successors established simple rules relating to the resumption of grants, to acquired land, and the augmentation of the revenues, insisting that holders not possessing a *sanad* were to be assessed at full revenue and not *chauth*. Armed with these they enforced cash payments to the value of the land occupied, and resumed any land in excess of the original grant. The Superintendents also settled long-standing disputes between major *ilaqadars* and Rewa State.

On completion of this gigantic task, the administration had an accurate record of the state's complex tenures for the first time in its history.[72] This enabled it to issue each grantee with *pattas* (even where these were missing) that contained a clear statement of his dues and rights and the rights of the *darbar*. To ensure compliance the state attached land when the holder died, and only regranted it to his heir after all dues had been paid. The main exception to these procedures related to the *paipakhar* grants to Brahmans, which the centre ruled in 1889 were to be assessed to *chauth* in the fourth generation, or resumed if there was no *patta*.

Agents and Superintendents took advantage of the enquiry into landed rights to redefine the state's claim to other revenues usurped by landholders during periods of slack administration.[73] Bannerman reserved permit, *abkari*, ferry, timber, mineral, and grazing dues to the *darbar*. In 1879 Berkeley placed the collection of customs in the hands of state officials, published the tariff, and authorized collection centres. Barr restated Bannerman's claims and insisted on Rewa's rights to excise revenue, recovering it from those who had established a claim to it. At the same time the state adjusted the claims of the Maharaja's many debtors.

The official claim that Superintendents carried out this massive exercise without opposition was generally correct.[74] Following warnings to the Thakur of Naigarhi in 1882, Barr reissued his *patta* in the old form; the *thakur* paid his dues and in 1882 attended the Dassehra ceremonies in Rewa for the first time for many years. In 1893 the Viceroy visited Rewa and personally interviewed com-

plainants, as a result of which the Superintendent could assert
that the authority of the *darbar* was 'now respected and enforced
throughout ... Rewah.'

The centre took advantage of direct rule and the
Superintendentcy to push Baghelkhand towards the national
market economy.[75] Basic to this was the state's first land revenue
settlement on the lines of those in British provinces, which assessed all *kothar* villages in the state and enhanced the revenue.
With rising revenues Agents and Superintendents expanded road
communications, the centre creating additional rail links and
postal facilities. These facilitated the export of wheat and other
products, and opened up Rewa's rich coal reserves, the *darbar*
handing over mining rights to the central government when private companies expressed disinterest in the venture. Political
Agents also sought to develop the estate's extensive forests, appointing W.H. McKee of the Central Provinces to advise on the
policies to be followed.

In addition, central officials intervened freely in Rewa's social
sector.[76] Nowhere was this more evident than in the field of health,
Agency Surgeon Dr H. Goldsmith laying the foundations of the
state's public health system and dealing with successive rounds of
disease. Despite local apathy, state and centre combined to put
education on to a sound footing. The central government also
dealt firmly with crime which continued on its usual lines, Barr
creating a new police force, building a jail, and introducing a
Western-style judicial system. At the same time he refused to allow
Christian missionaries to work in Rewa and so add to the region's
religious complexities, though as yet there was no hint of any
tension between Hindus and the tiny Muslim community which
was mostly urban-based.

V

THE CREATION OF A REGIONAL SPACE: MAHARAJA
VENKATRAMAN SINGH, 1895–1918

After two decades of central rule in Rewa, in November 1895 the
state came into its own when the Governor-General bestowed ruling powers on Maharaja Venkatraman Singh, who had by then
come of age. Though it was not immediately apparent, the ruler

went on to carve out a role for the region that partly retrieved the advantage gained by the central government during his minority. At the outset the government sought to retain the initiative.[77] Though terminating the Superintendentcy, it imposed conditions on the ruler that curbed his independence of action: he was to consult the Agent on important issues; uphold the reforms of the Superintendentcy; maintain the new roads system; and not modify or cancel orders or transfer officials without the Agent's approval. Venkatraman Singh perforce assented to these conditions, which the centre only revoked in 1907 as the ruler had observed them "on the whole".

Despite the transfer of power, Rewa remained embedded in the British central arena.[78] As earlier, the ruler received central officials, celebrated loyal occasions, and met the Prince of Wales in Indore in 1905. He also hosted regular viceregal visits to Rewa, and at these and other occasions the ruler and Viceroy met and interviews took place, sometimes on a formal basis—though one Viceroy debarred Venkatraman from staying at the Lodge in Simla because he did 'not live in European fashion'. The Maharaja also attended the Delhi *darbars* of 1903 and 1911, being received at the latter by the King–Emperor. From the Residency in Indore Barr's long shadow continued to envelop the region as he 'expostulated' with the ruler for heavy drinking.

However, reciprocation from the centre was not always forthcoming.[79] Although Queen Victoria created Venkatraman Singh a Knight Grand Commander of the Star of India, not previously accorded to a mere 20 year-old, officials later regretted that the centre had got nothing from the Maharaja in return, an ungracious reference to the ruler's refusal to commit troops to the Imperial Service scheme. The same issue resurfaced in the long debate preceding the War Office's appointment of the Maharaja as a Lieutenant Colonel of the land forces in 1914, an honour which Lord Hardinge firmly opposed.

Apart from resisting the Imperial Service scheme, Venkatraman Singh at first gave little hint of the regional initiatives he was to develop after the centre removed the restrictions on his powers.[80] In 1895 he appointed Lal Ramanuj Prasad, son of the late Lal Randaman Singh, as Diwan; and as secretary Lal Janardhan Singh of the Baghel family of Kasaunta *jagir*, whom he created a *sardar* of Rewa in 1898. However, as the Political Agent had the last word in

Figure: 5.3 Maharaja Venkatraman Singh, 1895–1918
(The Maharaja was installed in 1880; in 1895 the
Government of India bestowed him with ruling powers.)

important matters, the ruler lost interest in the administration and allowed 'the machinery ... to rust'. He also had occasional brushes with officers: one Agent in Indore found him 'vain, obstinate and wanting in manners'; and the Maharaja treated with disdain Political Agent Minchin who 'behaved foolishly' with him.

However, despite central pressures regional tendencies came to the fore.[81] Royal marriages were important state occasions, and the Maharaja made three such unions: the first in 1892 to a young Princess of Dumraon in Bihar, who was known as the Ujjainin Maharani; several years later to a Rathore Princess, sister of the Maharaja of Ratlam; and subsequently to the daughter of a Parihar *thakur* of Awadh. In 1903 the Ujjainin bore him a son, Gulab Singh. A second son, later known as Ravendra Sahib, was born to the Pariharin in 1917—seen by some as a threat to Gulab's Singh's position as heir. In 1919 the *yuvraj* himself married a Jodhpuri Princess. Outside family concerns, Venkatraman Singh toured his state and other parts of India, wintered in Govindgarh, bagged tigers, and visited exhibitions connected with his interest in horses and cattle.

Thwarted administratively before 1907, the ruler concentrated on making the state army a regional icon.[82] Though Hardinge dismissed the army as 'real rubbish', the Maharaja worked hard to restructure his forces, converting older bullock and elephant batteries into horse batteries, and incorporating former irregulars into the regular infantry, thereby increasing the army's size and annoying Agents and other central officials. Venkatraman also equipped his men with Enfield rifles and bought new cannon for the horse batteries, all with central approval. However, the centre refused to allow Rewa to cast saluting guns; and was alarmed to find that the ruler had clandestinely imported rifles of a prohibited bore in wartime for personal use!

Alone among the princes Venkatraman Singh held out against central pressure to bring Rewa troops into the Imperial Services scheme, and so render them liable for control by the Indian Army and for service in the field.[83] When officials first mooted the project in 1897, the Agent in Rewa and Barr in Indore claimed that Rewa could not afford the expense. Lord Curzon expressed official displeasure at the Maharaja's lack of response, and raised the matter again when he visited Rewa in 1903. The Maharaja told the Viceroy that he would be disloyal to Rewa and losing *izzat* if he approved the scheme. Curzon was cross:

He seemed reluctant ... mainly on the grounds that the State had never rendered military service to the Mogul Emperors, and that his own army, in which he took great pride, would be thereby weakened. I combated these very childish arguments.... [But] I declined to press him personally, since I attach great importance to the Imperial Service Troops continuing to be a voluntary movement.[84]

To deflect central annoyance, the Maharaja constantly offered his troops and state resources for use in wartime, but each time the government turned down the offer or slighted the ruler in some way.[85] Venkatraman also opened Rewa to recruitment by the Indian Army, but stories of recruits being sent ahead of other troops at the front created panic and paralysed the drive, and by 1919 the army had taken only 162 men from Rewa. In addition, the Maharaja ostentatiously joined other princes in funding a hospital ship; and presented two planes to form a Solanki squadron, though these came to no good: one was involved in an accident, and the other was 'destroyed' in 1917,

At home the Maharaja strengthened his administration, altering *tahsil* boundaries and creating the districts of North and South Rewa of five *tahsils* each.[86] Each *tahsil* was under a *tahsildar* who acted as revenue collector and magistrate, assisted by the local heads of government departments. At the same time Venkatraman Singh appointed Europeans to medical, forest, engineering and other posts.

As part of his quest for a strong regional state, the Maharaja maintained traditional ties with his nobility, appointing them to the administration, his personal service, and to positions in the army.[87] His Highness also visited *thakurs* on the birth of a son or the occasion of marriage, condoled the death of nobles, and performed *pagri bandhai* at an heir's succession. In 1915 he invested the state's premier noble, the Rao of Churhat, with a sword, *saropa*, *sarpech,* and *patta*. In return, most subordinate chiefs and nobles attended the Dassehra function in Rewa with its round of formal visits. Venkatraman Singh also occasionally invited his *sardars* to discuss public issues with him. However, where improving communications and the slow inroads of education were weakening feudal ties and creating noble dissent, the Maharaja dealt firmly with opposition or disobedience.

In other regional postures the Maharaja sought to open Rewa further to the market economy, partly assisting the centre's all-

India initiatives.[88] This included unsuccessful efforts to bring the capital on to the Indian rail network; building roads in the south and east of the state which had 'practically no means of communication'; and the expansion of postal and telephone services. In addition, the ruler bought back the Umaria coal mine from the central government, and backed a profitable agreement with the Bengal–Nagpur Railway to increase the traffic in coal. The extraction of other minerals also expanded.

In pursuit of the market economy the Maharaja moved to develop regional forests.[89] In 1906 he appointed R.M. Williamson Conservator of Forests, and the latter's report of 1906 like that of McKee in the nineteenth century became part of the history of forest management in Baghelkhand. Venkatraman Singh took a positive view of Williamson's criticisms and strategies, and allowed the Conservator to add to the state's reserved forests and begin demarcation. As a result, by 1916 Rewa's reserved forests had grown by over 70 per cent to cover 2,765 square kilometres spread over 33 forest blocks, most of which were surveyed and demarcated. At the same time, the *darbar* began the forest management in Mukundpur advised by Mckee, besides trying to curtail shifting cultivation and felling in reserved blocks, and building up the forest management staff.

The Maharaja, nobles, and distinguished guests continued to hunt in Rewa's reserved forests.[90] As earlier the ruler maintained his own *shikargarhs* there, and was keen to complete the bag of 109 tigers which was considered auspicious and thought to demonstrate princely chivalry. This target he achieved in 1914, celebrated in the capital by the firing of a 17-gun salute. His Highness also initiated his son Gulab Singh into the hunt, and on one expedition in 1916 the *yuvraj* captured Rewa's first recorded white tiger at the confluence of the Son and Tipan rivers. Most distinguished guests were sufficiently fortunate to bag their prey; but on one occasion in 1913 Lord Hardinge, who described Rewa's army as 'rubbish' and who opposed giving Venkatraman Singh a commission in the Indian Army, saw his bison retreat back through the beaters leaving him with a mere *chital*—though the Viceroy bagged his prey on other occasions!

Importantly for the state's finances, Venkatraman Singh endorsed the second land revenue settlement between 1903 to 1918, comprising a regular settlement in the north and summary opera-

tions in the south, both for a period of 12 years.[91] Despite the
problems that delayed proceedings, the settlement increased
Rewa's land revenues by 16.6 per cent, the largest increases occurring in the southern and eastern *tahsils* where the rates of the first
settlement had been low. At the same time, although the settlement did not disturb the Superintendentcy's arrangements for
alienated estates and villages, at the succession of an heir the
darbar took *nazarana* from *pawaidars* and increased the annual
mamla of *ilaqadars*, claiming the right to vary the terms of the *patta*
on that occasion.

Paradoxically, though Rewa's finances improved appreciably,
the state's fiscal position remained uncertain.[92] Fuelled by enhanced revenues from land, forests, customs and excise, coal-mining, and other ventures, Rewa's revenues reached a peak of 47.5
lakhs in 1916–7. Yet almost from the time Venkatraman Singh
assumed office the state spent heavily on famine relief, compelling
it to borrow from Gwalior and the central government. The Maharaja also outlaid more money on education and public works, and
spent lavishly on visits, subscriptions, new railway saloons, and the
grandiose Venkat Bhavan near the modest Nai Kothi of his child-
hood. Much of the centre's opposition to the ruler's army reforms
related to the vast sums expended on it; officials also labelled as
'outrageous' the outlay on the marriage of the Maharaja's sister.

The winding down of the central government's administrative
structures in central India strengthened Venkatraman's regional
stance. In 1911 Gwalior left the Central India Agency, reducing its
size and making Rewa the third most important state after Indore
and Bhopal. By then, too, there was noticeably less protocol about
visits to Rewa by the centre's Agent in Indore, as when Henry Daly
paid a flying visit in 1908 to see the state's famine works:

May I quote the facts as to a recent motor tour which I made in Rewa.
I was enabled by using my motor to travel in two days a distance of some
225 miles and to inspect a number of relief works on which some 10,000
persons were employed, and two poor houses. I was accompanied by the
Maharaja of Rewa, the Political Agent, and my Secretary in the PWD.
Had I been travelling in the ordinary way with a camp, I could scarcely
have carried out this tour and the combined inspections in less than 18
days.... The full expenditure ... may ... be put ... at Rs 500. On the other
hand, if I had been proceeding by camp .... the charges .... may be
estimated ... as .... Rs.2,550.[93]

Informality also marked the connections between the Maharaja and latter-day Agents from Indore such as O.V. Bosanquet, whose relations with Venkatraman Singh 'have been all that is desired', such that when he was to retire, the Maharaja asked that he be allowed to stay on until after the war. The centre granted the request.

Rewa itself was partly responsible for prising off central control by initiating a debate on its financial contribution to the Baghelkhand Political Agency.[94] After assuming office Venkatraman Singh challenged the legality of Rewa's annual payments which had doubled since 1870, and demanded that the centre reduce the Agent's status and his income. While officials demurred at first, in time they realized that as Rewa had its own ruler, the Political Agent's work was more or less confined to the petty states. It was clear from the records, too, that in the 1870s officials themselves had differed on the size of the state's financial contribution, much less committing Rewa to future increments. From 1912, therefore, the Government of India accepted financial responsibility for the Agency whose role in Rewa was then minimal, and permitted the Agent to correspond with the Political Department in certain matters related to the Maharaja. In 1921 the centre abolished the one post of the Agency still funded by Rewa, that of Agency Surgeon. With this, the buildings sold to the Government of India, surplus personnel transferred, and the Satna cantonment withdrawn, the Baghelkhand Agency was but a shadow of its former self.

Officials must have been glad that the Rewa work was much reduced.[95] Twentieth century bureaucrats had a negative view of the posting with its 'shy, suspicious and proud' people, and a ruler who required expert 'handling'. Senior officials believed it important to have at Rewa a man whom the Maharaja liked and who in turn understood him, and such were not always forthcoming. Agents, too, were often deprived of 'European company', while the loss of power after 1907 must have rendered the posting less attractive. Thus from 1907 to 1912

there have been no less than nine changes of Political Agent and six of Agency Surgeon. This is...fatal to efficient working.... His Highness...commented on the frequent transfers of political officers, and said he found it difficult to keep pace with them.... At present the first aim of an officer posted to Satna is to obtain a transfer.[96]

Despite the swing of power towards the region, Rewa's age-old problems persisted, foremost among which was the dominance of self-subsistent agriculture.[97] Large areas remained beyond the reach of road or rail. In a poor and largely illiterate population, the hill and forest people were poorer and more illiterate than the mainline peasant communities. Cholera, smallpox, malaria, and plague continued to ravage the region; while the terrible visitation of influenza in 1918–19 killed 11 per cent of the population and even the ruler himself. Social backwardness and ignorance thwarted efforts to control disease, as people resisted preventive measures. Under the impact of disease and periodic scarcity and famine, population growth rates plunged as people died or emigrated to neighbouring districts. In an environment of poverty, illiteracy, and disease, crime flourished, especially at times of dearth.

Communal tension made its first appearance during the reign of Venkatraman Singh.[98] Although the *darbar's* ban on Christian missionaries held, a church was built in the Satna railway area; while cow slaughter for Christians and others continued to annoy the ruler who banned the practice and forbade the export of beef, though slaughter continued. Tension largely affected the tiny Muslim community, for whom the ruler approved the building of village mosques, but who banned the conversion of Hindus to Islam without the *darbar's* permission. Disturbances over the route of *tazia* processions at Muharram began in Satna in 1902, and occurred again in 1906 when Muslims took the procession through the bazar at Umaria.

VI

THE CENTRAL STING IN THE TAIL: THE REGENCY, 1918–22

Maharaja Venkatraman Singh's death from influenza in October 1918 and subsequent events abruptly terminated the region's ascendancy and returned the initiative to the centre.[99] Before his death the ruler sought to circumvent central interference by urging his brother-in-law, the Maharaja of Ratlam, to administer the state until the 15-year old Gulab Singh came of age. To soothe his friend's last moments Ratlam agreed, though he had no wish to add to his responsibilities. Despite this manoeuvre, an officer from Indore temporarily assumed control of Rewa until the central government appointed A.J.D. Colvin as its Agent in Baghelkhand in 1918, amidst protests from the *darbar*. Ratlam only became Regent on 9 January 1919 with viceregal consent.

Though the Regent governed with a locally selected council, the arrangement proved unworkable due to his outside commitments and diffidence about the venture.[100] In 1919 the government permitted Ratlam to serve as Honorary ADC to the GOC on the Peshawar front, from which he returned in August 1920. In 1921 the centre noted that the Regent was 'frequently absent' from Rewa, and the Maharaja himself felt that his work in Rewa would be more effective if he were there more often. However, his wife's illness and the affairs of Ratlam prevented this, and in May 1921 the centre granted him leave for four months. When he returned in early 1922 his own health was causing problems. By then, too, the lack of 'mutual sympathy' between the Regent and the young Maharaja was making his visits to Rewa more and more unpleasant, though he found a supporter in Colvin.

To resolve these difficulties, the Maharaja of Ratlam suggested that Colvin act as president of the council, and even as Regent in his absence.[101] While this would not end the tension between Gulab Singh and those temporarily in charge of the state, the central government agreed, embarrassed though it was by the suggestion. Moreover, Colvin's style of functioning together with the appointment of Europeans to key posts in the administration aroused adverse comments in the press and probably inflamed local opinion, embarrassing the centre further.

The Rewa administration, whether under Ratlam or Colvin, had a wider than regional vision.[102] The council slashed the size of the army and curtailed the military projects of the late ruler. Colvin, for his part, introduced a budget in 1921–2 and implemented famine relief; spent 17½ lakhs on Gulab Singh's marriage and an initial three lakhs on a third land settlement, in addition to meeting the demands of various departments. The centre naturally approved Colvin's 'careful' husbanding of finances and even proclaimed Rewa 'free from debt'.

Colvin made several other moves that reflected the wider interests of the centre.[103] As noted above, he brought Rewa more into line with the 'British' districts by appointing British officers to head the new settlement operations and the police and other departments. The administration also introduced police and other reforms 'on lines prevalent in British India'. The Public Works Department developed main roads in the north and south of the state; the council approved the Belan canal scheme of United Provinces which the state had earlier rejected; and the Settlement Officer pushed ahead with operations.

Notwithstanding the new central thrust, the weaknesses of the system remained.[104] Accounts for 1921–2 showed a deficit. Those affected by famine still flocked to Jabalpur and Mandla, some dying before relief 'could have any effect'. Education continued at a low ebb in comparison to that of the larger states in central India; and Rewa's communications remained patchy, while the new heavier vehicles pounded roads not built to carry their load. A former Conservator of Forests declined to return to Rewa on the grounds that the administration had not implemented his reforms. Unfavourable seasons to 1921, high prices, and a wartime embargo on grain exports adversely affected trade; while a serious pit fire at Umaria slashed coal production and highlighted the need to put this and other coal fields on to a sound footing.

However, the dominant issue so far as the region was concerned was that Rewa did not have its own ruler.[105] Gulab Singh and his supporters opposed the land settlement and other reforms initiated by Ratlam and Colvin; and took a less rosy view of Rewa's finances than the central government. Also, even though Colvin associated the Maharaja closely with his administration, Gulab Singh was naturally anxious to come to power. Central officials agreed

that the maharaja is probably as well qualified as other youthful rulers. It is inadvisable and productive of harm to prolong the recognition beyond the next cold weather. The Viceroy Lord Reading concurred, and planned to invest Gulab Singh with ruling powers in Rewa in October 1922—though illness forced him to curtail his programme and transfer the ceremony to Indore instead.

Notes

1. FS, 1781, 5 Nov., W. Popham to W. Hastings, 19 Oct. 1781; V.A. Smith, *The Oxford History of India*, Oxford, 1961, pp. 508, 515; *Rewa Directory*, p. 30.

2. *Satna Gazetteer*, pp. 55–6; M.W. Burway, *Raja Sir Dinkur Rao, 1970*, p. 142; Baghel, 'Rewa ke Baghel rajya', PhD, 1991, pp. 121–2.

3. Nizami, 'Early British relations', p. 44; Nizami, *M.P. Chronicle*, pp. 1–2; Baghel, 'Rewa ke Baghel rajya', PhD, pp. 127–31; A. Bhargava,

'The relations of British paramount power with Rewa from 1858–1947', PhD thesis, APS University, Rewa, 1981, p. 84; *Shahdol Gazetteer*, pp. 53–4; H.N. Sinha, *Selections from the Nagpur Residency Records*, vol. III, Nagpur, 1953, J. Adam to R. Jenkins, 15 Apr. 1814.

4. FS, A, 13 Jan. 1777, 8, Lt. Col. Dow to General Clavering; FS, 19 Apr. 1799, 3, Capt. Osborne to GOI, 3 Apr. 1779; FP, 18 July 1805, 3, Raja Himmat Bahadur to GG, 22 May 1803; ibid., G. Grant to J. Ahmuty, 12 and 13 June 1803; FP, 15 Mar. 1811, 94, J. Richardson to N.B. Edmonstone, 28 Feb. 1811; *Sidhi Gazetteer*, p. 27; A.H. Nizami, 'Baghelkhand during the Great Rebellion of 1857', *Princely Historian*, Commemoration volume of Maharajkumar Dr Raghubir Singh, 1944, p. 428.

5. Bhargava, 'Relations of British paramount power', PhD, p. 1; C.U. Aitchison, *A Collection of Treaties, Engagements and Sanads, Relating to India and Neighbouring Countries*, Calcutta, 1909, p. 221; *Satna Gazetteer*, p. 56; Nizami, 'Early British relations', p. 42; Nizami, *Princely Historian*, p. 428. The Raja of Rewa declined to be treated as a vassal of Ali Bahadur of Banda.

6. FP, 15 Feb. 1817, 108, J. Wauchope to I. Lowther, 1 Feb. 1817; Nagpur Residency Records, vol. I, p. 78, Capt. Roughsedge to N.B. Edmonstone, 10 Mar. 1806; NRR, vol. XXVIII, 1812–17, L. 523, R. Jenkins to J. Warden, 18 Nov. 1816; B. Ghose, *British Policy towards the Pathans and Pindaris in Central India, 1805–1818*, Calcutta, 1966, p. 170.

7. Aitchison, *Collection of Treaties*, pp. 238–41; R. Ali, 'The Baghelas: An appraisal', *PP*, Vol. XII, nos 1–2, 1984, pp. 99–100.

8. Aitchison, *Collection of Treaties*, p. 241.

9. NRR, vol. XX, no. 16, J. Adam to R. Jenkins, 4 Apr. 1813; *Rewa Gazetteer*, p. 42; H.T. Prinsep, *History of the Political and Military Transactions in India during the Administration of the Marquess of Hastings, 1813–1823*, vol. I, London, 1825, p. 19.

10. JDR, 1806–59, vol. I, Second Treaty, 2 June 1813; Aitchison, *Collection of Treaties*, pp. 242–5.

11. CIA, Extracts from Typed Records, 207, 1814–55, Sec GOI to J. Wauchope, 15–20 Jan. 1814, and 25 Feb. 1814; NRR, vol. XV, no. 15, J. Wauchope to R. Jenkins, 24 Nov. 1813; Aitchison, *Collection of Treaties*, pp. 246–8; The Marchioness of Bute (ed.), *The Private Journal of the Marquess of Hastings, K.G., Governor General and Commander-in-Chief in India*, Allahabad, 1907, p. 24; O.S. Crofton, *List of Inscriptions on Tombs and Monuments in Rajputana and Central India*, Delhi, 1935, p. 216. The documents do not make it clear whether the action at Entauri was in response to further Sengar attacks, or a retaliation for the earlier incident at Sattini Itar.

12. CIA, Extracts from Typed Records, 207, 1814–55, Sec. GOI to J. Wauchope, 15 and 20 Jan. 1814, and 25 Feb. 1814; FP, 26 July 1814, 67, Raja Jai Singh and Vishwanath Singh to J. Wauchope, June 1814; Aitchison, *Collection of Treaties*, pp. 246–8.

13. JDR, BC, 1818–59, p. 17, 1820, T.H. Maddock to C.T. Metcalfe, 16 Nov. 1820; CIA, BA, 342, 1854, A. Ternan to D.A. Malcolm, 15 Apr. 1854; CIA, BA, 334, 1862–3, J.P. Stratton to R.J. Meade, 23 Mar. 1863; *Census of India, 1901*, vol. XIX, *Central India*, pt I, *Report*, Lucknow, 1902, p. 1; Bhattacharya, *Historical Geography*, pp. 47–8. For some time W.H. Sleeman seems to have held a post as Agent from an office in Jhansi.

14. FP, 1816, 16 Apr. 39–40, J. Wauchope to J. Adam, 18 Mar. 1816; JDR (pre-EIC), vol. 136, no. 626, 1828, A. Stirling to J.H. Maddock, 8 Nov. 1828; FP, A, Ootacumund, 11 July 1834, 17, Maharana Udaipur to GG, 2 May 1834; FP, 21 Nov. 1834, 228, Crown A, Agent SNT to GG, 21 Oct. 1834; FP, A, 1835, 23 Nov., 5, Agent SNT to R.H. Scott, 14 Oct. 1835; FPS, A, 26 Dec. 1846, 572 & KW, W.H. Sleeman to F. Currie, 23 Apr. 1846; Nizami, *Princely Historian*, p. 429.

15. FP, A, 1835, 23 Nov. 5, Agent SNT to R.H. Scott, 14 Oct. 1835.

16. Pre-1920 files, RDO, B. 5, 225–P, 1936, GOI to Maharaja Bishonath Singh, 21 Nov. 1834; Pre-1920 files, RDO, no. 5, 225–P, 1935, W. Bentinck to Maharaja Bishonath Singh, 12 June 1835; FP, C, 8 June 1844, 70, W.H. Sleeman to F. Currie, 25 May 1844; FP, C, 25 Apr. 1846, 262, W.H. Sleeman to F. Currie, 2 Mar. 1846; Baghel, 'Rewa ke Baghel rajya', PhD, p. 162.

17. FP, A, 1835, 23 Nov., 6, R.H. Scott to F.J. Shore, 31 Oct. 1835; ibid., GG's note, 23 Nov. 1835; FP, A, 21 Oct. 1843, W.H. Sleeman to J. Thomason, 13 June 1843.

18. Sleeman P, C. Browne to W.H. Sleeman, 24 Apr. 1835; Sleeman P, W.H. Sleeman to G. Tremlow, 31 Aug. 1842; Sleeman P, W.H. Sleeman to F. Currie, 14 Jan. 1845; Sleeman P, H. Rose to R. Lowther, 31 Dec. 1845; Sleeman P, W.H. Sleeman to G.A. Bushby, 19 Dec. 1852.

19. FP, 8 July 1820, 26, J.H. Maddock to C.T. Metcalfe, 25 May 1820; FP, A, 19 June 1847, 19, Messrs Hamilton Higginson to J. Thornton, 20 Mar. 1847; ibid., 19, W.H. Sleeman to J. Thornton, 6 May 1847; FP, A, 31 July 1847, 171, W.H. Sleeman to the Raja of Rewa, 6 May 1847; FP, A, 21 Oct. 1853, 22, D.A. Malcolm to W. Seton Karr, 10 Oct. 1853; V. Kumar, *India under Lord Hardinge*, New Delhi, 1978, p. 100; Barr, *Administration of Rewah*, p. 160.

20. FP, A, 110, 8 May 1847, W.H.M. Sutherland to W.H. Sleeman, 24 Mar. 1847; Sleeman P, W.H. Sleeman to H.M. Elliott, 8 Oct. 1847; FP, A, 20 Jan. 1855, 45, D.A. Malcolm to FSec, 27 Dec. 1853. Female

infanticide was especially prevalent in Kalachuri, Kushwaha, and Parihar Rajput villages in the Umarkoti *ilaqa.*

21. Sleeman P, Rajah of Rewa to AGG, SNT, 6th Bhadon 1847; CIA, Misc, 1248, 1871, AGGCI to PA Bukd., 17 July 1871. Brahmanae seems to be a word coined by officials, probably meaning 'Brahmans', using a schoolboy Latin form.

22. FP, 14 May 1819, 71, J.T. Maddock to C.T. Metcalfe, 19 Apr. 1819; JDR, P, 3, 1827, F.C. Smith to G. Swinton, 14 Dec. 1831; JDR, P, 1818–59, BC, 11, 1847, W.H. Sleeman to H.M. Elliott, 24 May 1847.

23. JDR, P, 3, 1827, F.C. Smith to G. Swinton, 14 Dec. 1831; JDR, p. 1818–59, BC, 11, 1847, W.H. Sleeman to H.M. Elliott, 24 May 1847. Among those so dealt with by Raja Vishwanath Singh were the Thakur of Jerowah, the Raja of Mau, the Thakurs of Naigarhi, Simeria, and Chandia, and the Raja of Singrauli.

24. JDR, P, 1818–59, BC 11, 1847, W.H. Sleeman to W.H. Elliott, 24 May 1847.

25. FS, A, 26 Dec. 1846, 572 KW, W.H. Sleeman to F. Currie, 23 Apr. 1846; CIA, Extracts from Typed Records, 207, 1814–55, R.N.C. Hamilton to G.F. Edmonstone, 20 Jan. 1855.

26. FP, A, 15 Sept. 1854, 35, R.N.C. Hamilton to G.F. Edmonstone, 25 Aug. 1854; *RMCI*, p. 7, pt VIII.

27. FP, B, 5 Dec. 1856, 30, Sec GOB to Sec GOI, 14 Nov. 1856; FP, C, 8 May 1857, 274, GG to Maharaja Rewa, 2 May 1857; A.H. Nizami, 'Baghelkhand's contribution to the 1857 revolt', *Amrit Bazar Patrika*, 22 Aug. 1957; Nizami, *Princely Historian*, p. 432; Aitchison, *Collection of Treaties*, p. 223.

28. FS, 25 Sept. 1857, 293, W. Osborne to R. Ellis, 9 Sept. 1857; E. Stokes, *The Peasant Armed: The Indian Revolt of 1857*, ed. C. Bayly, Oxford, 1986, pp. 37–8.

29. FPS, A, 31 July 1857, 188, W. Osborne to G.F. Edmonstone, 22 June 1857; FP, A, 30 Dec. 1859, supp. 1300, W. Osborne to G.F. Edmonstone, letters from July–Aug. 1857; FS, 25 Sept. 1857, W. Osborne to R.R. Ellis, 30 Aug. 1857; Nizami, *Princely Historian*, p. 433; Nizami, *Amrit Bazar Patrika*, p. 2; R.C. Majumdar, *The Sepoy Mutiny and the Revolt of 1857*, Calcutta, 1957, pp. 166–7; *Rewa Gazetteer*, pp. 13–14.

30. FS, 25 Sept. 1857, W. Osborne to R. Ellis, 9 Sept. 1857; FPS, 25 Sept. 1857, 303, W. Osborne to Sec GOI, 10 Sept. 1857; FP, A, 30 Dec. 1859, supp. 1300, W. Osborne to G.F. Edmonstone, 27 Sept. 1858; A.H. Nizami, 'Baghelkhand during 1857', *Durbar College Magazine, 1956–57*, p. 6; Nizami, *M.P. Chronicle*, pp. 2–4; Stokes, *The Peasant Armed*, p. 36; *Rewa Gazetteer*, pp. 43–4. Rewa had matrimonial connections with Nagod, Raghuraj Singh being the son of a Parihar

rani from the Nagod royal family married to Vishwanath Singh.

31. FS, A, 18 Dec. 1857, 617, B. Strachey to GG, 23 Sept. 1857; FP, A, 30 Dec. 1859, supp. 1300, W. Osborne to G.F. Edmonstone, 27 Sept. 1858; FS, A, 18 Dec. 1857, B. Strachey to GG, 28 Sept. 1857; FS, A, 18 Dec. 1857, 690, GG to Lt. Gov. Benares, 17 Oct. 1857; K. Jha, 'A study of some Mutiny letters of Sohagpur', *IHRC Proceedings*, vol. XXXIII, pt 2, 1958, pp. 105–8; D.P. Misra, *History of Freedom Movement in Madhya Pradesh*, Nagpur, 1956, p. 83; *Shahdol Gazetteer*, p 55; Nizami, *Durbar College Magazine*, p. 6; S.B. Chaudhuri, *Civil Rebellion in the Indian Mutinies, 1857–1859*, Calcutta, 1957, pp. 318–29.

32. FS, A, 27 Aug. 1858, 88, W. Osborne to G.F. Edmonstone, 6 July 1858; FP, A, 30 Dec. 1858, Supp. 1300, W. Osborne to G.F. Edmonstone, 27 Sept. 1858; FP, A, June 1862, encl. in 159, C.R. Denison to A. Shakespear, Oct.–Nov. 1858; FP, A, 31 Dec. 1858, 3829, R.B. Chapman to G.F. Edmonstone, 12 Nov. 1858; FP, A, 31 Dec. 1858, 2515, W. Osborne to G.F. Edmonstone, 17 Nov. 1858.

33. FS, H.M. Durand to G.F. Edmonstone, 29 Jan. 1858; R. Hilton, *The Indian Mutiny: A Centenary History*, London, 1957, p. 68; Nizami, *Durbar College Magazine*, p. 5; Stokes, *The Peasant Armed*, p. 37.

34. FP, 3 Sept. 1858, 283, G.F. Edmonstone to W. Osborne, 25 Aug. 1858; FP, A, 29 Oct. 1858, 106, W. Osborne to G.F. Edmonstone, 3 Sept. 1858; Nizami, *Durbar College Magazine*, pp. 3, 7–8, 10; Nizami, *Amrit Bazar Patrika*, p. 3; Nizami, *Princely Historian*, pp. 434, 436, 439; Bhargava, 'Relations of British paramount power; PhD, p. 93.

35. Nizami, *Durbar College Magazine*, pp. 5, 9; Nizami, *M.P. Chronicle*, p. 5; Ali, 'The Baghelas: an appraisal', p. 100; Bhargava, 'Relations of British paramount power', PhD, p. 94; Jha, 'Some Mutiny letters', p. 108. The subsidy paid to Rewa amounted to seven lakhs.

36. Jha, 'Some Mutiny letters', p. 108.

37. See FP, 13 Aug. 1858, 320 and KW, G.F. Edmonstone to PA Rewa, 8 Apr. 1858; Nizami, *Princely Historian*, pp. 437–8; Nizami, *Durbar College Magazine*, pp. 7, 9; Ali, 'The Baghelas: an appraisal', pp. 100–1; *Shahdol Gazetteer*, p. 55; *Rewa Gazetteer*, pp. 46–7; Baghel, 'Rewa ke Baghel rajya', PhD, p. 226.

38. FS, 25 Sept, 1857, 293, W. Osborne to R. Ellis, 9 Sept. 1857; FPS, 25 Sept. 1857, 303, W. Osborne to Sec GOI, 10 Sept. 1857; FS, 18 Dec. 1857, 688, Lt. Gov. to GG, 10 Oct. 1857; FPS 28 Nov. 1857, 154, W. Osborne to G.F. Edmonstone, 30 Oct. 1857; *Rewa Gazetteer*, p. 45.

39. FPS, 27 Nov. 1857, 154, W. Osborne to G.F. Edmonstone, 30 Oct. 1857.

40. FPS, 25 Sept. 1857, 304, W. Osborne to G.F. Edmonstone, 15 Sept. 1857; FS, A, 30 Oct. 1857, 216, W. Osborne to G.F. Edmonstone, 7 Oct. 1857; FPS, A, 30 Oct. 1857, 217, W. Osborne to G.F. Edmonstone, 11 Oct. 1857; FP, A, 30 Dec 1859, Supp. 1300, W. Osborne to G.F.

Edmonstone, 27 Sept. 1858; Nizami, *Durbar College Magazine*, p. 5.
41. FS, 27 Nov. 1857, 16, W. Osborne to G.F. Edmonstone, 9 Nov. 1857; FP, A, 30 Dec. 1859, Supp. 100, W. Osborne to G.F. Edmonstone, 17–20 Dec. 1857; FS, A, 26 Mar. 1858, 187, W. Osborne to C. Beadon, 9 Feb. 1858; FP, A, 13 Aug. 1858, 327–A, W. Osborne to G.F. Edmonstone, 27 Apr. 1858; FP, A, 30 Dec. 1859, Supp. 1300, W. Osborne to G.F. Edmonstone, 27 Sept. 1858; FP, A, 5 Nov. 1858, 98, W. Osborne to G.F. Edmonstone, 6 Oct. 1858; Nizami, *Princely Historian*, pp. 435–6; *Rewa Gazetteer*, p. 46; S.N. Sinha, *The Revolt of 1857 in Bundelkhand*, Lucknow, 1982, p. 112.
42. FP, A, 10 Oct. 1858, 17, G.F. Edmonstone to PA Rewah, 14 Sept. 1858; Nizami, *Princely Historian*, pp. 434, 439; Nizami, *Durbar College Magazine*, p. 9.
43. FG, A, Oct. 1862, 85, Resn no. 2013/7, 24 Oct. 1862; FG, A, Oct. 1862, 86, Notification, F, 24 Oct. 1862, FG, A, 87, GG to Maharaja Rewah, 24 Oct. 1862; CIA, BA, 334, 1862–3; E.C. Bayley to R.J. Meade, 4 Feb. 1863; Nizami, *Princely Historian*, p. 439.
44. FP, A, 66, Aug. 1870, H.D. Daly to C.U. Aitchison, 21 June 1870.
45. FP, 139, 3 Sept. 1858, R. Hamilton to G.F. Edmonstone, 7 July 1858; F, 18, SOS to GG, 8 Mar. 1860; F, A, 769, Dec. 1860, W. Osborne to W.H. Elliott, 2 July 1860; FG, A, Oct. 1862, 857–88, File note, Signature illegible, 5 Aug. 1862; CIA, BA, 344, 1862–3, J.P. Stratton to R.J. Meade, 12 Dec. 1862; CIA, BA, 334, 1862–3, E.C. Bayley to R.J. Meade, 4 Feb. 1863.
46. FG, B, June 1862, 149, C.R. Coles to FSec, 28 May 1862, and other such letters; CIA, BA, 359, 1865–6, W. Muir to AGGCI, 18 Oct. 1865; FP, A, Aug.1870, 68, Note by H. le P.W., 2 July 1870; Daly, *Memoirs*, p. 300.
47. Rousselet, *India and its Native Princes*, pp. 366, 371, 374.
48. BA, 7, 1867, R.J. Meade to I.W.S. Wyllie, 21 Jan. 1867; Barr, *Administration of Rewah*, pp. 9–10, 19; Daly, *Memoirs*, pp. 299–300; Burway, *Dinkur Rao*, pp. 144–5.
49. FP, A, 18 Apr. 1856, 29, PA Rewah to G.F. Edmonstone, 26 Mar. 1856; CIA, BA, 432, 1875–6, P.W. Bannerman to H. Daly, 6 Nov. 1875; pre-1920 files, RDO, B, 1, 1882–99, Sup., D.W.K. Barr to AGGCI, 27 Mar. 1885; FI, A, July 1890, 293, D. Robertson, Note on Rewah Re-Settlement, 31 Mar. 1890; *CIA Report, 1867–68*, pp. xxviii, 42; *CIA Report, 1868–69*, p. cxxix; Daly, *Memoirs*, p. 299.
50. BA, 7, 1867, R.J. Meade to I.W.S. Wyllie, 21 Jan. 1867; FP, A, July 1868, 63, AGGCI to FSec, 4 June 1868; BA, 4, 1870, AGGCI to FSec, 21 June 1870; FP, A, Aug. 1870, 68, Memo of J.P. Stratton, encl in H. Daly to C.U. Aitchison, 21 June 1870; Burway, *Dinkur Rao*, pp. 136, 144–5; *RMCI*, p. 7, pt VIII.
51. Barr, *Administration of Rewah*, p. 19.

52. FP, A, Dec. 1862, 282, Petition of Gooha, recd 27 Sept. 1862; FP, A, May 1865, 17, R. Simson to AGGCI, 13 Apr. 1865; CIA, PO, 942, 1867–8, Letters from 7–25 Mar. 1867; CIA, Misc, 1248, 1871, AGGCI to PA, 17 July 1871; FP, A, Dec. 1873, 104, AGGCI to FSec, 28 Oct. 1873; BA, 7, 1867, R.J. Meade to J.P. Stratton, 22 Feb. 1887; *CIA Report, 1865–66*, p. 54; *CIA Report, 1867–68*, pp. 34–5; Barr, *Administration of Rewah*, p. 126.

53. FG, A, Dec. 1864, 32, J.P. Stratton to R.J. Meade, 28 Nov. 1864; CIA, 6, 1869, C.R. Coles to J.P. Stratton, 24 June 1865; CIA, G(Fam), 697, 1869, PA Bukd to AGGCI, 30 June 1869; *CIA Report, 1865–66*, p. 54; *CIA Report, 1868–69*, p. xcv; *Rewa Gazetteer*, p. 234.

54. BA, 4, 1863, C.R. Coles to J.P. Stratton, 20 May 1863; CIA, 291, 1863–98, Dispensaries, R.J. Meade to J.P. Stratton, 3 June 1863, and J.P. Stratton to R.J. Meade, 19 Dec. 1863; FG, A, Jan 1864, 54–7, KW, File note, J.T.W., 15 Jan 1864; FP, A, Aug. 1869, 73, H. Daly to W.S. Seton Karr, 26 July 1869; *CIA Report, 1867–68*, p. 40; *CIA Report, 1869–70*, p. lxiii.

55. CIA, G(Fam), 690, 1869, T. Wakley to C.R. Coles, 3 June 1869.

56. F.A., 1861, 184, C.R. Coles to PS, GG. 25 July 1861; CIA, Railway, 1450, 1869, PA Bukd to AGGCI, 8 June 1869; *CIA Reports* for the 1860s and 1870s; *Census of India, 1961*, vol. VIII, *Madhya Pradesh*, p. 192; Barr, *Administration of Rewah*, p. 160. Both K. Fitze, *Twilight of the Maharajas*, London, 1956, p. 92, and Corfield, *Princely India*, p. 61, claim that the ruler was so horrified at the prospect of rail passengers eating beef while passing through Rewa that he pushed for the present western alignment. In all probability, Raghuraj Singh pressed the central government to agree to the alignment by conceding the abolition of transit dues.

57. CIA, Transit Duties, 499, 1856, F.J.H Helbert to R. Hamilton, 13 Aug. 1856; FR, A, Nov. 1861, 74–6, C.R. Coles to H.M. Durand, 17 Oct 1861; FR, A, Dec. 1863, 6, C.R. Coles to J.P. Stratton, 30 Oct. 1863; CIA, Transit Duties, 504, 1865, C.R. Coles to J.P. Stratton, 22 Mar. 1865; CIA, BA, 393, 1868, C.U. Aitchison to R.J. Meade, 6 July 1868; FP, A, Oct. 1868, 343, R.J. Meade to W.S. Seton Karr, 9 Oct. 1868; BA, 12, 1879, Asst Collector, Mirzapur, 20 Nov. 1978.

58. S.K. Sharma, 'Changing pattern of resources', PhD, p. 349.

59. CIA, PO, 942, 1867, 1867–68, PA Bukd to AGGCI, 16 Sept. 1867; *CIA Report, 1867–68*, pp. xcv–xcvi; *CIA Report, 1869–70*, p. lvii; Aitchison, *Collection of Treaties*, p. 223.

60. CIA, BA, 383, 1868–72, Maharaja Rewa to AGGCI, 3 July 1868; CIA, BA, 388, C.R. Coles to J.P. Stratton, 10 Aug. 1868; FP, A, 66, Aug. 1870, H. Daly to C.U. Aitchison, 21 June 1870; *CIA Report, 1867–68*, p. 42; *CIA Report, 1868–69*, p. xc; *CIA Report, 1869–70*, p. xlii; *IG*, vol.

XXI, p. 288. Dinkur Rao replaced the powerful Deenabandhu Pande, the Maharaja's right-hand man during the revolt of 1857–8.

61. BA, 7, 1867, R.J. Meade to C.U. Aitchison, 10 July 1868; CIA, BA, 383, 1868–72, H. Daly to H. le P. Gwynne, 2 Oct. 1872; *CIA Report, 1868–69*, pp. xc, cxxxii; *CIA Report, 1869–70*, pp. xlii–xliii; Aitchison, *Collection of Treaties*, p. 223.

62. FP, A, Aug. 1870, H. Daly to C.U. Aitchison, 21 June 1870; CIA, BA, 383, 1868–72, H. Daly to H. le P. Gwynne, 2 Oct. 1872; *CIA Report, 1874–75*, p. xli. The ruler spent heavily on pilgrimages, royal marriages, and jewellery.

63. FP, A, 66–8 KW, Aug. 1870, Mayo, 9 July 1870; FP, A, Dec. 1870, 5, H. Daly to C.U. Aitchison, 25 Aug. 1870; FP, A, Dec. 1870, 527–33 KW, C.U.A C.U. Aitchison, 29 Nov. 1870; FP, A, July 1871, 118, SOS to GOI, 2 Mar. 1871; FP, A, Jan. 1872, 69–71, H. Daly to C.U. Aitchison, 11 Dec. 1871; FP, B, Aug. 1874, 107–8, KW, File note, H.D., Aug. 1874.

64. FP, A, Mar. 1872, 379, SOS to GOI, 29 Feb. 1872; FP, A, Mar. 1872, 389–94 KW, P.D.H., 15 Mar. 1872; FP, B, May 1874, 92–4 KW, AGGCI, 4 Mar. 1874; FP, B, Aug. 1874, 107–8 KW, File note, H.D., Aug. 1874; CIA, BA, 432, 1875–76, P.W. Bannerman to H. Daly, 6 Nov. 1875.

65. FP, A, Mar. 1875, 398–401 KW, C.U. Aitchison to GG, 19 Feb. 1875; *Shahdol Gazetteer*, p. 56; Aitchison, *Collection of Treaties*, p. 250.

66. CIA, BA, 432, 1875–6, P.W. Bannerman to H. Daly, 6 Nov. 1875; BA, 2, 1875, H. Daly to FSec, 10 Apr. 1877; FG, B, Nov. 1877, 84, P.W. Bannerman to H. Daly, 1 Oct. 1877; FP, B, Feb. 1878, 131, H. Daly to C.U. Aitchison, 19 Nov. 1877; FP, B, Feb. 1878, 131–3 KW, C.M.D., 23 Jan. 1878; pre-1920 Files, RDO, B 1, 1882–99, 99, Sup, R.J. Meade to Col. Biddulph, 13 Sept. 1887; Barr, *Administration of Rewah*, pp. 17–8.

67. FP, A, Aug. 1880, 142, J.C. Berkeley to AGGCI, 6. Feb. 1880; FP, A, Aug. 1880. 137. AGGCI to FSec, 24 Mar. 1880; *CIA Report, 1880–81*, p. 149; *Rewa Gazetteer*, p. 48; Barr, *Administration of Rewah*, pp. 22–26; *RMCI*, p. 8, pt. VIII.

68. Barr, *Administration of Rewah*, p. ?

69. FP, A, May 1882, 121, L. Griffin to C. Grant, 6 Mar. 1882; FP, B, 1, Nov. 1882, 22–7 KW, J.H., 11 Oct. 1882; FI, B, Sept. 1887, 156, Shri Chandelin Maharani, 21 Aug. 1887; Barr, *Administration of Rewah*, p. 43.

70. FG, A, Nov. 1883, 12, D.W.K. Barr to AGGCI, 11 Sept. 1883; FGI, A, Nov. 1883, 11–4 KW, FSec, 29 Sept. 1883; FI, B, Mar. 1888, 41, Viceroy to Maharanis of Rewa, 28 Aug. 1888; FI, A, Jan. 1889, 140, Maharanis to Earl of Dufferin, 2 Oct. 1888; FI, A, Aug. 1889, 231–41 KW, M.L. Ghosh, 16 July 1889; FI, A, Aug. 1889, 239. A.H.T.

Martindale to FSec, 17 July 1889; FI, A, Aug. 1889, 241, W.H.
Cornish to AGGCI, 14 Aug. 1889; FI, A, June 1890, 87, D. Robertson
to AGGCI, 24 Feb. 1890.

71. FP, A, May 1882, 121, L. Griffin to C. Grant. 6 Mar. 1882; pre-1920
files, RDO, B. 6, 1882–99, 87, Sup, D.W.K. Barr, Mar. 1885; pre-1920
files, RDO, B 6, (II), 7/2, Rev I, 1887, D.W.K. Barr to Diwan of
Rewah, 13 Mar. 1888; FI, A, Sept. 1890, 91, Note on alienations of
land in Rewa, D. Robertson, 18 June 1890; FI, A, Aug. 1893, 27, D.
Robertson to AGGCI, 14 June 1893. Under the new arrangements
Superintendents settled old disputes with *ilaqadars* holding the
estates of Churhat, Singrauli, Sidhi, Bardi, Naigarhi, Marwas, and
Chandia, among others. See also the *Report of the Committee Ap-
pointed to Enquire into the Nature of Pawai Tenures in Rewa State,*
Allahabad, 1934.

72. Pre-1920 files, RDA, B 1, 1882–99, 129, Sup, Het Ram to D.W.K.
Barr, 9 Oct. 1884; FI, A, Sept. 1890, 91, D. Robertson, Note, 18 June
1890; FI, A, Aug. 1893, 27, D. Robertson to AGGCI, 14 June 1893;
Pre-1920 files, RDO, B 6(II), 7/2, Rev, I, 1906, J. Prasad to PA, 18
June 1906.

73. FP, A, Oct. 1881, 37, Proclamation of Maharaja Raghuraj Singh,
1873; FP, B, Apr. 1882, 126, encl. 12, D.W.K. Barr to AGGCI, 19 Sept.
1881; Barr, *Administration of Rewah,* pp. 41, 85, 88–9.

74. BA, Eng. files, pt III, 427, 1929, citing Vern. 246/133 of 1882; FS-I,
May 1893, 20–9 KW2, D. Robertson, 15 Apr. 1893; *CIA Report, 1889–
90,* p. 45; Barr, *Administration of Rewah,* pp. 37–9.

75. FI, A, Mar. 1886, 159, L. Griffin to H.M. Durand, 3 July 1885; *CIA
Report, 1883–84,* p. 168; T.W.H. Hughes, 'The southern coalfields
of the Rewah–Gondwana basin', *MGSI,* vol. XXI, pt 3, Calcutta,
1895, pp. 21–5; Govt of M.P., Forest Dept, *Working Plan for Rewa
Forest Division, Rewa Circle, M.P., 1982/3 to 1991/2,* vol. I, pt I, p. 191;
Forest Management Plan, North Shahdol and Umaria Divisions, vol. I, p.
81; *Rewa Gazetteer,* pp. 179–82; Aitchison, *Collection of Treaties,* p. 224;
Barr, *Administration of Rewah,* p. 199; Bomford, *Final Settlement
Report,* p. 18. For communications Barr made Rewa the hub of an
expanding road system, opening connections with the south across
the Kaimur. The chief new railway was that from Katni to Bilaspur
through Umaria, 1886–91. Coal mining began at Umaria in 1883.
In calling for private investment in coal mining, the government
insisted that companies develop the necessary rail links to the
mines. Companies were then unwilling to so invest, though they
were prepared to put money into mining. Rewa's revenues rose
from Rs 10 lakhs in 1872 to average Rs 14 lakhs from 1890–1900,
the collections in 1894–5 being over Rs 17 lakhs.

76. FG-I, A, Apr. 1883, D.W.K. Barr to Rev. G.W. Jackson, 26 Dec. 1882;
FI, B, May 1891, 578, Appx F to CIA Report, 1880–81; for education
and health see annual issues of the *CIA Reports, District Gazetteers,* and
Barr, *Administration of Rewah,* pp. 114, 116–17, 121. Crimes such as
murder, affray, theft, illegal distilling, *dakaiti* and cattle lifting continued.
77. FI, A, Dec. 1895, 157–64 KW2, D.W.K. Barr to W.J. Cunningham, 19
Aug. 1895; FI, A, Dec. 1895, 157, D.W.K. Barr to FSec, 16 Sept. 1895;
CIA (Calcutta files), 10, 1897, W.M. Cubitt to AGGCI, 3 Oct. 1905;
FI, A, Apr. 1907, Notes, J.B., 21 Feb. 1907; ibid., M(into), 3 Mar.
1907; *RMCI,* p. 8, Pt VIII; Aitchison, *Collection of Treaties,* p. 224.
78. FI, B, Mar. 1892, 427, TG, W.J.C. to CI, 23 Mar. 1892; FE, A, Sept.
1902, 68, Viceroy to SOS, 15 Aug. 1902; FI, A, Apr. 1907, 87–8,
Notes, J.B., 21 Feb. 1907; FI, B, May 1913, Notes, A.H. MacMahon,
28 Feb. 1913; CIA, P.A., 1902–47, 104–A, 1916. O.V. Bosanquet to
J.B. Wood, 30 Aug. 1916; *RSA, 1911–12,* pp. 2–5; S. Playne, *Indian
States: A Biographical, Historical and Administrative Survey,* London,
1921–2, p. 246. Lord Hardinge vetoed Venkatraman Singh's stay
in the Lodge at Simla.
79. FS-I, Oct. 1903, 1–3 KW, C.S. Bayley to W. Lawrence, 1 June 1903;
FS-I, July 1913, 134, M.F. O'Dwyer, Mar. 1913; ibid., Notes, H.
Wilkinson, 1 May 1913, and H(ardinge), 19 May 1913; FPSI, Apr.
1915, 12, GOI to SOS, 29 Oct. 1914; Aitchison, *Collection of Treaties,*
p. 224; *RMCI,* p. 8, pt VIII.
80. FI, A, 1907, 87–8, Notes, J.B., 21 Feb. 1907; FE, B, Jan. 1909, 212–
61, E.H.S. Clarke, 17 Aug. 1908; FE, D, Oct. 1908, 9, H. Daly to H.
Butler, 10 Oct. 1908; Indian States Committee, *Evidence,* vol. II,
London, 1928, pp. 1279–81; *RMCI,* pp. 11, 13, pt VIII.
81. CIA, BA, 702, 1901–3, Maharaja Rewa to AGGCI, 12 Mar. 1903; FPI,
D, July 1919, 30, Gulab Singh to GG, 11 June 1919; *RSA, 1909–10,*
p. 1; *RSA, 1916–17,* p. 1.
82. FS-I, Apr. 1909, 2–5, Notes, J.B. Wood, 15 Sept. 1908; FS-I, Oct. 1910,
57–8, Notes, F.A.E., 31 Aug. 1910; FPSI, Sept. 1915, 7–10, Notes,
G.P.D., 8 July 1915, and H (ardinge), 13 Aug. 1915; FPG, A, Nov.
1915, 14–16, Notes, G.B.T., 23 Sept. 1915; ibid., 16, H.V. Biscoe to
AGGCI, 9 Nov. 1915; FPI, B, Sept. 1916, 25, R.E. Holland to AGGCI,
4 Aug. 1916; FPI, B, May 1920, 10, F.G. Beville to J. Wood, 14
Mar. 1920; *RSA, 1906–07,* pp. 5–6. Between 1895 and 1914 enrol-
ments in the Rewa Army rose as follows: cavalry, from 283 to 706;
infantry, from 579 to 3,450; and artillery, from 68 to 124.
83. FI, A, Oct. 1896, 470–528 KW2, D.W.K. Barr to W.J. Cunningham,
24 Sept. 1897; FS-I, Oct. 1903, 1–3 KW, Curzon, 11 Dec. 1902; ibid.,
Maharaja Rewa to C.S. Bayley, June 1903; Bhargava, 'Relations of
British paramount power', PhD, p. 126.

84. FS-I, Oct. 1903, 1–3 KW, C(urzon), 24 Apr. 1903.
85. FI, A, Oct. 1897, 470–528 KW2, Maharaja Rewa to A.F. Pinhey, 18
Sept. 1897; FI, B, Sept. 1913, 210–11, Notes, F.A.E., 22 May 1913; FPI,
B, May 1915, 914, Viceroy to SOS, 15 Aug. 1914; FPI, B, May 1915,
Notes, O.V. Bosanquet to J.B. Wood, 1 Sept. 1914; FP, June 1915,
223, AGGCI to FSec, 9 Oct. 1914; FPI, B, Nov. 1915, 129–41, R.E.
Holland to O.V. Bosanquet, 6 Feb. 1915; FPG, A, 191, Nov. 1915,
14–6, Notes, G.B.T., 23 Sept. 1915; FPI, B, May 1917, 268–70, Notes,
GOC IEF to C-in-C, India, 11 June 1916; FPI, B, June 1917, 273–5,
Notes, Maharaja Rewa to O.V. Bosanquet, 16 Apr. 1917; BA, 352,
1919, P.B. Warburton, from *RSA, 1918–19*; Zutshi, *Rewa and Ruler*,
p. 25; *Rewa Gazetteer*, p. 48.
86. FG, B, Jan. 1906, 20, H. Daly to V. Gabriel, 25 July 1905; *Rewa State
Census, 1921, Report*, p. 1; *Shahdol Gazetteer*, p. 3; *Sidhi Gazetteer*, p. 2;
Rewa Gazetteer, p. 171; *IG*, vol. XXI, p. 287.
87. FI, B, June 1909, 45, H. Daly to FSec, 23 Apr. 1909; FI, D, Mar. 1915,
59, R.E. Holland, 17 Dec. 1914; VP, RDO, 1928, 29, Rev, Note on
Silpara Chandels, 17 Feb. 1930; *RSA, 1906–07*, p. 2; *RSA, 1910–11*,
pp. 1, 4; *RSA, 1913–14*, p. 5; *RSA, 1915–16*, pp. 2, 4; *RSA, 1916–17*,
p. 3; *RMCI*, pp. 11, 13, pt VIII.
88. FPI, B, June 1916, 47, Encl II, Messrs Killick Nixon to Sec Railway
Board, 7 Feb. 1916; *RSA, 1904–05*, p. 7; *RSA, 1909–10*, p. 17; *RSA,
1916–17*, pp. 13–14, 18; *Satna Gazetteer*, p. 185; *Shahdol Gazetteer*, pp.
57, 161, 175; Aitchison, *Collection of Treaties*, p. 224; *Ruling Princes and
Chiefs of India*, Bombay, 1930, p. 310; *RMCI*, p. 9, pt VIII.
89. FI, B, Dec., 1906, 344, R.M. Williamson to Maharaja Rewa, 6 Jan
1906; FI, A, Dec. 1907, 9, AGGCI to FSec, 10 July 1907; *RSA, 1906–
07*, p. 11; *RSA, 1907–08*, p. 16; *RSA, 1909–10*, p. 13; *RSA, 1913–14*,
p. 13; *RSA, 1915–16*, p. 10; *Working Plan for Rewa Forest Division*, vol.
I, pp. 192, 200–1.
90. *RSA, 1909–10*, p. 2; *RSA, 1913–14*, pp. 2–3; *Forest Management Plan,
North Shahdol and Umaria Divisions*, vol. I, p. 121. Kitchener bagged
four tigers in Rewa in 1909.
91. *RSA, 1905–06*, p. 3; *RSA, 1906–07*, p. 4; *RSA, 1907–08*, pp. 4–5; *RSA,
1909–10*, p. 3; *Satna Gazetteer*, p. 243; *Shahdol Gazetteer*, p. 202; *Rewa
Gazetteer*, pp. 180–1; Bomford, *Final Settlement Report*, pp. 19–20.
92. BA, Fam, 1895–97, 8, 1896, A.F. Pinhey to Newmarch, 12 Oct. 1896;
CIA, Excise, J.H. Cox, 17 Apr. 1913; FI, A, Mar. 1919, 23, O.V.
Bosanquet to J.B. Wood, 20 Nov. 1918; FPIS, 1160, 1922, 1–6, Notes,
D.B.B. to FSec, 25 Sept. 1922; *CIA Report, 1905–06*, p. 17; *RSA, 1905–
06*, p. 12 *RSA, 1906–07*, p. 13; *RSA, 1916–17*, p. 4; *Rewa Gazetteer*, pp.
187, 195. Nearly 17½ lakhs were spent on the Maharaja's marriages,
though famine expenditure was also heavy. Rewa borrowed 6 lakhs
from Gwalior, and took two loans of Rs 9.38 lakhs and Rs 8 lakhs

from the Government of India between 1897–1900. See FI, A, June 1897, 362, encl. in D.W.K. Barr to FSec, 5 June 1897; BA, 122, 1909, V. Gabriel to PA, nd.

93. FI, A, Apr. 1908, 43, H. Daly to FSec, 17 Feb. 1908; FPE, D, May 1918, 51, Notes, Maharaja Rewa to Viceroy, 1 Apr. 1918; and Lord Chelmsford to Maharaja Rewa, 17 Apr. 1918; Bhattacharya, *Historical Geography*, p. 48.

94. FS-I, Mar. 1908, 43, Maharaja Rewa to PA, 6 Oct. 1906; and encl. W.M. Cubitt to AGGCI, 3 Nov. 1906; FS-I, Mar. 1908, 43–4, Notes, J.R., 1 June 1907; FS–I, Mar. 1908, 44, R.E. Holland to H. Daly, 2 Mar. 1908; CIA, BA, 82, 1905, P.B. Warburton to AGGCI, 18 July 1908; FE, A, Sept. 1912, 1–5, Notes, L.W. Reynolds, 31 May 1910; and H.G. Stokes, 14 Oct. 1911; FPE, B, Mar. 1914, 132–4, Notes, B.H., 12 Jan. 1914; BA, 283, 1916, AGGCI to PA, 11 May 1916; FPE, B, Nov. 1921, 173, SOS, 2 June 1921; ISC, vol. IV, Maharaja Rewa to PA, 6 July 1908; *ISC*, vol. IV, PA to See Maharaja Rewa, 12 Dec. 1912.

95. FG, A, July 1886, 29–50 KW2, L. Griffin to H.M. Durand, 20 Jan. 1886; FI, B, Aug. 1908; 436, W.M. Cubitt, Sept. 1903; FPE, B, Jan. 1909, E.H.S. Clarke, 17 Aug. 1908; FE, B, Mar. 1910, 184–202, Notes, S.H. Butler, 5 Sept. 1909.

96. FDE, July 1912, 32, M.F. O'Dwyer to A.H. MacMahon, 15 Apr. 1912.

97. FI, A, June 1897, 203, A.F. Pinhey to AGGCI, 15 Mar. 1897; CIA, CMO, 7/Misc, 1913–31, pt II, Influenza and Health Synopsis, 1917–18; *Rewa State Census, 1921, Report*, p. 43; *RSA, 1905–06*, pp. 12–13; *RSA, 1908–09*, pp. 16–17; *RSA, 1913–14*, p. 7; *RSA, 1916–17*, p. 5; *CIA Report, 1907–08*, p. 22; *CP Police Report, 1893*, pp. 14–15; *Satna Gazetteer*, p. 225; Bhattacharya and Verma, 'Rural settlement forms', pp. 299–300; Dube, *Population of Rewa*, p. 21; Bomford, *Final Settlement Report*, p. 10, notes that while Rewa's population was 15,08,943 in 1891, in 1921 it was only 14, 01, 524. By 1921 only 19 males per 1000 in Rewa State were literate.

98. FI, A, July 1898, 76, D.W.K. Barr to FSec, 8 June 1898; RDO, B 3/24–5, 19, Police, 1924, Maharaja's Order, 7 Aug. 1900; Pre-1920 files, RDO, B 4, 14, Police, 1902, F.C, Bayley to J.Singh, 18 Apr. 1902; Pre-1920 files, RDO, 14, Police, 1920, Mgr Rewah Collieries to J. Prasad, 20 Apr. 1906; CIA, PWD, 1–41, 1916–7, H.B. Learoyd to Jt Sec CC CP, 27 Apr. 1917; pre-1920 files, RDO, B 3/24–5, 19, Police, 1924, Note by J. Prasad, 19 July 1924; BA, Eng files, pt III, 167, 1926, J. Prasad to D.G. Wilson, 23 June 1926.

99. FPI A, Mar. 1919, 23, Note by the Maharaja of Ratlam, in O.V. Bosanquet to J.B. Wood, 20 Nov. 1918; *Papers Relating to the States Committee, Evidence*, vol. II, A(a), VII, Note on Minority Administration, Rewa, 1928, p. 2; FPE, B, 120a, G.N.S., 31 Dec. 1918; *Rewa Gazetteer*, p. 48. P.B. Warburton was the officer on special duty whom Colvin replaced.

100. FPI, B, Oct. 1919, 302, Viceroy to Maharaja Ratlam, 22 May 1919; FPI, B. Sept. 1919, 289, AGGCI to Polindia, 26 Aug. 1919; FPI, B, Aug. 1921, Notes, G.F. de Montmorency, 22 Apr. 1921; FPI, B, Aug. 1921, 14, F.G. Beville to PSec, 30 Apr. 1921; FPI, B, Sept. 1921, 348, D.B. Blakeway to PSec, 20 Aug. 1921; FPGI, 195, 1922, AGGCI to PSec, 21 Jan. 1922; FPIS, 1922, 1–6, Notes, D.B. Blakeway to FSec, 8 Apr. 1922. Colvin's sympathy for the Maharaja of Ratlam was evident in their common differences with the so-called 'Rewa group' in the Regency council on the land revenue settlement and other issues.

101. FPI, B, Sept. 1921, 348, D.B. Blakeway to PSec, 20 Aug. 1921; FPI, B, 264, F.G. Beville to PSec, 3 Oct. 1921; FPE, B, Dec 1921, 350, J.B. Wood to D.B. Blakeway, 15 Dec. 1921; BA, 400, 1921, 'Rewa miracles', *Pratap* (Kanpur), 5 Dec. 1921. When Colvin became acting Regent, he resigned from the Regency council, his place being taken by an 'Indian official'. Of European bureaucrats, I. Bomford took charge of settlement operations; and A.G. Scott became I.G. Police.

102. FPIS, 1160, 1922, 1–6, Notes, D.B. Blakeway to FSec, 25 Sept. 1922; *RSA, 1922–23*, pp. 9–10; Bhargava, 'Relations of British paramount power', PhD, pp. 100–01; Zutshi, *Report on the Administration of the Rewa State during the Minority of His Highness Maharaja Gulab Singh Bahadur, 1918–22*, Bombay, 1922, pp. 32–3. Gulab Singh and the Rewa group had a contrasting view of the state's finances.

103. FS-I, Mar. 1910, H.B. Peacock to AGGCI, 2 Dec. 1909; FPI, B, June 1920, 86, F.G. Beville to PSec, 25 Mar. 1920; CIA, PWD, Communications, A, 185, P.B. Warburton to AGGCI, 23 Nov. 1920; FPI, A, Jan 1921, 61. H.B. Learoyd to J.B. Wood, 16 Dec. 1920; FPIS, 1160, 1922, 1–6, Notes, D.B. Blakeway to FSec, 25 Sept. 1922; *RSA, 1918–22*, pp. 55, 71, 73, 78; Zutshi, *Report on the Administration*, pp. 32–3; Bhargava, 'Relations of British paramount power', PhD, p. 101.

104. HP, D, Mar. 1919, 16, CP FR 1/Feb. 1919; FP, Sept. 1919, 105–7, PSec to D.S., 2 Apr. 1919; FPI, B, Oct. 1919, 431, O.V. Bosanquet to PSec, 14 June 1919; BA, 420, 1920, P.B. Warburton to President, Regency Council, 26 Oct. 1920; FPI, B, Apr. 1921, 253–6, Notes, R.L. Simpson, 16 Mar. 1921; BA, 400, 1921, 'Education department of Rewa', *Pratap* (Kanpur), 4 Aug. 1921; BA, 352, 1919, *RSA, 1918–19; RSA, 1922–23*, pp. 9–10; *RSA, 1923–24*, p. 9, claimed a deficit of Rs 2,01,918 for the year 1921–22; *Rewa Gazetteer*, p. 135; *Satna Gazetteer*, pp. 73, 219; *Shahdol Gazetter*, p. 187.

105. FPIS, 1160, 1922, 1–6, Notes, D.B. Blakeway to FSec, 8 Apr. 1922; ibid., J.P. Thompson, 21 Apr. 1922; ibid., FSec to D.B. Blakeway, 25 Apr. 1922; ibid., J.P. Thompson, 8 Nov. 1922; *RSA, 1922–23*, pp. 9–10; Bomford, *Final Settlement* Report, p. 30; Bhargava, 'Relations of British paramount power', PhD, pp. 176–7.

6

An Assertion of the Region: Maharaja Gulab Singh, 1922–46

☙❧

Maharaja Gulab Singh (1922–46) played a key role in the quickening interchange between the centralizing British Raj and the region of Baghelkhand focused in Rewa state. Emphasizing the primacy of region over central government, the Maharaja strengthened Rewa's traditional autocracy and held at bay central proposals regarding his administration. In similar vein he opposed attempts by the Congress and other forces to bring Rewa into the circle of nationalist politics; and thereafter defended his state against inclusion in the proposed Indian federation. At the same time Gulab Singh maintained links with the central government, though these were coming under strain by 1939. The Maharaja's reign may thus be seen as an attempt to create a regional autonomy, isolating Rewa as far as possible from national initiatives.

I

THE AUTOCRATIC BASE OF AUTONOMY

Born in 1903 and educated by English tutors and at Daly College, Indore, Gulab Singh succeeded to the throne of Rewa as a minor in October 1918 on the death of his father.[1] The following year he married the Maharaja of Jodhpur's sister, who bore him an heir, Martand Singh, in 1923; four years later he married a daughter of the Maharaja of Kishengarh. Although he ascended the Rewa *gaddi* in 1918, Gulab Singh's reign began officially on 31 October 1922 at Indore when Lord Reading invested him with full powers in the presence of officers of the Central India Agency and a large company of nobles and other representatives from Rewa.

Thereafter Gulab Singh seemed fixed within the ambit of the Raj.[2] Reading had had to cancel a visit to Rewa in 1922; in 1925 Gulab Singh renewed the invitation but this, too, had to be cancelled, making the Maharaja 'very touchy' on the subject. Irwin's visit several years later somewhat made amends for these false starts, but his remarks when opening the new bridge across the Ghoghar river, ending Rewa's isolation from Satna and elsewhere during floods, could not have been welcome. There Irwin spoke of the passing of the old order and Rewa's need to end its aloofness from the world beyond its borders.

Irwin's royal host did not at all envisage the passing of the old order, but proceeded to deepen the region's autocracy inherited from his father.[3] Early on, officials noticed that he relied on his own opinions which they claimed owed much to the 'conservative prejudices' of Venkatraman Singh. Once in office Gulab Singh constructed a centralized administration whose officials were to mix with the people, the ruler himself travelling to the remoter parts of his state. Although pained to discover that the population there was poor and illiterate, for him autocracy and regional autonomy seemed the paths by which Rewa and its people might progress.

In consequence Gulab Singh took all decisions and relied on as few people as possible.[4] His officials had to refer all important matters to him: a *tahsildar* could not pass orders even in petty matters without the permission of His Highness; and no state building could be constructed without the Maharaja's approval. Gulab Singh claimed the entire land, its minerals and water resources as his property, together with all customs and excise. He also laid down that

the Ruler can spare or not the lives of any one of his subjects, can remove anyone's property without assigning any reason, can stop all national-building activities ... can levy tax at his own free will, and enact any law which catches his fancy without consultation, the Ruler of course being ready to confront all consequences with the help of a large army.[5]

In such circumstances it was not surprising that 'everybody looked for inspiration and guidance to His Highness'.

Nor was it surprising that centre and region eyed each other with some suspicion.[6] For his part, Gulab Singh rejected advice from the centre, and once refused to allow a British official to inspect Rewa's schools. Even though some officers dubbed the Maharaja 'mediaeval' compared to other princes, Gulab Singh believed that the treaties of the nineteenth century together with his sovereign powers as ruler gave him freedom of action within his state. This was evident from 1927 on in his refusal to publish the customary administration reports detailing Rewa's progress in various fields. As he explained to Kenneth Fitze, the Agent in Rewa in the late 1920s:

Since it was in the capacity of conquerors, and not as guests or philanthropists, that his ancestors had come to Rewa, he regarded his vast domains as a kind of private property, and saw no reason why he should administer them on a democratic system, which from his observation of events in British India, produced neither gratitude or contentment.[7]

However, Gulab Singh's reign was not the monolith the above might suggest, but divided into two parts—one more consultative until about 1932, and the other more autocratic, from about 1932 to 1946.[8] In the first period, besides Indian officials the state had several European heads of department; and until 1932 the Maharaja used the services of European advisers, one of whom was E.J.D. Colvin, who had acted as Regent during his minority. The Maharaja also closely associated his *darbar* secretary Janki Prasad with decision-making, a relationship that replaced that of the earlier advisers. Moreover, Gulab Singh widened the administration by forming the East district from *tahsils* taken from the North and South districts, and creating a new *tahsil* in the latter district.

The Maharaja's visits to England and Europe for the Round Table Conferences between 1930–32 formed a watershed in the evolution of his regional autocracy.[9] Paradoxically, the second phase began with Gulab Singh announcing reforms to counter a civil disobedience movement that had taken place while he was away from Rewa. These comprised a consultative council to advise the ruler; and a *raj parishad*, a type of legislature that could raise matters for discussion and make proposals which the Maharaja was free to accept or reject.

These phantom-like concessions introduced a period of heightened autocracy where the ruler dispensed with European officials and relied less on advice.[10] Several trusted ministers assisted him in this phase: Brajendranath Chaturvedi, nephew of Janki Prasad, who served as Finance Minister and the Maharaja's right hand man; and Visheshwar Prasad the Political Minister. Central to the new political style was a 'news section' staffed by low class men, whose task was to obtain information on *ilaqadars*, officials, and others about whom Gulab Singh wished to be informed. The police and officials resented this section which was disbanded in 1937, though its personnel formed a power centre close to the ruler, some of them becoming his ADCs. Central officials were scornful of the results:

> By surrounding himself with a circle of men of the lowest social standing, and confiding in them more than in his senior officials, by centralizing power in himself, and having direct contact with all ranks of state servants, the Ruler encouraged intrigue, indiscipline and dissension among all classes.[11]

Using these methods Gulab Singh sought to create an obedient bureaucracy.[12] Two cases were notable. In 1937 Santokh Singh, who had been Home Minister for 11 years, found that the ruler had transferred his portfolio to the Finance Minister without warning. Gulab Singh also publicly humiliated his army chief, encouraging his resignation. In general, too, the ruler selected local men over outsiders, regarding the latter as less loyal to the state and taking jobs from those whose birthright they were. The Maharaja personally selected candidates at parades, posting them to departments regardless of the wishes of departmental heads, and sometimes consulting them over the same heads! He frequently kept appointments pending, and then paid appointees less than the prescribed scales, filling his services with inefficient if subservient men.[13]

Gulab Singh also controlled the press in Rewa, and to some degree in the neighbouring United Provinces.[14] Apart from the official *Rewa Raj Gazette*, he sponsored an illustrated weekly, *Prakash*, to encourage 'contentment and loyalty' among his subjects. With unpleasant rumours circulating, in 1940 the Maharaja came to an understanding with the editor of the *Leader* of Allahabad, whereby the paper would publish material sent from Rewa and suppress news reflecting adversely on the Rewa administration. To finance the scheme the ruler authorized an annual payment of Rs 6–700.

Though the Maharaja maintained an army as a basis for his regional autocracy, the centre scored a notable military coup in the state.[15] In 1926 Gulab Singh appointed Colonel Bayley of the Indian Army as his Commander-in-Chief, his brief being to recast the force for possible service with that army. The following year Rewa dressed its more compact force in new uniforms and applied to the central government for new weapons. However, the centre made these conditional on the Maharaja joining the Indian States Forces scheme for service with the Indian Army in wartime, leaving him with virtually no choice. When a central officer came to inspect Rewa's army in 1934, he found that the Chief of General Staff had resigned, his place being taken by Chaturvedi, the Finance Minister. He also reported that the men did not know how to use their new weapons, and suggested a central training programme. In the ensuing discussion the Maharaja and the central government took opposing sides, but in the end Gulab Singh bowed to the army's demands and so retained his links with the government. Thereafter, however, he took little interest in his forces which he then regarded as outside his control.

Gulab Singh's regional autocracy would have been incomplete without his attempted subjection of the *ilaqadars* and other powerful grantees of the state.[16] To this end he emphasized a ruler's claims to the soil including minerals, and regarded the *ilaqadars* as virtual tenants of the *darbar*. He insisted that they appear before him at the Dassehra ceremony in the capital with their levies of troops in keeping with their service obligations.

The *ilaqadars* fiercely opposed Gulab Singh's attempts to diminish their status and his use of resumption to compel obedience.[17] Moreover, though the ruler initially excluded major grantees from Rewa's third land settlement, he later directed that villages on their estates also be surveyed and settled. Landholders obstructed these proceedings, forcing the Maharaja to assess the revenue by estates rather than individual villages, using an *ilaqa*'s cash rents as a basis for the settlement. Under this compromise the state bestowed *pattas* on villages of the major estates, on the villages of ordinary *pawai* and lesser grantees, and on Baghel villages in Beohari that claimed 'better treatment'.

Bomford, the Settlement Commissioner, maintained that the grantees' principal grievance was financial.[18] They had opposed a *daijawan* tax in 1925, and resented paying *nazarana* at entry to a lease. *Ilaqadars* also found the cost of bringing soldiers, horses and elephants to Rewa for Dassehra burdensome, and rejected the monetary equivalent conceded by the *darbar* as too heavy.

The Maharaja and his *ilaqadars* also bitterly contested issues beyond those related merely to land.[19] The ruler regarded his opponents as dangerous rivals for power, scorning them as uneducated, spendthrift and open to 'baneful company', besides being poor managers of their estates. The landed resented these attacks, the more so as they could no longer defend themselves at court where the lowly born had usurped their place. The result was a dangerous divide, evident

Not only among the higher state officials, from whom His Highness shuts himself off and practically refuses to see, but also among the landed aristocracy who are no longer in the Ruler's confidence, and who avoid his presence except when they are summoned to ceremonial functions.[20]

To strengthen their position, in 1931 leading *ilaqadars* sought the help of political organizations while the ruler was away at the second Round Table Conference.[21] *Ilaqadars* and *pawaidars* had formed the Pawaidar Sangh in the twenties to represent their grievances to the central government; and in 1931 they used the Sangh's platform to target the *darbar*. The landowners were also in touch with leaders of the Indian National Congress in Allahabad, complaining that the Maharaja was threatening their established rights. Some Congressmen encouraged these approaches, anxious as they were to obtain a foothold in Baghelkhand. *Ilaqadars* also reportedly financed the Praja Mandal, an organization seeking political rights for the subjects of princely states.

Before going abroad Gulab Singh appointed Conrad Corfield, a shrewd political officer, as Adviser and vice-president of the council, a posting that took effect as the tension between the ruler and the landed nobles was nearing its climax.[22] Corfield tackled the landowners on two fronts. While arresting leaders of the proposed civil disobedience campaign, he also sought to conciliate them by moving to reform the rules relating to land grants. With Gulab Singh's approval Corfield probed the grounds of the hostility between the Maharaja and his landholders, tracing its immediate rise to the rules relating to land grants sanctioned (though not promulgated) by the ruler in 1925. These rules led to the creation of the Pawaidar Sangh under the Rao of Churhat, 'a ruthless ... man and implacable enemy' of his royal kinsman. Corfield believed that he had found a solution to the conflict:

Gulab Singh wanted to reduce the Pawaidars' privileges because of their disloyalty, and I pressed him to make their legitimate rights secure, so that they would remain loyal next time. I toiled through these enquiries throughout the rest of the hot weather, and eventually produced recommendations.[23]

The resulting Pawai Report was a compromise, the aim of which was to strengthen the state.[24] While differentiating between the privileged *ilaqadars* holding older service grants and the less prestigious *pawaidars*, including those with smaller estates and paying less revenue, the report held that all must share the cost of administering Rewa, together with the *khalsa* villages. For landholders, Corfield defined the cesses to be paid; permitted their automatic adoption of an heir; relaxed the need for *pawaidars* to seek the ruler's approval before leaving their estates; gave larger *ilaqadars* the power to eject tenants for not paying their rents, and the right of *nistar* in forests on their estates.

For the *darbar*,[25] Corfield awarded civil and criminal jurisdiction and the right to excise and forests on estates; heirless property was to escheat to the *darbar*; the *darbar* was to treat attendance at Dassehra as a ceremonial practice and not a test of noble loyalty, converting the *sewa* of small *muafidar*s to cash, reducing the payment for other tenures, and abolishing it for life grantees. The *darbar* was also to be responsible for famine relief throughout the state.

Both sides accepted the recommendations, if with some qualifications.[26] Initially the Maharaja delayed sanctioning the report, but three hours before Corfield's brief tenure ended, he induced the ruler to do so. The landholders did not endorse the new rules entirely, but declared that they would obey *darbar* orders if based on the report; though some felt privately that the Maharaja would not implement it. Thus, though the proposed rules did not completely heal the rift between the ruler and his landed gentry, they did lessen tension, Gulab Singh reporting to a senior central officer that his relations with the *pawaidars* had taken a turn for the better by 1939.

II

EXPANDING THE MARKET ECONOMY 1922–42

Economic development occupied a prominent place in Gulab Singh's efforts to build a strong regional state despite post-war uncertainties and the ensuing economic depression.[27] Though grain prices rose and exports were buoyant during the 1920s, the trade in coal remained depressed and buyers pressed the state to reduce its sale price. During the depression coal companies at Burhar near Umaria went into liquidation, and exports of coal and imports generally declined. The situation in Rewa only improved with the onset of the Second World War, though this brought chronic shortages and rising prices in its wake.

To meet the exigencies of the inter-war years, Gulab Singh brought coal mining under state control on the grounds that foreign companies should not profit from Rewa's resources.[28] In 1923 he took over the mine at Burhar leased to Villiers and Company of Calcutta, amalgamating it with the state colliery at Umaria in 1930 to form the Rewa Coalfields Company, in which the state and Shaw Wallace of Calcutta held shares. With the upturn in the coal trade the venture succeeded, bringing the state royalties and surface rents which were paid into the Maharaja's account.

Like his father Gulab Singh also sought to extend the region's communications to bring traders closer to villages and food grains to markets.[29] This included a liberal road construction programme in the East district, as a result of which

Deosar and Singrauli tahsils, where wheeled traffic was unknown, and which had not a single mile of road of any kind ... have been connected to Rewa, and buses run from Rewa once a week.[30]

New fair weather roads also began connecting the capital with places as far apart as Dabhaura, Umaria, Amarkantak, and Waidhan; and linking Satna with Amarpatan, Simeria, Nagod, and Kothi. These roads, together with new bridges across the Tons and the Son, the Ghoghar bridge at the entry to Rewa, and pontoon bridges at various places, filled key gaps in the state's communications, stepping up motor and lorry traffic between Rewa, Satna, and other towns in the state as well as with the neighbouring United and Central Provinces.

The Maharaja also endorsed several rail projects, which sought to redress his state's isolation from the Indian rail system and ecourage trade.[31] Following Irwin's visit the Railway Board re-examined proposals for lines linking Rewa with Satna and Katni with Singrauli, but again turned them down on the grounds that neither would be remunerative. Promising coal surveys, however, led the Board to build a branch line from Anuppur on the Bilaspur line to Korea, though the *darbar* refused to cede territory or jurisdiction as previously. At the same time the central government expanded Rewa's telephone and postal services, with the state contributing towards the cost.

As agriculture remained the region's main source of wealth, crop out-turns were vital to the state's economic well-being.[32] In the 1920s the state enjoyed fair to good seasons, the first failure occurring in 1928–9 when a break in the rains harmed the rice crop, while rust damaged *rabi* linseed and wheat, and blight the gram crop, compelling the state to begin relief measures and suspend revenue. Thereafter over-heavy or too little rain harmed crops, leading to further suspensions. (Subsequent information on crops is meagre as the state ceased to publish administration reports, though crops were unsatisfactory in 1941 due to poor rainfall.)

The main development in agriculture was the Maharaja's decision to continue the third land revenue settlement begun during the Regency.[33] Though the 'Rewa group' in the Regency council strenuously opposed the settlement, once Gulab Singh became Maharaja he confirmed Bomford as Settlement Commissioner. Completed by 1926–7, the settlement surpassed the two previous settlements in accuracy, bringing Rewa more or less to the standard of British districts, and thereby confirming the integrative process favoured by the centre. Though Bomford realized that it was a 'mistake to divide settlement operations between the northern and southern districts', proceedings moved quickly in the north which had had two regular settlements previously; but took much longer in the south where records were scanty, and many lots were 'cultivated temporarily' or were 'buried in jungles'. Famine and inexperience also delayed proceedings in the south, as did the lack of landmarks demarcating holdings in the villages of Shahdol.

Apart from increasing the land revenue, Bomford's settlement helped improve the position of peasants, aiding the ruler's efforts to strengthen the regional economy.[34] The settlement broke the power of the revenue *thekedars* by appointing *patwaris* to collect the revenue in *kothar* villages, besides giving security of tenure and stable rents for the duration of the settlement. The state also allowed peasants to cultivate *chheola* trees from which it collected *lac*, and provided relief for peasants at times of seasonal difficulty. At the same time the Rewa Land Revenue and Tenancy Code of 1935 equalized the position of tenants on alienated estates with those of the *kothar* villages by bestowing them with *pattas*, and providing them with similar security of tenure and stable rents, together with the right to improve their holdings and gain associated revenue benefits. *Patwaris* were similarly to prepare annual papers for estate villages and collect the revenue.

As part of his strong regional policy, Gulab Singh put forest management on to a more permanent basis than earlier.[35] This resulted partly from his appointment of C.M. Harlow of the Central Provinces as Conservator of Forests from 1929–36. As Mckee and Williamson had done, Harlow criticized the state for felling timber in reserved forests to obtain revenue, and recommended forest management on lines laid down in the Central Provinces. In this vein he prepared working plans for various forests with coupes which were to be felled by rotation and then closed. These measures were enshrined in the Forest Rules of 1930 and in Rewa's adoption of the Indian Forest Act in 1935. At the same time the state gradually replaced untrained with trained forest officers, and enlarged its reserved forests from 4,613 to 7,115 square kilometres between 1926 and 1937.

Like his forbears the Maharaja used his reserved forests as shooting blocks for *shikar*.[36] He was a good shot, and attained the coveted *mala* of 109 tigers as early as 1924; by 1937 the Maharaja had bagged 154 male tigers and cubs, and 166 tigresses with cubs. By the end of his reign Gulab Singh had accounted for the astonishing kill of over 800 tigers, probably because he had 'reduced the business of big game-shooting to a fine art':

He would relax in the machan and read, relying on his monkey on a lead to alert him to a tiger. The monkey would give a discreet cough, and the Maharaja would reach for his gun; in a few seconds it would all be over.[37]

Gulab Singh reserved the mutant white tigers for his own rifle.

As his predecessors had done, the ruler entertained distinguished visitors to the state at *shikar* in the region's forests, though there were those who did not belong to official parties:

Ram Jam was a rascal.... Officially ... he was the contractor in charge of the coaling of the Bengal–Nagpur Railway's locomotives at Sahdol. Actually he was a deep-dyed poacher and a night-flitter, a doer of dark and mysterious deeds in the jungles of his Lordship, the Maharaja of Rewa.... He went round the nearby reserves and jungles like Halley's comet, leaving a trail of death and destruction in his wake and occasionally falling foul of the Maharaja's game wardens.... On one particular occasion we penetrated into the Sahdol jungles for some miles. We had not long to wait. We heard the cry of '*Bagh*', and every native ... shinned up the first available tree.... From the nearby forest walked the lord of the jungle to stand under the tree in which Ram Jam had perched himself.... Eventually the tiger moved off again, and he was most indignant because I had not shot the tiger.

'What about the ... fine, Ram Jam?' I asked....

'I'd have fixed things', he said, with an air that seemed to convey that he and the Maharaja of Rewa were as one.[38]

III

THE FINANCIAL COMPONENT OF REGIONAL AUTOCRACY

Creating a financially strong state was integral to Gulab Singh's notions of autonomous regional power.[39] In the 1920s rising revenues reached heights not previously attained, before being threatened by bad seasons and the trade depression. As a result, revenues plummeted from 63 lakhs in 1926–7 to 37 lakhs in 1932–3, though by 1936 the rising trend had reasserted itself, the revenue total crossing 44 lakhs. The enhanced revenues of the third land settlement (to the extent of about five lakhs) added to Rewa's buoyant financial position before as after the depression.

Rewa's financial policy differed in one crucial aspect from that of other important princely states.[40] By the 1930s the centre had persuaded the more important rulers that state revenues were public funds, from which they should set aside a civil list for their own expenses, the remainder being spent on public works. Gulab Singh declined to distinguish between state money and a civil list, defending this as Rewa's practice, and attacking any division of revenues as a recent invention. Thus even before the depression Gulab Singh paid surplus revenues into his private account, and from 1927 ceased to publish administration reports so that the central government could not discover what revenue was surplus, and whether or where it was being spent. As a result Rewa's opening balances always began with a zero, a figure that astounded Lord Willingdon, but worried Corfield who was responsible for certain items of expenditure:

I had to tour the State, and decide where roads and bridges should be built. I found that the south of the State was almost inaccessible, and an expensive bridge would be required. So I asked the Finance Minister what the position was. If the Maharaja approved a project, its cost would be included in the Budget; but none of the money would be spent without another order allowing the work to begin. At the end of the year money not spent went into the Maharaja's private account, and the state budget for the following year started again from scratch. The Maharaja had only to postpone a project to make sure that his private account grew.[41]

Maharaja Gulab Singh thus proved himself an astute manager of Rewa's finances.[42] While this was partly due to the near bankruptcy of the state when he assumed office and to the alarming fall in revenue across the depression, critics cast him in the role of a miser who even made the Jodhpuri Maharani pay for the electricity she used in Venkat Bhavan! Some of the monies harvested by the Maharaja were indeed private, but much of his income came from state funds and comprised the unspent revenue balance which was put into promissory notes, bonds, cash certificates, fixed deposits, and war loans. As early as 1927 such investments stood at over 27 lakhs.

The Maharaja's savings burgeoned in the 1930s as his control over Rewa became more absolute.[43] British officials claimed that he employed an army of money-saving devices, which included falsifying departmental accounts, retaining monies shown as expenditure in various departments, delaying departmental purchases, reducing the salaries of posts held by Rewa appointees, and transferring unexpended monies from the annual budget to himself. To harvest this increasing cash flow, Gulab Singh opened a number of accounts in India and abroad, which by conservative estimates held over one crore rupees by 1940.

Figure: 6.1 Maharaja Gulab Singh, 1922–1946 (acceded in Oct. 1918 but owing to the Regency did not assume power till 1922)

The transactions of the Rewa Coalfields Company highlighted the indivisibility of state monies and the Maharaja's personal income.[44] Although the *darbar* purchased shares in the company from state revenues, Shaw Wallace allotted the shares to the Maharaja, who directed his officials not to mix up the company account kept in his private office with state accounts. When questioned later by the central Income-Tax Department, Gulab Singh stated that the shares belonged to Rewa State; yet Shaw Wallace paid royalties and surface rents into the ruler's current account in the Imperial Bank in Calcutta. Central authorities investigating Gulab Singh's finances in 1945–6 claimed that the shares and dividends were state property, but the ruler asserted that he was 'constitutionally fit' to hold the shares in his name, and declined to transfer them to a government agency as directed.

The activities of the Bank of Baghelkhand displayed the same mingling of state financial policy with the personal interests of the Maharaja.[45] Gulab Singh founded the bank in 1933 to 'finance trade' in Rewa state, and as its first Managing Director he appealed for subscriptions. Leading Mahajans and others subscribed a capital of three lakhs—a safe investment as the *darbar* ordered that any dues outstanding against the bank were to form an 'ultimate charge to the state treasury', to be realized through government departments like state dues. Bank officials thus sought recovery of debts by auctioning clients' property or disposing of it in any way they chose.

The ruler contributed to the bank's business as to his own profits.[46] The state held a current account with the bank; and in 1934 he directed it to take over all *tahsil* treasuries, hitherto under the management of one Ganeshdas Krishnaji. With the ruler at the helm, the bank expanded its operations throughout the state to hold deposits of 2.5 crores by 1946, with pay offices and branches in the main commercial centres. Apart from its normal functions as a bank, the institution would seem to have played an important part in placing state monies at the Maharaja's disposal. State accounts would have earned substantial amounts in interest, which probably accrued to the ruler. He certainly directed the treasuries under the bank's purview to transfer their surpluses to his personal accounts.

IV

STATE AUTONOMY WITHIN THE CENTRAL ARENA OF THE RAJ

With considerable panache, Maharaja Gulab Singh took his policy of state autonomy to the heart of the British political arena. He clearly saw this as a type of 'nationalist movement', as he sought to advance Rewa's status and power with the aid, and yet at the expense, of the central government.

In recognition of Gulab Singh's relations with the British arena, the centre created him a Knight Commander of the Star of India in 1927, and later suggested that he be awarded a Grand Commandership of the Indian Empire, which the Maharaja tried unsuccessfully to deflect in favour of enhancing his 17-gun salute.[47] He also won central approval to use the Indian title of Maharajadhiraja,

not only on the grounds of ancient usage of the title in His Highness's family, and of the probability that it was recognised by the Mughal Emperors, but also in view of His Highness's character and good administration.

However, the government stopped short of recognizing the title of Bandhvesh or Lord of Bandhavgarh, though the Maharaja used the appellation especially towards the end of his reign.

Rewa State grew further in stature when the Government of India withdrew its Agent from Baghelkhand in 1932.[48] The centre debated this move through the twenties, finally accepting it as a measure of retrenchment during the depression. With this the government merged the charges of Bundelkhand and Baghelkhand, placing them under its Agent for Bundelkhand based in Navgaon, who was to handle minor matters pertaining to Rewa. In 1934 the centre handed back the Agency area in Satna to Rewa State.

With the centre's withdrawal from the region, the Maharaja requested that he correspond directly with the Agent in Indore, rather than the local Agent in Navgaon,

solely on grounds of prestige. Rewa is a single greater state among many smaller states.... Now that the Political Agent is gone, Rewa is not properly placed in the area, with a status much above the rest.... Direct relations with important states has long been the policy of the Government of India.[49]

The Political Department thus sanctioned the measure, but the Maharaja carried his independent stance further by occasionally corresponding with the Viceroy himself, bypassing the Agent's office in Indore and inviting comparison with his forbear Vishwanath Singh, who corresponded directly with the Government of India rather than with any intermediary.

The visit to India of the Butler Committee in 1928 gave Gulab Singh a further opportunity to voice state interests vis-à-vis those of the central government.[50] Concerned about the future connection between the princely states and British India, in 1927 Irwin convened a conference which appointed a committee under Sir Harcourt Butler to examine the question. Gulab Singh used the committee's visit to Rewa to project a regional stance towards the centre, the main thrust of his argument being that the Paramount Power was infringing the state's sovereignty guaranteed by the treaties of the nineteenth century, as when it committed India to international agreements without consulting the princes.

Rewa aggressively raised other issues before the Butler Committee.[51] Among these were the intemperate language used by central officials in communications with the *darbar*; the centre's demand for reports and statistical returns; the jurisdiction of British courts over Rewa subjects; and the state's rights in the land given for railway construction.

On the latter issue Gulab Singh won a signal victory.[52] In the 1930s Rewa declined to surrender the 'full and exclusive power and jurisdiction' over such land it had given earlier, favouring a 'minimum jurisdiction ... necessary to secure effective working of railways and detection of crime'. With the Political Department supporting Gulab Singh, the Railway Board accepted a compromise whereby the Rewa *darbar* would exercise civil and criminal jurisdiction over railway land in return for adopting the Indian Railways Act of 1890.

V

REWA AS A PROPONENT OF REGIONAL AUTONOMY
AGAINST A FEDERAL INDIA

Gulab Singh added to Rewa's status as a regional power by leading conservative princes against the states' inclusion in a proposed federal constitution for India.[53] To voice his views, the Maharaja used the Chamber of Princes set up in 1921 to discuss the Montagu–Chelmsford reforms and other matters of common interest. The Chamber, which formed a secretariat in Delhi, held its annual sessions in the princes' section of the new parliament house under the presidentship of the Viceroy. As the forum concerned itself mainly with grievances and lacked support from some major states, it came to be 'dominated by a group of middle-sized, mainly Rajput rulers, ... who ... had...much to gain by moving into a wider political arena'. Gulab Singh was one such ruler.

The Maharaja used the Chamber to oppose the views of more moderate princes and the role the centre envisaged for the Chamber in giving the states the vision of a wider India. In so doing he became the spokesman for other like-minded rulers.[54] Gulab Singh crossed swords most often with the rulers of Patiala and Bikaner who claimed to speak for the princes as a whole, and who used the Chamber to represent such views to the Government of India. Gulab Singh fought these attempts to compel individual states to adopt a majority view, and urged that the Viceroy alone could handle issues arising between individual states and the Paramount Power. On many occasions a foe of Paramountcy, in 1932 Gulab Singh defended the concept when Bikaner and Bhopal sought to reduce Paramountcy's discretionary powers, arguing that

it would be suicidal for princes themselves to weaken the protective functions of the Paramount Power at a time when autocratic systems of government are being openly challenged in British India circles.[55]

However, the main thrust of Rewa's hostility to the Maharaja of Patiala and other rulers turned on the question of reforms in the princely states espoused by the centre.[56] A special committee of the Chamber had opined that the princes could best survive the challenge of democracy by forming closer connections with the British Indian provinces rather than relying on British guarantees.

This included responding to the demands of people in the states for reforming royal administrations. As leading autocrats, Gulab Singh and the Maharaja of Dhaulpur opposed these suggestions in the 1920s, but appear not to have pressed the matter, allowing Patiala and other reformist princes to dominate the proceedings.

However, the gap between Rewa and Patiala narrowed in the 1930s as the latter came to share Gulab Singh's views on introducing reforms into the states.[57] Gulab Singh and, by then, most rulers did not regard themselves as accountable to their people, but preferred to rely on the loyalty or indifference of their subjects. Thus, Gulab Singh defended his refusal to publish administration reports with details of monies spent on public works on the grounds that no one would be interested.

Gulab Singh took the conservative anti-federal viewpoint to the heart of Empire by attending the Round Table Conferences held in London between 1930 and 1932.[58] These conferences focused on a new constitution for India, and in particular the relationship of the states and provinces to the centre in a proposed federal scheme. When the first Conference opened in 1930 the princes generally endorsed the federation of provinces and states envisaged by the British Government, though Gulab Singh, the ruler of Dhaulpur, and others were convinced that such a combination would introduce democracy and so spell the doom of their autocratic states. Representing the conservative princes, the Maharaja counselled caution, asserting that

the Conservative element ... wish to safeguard their individual existence. They ask for guarantees that changes in the Government of India ... will leave them free to pursue their own ideals in the manner of their heritage.... [and that] their position will not be modified without their own consent.... We do not desire to stand in the way of reforms for British India. We wish to preserve the individual and historical identity of the States.... We wish to know the nature of our destination.... We do not desire federation if that involves the gradual disappearance of all that the States have stood for.[59]

Gulab Singh's plea was thus for an unlikely India in which autonomous autocratic states mingled with former British provinces enjoying a parliamentary system of government.

Gulab Singh's princely opponents accused officers of the Political Department accompanying the Maharaja to the conferences of shaping his views on federation.[60] Princes especially resented serving officers attending their meetings, and charged the Political Department with interference. However while Gulab Singh's views reflected his political style in Rewa, permission to Political Officers to accompany the Maharaja to the Conference, and Willingdon's request that he attend the third Conference in 1932, create the impression that an official lobby supported the conservative princes.

However, notwithstanding the opposition of Gulab Singh and others to federation at the Round Table Conference in 1931, at its conclusion the British Government despatched committees to India to collect evidence relating to the framing of a federal constitution, particularly the financial arrangements.[61] Rewa and Dhaulpur criticized these delegations, condemning democracy and any subordination of the states to majority rule from British India. Rewa also came out strongly against any financial nexus between the states and a future federal Government of India.

For Gulab Singh the third Round Table Conference in November–December 1932 was something of an anticlimax.[62] By then many princes shared Rewa's views on federation and abstained from the meeting, sending delegates who were powerless to influence the proceedings. An indifferent Gulab Singh attended the conference at Willingdon's request, though by then the central government had come out against harnessing India's future to the views of the princes. Willingdon also permitted Corfield, then on duty in Rewa, to accompany the Maharaja to London. Corfield later recalled the lacklustre proceedings:

The Conservatives had returned to power and many of them were unsympathetic to Indian aspirations. The Indian National Congress was not represented, and the Labour party took no share in the proceedings.... When the Conservative members ... put forward a proposal, the Indian members...raised every objection.... When Lord Irwin made a proposition, they tried to accept it.... It was quite clear at this conference that any enthusiasm the Rulers ever felt for federation had evaporated.... The Maharaja showed little interest in its proceedings.[63]

Gulab Singh and many princes continued to oppose federation after the conference was over.[64] In 1933 the Maharaja declined to attend a meeting in Indore to allocate seats in a proposed federal legislature; and later objected to any federal agency interfering in his administration, demanding of central representatives visiting Rewa that the proposed constitution reserve 'almost every item of administration to the state'. He also made any state agreement on fiscal and other matters conditional on his signing an instrument of accession to a federal India. Further, Rewa refused to federate until the 'great majority' of states accepted the scheme; and by 1935 only the greater Rajput states had endorsed it.

Regardless of princely opposition, the British Government embodied the federal scheme in the Government of India Act of 1935, though the federal clauses remained inoperative so far as the states were concerned.[65] Despite this, the princes maintained their stance until war broke out in 1939, when the central government suspended further negotiations with them, requiring their contributions to the war effort. But by then Rewa and other princes had forfeited any prospect of shaping their future in a united and independent India, though they were not aware of this at the time.

VI

THE REGION AND THE NATIONALIST CHALLENGE

Besides combating the central government's plans for an Indian federation, Rewa also had to come to terms with the activities of the Indian National Congress and other organizations which threatened to bring their own national currents to bear on regional politics.[66] The outbreak of nationalist agitation in Rewa in 1930–1 confirmed Gulab Singh's fears about democratic trends in British India overflowing to neighbouring states, and he was quick to defend his state's autonomous autocracy against them.

The Congress opened its account in Rewa during the non-cooperation movement, as a result of which the organization entrusted the work of developing nationalism there to the Ajmer Provincial Congress Committee.[67] The Karachi Congress of 1931 brought this objective closer by authorizing Baghelkhand's first District Congress Committee. Within a short time *mahajans*, pleaders, and landowners formed the committee and enrolled members, mostly from Rewa State. This done, the national Congress placed the committee under the jurisdiction of the Mahakoshal Provincial Committee in the neighbouring Hindi-speaking districts of the Central Provinces.

The leading *ilaqadars* of Rewa identified themselves closely with the infant Congress in Baghelkhand, forming a majority on the District Committee.[68] Apart from ventilating landed issues, the new Congressmen ranged themselves against the Maharaja's autocratic system, whereby they could not hold meetings without permission, there was no freedom of speech or the press, and where they could not form trade unions or political parties without seeking registration from the state.

While the doyen of the *ilaqadars*, the Rao of Churhat, sympathized with the Congress, two men especially played a key role in the organization.[69] One was Narmada Prasad Singh of the Baikunthpur *ilaqa*, whom the ruler had expelled from Rewa in 1924 for disloyalty. Thereafter Singh settled in Allahabad, where he joined the Congress and from where he penned newspaper articles attacking Rewa and advocating non-payment of taxes. Narmada subsequently became a member of the UP Provincial Congress Committee, and in 1932 the UP government imprisoned him for a year as posing a danger to Rewa State and its ruler.

The Congressman on the spot, so to speak, was Awadesh Pratap Singh of Rampur Baghelan *ilaqa* in Satna district.[70] Formerly a captain in the Rewa State Army, Singh joined college in Allahabad in 1914, and in 1920 became a member of the Congress. Nominated to represent Rewa State at the Karachi Congress, Singh became president of the Baghelkhand Congress Committee, and played a leading part in the agitation of 1932:

on his invitation, between 12,000 and 15,000 people converged on Rewa from the rural areas.... Alarmed at this new development, the State authorities arrested him. This created a stir in the army and police force, and a number of officers ... resigned in protest. Every day processions were taken out and satyagraha offered at the jail gates. But observing the signs of revolt in the army, the authorities released Captain Saheb within a month.[71]

From 1934–7 the captain was a member of the All-India Congress Committee; and from 1934 also secretary of the All-India State People's Conference or Praja Mandal. He became president of the Mahakoshal Provincial Congress Committee in 1937.

The Baghelkhand Congress opened its innings against Maharaja Gulab Singh in 1930, selling Gandhi caps and badges and distributing pamphlets in Rewa town where there was 'considerable sympathy' for the movement.[72] The situation was more volatile in Satna where some peasants refused to pay land revenue during the 1931 famine, compelling the state to remit payments. Between March and July 1931 Satna town was the focus of the civil disobedience movement, when Congressman organized hartals and obstructed the sale of foreign cloth, burning one shop and threatening those selling it. In July a large procession passed through the bazar, and at a later meeting Awadesh Pratap Singh demanded responsible government in Rewa. Singh's arrest led to a hartal in Rewa and a protest march from Satna to the capital together with agitations in some of the region's petty states.

Before leaving for the second Round Table Conference in 1931, the Maharaja sought to conciliate his opponents, releasing detainees and appointing a commission to enquire into the incidents in Satna.[73] He also permitted small meetings and occasional processions, provided speakers did not adversely criticise the *darbar*. At the same time the Maharaja appointed Colonel Loch of the Rewa Army President of the council with powers to deal with any trouble during his absence, thereby shifting the odium of repressing agitation onto British shoulders. He also set up a committee to investigate the grievances of *ilaqadars*.

While not openly confronting the *darbar*, the Baghelkhand Congress kept up pressure on the administration in Rewa.[74] From October 1931 the Congress enrolled members and celebrated Gandhi week with flag processions and meetings. There were also reports of activity in Nagod and other states. However, when Gulab Singh returned from abroad in February 1932, the Congress presented him with a written demand for responsible government, which the Maharaja refused, instituting instead representative but powerless councils.

The Maharaja's hostility to nationalist and *ilaqadari* politics reached a climax in April 1932 when Corfield, as Vice-President of the council, promulgated ordinances similar to those imposed in British provinces to deal with agitation.[75] Under these measures the *darbar* arrested the Baghelkhand Congress executive and many volunteers, lodging them in various forts and requisitioning the Congress office in Rewa town. As Congress members replied with flag processions, picketing cloth shops, and urging non-payment of revenue, the *darbar* retaliated with further arrests, while releasing those who apologised. By August 1932 the position was sufficiently calm for the *darbar* to withdraw the ordinances, though it declared the Baghelkhand Congress unlawful in May 1933.

The Praja Mandal or State Peoples' Conference similarly brought pressure to bear on the Maharaja.[76] This organization which also enjoyed *ilaqadari* support was formed in Rewa in 1931 and affiliated to the Congress. Its leaders had planned to join the agitation in 1932, but Corfield foiled the move by jailing them. In 1934 Awadesh Pratap Singh became Secretary of the All-India States Peoples' Conference, which aimed at coordinating activities in the princely states, and also sat on the subcommittee of the Congress dealing with the states. In 1934 he sought to link the two organizations by proposing at the Congress annual session in Bombay that the Congress actively support the Praja Mandal.

Singh's proposal fuelled a long debate that was still unresolved in 1939.[77] Up to 1927 the Congress had declined to interfere in the affairs of the princely states, though the following year it assured people there that it supported their struggle for responsible government. However, despite Singh's pleas at Bombay, Gandhi maintained that

the policy of non-interference in the affairs of the Indian States that the Congress has followed is wise and sound. The States are independent entities.... Any attempt on the part of the Congress at interference can only damage the cause of the people in the States.

The Congress thus rebuffed Awadesh Pratap Singh: no Congress committee was to be formed in the princely states, though existing organizations could continue. In 1935 the Congress annual session went further by shifting the task of winning responsible government in the states to the states' people themselves.

Despite minor changes, this remained substantially the view of the Congress.[78] The Congress session at Haripura in 1937 permitted its members to aid the Praja Mandal 'in their individual capacities', though this was already established practice; and at Tripuri in 1938 it 'supported' movements in the states, with Nehru himself becoming President of the States' Peoples Conference that year. However, the intervention of the war and the resignation of the Congress ministries put a damper on any further movement; and the two camps at the Mysore session of the Congress in 1939, one led by Gandhi and the other by Nehru, remained as unreconciled as ever.

VII

FLAWS IN THE REGIONAL GLASS

Serious problems undermined Gulab Singh's efforts to promote regional autonomy.[79] For communications, Rewa remained ill-served by railways; and many, if not most, villages remained unconnected to the regional road system; Bomford was scathing about roads south of the Kaimur. Many of the state's post offices could not maintain a daily service; while telephonic communications served the *darbar's* needs alone.

Problems also affected two potentially valuable sources of regional wealth—mining and forests.[80] As we have seen, the trade depression seriously damaged the coal-mining industry which recovered only towards the end of the 1930s. As for forests, despite Harlow's work gaps remained in forest management: undemarcated forests were victims of felling and encroachment; grazing and *nistar* rules were too liberal, and not adequately supervised, so that offences were easy to commit and difficult to detect immediately. For many 'bribery was a better method than resistance'.

However, whether Rewa was wise to rely heavily on forests and mining was debatable. Between the railways skirting the state's western and southern borders lay a huge area, deficient in communications and poor in literacy, with the southern part largely undeveloped. A central official remained sceptical about economic progress under such conditions:

I consider both the Political Agent and the Darbar over-optimistic as to the resources of the State. It is a very common delusion in Indian States that great mineral wealth has only to be tapped, and the whole place will be transformed. There are no doubt ... minerals in Rewa..... The hard facts are that people do not come forward to take prospecting licences.... For the present the State would do better to concentrate on agriculture.[81]

Yet, despite the third land settlement and attendant legislation, the condition of Rewa's peasantry ruled out any immediate advance in agriculture.[82] As earlier, agriculture remained largely self-subsistent, with peasants lacking the capital and incentive to improve. In 1926 Gulab Singh discovered that his peasants were debt-ridden; eight years later in Sidhi he was dismayed to see that they were oppressed by *thakurs* and corrupt officials: The results were there for all to see:

In our place the human beings of the lower strata wander about in a semi-nude form ... because they cannot afford anything better.... We give no security whatsoever to the tenants. We have ... been busy for genera- tions in endeavouring to placate the rich.... We should now realise that our security and prosperity lie in doing the greatest good to the greatest number.[83]

The problem of the debt-bonded was far worse and, though the Maharaja abolished *harwahi* in 1935, the agricultural problem lay far beyond a ruler whose thoughts, however well-intentioned, were a mere 'palliative in the face of ... a declining, stagnant and inef- ficient rural economy'.

Population statistics for the region tell a mixed story.[84] After the combined influenza and famine of Gulab Singh's minority, the population recovered slowly, picking up further in the 1930s prob- ably due to improving control over disease, some movement in agriculture and forests, together with developments in transport and communications. However, while poverty, lack of economic growth, periodic scarcity, and the lure of wages pushed Rewa's unemployed as far afield as Nimar, Nagpur, and Amravati, 94 per cent of the population remained in the *tahsils* of their birth, a chilling comment on the restricted outlook of the mass of people and the state's lack of development.

Minor advances in education between the two wars masked a degree of illiteracy far below that of central India as a whole.[85] However, while student totals increased, the number of schools fell marginally between 1926–37. As a result by 1943 schools were overcrowded with classes of 80 pupils, described by one observer as 'illiterate children ... being taught by a semi-illiterate tutor'. The vast majority of people did not send their children to school at all. In 1942 a committee touring the Amarkantak *patha* could not find a single village that had even one literate inhabitant! Due to the prevailing illiteracy, newspapers were few, and those confined to the capital and under the control of the *darbar*. All ceased public- ation at the time of Independence.

Health care similarly made slow progress during Gulab Singh's reign.[86] Between 1921–41 the number of outpatients in state hos- pitals and dispensaries, and expenditure on health, doubled.

However, in the prevailing poverty, illiteracy and disinterest in public cleanliness, epidemics continued to wreak havoc, the *darbar's* thinly spread health network being poorly equipped to handle the onslaught.

Rewa's social and economic backwardness severely limited urban growth after the First World War.[87] Due to the mining and export of coal, some towns on the railway in south Rewa came into focus; and Satna, too, surged due to its railway location and the consequent growth of trade and industry, though it remained dirty and congested. Rewa was perhaps more typical of the urban scene in the state. Electrified as late as 1934, it had no industry and spawned numbers of insanitary mud huts; its population in 1941 was lower than that in 1911.

Social oppression and crime flourished in a society where a few held most land, and the many comprised the rural poor, illiterate and vulnerable to disease. The ruler himself witnessed the gap between the peasantry and his nobility when visiting Singrauli in 1933:

Being too far from headquarters and inaccessible owing to lack of communications, Singrauli is to Rewa what Siberia is to Russia. The result is that high-caste people, who are either rich private individuals or Pawaidars, and who ... are better educated than the lower castes which is[sic] both poor and illiterate ... continued ceaselessly to harass and oppress the latter. The general difficulty of lack of communications, the inaccessibility of the tract ... added to the illiteracy of the residents, provides a prominent sphere for harassment and loot.[88]

Social divisiveness also encompassed a growing communal consciousness, particularly in Satna with its links beyond Baghelkhand.[89] Up to 1921 Hindus and Muslims lived together more or less amicably, but outside influences combined with competition for resources among a growing urban population led to a projection of identity as a way of advancing group interests. After the First World War relations between Hindus and Muslims in Satna became strained due to talk of *jihad*, instances of conversion to Islam, and tension over *tazia* processions. In the 1930s national political pressures entered the state, such that in 1940 Muslims in Satna sought to organize themselves politically with help from the Central Provinces Muslim League. Gulab Singh spoke forcibly against some of these developments, while disallowing Hindu organizations to work in the state. Nonetheless, communal tension mounted, for when turning down further requests by Christians to work in the state, he noted that 'we have already got sufficient divisions'.

However, by then Rewa was involved in more compelling tensions with the central government, and it is to this crisis in the relations between centre and region that we now turn.

Notes

1. K.S. Fitze, *Rulers, Leading Families and Officials in the States of Central India*, Calcutta, 1928, p. 33.
2. FP*Hons*, 18(7)—H, 1925, CI to Polindia, 28 Mar. 1925; CIA, P, A, 1902–47, 82–A, 1927, R.I.R, Glancy to MSec, 28 Oct. 1927; FP, 10(20)-H, 1927, R.I.R. Glancy to Polindia, 21 Nov. 1927; FP, 557(2)-P, 1927, Irwin's speech at Rewa, 9 Jan. 1928; Fitze, *Twilight*, p. 91.
3. FPIS, 1160, 1922, D.B. Blakeway to FSec, 8 Apr. 1922; RS, Dak Office, 1924–42, 80, 1925, P, Maharaja's note, 8 June 1933; *RSA, 1922–23*, p. xi.
4. FP, 557(2)-P. 1927, Memo of K.S. Fitze, 24 Nov. 1927; VP, RDO, 34–35, SN–151, FX, 1934–35, Maharaja's circular, 28 Jan. 1935; CRR, CI, 18(7)-P(S)/42, L.C.F. Robins' report, 1942; *The Rewa Land Revenue and Tenancy Code, 1935*, Allahabad, 1935; p. 11; Bomford, *Final Settlement Report*, p. 29.
5. RDO, B 8/32–33, Admin (Confdl), Sardars, 3, 1932, Maharaja's note, n. d.
6. FP, P, 692–P(S)/33, 186, R.J. MacNabb to B.J. Glancy, 6 Dec. 1933; RDO, B, 15/45–46, 172, Confdl, 1946, K.S. Fitze to Maharaja Rewa, 8 Mar. 1939; CRR, CI, P, 18–P(S)/42, G.T. Fisher to K.S. Fitze, 14 Feb. 1942.
7. Fitze, *Twilight*, pp. 92–3.
8. FPIS, 1160, 1922, 1–6, Notes, D.B. Blakeway to FSec, 25 Sept. 1922; BA, Eng files, pt III, 106, 1926, Return of Europeans, Eurasians, 12 Feb. 1926; FPE, 241–E, 1929, Maharaja Rewa to R. Glancy, 16 Jan. 1929; *RSA, 1922–23*, p. 1; *Shahdol Gazetteer*, p. 3; information supplied by R.S. Misra. The East district subsequently became Sidhi district. Gulab Singh created Pushprajgarh *tahsil* in the south district in 1935.
9. Information supplied by R.S. Misra. For the civil disobedience and related movements see pp. 241–4. A. Siddiqui, 'An assessment of the working of the former Vindhya Pradesh legislative assembly', PhD, Rewa, 1978, pp. 43–5; *Rewa Commission of Enquiry*, appx. IV,

vol. I, Opening address by A.N. Chaudhury for the Crown, pp. 13–14, 18. The *raj parishad* had 41 members: 21 officials and 20 non-officials. It had no legislative powers, and questions were disallowed. Ministers and departmental heads were members ex-officio. The ruler himself selected the members from a list of recommended names.

10. CRR, CI, 45-P(S)/36, K.S. Fitze to B.J. Glancy, 22 Feb. 1936; *ibid.*, J. Robson to B.J. Glancy, 23 Nov. 1936; CRR, CI, 18(7)-P(S)/42, Robins' report, 1942; *RCE*, appx. I, vol. I, pp. 12–13, 21.

11. CRR, CI, 18(7)-P(S)/42, Robins' report. The report claimed that the ADC power centre split the ministers, some of whom threw in their lot with the ADCs, others forming a 'party of their own'.

12. RDO, B 8, 32–3, G, 4, 32–3, C.L. Corfield, 26 July 1933; RDO, B 13, 1934–41, Rev, 281, Maharaja to Rev Min, 4 May 1935; CRR, CI, P, P branch, 30-P(S)/37, FR Bgkd 2/Feb. 1937; CRR, CI, 18(7)-P(S)/42, Robins' report; *RCE*, appx. I, vol. 3, HH, 16 Oct. 1936; Fitze, *Twilight*, pp. 93–4. The ruler's policies were probably counter-productive, as they created unrest and discontent, not the least because he had no time for a bureaucracy which he regarded as corrupt and inefficient.

13. *RCE*, vol. I, p. 14.

14. BA, 119–C, 1932, Brajendranath to PA, 24 Oct. 1932; RS, PM and Council, 1932–46/47, Aliya office, 20, 1940, Illegible, 5 Apr. 1935; ibid., Sahi (Gulab Singh), 19 Apr. 1935; *Rewa Gazetteer*, p. 291.

15. BA, P, A, 99–A, 1931, F. Bailley to E. Egerton, 8 Sept. 1931; RDO, B 14, 7, 1930–2, 175 I, Army, 1931–2, G.S., 17 Sept. 1932; Ibid., PSec to PA, 19 Sept. 1931; BA, P, A, 99–A, 1931, G.S. to B.J. Glancy, 10 May 1933; CIA, P, A, 72–A, 1935, E. Egerton, 19 Sept. 1934; CIA, P, A, 72–A, 1935, J.A. Blood to Military Adviser, 11 Dec. 1934; CRR, CI, P, 45-P(S)/36, K.S. Fitze to A.M. Mills, 21 Feb. 1938; P, P Branch, 3(7)-P(S)/40, G.T. Fisher to F.V. Wylie, 31 Jan. 1941; *RSA, 1925–26*, p. 2; *RSA, 1926–27*, pp. 13–14. In 1926–27 the Rewa Army had a total of 1521 officers, other ranks, and followers, the amalgamation of battalions and regiments taking place that year. So far as differences with the central government over the State Army were concerned, the Maharaja realized that he needed to maintain good relations with the government as his regime began to come under closer scrutiny.

16. RDO, B 8, 32–3, Admin (confdl), 3, 1932, Gulab Singh's note, n. d.; RDO, B 10, 1934–5, 191, R, 1934–5, Maharaja Surguja to Maharaja Rewa, 28 Nov, 1934; *Report of the Committee Appointed to Enquire into the Nature of Pawai Tenures in Rewa State*, Allahabad, 1934, pp. 6–7, 46–8. The Maharaja allowed landholders to request compensation

for land taken for road or rail communications, or for reserved forests.

17. AICC P, G-17, 1930–1, Maharaja's order, 353 B.D., 29 Mar. 1928; RDO, B 10, 1934–5, 191–R, 1934–5, Maharaja Surguja to Maharaja Rewa, 28 Nov. 1934; *Rewa State Census, 1941, Report,* pp. 17–18; *Sidhi Gazetteer,* p. 146; Bomford, *Final Settlement Report,* pp. 23–4, 32, 24, 43.

18. RDO, 1920–2, B 3, 1924–5, 5, R(Confdl), 1924, Maharaja's note, 12 Aug. 1924; ibid., H. Bomford to Sec Darbar, 24 Feb. 1925; FP, P, 60–P(S)/31, AGGCI to PSec, 20 Dec. 1930; Bomford, *Final Settlement Report,* p. 24. *Daijawan* was a cess levied at the time of the marriage of a ruler's daughter.

19. RDO, 1930–44, Rev, 111, Gulab Singh to Darbar Sec, 10 June 1926; CIA, 296–C, 1931, Maharaja Rewa to R.J. Heale, 6 Aug. 1931; *RSA, 1918–22,* p. 64; Corfield, *Princely India,* p. 62; E. Wakefield, *Past Imperative: My Life in India, 1927–1947,* London, 1966, pp. 197–8.

20. CRR, CI, P, 45-P(S)/36, J. Robson to B. Glancy, 23 Nov. 1936.

21. CIA, Confdl, 424–C, 1930, Gulab Singh to R.J.W. Heale, 19 Aug. 1930; FP, P, 32-P(S)/31, FR Bgkd 1/July 1931; FP, P, 60-P(S)/31, H.A.L. Metcalf, 22 Nov. 1931; CIA, P, A, 81-A/31, AGGCI to PSec, 20 Jan. 1932; AICC P, G-27, pt. II, 1934–5, A.P. Singh, 8 Oct. 1935; AICC P, G-17, 1930–1, A brief statement of the case of a number of elakadars in Rewah, nd; *Shahdol Gazetteer,* p. 314; Bhargava, 'Relations of British paramount power', PhD, p. 101.

22. RDO, B 3, 1924–5, 5, Confdl, Rev, 1924, Maharaja to Sec Saheb, 20 Aug. 1925; CIA, 296-C, 1931, Gulab Singh to R.J.W. Heale, 6 Aug. 1931; C. Allen and S. Dwivedi, *Lives of the Indian Princes,* London, 1984, p. 234; Corfield, *Princely India,* p. 62; Wakefield, *Past Imperative,* pp. 197–8.

23. Corfield, *Princely India,* pp. 66–7.

24. CIA, 296–C, 1931, Gulab Singh to R.J.W. Heale, 6 Aug. 1931; Allen and Dwivedi, *Lives of Indian Princes* p. 234; *Pawai Report,* pp. 31–2, 36–8, 60–2; Corfield, *Princely India,* pp. 66–7. In his settlement Bomford distinguished between *ilaqadars* holding the older *jagirs* which were essentially military service grants; and the *pawaidars* and other holders, some of whom held large estates in south Rewa.

25. *Pawai Report,* pp. 35, 40–1, 44, 50–2, 57–8; *Rewa Directory,* p. 213.

26. RDO,9/32–34, 6, Pawai Commitee, Ramgovind Singh, 20 Nov. 1933; P, P branch, 22-P(S)/34, C.L. Corfield to B.J. Glancy, 30 Nov. 1933; ibid., C.L. Corfield, 11 June 1934; P, P branch, 248–P(S)/39, B.J. Glancy, 18 Apr. 1936; Corfield, *Princely India,* p. 71. Corfield mentioned to the Maharaja that he was to meet the Political Secretary, Sir Bertram Glancy, in Delhi, and this seems to have induced Gulab

Singh to sign the report which had been lying on his table 'for months'.

27. BA, Eng files III, 190, 1927, PA, 9 Mar. 1928; BA, Eng files, pt III, 462, 1929, Janki Prasad to PA, 30 Dec. 1929; BA, 242–A, 1931, Synopsis of important events; *RSA, 1926–27*, p. 39; *Rewa Gazetteer*, pp. 158–9; *Satna Gazetteer*, p. 219.

28. CIA, PWD, Misc, H-14, vol. I, 1921; VP, RDO, B 3, 1922–3, 65-II, 1922–3, Mining, Mgr RS Collieries to Maharaja Rewa, 13 Nov. 1922; VP, RDO, 1928, Mine, 175, 1928–9, Maharaja's note, n.d; VP, RDO. 1929–30, 181, Mine, 1929–30, Shaw Wallace to Sec Darbar, 16 May 1930; RS, Aliya office, 1935–7, Minerals, 1939, no. 4196, Ind Min, 12 Aug. 1939; *RSA, 1926–27*, pp. 38–40. The state held shares in Rewa Coalfields worth Rs 8.65 lakhs, comprising the capital value of the colleries. Royalties and rent could fetch the ruler up to a lakh each year.

29. BA, Eng files, pt. III, 402, 1925, Dewan of Nagod to PA, 18 May 1925; BA, Eng files, pt. III, 409, 1927, J. Prasad to PA, 9 Jan. 1928; CIA, P, A, 1902–47, 82–A, 1927, Proposed speech of state engineer; CIA, PWD, Communics, A-135, PSec Rewa to Sec AGGCI, 3 Sept. 1934; *RSA, 1926–27*, pp. 52–4; Bomford, *Final Settlement Report*, pp. 6–8; A.K. Roy, 'Myth, fable and guile: the art of survival in Shahdol', *India International Centre Quarterly*, vol. 19, nos 1–2, Spring-Summer, 1992, p. 245. Bridges across the Tons included the low-level bridge at Madhogarh and the bridge at Chakghat on the Allahabad road. Between 1921 and 1941 metalled roads in Rewa State expanded from 373 to 717 kilometres, and fair weather roads from 337.4 to 1008 kilometres.

30. *Rewa State Census, 1941, Report*, p. 20.

31. For rail communications see BA, 531-B, 1924, Rewa Darbar to Engineer, CIC Railway, 14 Apr. 1924, with note by PA; FPI, 272–I, 1928, J. Kaul, 7 Jan. 1928; RDO, B 6, 1927–30, 123–B, Railway, 1928– 29, K. Haksar to E. Colvin, 3 Mar. 1932; CIA, PWD, PW branch, 47– S, 1935, PSec Rewa to Sec AGGCI, 17 Apr. 1935; RDO, B 11, 1935–6, Railway, 158, 35–6, Report on the proposed Katni–Singrauli railway, W. Gurney, Dec. 1939. (Indian Railways built the Singrauli line in the 1950s and the Satna–Rewa spur in the 1990s. The former is a case where building a line through a remote, poorly populated tract has not led to the development of the area.) For telephone and postal services, see FPI, 1202, 1923, 1, D.B. Blakeway to PSec, Delhi, 6 Jan. 1923; BA, Eng files, pt III, 424, 1930, Supt POs, Jubbulpore to PA, 3 Oct. 1930; CIA, PWD, 6-S, 1941, V. Prasad to AGGCI, 8 Feb. 1936; CIA, Fin, C, 27–C, 1935, pt I, PMG, Nagpur to Rev Min, Rewa, 5 Aug. 1936. The central government added to the number of post offices provided Rewa contributed towards their

cost; and converted some post offices to an alternate-day service, where these were running at a loss.

32. For seasons and crop reports see *RSA*, 1922 to 1927; FP, P, 207–P(S)/28, CIA FR 2/Sept. 1928; CIA, P, A, 1902–47, 119-A, 1928, Synopsis for year ending 31 Dec. 1928; CIA, P, 98–A/29, 1929, K.A.G. Evans-Gordon to Sec AGGCI, 4 Jan. 1930; BA, 242–A, 1931, Synopsis of important events, 1931; CIA, P, A, 81–A/31, 1931, Synopsis of events in Baghelkhand; P, P branch, 5(13)-P(S)/41, CIA FR 1/Dec. 1941.

33. *Notes and Orders on the Introduction of Regular Survey and Settlement Operations in the Rewa State*, Lucknow, 1922, Confdl note of V.K. Mulye, 11 June 1919, pp. 4–5; ibid., Order, Regent of Rewa, no. 107, 1919, 22 June 1919, p. 32; ibid., Order, Regent of Rewa, no. 4, 1920, 18 Mar. 1920, pp. 17–21; *RSA, 1922–23*, p. 31; *Satna Gazetteer*, pp. 250–1; *Shahdol Gazetteer*, pp. 205–6; *Sidhi Gazetteer*, pp. 144–5; Zutshi, *Rewa and its Ruler*, Extract from Lord Reading's speech; Bomford, *Final Setlement Report*, pp. 30–1; Roy, *Planning the Environment*, 1982. p. 5.

34. RDO, B 3, 1924–25, 1/2C, Rev Coop, 1925, Note, Maharaja Rewa, Oct. 1926; *Survey and Settlement Operations*, Regent's Order, 22 June 1919, p. 32; *Rewa State Census, 1941, Report*, pp. 17–18; *Satna Gazetteer*, pp. 250–1; *Rewa Directory*, pp. 149–50. See p. 132.

35. RDO, P, 105, CC, 1930–1, Note by C.M. Harlow, 10 Mar. 1930; RS, Pr Sec's office, 1940–1, 227, 1930, Misc, Working plan of Dhatura reserved forest, C. M. Harlow; *RSA, 1922–23*, pp. 32–3; *RSA, 1926–27*, pp. 35–6; *Working Plan, Rewa Forest Divn*, vol. I, pp. lxii, 193–5, 201–2, 205–6; *Working Scheme for West Sidhi Forest Divn*, pp. 63–4, 128; *Forest Management Plan, North Shahdol and Umaria*, vol. I, pp. 83–5; *Working Plan, South Shahdol*, vol. I, pp. 73–4; *Path Enquiry Commission*, pp. 113–14; *Rewa Gazetteer*, p. 15; *Sidhi Gazetteer*, p. 15. The rules of 1930 sanctioned *nistar* and grazing for *aam* jungles, peasants having to pay for produce taken from reserved forests; and regulated the cutting of bamboo and shifting cultivation. In 1930 the state also introduced the concept of fire prevention in its forests. The 1935 Act distinguished between reserved forests and *aam* jungle or waste, termed protected forest in Rewa. Saklani, Conservator from 1936 to 1947, largely continued Harlow's policies.

36. BA, Eng Files, pt III, 309, 1928, J. Prasad to PA, 5 Nov. 1928; *RSA, 1923–4*, pp. 3–4; K. Sankalia, *Tiger! The Story of the Indian Tiger*, London, 1978, p. 171; Fitze, *Twilight*, p. 145.

37. A. Morrow, *Highness: The Maharajahs of India*, London, 1986, pp. 140–1; Gaekwad, *Palaces*, p. 106.

38. J. Mitchell, *The Wheels of Ind*, London, 1934, pp. 151–4.

39. BA, A branch, 219–A, 31, 1931, J. Prasad to PA, 10 Nov. 1931; RDO, B 8, 32–3, File IV, Stdg Orders, 32–3, Darbar Order 189 B.D., 21,

21 Nov. 1933; *RSA, 1926–27*, pp. 5–7; *Rewa Directory*, np. For land revenue, see *RSA, 1925–26*, p. 24; *RSA, 1926–27*, p. 27; *Satna Gazetteer*, p. 244. With the third settlement, the revenue from north Rewa yielded an additional 3.6 lakhs, and from south Rewa about 1.5 lakhs. Land revenue fell owing to remissions in the bad seasons which, with the non-payment of arrears, in 1931 totalled Rs 28.56 lakhs.

40. HP, 1922, 544, D.B. Blakeway to HSec, 27 June 1922; VP, RDO, 1921–2, Fin, 83, 1921–2, Maharaja Rewa to Regent, 17 Oct. 1922; VP, RDO, 1929–30, 181, Mine, 1929–30, Shaw Wallace to Sec Darbar, 11 June 1931; CRR, CI, P, 45-P(S)/36, J. Robson to B.J. Glancy, 23 Nov. 1936; RDO, B 15/45–46, 172, Confdl, 1946, V. Prasad, 19 Feb. 1939; RDO, P, 1937–8, P Office, Conversation between Lord Willingdon and Maharaja Rewa, 11 Dec. 1939; Corfield, *Princely India* p. 125.

41. Ibid p. 70.

42. Information supplied by R.S. Misra. Gulab Singh's private income included money on account of his mother's dowry and her share in the estate of the Dumraon Raj. See FP, P, III-P, 1924, 1–3, passim. Most of the transfers of state money appear to have taken place after 1927, when Rewa ceased to publish the annual administration reports. *RSA, 1926–27*, p. 10. G.T. Fisher, AGGCI in the early 1940s, assumed that the Maharaja 'put away Rs 20 lakhs per year'. See CRR, CI, P, P branch, 18(3)–P(S)/42, G.T. Fisher to K.S. Fitze, 29 Jan. 1942.

43. RDO, B 8, 32–33, File IV, Stdg Orders, H.H., 21 Nov. 1932; CRR, CI, P, 45-P(S)/36, J. Robson to B. Glancy, 23 Nov. 1936; RS, Aliya Office, 1935–7, Mine, 1939; CRR, CI, P, P branch, 18(3)-P(S)/42, K.S. Fitze, 13 Jan. 1942; CRR, CI, P, P branch, 18(3)-P(S)/42, G.T. Fisher to K.S. Fitze, 29 Jan. 1942; *RCE*, vol. I, Statement of Finance Minister, p. 16, notes that from 1931–40 a sum of Rs 1,08,54,653 was transferred from the state to Gulab Singh's personal account. In 1932 Corfield claimed that the Maharaja had told him that he had invested Rs 110 lakhs in British and Greek loans.

44. VPR, RDO, 1929–30, 181, Mine, 29–30, Shaw Wallace to Sec Darbar, 16 May 1930; RDO, B 8, 32–33, File IV, Stdg Orders, H.H., 21 Nov. 1932; RS, P, 1924–35, 193, Mine (Coal), II, 1933–4, passim; RS, Aliya Office, 1935–7, Mine, 1939; CRR, CI, P,P branch, 15(15)-P(S)/45, Report on Rewa finances, Rai Bahadur Chatterji, Jan. 1946; CRR, CI, P, P branch, 15(15)-P(S)/46, M. Prasad, 22 July 1946.

45. RDC, B 8/32–3, Admin, 1932–3, BOB file, Circular 89, Maharaja Rewa, 26 Sept. 1933; CRR, CI, P, 45–P(S)/36, J. Robson to B. Glancy, 23 Nov. 1936; RDO, 8/32–33, Admin, 1932–3, BOB file,

L.W. Wooldridge, Administrator RS, 16 June 1942, on Darbar Order of 1 May 1933, citing clause 2, para 1; *Rewa Directory*, p. 177.

46. RDO, Admin, B 8, 1932–3, S.B. Kelkar, 14 Oct. 1933; RDO, Admin, B 8, 1932–3, Brajendranath to Maharaja Rewa, 2 Feb. 1937; MS, P, Group III, 6(31)-P/49, S.N. Mehta to DepSec MS, 12 June 1949; *Rewa Directory*, p. 177.

47. FP, 1926, 28(S)-H, AGGCI to PSec, 24 Dec. 1926; FPS, 33-H, 1929, Cusnawen (?), 7 Aug. 1929; ibid., PSec to AGGCI, 14 Jan. 1930; CRR, CI, P, 35(3)-H(S)/30, A.H., 7 Feb. 1931; *RSA, 1926–27*, p. 3. Gulab Singh's full title in 1930 was His Highness Maharajadhiraja Sir Gulab Singh Bahadur, KCSI, Maharaja of Rewa.

48. FP, 92-P, 1924, 1–2, G.D. Ogilvie, 21 Oct. 1924; CIA, G, 343–C, 1931, CI to PA, Bgkd, 14 Nov. 1931; CIA, 164B, 1931, AGGCI to PA Bgkd, 27 Nov. 1931; CIA, 127 B, 9, 1933, AGGCI to PA Bukd, 24 Jan. 1933. The Political Agent in Navgaon was to handle extradition, arms licences, post office offences, succession certificates, and the registration of births, deaths and marriages in Rewa State. See FP, Accts, 386-A, 1933, B.D., 12 May 1933.

49. FP, 5 Feb. 1835, 24, W.H. MacNaghten to L.C. MacSween, encl. R.C. Smith to G.A. Bushby with a translation of a *khureeta* from the Raja of Rewa, 21 Jan. 1835; CIA, Fin, 390–C/31, 1931, G.D. Ogilvie to JSec FP, 10 Sept. 1932; FPI, 355–I, 1932, G.D. Ogilvie to FSec, 5 Oct. 1932; CIA, G, 343–G, 1931, DSec FP to AGGCI, 24 May 1933.

50. ISC, vol. I, *Evidence*, pp. 735–6; ISC, vol. III, *Evidence*, pp. 1427–8; N. Gangulee, *The Making of Federal India*, London, 1936, pp. 57–8; Bhargava, 'Relations of British paramount power', PhD, pp. 239–40.

51. ISC, vol. I, *Evidence*, pp. 688, 694; ISC, vol. II, *Evidence*, p. 1272; ISC, vol. III, *Evidence*, pp. 1374–93, passim; Bhargava, 'Relations of British paramount power', PhD, p. 202.

52. CIA, J, 150-B, 1927, Sec Darbar to PA, 5 Aug. 1927; FPI, 202–I, 1929, pt I, J. Prasad, 9 Jan. 1930; ibid., J.P., 14 May 1930; CIA, J, 150–B, 1929, illegible, 21 Oct. 1932; FPI, 202-I, 1929, A.M. Ali, 2 Dec. 1932; ISC, vol. I, *Evidence*, pp. 527–9. Much of the discussion on railway land turned on Rewa's insistence that it collect *lac* on such land. The compromise permitted the *darbar* to exercise civil and criminal jurisdiction over railway land, pending a general discussion of the question of jurisdiction.

53. Gangulee, *Making of Federal India*, pp. 53–4; Fitze, *Twilight*, p. 26; Corfield, *Princely India*, p. 4; I, Copland, *The Princes of India in the Endgame of Empire, 1917–1947*, Cambridge, 1997, p. 46. States supporting the chamber included Alwar, Dhaulpur, Nawanagar, Palampur, Kachchh, Rewa, Bikaner, and Patiala.

54. FP, P, 654-P(S), 1927, MS, 29 Apr. 1927; Copland, *Princes of India*, p. 59; S.R. Ashton, *British Policy Towards the Indian States, 1905–1939*, London, 1982, p. 139.
55. Ibid., p. 144.
56. Copland, *Princes of India.*, pp. 62–3, 96.
57. HP, 1922, 544, D.B. Blakeway to HSec, 27 June 1922; RS, P, 1937–38, P Office, Maharaja Rewa's conversation with Viceroy, 11 Dec. 1939; CRR, CI, P., P branch, 179-P(S)/H, G.T. Fisher, to Maharaja Rewa, 17 Sept. 1941; Copland, *Princes of India*, p. 96.
58. H. Montgomery Hyde, *Lord Reading: The Life of Rufus Isaacs, First Marquess of Reading*, London, 1967, p. 404; *The Round Table Conference: India's Demand for Dominion Status: Speeches*, Madras, 1931, pp. 66–72; Copland, *Princes of India*, p. 87.
59. VPR, RDO, 101–20, 1 RTC(6), 1918–19, Maharaja Rewa, 18 Nov. 1930.
60. FP, P, 412-P, 1930, 1–2, SOS to Viceroy, 19 Sept. 1930; CIA, Confdl, 424–C, 1930, FDept to CI, 28 Sept. 1930; FP, P, 395–P(S)/31, 1931, SOS to Viceroy, 6 Aug. 1931; CIA, Confdl, 146-A/32, Polindia to CI, 13 Oct. 1932; B. Ramusack, 'The civil disobedience movement and the Round Table Conferences; the princes' response', B.R. Nanda, *Essays in Modern Indian History*, New Delhi, 1980, also claims that political officers influenced Gulab Singh's opinions.
61. FP, P, 395-P(S)/31, 1931, SOS to Viceroy, 4 Nov. 1931; U. Phadnis, *Towards the Integration of the Indian States, 1919–1947*, New Delhi, 1968, p. 64; Copland, *Princes of India*, pp. 92, 102; Fitze, *Twilight*, p. 80.
62. CIA, Confdl, 146–A, 1932, Maharaja Rewa to Col. Ogilvie, 21 Oct. 1932; ibid., PA to AGGCI, 16 Nov. 1932; Fitze, *Twilight*, p. 83; R.J. Moore, *The Crisis of Indian Unity*, Delhi, 1974, pp. 280, 283; Corfield, *Princes India*, pp. 68–9. Corfield emerged as a defender of princely interests in the months before Independence in 1947.
63. Corfield, *Princely India*, pp. 68–9.
64. VPR, P, 1935–36, 24, PC, 1927, P, Maharaja Rewa to 'Your Highness', 25 Mar. 1927; CIA, P, A, 112–A, 1933, Rewa to CI, 16 Sept. 1933; P, Federation I, 357(18), 1936, Maharaja Rewa to Lord Linlithgow, 11 Sept. 1936; ibid., A.C. Lothian to J.B. Glancy, 19 Sept. 1937; Copland, *Princes of India*, p. 102; Corfield, *Princely India*, p. 94.
65. Fitze, *Twilight*, p. 33; Corfield, *Princely India*, p. 5; Bhargava, 'Relations of British paramount power', PhD, p. 41.
66. FP, P, 148-P(S), 1930, Maharaja Rewa to Lord Irwin, 12 Mar 1930; RS, P, 1932-46, 225, 1941, P, H.H., note, 13 Apr. 1941; ibid., Brajendranath, 17 Apr. 1941; Fitze, *Twilight*, p. 93.
67. FPI, B(S), Aug. 1920, 164, A.B. Scott to Chief, Gen Staff, 10 May 1920; FPI, B, Aug. 1921, 13, F.G. Beville to PSec, 15 Apr. 1921; FP,

O, 32-P(S), 1931, FR Bgkd, 1/July 1931; MPCC P, G-32, 1939–49, L.A.P. Singh to GSec, AICC, 10 Aug. 1939; *Rewa Gazetteer*, p. 49; *Shahdol Gazetteer*, p. 314; Dubey, 'Establishment of democratic political system', PhD, p. 55.

68. AICC, P, G-17, 1930–31, J.L. Nehru to Sec RDarbar, 25 Feb. 1930; FP, P, 148-P(S), 1930, Gulab Singh to C. Watson, 15 July 1930. RDO, B 12, 1936–37, 46, S, 1936, D Order, 342 B.D., 6 May 1933; Dubey, 'Establishment of democratic political system', PhD, pp. 54–5.

69. RDO, B 6/27–30(S), 14, Sec Darbar to Maharaja Sarguja, 17 July 1929; FP, P, 148-P(S), 1930. Gulab Singh to C.Watson, 15 July 1930; FPI, 321-I, 1930, R.J. W. Heale to PSec, 27 Oct. 1930; FPI, 31-I, 1932, J.M. Clay to C. Watson, 12 Feb. 1932; CRR, CI, P, P branch, 11(30)-P(S)/40, CIO, Nagpur, 30 Nov. 1940; *Rewa Directory*, p. 230. In 1932 Rewa requested the government to detain Narmada Prasad Singh.

70. VPR, RDO, 1923–4, P, 50, Pawaidars, Maharaja Rewa, 7 Aug. 1932; *Dictionary of National Biography*, vol. IV, pp. 205–7; *Rewa Gazetteer*, p. 7; *Rewa Directory*, p. 248. Satna district did not come into being until 1947, but the phrase is used here as a convenient marker.

71. *DNB*, vol. IV, p. 206.

72. FP, P, 18-P(S), 1930, 191, FR Bgkd 1/Aug 1930; RDO, B 6/27–30, 162-Rev, 1930–1, City Inspector Satna to SP North, 10 Dec. 1930; FP, P, 32-P(S), 1931, FR Bgkd, 2/Mar., 2/Apr., 1/July 1931; AICC P, 1930–1, J. Nehru to Sec Darbar, Rewa, 17 July 1931; AICC P, G-17, N.P. Singh to J. Nehru, 17 Aug. 1931; FP, P, 32-P(S), 1931, 192, FR Bgkd, 1/Nov., 2/Nov., 1/Dec. 1931; BA, 252-A, 1931–32, *Lokmat*, 20 Nov. 1931; *Rewa Gazetteer*, p. 49.

73. CIA, 296-C, 1931, Pol Rewa to CI, 9 Aug. 1931; AICC P, G-17, 1930–1, B. Joshi to J.L. Nehru, 10 Aug. 1931; FP, P, 32-P(S), 1931, FR Bgkd 1/Aug. 1931: FPP, 60–P(S)/31, 1931, SOS to Viceroy, 26 Sept 1931; *ibid.*, PA to AGGCI, 26 Sept. 1931; *ibid.*, G.D. Ogilvie to C. Watson, 21 Oct. 1931; FPP, 32-P(S), 1931, 192, FR Bgkd 2/Oct. 1931.

74. FP, P,32-P(S), 1931, 192, FR Bgkd 1/Oct., 2/Oct., 1/Nov., 2/Nov., 1/Dec. 1931; BA, 252/A, 31–32, *Lokmat*, 10 Dec. 1931; P, P branch, 5(13)-P(S)/41, FR CIA 2/Jan. 1932; *Rewa Gazetteer*, p. 50; Dubey, 'Establishment of democratic political system, PhD, p. 61. For the Maharaja's reforms see p. 225.

75. P, P branch, 32-P(S)/32, FR CIA 1/Apr., 2/Apr., 1/May, 2/May, 1/June, 1/Aug. 1932; MPCC, G. 32, 1939–48, Report of MPCC; RDO, B 12, 1936–37, 46, S, 1936, C.L. Corfield to Congress office in-charge, 6 May 1932; CIA, P, A, 130-A/32, 1932, CIA synopsis for 1932; RDO, B 8, 32–3, 106 (Admin), 32–33, Circular, C.L. Corfield, 10 May 1933; Dubey, 'Establishment of democratic political system', PhD, pp. 67, 115. There was a minor flurry in September 1932 when students in Satna boycotted their schools, and the temple of

Keshavdass was opened to Harijans; the Baghelkhand Congress
Commitee remained illegal until 1939.

76. AICC P, G-27, pt II, 1934–5, Note by A.P. Singh, 1934; RS, P, 1924–
35, 93, Confdl, IGP Rewa to V. Prasad, 11 Feb. 1935; *Rewa Gazetteer*,
p. 50; Corfield, *Princely India*, pp. 64–5; *Rewa Directory*, p. 107.

77. AICC P, G-27, pt *Final Settlement* II, 1934–5, M. Gandhi to N.C.
Kelkar, June 1934; AICC P, G-27, pt 1, 1934–5, J. Kripalani to G. Sec,
Karnataka PCC, 11 Dec. 1934; AICC P, G-27, pt I, 1934–5, R. Prasad
to Amritlal, 1 Aug. 1935; Siddiqui, 'Former Vindhya Pradesh legislature', PhD, p. 35; Dubey, 'Establishment of democratic political
system', PhD, p. 68.

78. AICC P, G-12, 1937–9, Mysore resolution; Dubey, 'Establishment of
democratic political system', PhD, pp. 105–7, 109, 111, 119. Awadesh
Pratap Singh made another unsuccessful appeal to Congressmen
at the Ramgarh session in 1940 to lift the ban on forming Congress
committees in princely states.

79. CIA, Fin-C, 27-C, 1935, pt I, PMG to Sec AGGCI, 31 Oct. 1935; *RSA,
1925–26*, p. 42; *Rewa State Census, 1941, Report*, p. 18; Bomford, *Final
Settlement Report*, p. 17; Corfield, *Princely India*, p. 70.

80. For coal see p. 230. For forests, *Sidhi Gazetteer*, p. 15; *Report of Path
Enquiry Commission*, pp. 113–14.

81. RDO, B 10, 1934–5, 300–31, 58-I, Railway, 1934–5, E. Digby to K.G.
Evans-Gordon, 31 Aug. 1922; FP, 557(2)-P, 1927, R.I.R. Glancy to C.
Watson, 28 Nov. 1927; RS, Pr Sec's office, 1944–45, Maharaja Rewa,
5 Jan. 1934; CRR, CI, P, P branch, 79-P(S)/41, G.T. Fisher to H.
Craik, 11 Dec. 1941. According to the Rewa census of 1941 2.7 per
cent of the state's population was literate in 1931, and 4.62 per cent
in 1941, contrasting with the 8 per cent average for the Central
India Agency. The northern *tahsils* had the highest literacy rates.

82. RDO, B 3, 1924–25, 1/2C, Rev Coop, 1925, Note by Maharaja Rewa,
Oct. 1926; RS, Pr Sec's office, 1944–5, Maharaja Rewa, 5 Jan. 1934;
Rewa State Census, 1941, p. 53; *Shahdol Gazetteer*, p. 211.

83. RDO, B 10, 1934–5, 200R, 1934–5, Note by Maharaja Rewa on
tenancy, 3 Mar. 1935. The Maharaja wrote this note before the
passage of the tenancy legislation.

84. CIA, War, 150-W/1942, N.J. Thompson to Milit 10, 11 May 1942;
Rewa State Census, 1941, Report, pp. 24–5; *Census of India, 1931*, vol.
XII, *CP and Berar*, pt. I, *Report*, pp. 96, 100–1; *Rewa Gazetteer*, p. 59;
Sidhi Gazetteer, p. 36; Bomford, *Final Settlement Report*, p. 10; Dube,
Population of Rewa, pp. 20–2; Lal, 'Settlement geography', PhD, p.
96.

85. See note 81 for literacy rates. *Rewa State Census, 1941, Report*, pp.
41–4; *Report of Path Enquiry Commission*, pp. 128, 236, 291; *Rewa
Gazetteer*, p. 291; *Satna Gazetteer*, p. 358. The number of students in

schools in Rewa rose from 9931 to 17,000 between 1923–7. In 1926 there were 152 schools, and in 1937 150! For education, see *RSA* between 1922–7; *Rewa Directory*, p. 188; Wakefield, *Past Imperative*, p. 198. For higher education, by 1923 high schools in Rewa and Satna were preparing students for the matriculation exam. In 1935 the Darbar High School in Rewa became an intermediate college, and in 1944 a degree college teaching arts and science. College students rose from 222 in 1936–7 to 358 in 1945. Among publications, the English *Prakash* had a circulation of 500; the *Rewa Raj Gazette* appeared fortnightly; and *Bandhava*, an official Hindi monthly, began circulating from 1943. See CIA, Police, R-2/47, 1933; and CIA, Police, R-2/49, 1934. Several libraries opened in Rewa town during this period.

86. CIA, CMO, 118/Misc, PMin to CMO, CI, 18 Aug. 1941, notes that there were 24 dispensaries and hospitals in the state handling 2,29,284 outpatients for that year, with a health budget of Rs 1.33 lakhs. In 1921 outpatients totalled 1,12,788, and expenditure on health was Rs 55,682. The number of vaccinations rose from 44,343 in 1931–2 to 62,644 in 1939–40. *RSA, 1922–23*, pp. 44–5; *Report of Path Enquiry Commission*, p. 124. For disease, see files of CIA, CMO, Misc, 1913–31; CIA, P, A, 81-A/31, R.McGregor to L.G.L. Evans, 2 Jan. 1932; issues of *RSA, 1922–23* to *1926–27*; *Rewa State Census, 1941, Report*, pp. 54–55; *Rewa Gazetteer*, pp. 254–6; *Satna Gazetteer*, p. 331; McCombie Young, 'Lathyrism'.

87. RDO, 50, Ind, B 11, 1935–6, Towns; CIA, War, 139-W, 1945, C.C.H. Smith to Res CI, 24 May 1941; *Rewa State Census, 1941, Report*, pp. 23–4; *Census of India, 1961*, vol. VIII, *Madhya Pradesh*, 1974, p. 151; *Rewa Gazetteer*, pp. 61–76; *Shahdol Gazetteer*, pp. 241, 323, 330–1; Lal, 'Settlement geography', PhD, pp. 315, 320–1.

88. RS, Dak office, 1924–42, 80, 1925, Postal, Note of Maharaja Rewa, June 1933; For crime see CIA, Police files, R-2 series from 1923 to 1932; and *RSA, 1922–23* to *1926–27*. Crime included theft, smuggling and *dakaiti*.

89. RDO, B 3, 1924–25/19, Police, 1924, Note by J. Prasad, 19 July 1924; ibid., J. Fitzpatrick to Sec Darbar, 22 Sept. 1924; ibid., Maharaja's note, nd; FPP, 411-P(S), 1927, FR CIA 1/July 1927; P, P branch, 5(24)-P(S)/41, CIO, 10 Mar. 1941; CRR, CI, 18(7)-P(S)/42, Robins' report, 1942.

7

The Triumph of the Centre: Baghelkhand's Integration into the Indian Nation, 1942–56

Cℜℰ⊃

Nationalizing forces achieved their final goal between 1942–56 with Baghelkhand's integration into the Indian State. Early in this period the central government externed, launched an enquiry against, and finally deposed Maharaja Gulab Singh, appointing central officials to administer the state. In 1946 the centre welcomed Gulab Singh's heir, Martand Singh, as a more pliant regional ruler in place of his father. Following India's Independence from Britain, central interference in Rewa and other states in Baghelkhand deepened when the government merged the region with princely Bundelkhand to form the Union of Vindhya Pradesh.

This heralded a round of greater central intervention in Baghelkhand. Among other reforms, the constitution of Vindhya Pradesh introduced universal suffrage and a parliamentary system in which power shifted from Martand Singh and other princes to a Prime Minister and cabinet. Despite this the experiment of Vindhya Pradesh failed, and as a final solution in 1956 the central government united the area with Madhya Bharat and the Hindi districts of the old Central Provinces to form the state of Madhya Pradesh, locating Baghelkhand within its Rewa division. With this, the region's nationalization was complete—an arrival that does not rule out a future alteration of boundaries in the area.

I

INCREASING TENSION BETWEEN CENTRE AND REGION, 1939–42

By 1939 the central government had become uneasy about the administration of Rewa State, pitted as it appeared against the forces of integration.[1] Initially this was because the ruler declined to publish the usual administration reports, showing details of income and expenditure in various departments. Despite central pressure Gulab Singh refused to divulge the state of Rewa's finances; but as the central government was pursuing a policy of non-intervention in princely states, the impasse continued.

Rumours about Gulab Singh emanating from Rewa fuelled central unease.[2] Those who met the ruler from the mid-1930s found that his behaviour had changed. In the interim he attended the Round Table Conferences and visited various European countries including Germany, where he appreciated Hitler's national socialism. While there the Maharaja reportedly developed relations with a German lady, which some claimed led to the birth of a child. Others asserted that following this visit the ruler became impotent. Whatever the reason, when Fitze (then the Resident for Central India) met the Maharaja in Rewa in 1936, he, too

was conscious of a change in his demeanour, which on previous occasions had been genial to the point of joviality. He seemed to be defending himself against various charges, which were certainly not inherent in anything I said to him. His Highness kept on reverting to his resentment at the entertainment of complaints from his own disloyal employees.[3]

Fitze also found the air in Rewa thick with talk of the Maharaja's indulging in 'degrading vices'.

The ruler put a different gloss on his changed behaviour and the rumours concerning his private life.[4] He claimed that he had once been a 'drone' interested only in tiger shooting, but that he was now a ruler who had begun to 'take his responsibilities seriously'. Gulab Singh also emphasized to Fitze that the state was his property, and that its financial policy was his concern alone.

Subsequent events deepened the anxiety of the central government.[5] In 1937 the Maharaja had a 'mental breakdown', which a state official attributed to his hard work as well as to the 'shock and anxiety' resulting from the violent deaths of two members of his personal staff. Following medical treatment in Calcutta, the Maharaja visited religious sites in south India, after which his health reportedly improved; though several years later G.T. Fisher, the then Resident in Central India and Gulab Singh's severest critic, found him 'desperate and ... quite unbalanced'.

The visit of the Crown Representative Lord Linlithgow to Rewa in December 1939 brought the tension between centre and region into the open, despite the round of ritual dinners and tiger shoots.[6] Before welcoming Linlithgow at Satna, the Maharaja had a sharp exchange with Sir Bertram Glancy of the Political Department. Subsequently Maharaja and Crown Representative disagreed on the issues of political reform, administration reports, an annual budget, and Rewa's alleged backwardness. Fitze, an old friend of Gulab Singh, also crossed swords with the ruler on the subject of rising wheat prices in the state.

Fisher's appointment as Resident for Central India in 1940, together with that of the controversial F.V. Wylie at the Political Department, raised the political temperature further.[7] Almost from the outset Fisher launched a moral crusade against the Maharaja, drawing the centre's attention to the alleged ills of Rewa, the reviving Congress agitation there, and reports that the *yuvraj* was taking an anti-British line at Mayo College. For his part, Wylie was concerned about the Maharaja's private life, having dealt with what seemed to him a similar situation in Alwar. The earlier death in Ranikhet of Gulab Singh's half-brother, Ravendra, deepened central concern, especially as tension had reportedly existed between the two; and rumour-mongers claimed that the Maharaja had had him murdered, though officially his death was due to heat-stroke.

To communicate the centre's disquiet, Fisher called the Maharaja to Indore for an interview in August 1941, where he told Gulab Singh that several murders had taken place in Rewa in doubtful circumstances, and with the ruler's knowledge.[8] Fisher again adverted to Gulab Singh's refusal to publish administration reports, and claimed that the Maharaja's Bank of Baghelkhand was holding Rewa's revenue surplus. Complaining about the unsatisfactory administration in the state, Fisher advised Gulab Singh to reconstruct his council and appoint European or I.C.S. officials to his service. The Maharaja claimed that his administration was sound, and urged that the criticisms and rumours emanated mainly from his opponents. Both men corresponded on these topics for a further five months—with the same inconclusive result, such that Linlithgow asked the Resident to meet the ruler again in December 1941.

The meeting did not take place, for by then Fisher had broached the holding of an enquiry against Gulab Singh.[9] Amidst further complaints from Rewa, in October 1941 a court in Indore sentenced a Rewa clerk, Baldev, to jail for 'being deputed' to obtain confidential information from the Resident's office. Two months later police arrested Kallu, a person of doubtful character, and charged him with murdering Gulab Singh's ADC Shanker Prasad in 1937. Sensing the trend of events, Gulab Singh sought an interview with Linlithgow who declined, asking Fisher to meet the Maharaja instead. By then, thoroughly worked up, Fisher postponed the meeting:

While I was preparing the case, I saw the Thakur of Chandia and one of the chief Pawaidars of Rewa. Amongst other complaints of his own regarding confiscation of his villages, stories of glaring misrule and oppression, he gave me details of the death of two ADCs of His Highness, Uma Prasad and Shanker Prasad.... The allegations were so startling and so circumstantial and categorical in their nature that I sent Robins to the U.P. to get in touch with their Special Branch.... [I] ask that the ... facts may be placed before His Excellency, as I believe they constitute ample grounds for facing His Highness immediately with the option of a regular enquiry, that might include the question of his mental balance, and even a criminal liability in which he is undoubtedly involved.[10]

With these revelations Linlithgow joined Fisher in his moral crusade against the region's ruler.[11] Months previously the Crown Representative had forecast 'serious trouble' in Rewa, which the centre could not ignore, with the war causing anxiety and nationalist forces bent on agitation in Rewa and elsewhere in India. After an exchange of views, Linlithgow obtained the Secretary of State's permission to launch an enquiry against Gulab Singh, though the Secretary found the evidence unconvincing, and advised Linlithgow to proceed with caution. The latter's advisers also regarded the evidence as nothing more than a series of allegations, many of them irrelevant and unreliable.

Undeterred, the Crown Representative moved towards an enquiry against a regional ruler with a case resting largely on rumour.[12] By 17 January 1942, with a second interview between Resident and Maharaja still weeks away, Linlithgow decided that he had sufficient material to hold an enquiry against Gulab Singh; material which would also form the subject of the interview. His comments, like those of Fisher, took on the appearance of a personal vendetta against the ruler:

I find myself after the fullest and most anxious consideration definitely unable to desist from whatever actions seem best calculated to turn into certainty the strong suspicion of the Maharaja's complicity...in singularly sordid murders.[13]

With the Secretary of State still counselling caution, on 11 February 1942 Linlithgow suspended the Maharaja's powers for two weeks.[14] The Resident informed Gulab Singh of this decision, and presented him with a charge-sheet, requesting him to reply to the charges within the fortnight. He also told the ruler that the government had decided to hold an enquiry into the charges, and that he was to say whether he accepted such an enquiry or not. If the Maharaja did not respond to these communications, the Resident informed him that the Crown Representative would take further action against him.

Though perturbed at the turn of events, Gulab Singh was not prepared to surrender throne and region without a fight.[15] When Linlithgow granted him an interview on 17 February, advancing his response to the above communications by a week, Gulab Singh sought the advice of his counsel, T.B. Sapru of Allahabad, as the development was 'fraught with grave consequences for the sovereignty of my state and the prestige of the dynasty'. When Sapru advised him to 'hold out', Gulab Singh declined to meet the Crown Representative; and on 18 February the latter announced the holding of an enquiry and suspended the Maharaja's powers, externing him from the state until the enquiry was complete. In place of the ruler, Linlithgow announced the appointment of L.W. Wooldridge of the Political Service as Administrator.

Regional reactions to central rule in Rewa varied.[16] Within his fort Gulab Singh burnt material likely to embarrass him, and appointed his loyal minister Brajendranath to guard his interests. One report claimed that the suspension came as a shock to the people of Rewa State. There were widespread hartals, meetings and processions ... in all major towns of the state. The Rewa State People's Representative Committee was set up to spearhead the movement demanding the restoration of the Maharaja. A delegation ... was sent to meet Sir Stafford Cripps [and]....the Viceroy, (but)....with little success.[17]

The ruler's critics alleged that money was 'freely spent' to organize the state-wide strike; while the *ilaqadars* and other landed foes of Gulab Singh claimed that an 'overwhelming section of the public' welcomed the ruler's suspension and his replacement by a central official. Though the agitation continued until June, the centre withdrew its platoon of troops several months previously, indicating that the situation was under control.

Gathering evidence for the enquiry took longer than expected, and it was only on 4 June 1942 that the government announced the formation of the Enquiry Committee headed by Justice F.W. Gentle of the Calcutta High Court.[18] Issues before the Committee included the Maharaja's part in the murder of the ADCs in 1937; whether in connection with those deaths he had shielded persons whom he knew to be guilty, and implicated those he knew to be innocent; and whether he had instigated the theft of confidential material from the Resident's office in Indore. The enquiry was to be held in camera in the Residency area, Indore, the government overruling the Maharaja's requests to change the venue and to hold the meetings in public.

II

A CENTRAL ENQUIRY INTO A REGIONAL RULER, 1942–3

The immediate outcome of the enquiry represented a defeat for the central government.[19] The hearing examined the prosecution's evidence relating to the murder of Uma and Shanker Prasad, favourites of, and in constant attention upon, the Maharaja. For Uma's murder, the two ADCs had been travelling in the same car as part of a motorcade conveying the Maharaja to Satna en route to Calcutta. Uma was in front with the driver, his friend Shanker occupying a rear seat with a rifle on his knee. Near Durjanpur in Sohawal State Uma died of a gun-shot, and the party returned immediately to Rewa, where the prosecution asserted correctly that

the body was burnt hurriedly.... The doctor ... pushed a stick into the wound....a sort of twig.... That was ... the total extent of the medical examination....No post-mortem examination was ever held, no ... report was ever made.... The I.G.P. asked if anybody had seen the dead body, and ... that the usual procedure was to hold a post-mortem examination, and then to prepare the police inquest report.... The Judicial ... and Political Minister ... said that an inquest can be held by a Magistrate.... He did not examine the rifle....[or] the body....(yet) came to the conclusion that it was an accident.... The whole thing was stifled as if nothing had happened.... The body was cremated without delay.[20]

However, the prosecution failed to prove conclusively that Uma was murdered, and by Shanker; nor could they find any motive or evidence suggesting the ruler's complicity.[21] They thus withdrew the charge, casting a cloud on their case as a whole. Much later Gulab Singh disclosed that he had no hand in the murder, which was an act of jealousy on the part of Shanker; and that the events after the death as reported above were designed to shield his ADC from trouble.

On the murder of Shanker Prasad, the prosecution was again unable to establish that the ruler had instigated the crime, and so declined to press the charge.[22] Years later Gulab Singh admitted that he had arranged the killing, as Shanker was carrying on an affair with his second wife, the Kishengarhi Maharani. In 1935 an enraged Maharaja personally whipped his ADC; and ceased to visit his wife as a sign of displeasure, appointing Narbada Prasad Patwa, his long-time associate, to manage the *deorhi* with orders to stop any intrigue in the *zenana*. Despite this the relationship continued and, as the prosecution rightly charged, Gulab Singh appointed Kallu, an associate of Patwa, to murder Shanker with the help of two ADCs. Following the killing near Amahiya House in Rewa town, Gulab Singh sent Kallu to Bombay, and forced Narbada to confess to the crime. However, with the prosecution's failure to press the charge against the Maharaja, the associated charges of shielding the guilty and securing the conviction of the innocent also failed to stand.

Other factors besides weakened the case for the Crown.[23] Buoyed by the prosecution's weak position, Sapru went on the offensive, destroying the evidence presented by 'blackguards of the worst type', and highlighting the defects of other witnesses, some of whom retracted their previous statements, some failing to give evidence at all. Moreover, though on the Enquiry Committee, Justice Rangnekar openly favoured the Maharaja and made somewhat vituperative interventions in his favour. By contrast, the Crown prosecutor Sir Nripen Sircar was in poor health, and found the strain of the proceedings difficult to bear. It was further unlikely that the princes on the Committee would condemn a member of their order.

Ironically, Maharaja Gulab Singh played a key role in defeating the case for the prosecution:

His Highness Rewa was present throughout the trial. The witnesses from Rewa had to face His Highness who was given a seat opposite the witness box. This was undesirable. All we could do was to induce the President to make the witnesses face him and not His Highness.... The atmosphere here is one of violent bias in favour of His Highness.[24]

The prosecution claimed that witnesses went back on their previous statements because they had become 'friendly' to the ruler. A crown informant, B.C. Awasthi of the Rewa police, exp-lained how this could happen:

The Maharaja has so far spent ... 18 lacs of rupees over this first real fight between a Native prince and the Government of India, and ... persons have made fortunes—not thousands—on petty help ... giving false statements ... or trying to make other Prosecution witnesses change their statements.[25]

Awasthi alleged that he himself had turned down several royal offers, together with thousands of rupees as 'advance'.

A master of tactics, Gulab Singh prevented other incriminating evidence from reaching the court by silencing one of his most bitter *ilaqadari* foes, Narmada Prasad Singh of Baikunthpur.[26] In the aftermath of Shanker's murder, Narbada Patwa drew up an affidavit detailing the events leading to the murder, and for safe-keeping gave it to Singh, then in Allahabad. Kallu, likewise, filed an affidavit on the ruler's complicity in the murder, also lodging it with Narmada Prasad Singh. On hearing of these transactions, Gulab Singh used the death of Narmada Singh's father, the Thakur of Baikunthpur, to intrude an illegally adopted heir into the *ilaqa* in place of Narmada, and refused to admit the latter until he surrendered the affidavits. The exchange duly took place and, after permitting Narmada to re-enter Rewa from where he had been exiled in 1924, the ruler himself performed the traditional *pagri* ceremony on 12 September 1938, declaring Narmada Prasad Singh as Harol and Thakur of Baikunthpur.

However, though the outcome of the case appeared to favour the regional ruler, his victory was by no means assured.[27] The findings of the Enquiry Committee comprised two reports divided on ethnic lines. The British members' minority report found the Maharaja guilty of instigating the murder of Shanker Prasad; of shielding persons he knew to be guilty; and of obstructing the course of justice by seeking to obtain confidential evidence by bribery—charges subsequently found to be correct. The report emphasized that though certain charges were withdrawn, they revealed the unsavoury nature of Rewa's administration and indicated that Gulab Singh was unfit to rule. The report accordingly recommended that he be deprived of his ruling powers.

The Indian members, who were in a majority, drew up a contrary report which held that the Crown had failed to prove its case; and condemned its witnesses for their 'groundless lies, filthy perjury, abominable inventions, glaring contradictions, inconsistencies and improbabilities'.[28] The majority view was that the centre should restore Gulab Singh to Rewa, with the rider that he should reorganize his administration along professional lines.

Though dismayed by the outcome, the central government continued to stalk its regional prey, the stakes being the centre's authority and the unity of the country.[29] From the outset Linlithgow emphasized that he could not permit the Maharaja to return to Rewa until the government had considered the reports. Early on, the Crown Representative distanced himself from the majority report, holding the Maharaja guilty of improperly obtaining confidential material by bribery. It followed from this that the centre could not allow the conditions leading to such an incident to persist, but must establish a regime in Rewa that would usher in the reforms which Gulab Singh had so long delayed, and which it desired for the princely states as a whole.

Kenneth Fitze, long-time friend of the Maharaja but then Private Secretary to the Crown Representative, clarified how the latter might implement the plan he had in mind.[30] On 3 February 1943 Fitze noted:

It has only now occurred to me that further procedure will have to be governed by the...passage of the Foreign Political Resolution of 1920.... If the Government of India disagrees with the findings of the Committee, the matter will be referred to His Majesty's Secretary of State for decision. The Government of India will communicate to the ruler, ... whose condition is under enquiry, the reasons for disagreeing with the recommendations.... The Report by the majority ... must be regarded as the findings of the Committee.

In addition to the disputed charges, the centre complained that Maharaja Gulab Singh interfered in the mutation case of Narmada Prasad Singh; passed a savage sentence on Narbada Patwa to shift the blame for Shanker's murder; and appropriated 'wholesale' the revenues of his state.

Having accepted Fitze's advice, the Political Department outlined the conditions for Gulab Singh's return to Rewa.[31] Central to these conditions was the Maharaja's position as nominal head of state in place of the royal autocracy he had nurtured since 1922. The central government was to appoint a Chief Minister and approve a council of Ministers to handle all state business, including the training of the Heir-Apparent, pushing the state in the direction of reforms common to the British-ruled districts. The administration would submit an annual budget for the Resident's approval, besides controlling appointments to and dismissals from the state service. On the question of the revenues, the centre permitted the Maharaja to enjoy a civil list of five lakhs, conditional on his disclosing the monies he had appropriated and returning 'the balance or portion thereof'. The ruler was to follow the advice of the council, but where he disagreed with it the matter was to be referred to the Resident in Indore. The centre further clarified that the ruler could not return to Rewa until the administration was firmly established.

In August 1943 the centre communicated its decisions to Maharaja Gulab Singh, together with the conditions necessary for his return to Rewa.[32] The government stated that if the Maharaja broke these conditions, he would render himself liable to deposition. Gulab Singh intimated his 'general acceptance', thereby paving the way for his return at a time to be decided by the centre.

III

CENTRAL RULE IN REWA, 1942–4

In the meantime the central administration in Rewa under Wooldridge could do little more than tackle immediate problems.[33] One concerned the tragic figure of the senior Maharani, her health shattered by events outside her control. Another related to the presence in the fort of Gulab Singh's personal secretary, Kaushal Prasad, whom Wooldridge claimed financed the agitation to secure the ruler's return to Rewa. On both counts the administration failed. The Maharani's psychological problems thwarted solution; and officials failed to seize Prasad, leaving it to a later Administrator to resolve the problem.

Similarly, Wooldridge could do little to gain control of the Maharaja's hidden wealth.[34] He began by freezing a sum of 60 lakhs which Gulab Singh had given his wife before he was suspended. He also compelled Dadu Jagdish Prasad, said to be the ruler's illegitimate son, installed in the royal *ilaqa* of Anandgarh to return monies taken from the Bank of Baghelkhand; and to restore jewellery removed from the state Bhandar—both possibly for the Maharaja's use. At the same time, however, Gulab Singh continued to operate his bank accounts and sell securities, ignoring central orders for details of his transactions. Wooldridge did prevent the Bank of Baghelkhand from using official machinery to recover its debts, though the bank refused to admit his claim to replace Gulab Singh as Director-General of its operations.

The Administrator also had to deal with the agitation demanding the Maharaja's return to Rewa following his suspension in February 1942.[35] Students, supported by *mahajans* and Muslims were prominent in the agitation whose focus was Rewa city, though it spread to other towns and villages as well. The Praja Mandal sponsored a parallel movement for the same cause. The situation deteriorated markedly from August 1942 when the *ilaqadar*-led Baghelkhand Congress joined the agitation on behalf of the nationwide Quit India movement.[36]

Wooldridge took a strong line against the combined student and Quit India campaign in a manner reminiscent of Corfield's handling of civil disobedience ten years earlier.[37] In August 1942 he invoked wartime security rules to declare the local and national

Congress unlawful and seized their office in Rewa, arresting Awadesh Pratap Singh and Narmada Prasad Singh, the latter for leading a no-rent campaign. The administration also banned certain publications, acted against speeches deemed objectionable, and requisitioned troops from Allahabad and elsewhere to enforce its authority.

The embattled administration, however, gained strength from the fact that by and large the *ilaqadars* of Rewa under the leadership of Shiva Bahadur Singh, the Rao of Churhat, backed central intervention and the action taken by Wooldridge in Rewa.[38] Even Narmada Prasad Singh agreed to testify against the Maharaja at the enquiry yet to begin. For these men the administration provided the platform denied them by the ruler, besides fuelling the hope that the central government would protect their interests in the future. Wooldridge responded by registering the Pawaidar Sangh, which Gulab Singh had refused to recognize, and by associating the Rao of Churhat, the Thakur of Tala, and other prominent *ilaqadars* with the recruitment drive and the wider war effort.

The conclusion of the Rewa Enquiry and the holding nature of Wooldridge's administration paved the way for a deepening of central rule in Rewa.[39] By early 1944 Gulab Singh was pressing the government to permit him to return to his state; and officials realized that the new Crown Representative, Lord Wavell, could not withhold permission indefinitely as the Maharaja had accepted the conditions for his return. However, well before this took place, the centre installed a more permanent administration to introduce the reforms that made Rewa a limited and not an autocratic monarchy.

The centre chose its first Chief Minister in Rewa with care.[40] In November 1943 Wylie, then Political Adviser to Wavell besides heading the Political Department, invited Edward Wakefield of the Political Service to fill the post. Before accepting the position, described as one of 'extreme difficulty and delicacy', Wakefield sought the advice of Conrad Corfield, a former Adviser to Gulab Singh but then in Lahore. Corfield

warned me that ... Sir Gulab Singh would try to provoke or entice me into indiscreet words or conduct and would seek every possible means of discrediting me. He would probe for my weaknesses, exploit them, and try to compromise me in order to establish some kind of hold over me. He would use his wealth and influence to undermine my position in the State and, finally, he would employ against me all the resources of his elaborate system of espionage. Corfield ... advised me to treat the Maharaja with the courtesy due to a person of his rank, and to be helpful and accommodating in minor matters or in matters touching his comfort and convenience, but to be absolutely unyielding ... in important matters.[41]

Wakefield accepted the challenge, and on 2 December 1943 assumed charge of Rewa State.

As intended by the centre, Wakefield's regime signalled the shift of power from Maharaja to Chief Minister and nominated council.[42] At another level it signified a shift from a wholly regional power to an administration representing the central government. Wakefield took seven months to build a council proof against attack by the Maharaja. Some ministers came from outside the State; others were from Rewa itself, among them the Rao of Churhat as Minister for Education. All ministers had financial powers relating to their departments, and were to meet once a week under the Chief Minister instead of the Maharaja, who had presided at meetings of his council from 1932. The Chief Minister also had powers to pass orders in case of obstruction by Gulab Singh.

Wakefield and his ministers faced immediate problems with the state's ravaged bureaucracy.[43] Most departments were understaffed, and had no secretaries, personal assistants, or stenographers. Work in the courts was reportedly 'dilatory and slip shod'. Police officials complained at their low rates of pay. The army, too, was underpaid, and even feeding it at times posed problems. The state garage with its fleet of limousines had no competent mechanic. Thousands of cases awaited hearing in the Revenue Department, many of whose officials were illiterate and dishonest. The Audits and Accounts Department required furniture for its staff who earlier sat on the ground 'in serried ranks'. Most services provided by the Health Department went to assist the small urban population.

Despite such handicaps, ministers sought to initiate social and economic reforms[44] on a wider scale than the ruler had done, while struggling to provide people with food and other basic commodities.[45] Early in the Second World War Rewa faced shortages of food brought on by poor crops, hoarding, and consequent high prices, all encouraging the growth of a black market. In 1943 Wooldridge prosecuted those hoarding coins, thereby releasing them into the market. Also, though the administration banned grain exports, smugglers connived with officials to shift grain to outside markets. In 1943 the centre directed Rewa to export its surplus rice to famine-hit Bengal in a move linking Rewa more fully to the national economy. In the face of determined opposition, Wakefield bought up the entire surplus and delivered it to railway stations, from where Bengal officials helped it to reach its destination. Then, as the war closed Rewa experienced an acute shortage of cloth.

However, in spite of the administration's efforts and minor advances, the same conditions of social and economic underdevelopment thwarted Wakefield's ministry as they had done earlier rulers and administrators.[46] For although Rewa made incursions into the market, it remained basically a subsistence economy, its people mired in illiteracy and disease. Poor communications still isolated the region from the rest of India, and even in the more advanced north Rewa the lack of communications quenched 'the incentive for development'.

IV

REGION AND CENTRE IN CONFLICT, 1944–46

Maharaja Gulab Singh's return to Rewa on 25 July 1944 set the stage for the 'inevitable duel' between region and nationalizing centre.[47] The ruler opened his innings by ignoring his new Chief Minister who had come to welcome him at Satna station, though he did meet the ministers at a halt on the road to Rewa. The Maharaja was also expected to return quietly to the capital, but

it was characteristic ... that he should choose for the day of his return a Hindu holiday, Nag Punchami, when the Rewa population would be thronging the streets in festive mood.[48]

Once installed in the fort, the Maharaja widened his attack against a central administration that had usurped his place as ruler of Rewa.[49] Behind the scenes he began a whispering campaign against Wakefield and the ministers, especially Churhat whom he described as 'a snake'. Gulab Singh also insisted that the Chief Minister dismiss his army chief for allegedly not saluting him in the street, but dropped the demand when Wakefield threatened to send a report on his finances to Delhi. However, despite being at a disadvantage, the Maharaja remained implacable in his bid to demolish central rule in Rewa—a stance that could also be seen as a nationalist's opposition to colonial rule.

As Chief Minister Wakefield inevitably became the focus of Gulab Singh's battle with the central government.[50] As expected, the Maharaja did not attend council meetings but organized a rival power centre in the fort. Initially he made suggestions on policy to the Chief Minister, but the latter remained on guard against any proposals that, however innocent, might conceal some 'ulterior, perhaps sinister design'. When Wakefield vetoed his suggestions, Gulab Singh contested council decisions and publicly outlined rival policies, such as that on education in August 1944. These the Chief Minister again vetoed, secure in Fitze's ruling that in any conflict the Resident was to arbitrate, it being unlikely that he would award a decision in favour of the Maharaja.

However the Maharaja's campaign against Wakefield's person was more subtle than his exchanges with the administration.[51] At the Chief Minister's first shoot, he was alarmed to find the Maharaja pointing his rifle at him, and he thereafter arranged for someone to sit between him and Gulab Singh in the *machan*. As predicted, the Maharaja probed for Wakefield's weak points. The latter sent back

two cartloads of toys for the children at Christmas.... His Highness said that he would like to show his friendly feelings for me.... He held out to me a thin envelope containing ... a cheque.... Putting my hands behind my back to avoid so much as touching the bribe, I took a step backwards....

'But your father is alive, isn't he? I could make it out in his name, or anyone else's.' Believing that his £2 million was at stake, he should have made the cheque a larger one.... My curiosity ... will never now be satisfied.[52]

Sensing that its greatest struggle lay ahead, in February 1945 the centre replaced an exhausted Wakefield with an army man, Lieutenant Colonel C.C.H. Smith.[53] As Smith realized from the outset, the Maharaja would freely intrigue against him, contesting the reforms and denouncing the administration on his frequent tours through the state. Gulab Singh also continued to malign the ministers, some of whom believed that their lives were in danger; and sought to build a rival constituency among *ilaqadars* and non-Baghel Rajputs by bestowing them with titles and by admitting non-Baghels to intermarriage with his clan.

Like his predecessors, Smith remained at a disadvantage in attempts to secure the Maharaja's assets.[54] Central officers knew that Gulab Singh would never disgorge his wealth and live on the paltry sum of five lakhs per year. As the ruler's banks declined to disclose details of his accounts, the centre appointed a special Accounts Officer to scrutinize the records and estimate the monies held by Gulab Singh. However, the investigation made little progress, and in September 1945 the central government gave the Maharaja two months in which to produce a financial statement, failing which the Crown Representative would decide on a course of action. During an interview with Smith in February 1945

His Highness ... tried to argue that he was being treated differently to other princes who had accumulated money prior to the fixation of a Civil List.... I pointed out to His Highness that the settlement of outstanding accounts was one of the conditions on which he was permitted to return [yet]....no collaboration whatever had taken place from His Highness's side .... He was...putting off an issue that he, in his own interests, should honour.[55]

Smith similarly failed to gain control over the Bank of Baghelkhand—a difficult task as the Bank had no constitutional basis.[56] The Maharaja treated it as his own business, and hotly contested the claim by central officials to direct the institution. The bank thus disregarded government orders and notifications, including Smith's attempts to control the accounts and transactions standing in Gulab Singh's name, especially those dealing with the Bank of England. The Bank also vetoed Smith's suggestion that he employ accountants to reconstitute the organization, and that it invest the Maharani's 60 lakhs, then frozen, in government securities.

Nevertheless, the Chief Minister and council did have access to current revenues, enabling them to produce the first annual budget for many years.[57] Following the ruler's suspension revenues rose rapidly to reach 92 lakhs in 1946, underlining the centre's view that the Maharaja was appropriating large sums of state money. Favourable balances at the end of each year also increased, at least up to 1945, instead of disappearing as earlier. The administration was thus able to spend more on education, communications, and other necessary projects.

One positive development for the administration was that the *ilaqadars* continued to side with Smith in their battle with the Maharaja.[58] Most landholders regarded the ruler as hostile to their cause, interpreting Corfield's *pawai* rules as he chose and on occasion even disregarding them. Grantees still suspected that the Maharaja aimed to extinguish their rights to land, and for personal benefit rather than for reasons of state. For his part Gulab Singh continued to criticize the nobility for not attending the Dassehra celebrations and not producing their quotas of men and animals on that occasion. He also accused some of not making 'full obeisance' as he sat on his gorgeously caparisoned elephant at the centre of the festivities.

The large body of landowners thus supported the central administration, and Smith responded by including the Rao of Churhat in the Birthday Honours list for 1945.[59] The *ilaqadars*, however, wanted more than titles. Outside the council their principal spokesman remained Narmada Prasad Singh, who had given Fisher information on Gulab Singh's officials in 1941, and in August 1942 helped Wooldridge win over the *ilaqadars*. The alliance held firm during Smith's tussle with the Maharaja, but from 1944–6 Singh urged Wakefield and Smith to effect Corfield's assurances to the landholders. However, central administrators failed to address these claims, preoccupied as they were with the contest with Gulab Singh.

The administration's understanding with the *ilaqadars* probably encouraged it to adopt a softer line towards the *ilaqadar*-led Congress.[60] In May 1944 Wakefield released Awadesh Pratap Singh from jail; and Congressmen for their part busied themselves with Gandhi's constructive programme. A student-led agitation in August 1945 notwithstanding, in September Smith lifted the ban on the Congress, though it continued to press for responsible government in Rewa.

V

THE CENTRE DEPOSES A REGIONAL RULER

The alliance with the landowners and truce with the Congress strengthened Smith's hand in dealing with an increasingly desperate Gulab Singh.[61] Irked at being a 'captain without a ship', from mid-1945 the Maharaja raised the political stakes. Belittling the Rao of Churhat as Minister for Education, Gulab Singh campaigned extensively for more schools and greater literacy, though Smith ignored the campaign as not involving any question of principle. The Maharaja also disputed the council's decision to build a bridge across the Son at Kuldahaghat near Churhat, compelling Smith to submit the scheme to the Resident for approval. The Chief Minister also discerned the ruler's hand in the student agitation of 1945.

In the later months of 1945 the Maharaja stepped up his campaign against the central administration, apparently insensitive to the issues at stake.[62] In October he used the Dassehra celebrations in the capital to announce the grant of responsible government to the state, risking central action for breaking a condition of his return which disallowed him from initiating policy. With this the situation in Rewa worsened, as the Maharaja must have hoped, compelling the Resident to visit the state in December. However, though the Crown Representative advocated intervention, the Secretary of State adopted a wait and see policy.

Sensing hesitation or indecisiveness at the highest level, Gulab Singh pushed events towards a showdown by contesting the centre's plans for the *yuvraj*, Martand Singh.[63] Conditional on the return of the Maharaja to Rewa in 1944, the centre assumed responsibility for his son in preparation for his one day becoming the ruler. Officials engaged the young man in a number of training programmes, and in 1945 planned to send him abroad to widen his perspectives and to keep him away from his father. The Maharaja publicly condemned the tour and attempted to seal the son off from his mother, of whom he was fond. In December 1945, to thwart the foreign tour (which he believed imminent) and to destabilize the Rewa administration, Gulab Singh warned Smith that

If offices are not closed by 16th December, then on 17th I will visit all officers personally and will persuade all my servants to get out of all offices.... I will visit all my tehsils on the same mission.[64]

The ruler also sought to convene a meeting of the council while Smith was away from the capital.

Though Smith's will in both matters prevailed,[65] the situation in Rewa compelled the central government to show its hand.[66] Unrest spread to villages around the capital, and the Resident reported that the administration could not rely on the full loyalty of the army and the police. For some weeks he had been urging the centre to support Smith, and the Crown Representative had recommended to the Secretary of State that the Maharaja be deposed. However, it was not until 1 January 1946 that Wavell informed the Secretary of State that central authority in Rewa could only survive if Gulab Singh were deposed. The British government endorsed the deposition; and preliminary contacts with Martand Singh indicated that he was willing to accede to the throne. In preparation for the central coup, the Political Secretary ordered an army company and tear-gas squad to Rewa by 29 January.

As grounds for deposition, the central government highlighted the Maharaja's failure to disclose his financial assets together with his interference with the state administration.[67] As for the former, the centre's deadline for financial disclosure came and went in November 1945, such that the investigating officer closed his enquiries and in his report of January 1946 concluded that Gulab Singh's assets amounted to well over three crores. Armed with the report the centre made ready to act, and on 31 January the following appeared in the *Rewa Raj Gazette*:

The Crown Representative on considering the report of the Committee permitted His Highness to return to the State on certain conditions.... No civil list allotment would be made to His Highness unless he made full disclosure of his disposal of the sums appropriated by him in the past to his personal control, and returned the balance to the State. This condition has not yet been fulfilled;...[nor has] an undertaking by which all State business should be initiated in Council.... It was ... made clear to His Highness that in the event of his failing to abide by these conditions, he would render himself liable to deposition. His Highness accepted these conditions and returned to the State.... His Highness has recently committed several gross breaches of this undertaking to the

Crown Representative.... In the circumstances, the Crown Representative with the approval of the Secretary of State has come to the conclusion that it will not be possible to carry through the reforms while the present Ruler is on the *gaddi*, and therefore in the interests of the State and his people the Maharaja is being deposed and the Heir Apparent recognised as his successor.[68]

The Rewa council received the announcement 'with regret', while offering its 'loyal and respectful congratulations' to Martand Singh as the new Maharaja of Rewa.

Ahead of his impending deposition, Gulab Singh left Rewa by the Allahabad road, turning from Chak into the interior of Teonthar. The Resident and Smith, accompanied by police, took the same route to deliver Wavell's order of deposition, finally coming upon the Maharaja in his camp at Rampur Sonouri. The Resident described what followed:

Smith told the Maharaja that I had come to see him, and to tell the people to depart as I wished to see him alone. I then entered the tent and handed His Highness the letter. The Maharaja opened the letter with trembling fingers and read it through very hastily. He fastened onto the significant sentence that he had been deposed and must leave the state within 24 hours. He appeared to be completely stunned by the news, ... and was quite unable to say anything for some considerable time. He then asked to be allowed to go to Rewa, a request which I refused. I suggested that he give instructions for the kit he had with him to be packed up, and such servants ... whom he wished to take prepare themselves for the journey.... I had to be a little brusque.... When his belongings were packed up, ... I took him to my car, and seated myself alongside him.... It was about 10 p.m. when the whole party left the camp.... One of His Highness' well known supporters ... had come from Rewa and....tried to make a demonstration ... but were [sic] quickly removed....[we] met a car containing the Junior Maharani.... His Highness then saw the Junior Maharani for a few minutes...and returned to my car.... Some ten miles on another car met us. This contained the Senior Maharani.... Again the same procedure was gone through, and His Highness returned to my car.... One mile from the main road we came across a very poor attempt at a road block.... At the border, I told His Highness that I would be taking leave of him, and.... Major Jai Singh ... would assist him on his journey to Allahabad.... He then insisted on getting out of his car to wish me good-bye.... We reached Rewa at 2.30 a.m..... No incident had taken place the previous night....[but] there was an air of suppressed excitement throughout the town.[69]

Subsequently also 'not a single dog barked', as Narmada Prasad Singh put it; and on 4 February the Crown Representative's Police returned to headquarters. Several student demonstrations followed, but the Rewa public seemed to accept the situation and the police and State Army remained 'steady'.

The central government added further strictures to the act of deposition.[70] It externed the former ruler from Rewa, forbidding him to visit any adjoining province or state; and cancelled his 17-gun salute and the title of His Highness, while permitting him to retain his British honours.

Though the incoming Indian Government permitted Gulab Singh to return to Allahabad, the same compulsions made it act as decisively against the former Maharaja as its British predecessor.[71] On 22 August 1947 Gulab Singh paid the first of several unauthorized visits to Rewa. As the British restrictions on his visiting Rewa remained in force, the head of the new States Ministry, Vallabhbhai Patel, ordered him to Delhi. Though complying with this, once the ex-Maharaja learnt of the ministry's plan to unite Bundelkhand and Baghelkhand to form Vindhya Pradesh, he again went to Rewa on 3 March 1948 to protest the scheme, crowds accompanying Gulab Singh to the fort where he met Martand Singh.

Firm on quashing any opposition to Delhi's plans for central India, Patel again ordered Gulab Singh out of Rewa, and on 19 March sent a police official to arrest him and bring him to Delhi.[72] However, security in Marina Hotel where the centre detained Gulab Singh was lax, and the former ruler once more slipped away to Rewa, where on 12 April night

A warm reception was accorded him by the people in the Laxman Bagh. Next day he addressed a public meeting ... where 6,000 people were present.... A news spread that Crown Police have arrived to arrest the ex-ruler, nearly 7,000 persons assembled ... to protect (him).... All the shops were closed, and a partial strike was observed in the offices.... He expressed his firm loyalty to the Central Government. He declared that he was a socialist and the Ruler was a toady.[73]

The States Ministry ordered a reluctant local government to deliver the former Maharaja to central police on the Rewa border, where he was remanded to Delhi as a state prisoner.[74] To prevent Gulab Singh from further destabilizing Vindhya Pradesh, the centre interned him in far-off Dehra Dun and froze all his bank accounts in Rewa State.

However, the long conflict with central governments had shattered Gulab Singh's health, and on 31 October 1949 the centre released him from detention on condition that he did not engage in any undesirable activity or reside in Vindhya Pradesh, Uttar Pradesh, or Jabalpur district.[75] The former ruler spent some time in Bikaner, where his doctor advised complete rest; but on 22 March 1950 he went to Bombay, and about three weeks later the *Hindustan Times* announced that the

> former ruler of Rewa, succumbed today to injuries he received from a fall while having his morning walk at the Bikaner Palace here. The former Maharaja Rewa was 47 years old ... [and] was not suffering from any ailment.... At 7.30 this morning he went up to the Terrace of the Bikaner House ... for a walk. He slipped and fell down on the pavement. He was found unconscious and removed to the Polish Hospital. He died on the way.[76]

With the centre delaying permission, the senior Maharani ordered her late husband's private secretary to take the body to Allahabad by plane. From there it was brought by car to Rewa to be cremated in the presence of a huge crowd.

VI

Martand Singh—Central or Regional Prince?

Well before this the centre completed its regional coup by installing Martand Singh as Maharaja of Rewa in place of his father.[77] This was a greater triumph than appeared, for the *yuvraj's* accession meant that the centre had succeeded in its long effort to wean the son from his father, and establish further control over Rewa. At first the government had merely assumed responsibility for his tutoring, but by the forties it was concerned to remove Martand Singh from the supposedly evil atmosphere of the Rewa court. In 1941 Gulab Singh took charge of the prince after dismissing his English guardian, though the latter believed the move was aimed at removing the boy from contact with his mother and bringing him under his father's control.

Following Gulab Singh's suspension in February 1942, the centre once again took charge of Martand Singh, getting him away to Bikaner, and in October to Kashmir with the Jodhpur family.[78] For a year thereafter the *yuvraj* remained in Jodhpur with his mother's brother. Subsequently, the centre sent the young man for several training programmes, but when the Maharaja returned to Rewa in mid-1944 he desired his son to rejoin him. By then, the centre had appointed W. Owens as special officer with the *yuvraj* in order to retain some control over the future ruler, but the young prince grew increasingly restless under the outdated training regimes, and central officials planned to send him off on a tour of Egypt— a venture only postponed with the impending deposition of his father.

Despite the central initiatives, Martand Singh remained beyond reach. Owens described the youth as a dandy,

with about eighty pairs of shoes, a considerable collection of wrist watches, and a nauseating fondness for scents of which he has over 100 bottles of different kinds ... his dressing table is crowded with hair oils, lotions ... [and] face creams.... His dominating ideas are to spend lots of money, and to lead an effortless, irresponsible and feckless existence.[79]

Old war horses in the Political Department such as Lepel Griffin described the *yuvraj* as a 'revolting young man'; and Wylie, ever the martinet, was 'afraid that we will never make a ruler out of him'. Other comments were even more dismissive.

Martand Singh's marriage to Pravinba, a Princess of Kachchh, in 1943 struck a more positive note.[80] Negotiations for the marriage were complete in 1941, but the death of the Maharrao of Kachchh postponed the ceremony. The following year Gulab Singh refused to permit the marriage until the Enquiry Committee had published its report. Early in 1943 Pravinba's parents urged that the marriage take place, though the Maharaja again refused permission unless the government allowed him to return to Rewa. To settle the impasse, the Maharaja of Jodhpur supported by the *ilaqadars* of Rewa suggested a quiet wedding in Bombay in August. In deference to his wife's ill-health, Gulab Singh agreed, and he and a party from Rewa were present at the occasion.

Several years later after Martand Singh had succeeded his father as Maharaja, the young Pravinba found herself Maharani of

Rewa.[81] From the outset her presence in the palace added a new dimension to the tensions of the royal family. Ignorant of Hindi, Pravinba arrived in 'unbeautiful' Rewa amidst the strains of her father-in-law's externment. Her husband strictly enforced *parda*, a system she was unused to, and warned her that 'any part of her anatomy shown in public would be cut off'. 'I was fighting the system all the time,' she exclaimed later. Even her maids could 'not fathom' her. Pravinba was also apprehensive at becoming Maharani so soon after her marriage:

She is not sure of her husband's future attitude to her, for she asserted that she does not know him. She is particularly fearful of the treatment she is likely to receive at the hands of the Dowager-Maharani ... her strong personality dominating her weaker son.[82]

Matters could have been no less difficult for her husband, whose throne was tied to the central government more securely than at any time in Rewa's history.[83] Martand Singh willingly occupied the position of constitutional ruler that the centre had tried to force on his father: he was to submit his choice of Chief Minister to the Crown Representative for approval, and was to be guided in all matters by the Chief Minister, referring any differences to the Resident in Indore. Martand Singh assented to these conditions on 30 January 1946, and in a stroke removed overnight many of the gaps between the British provinces and the princely states, a long-desired objective of the central government. A few days later the Maharaja was enthroned in Rewa; the King-Emperor recognized the succession, and on 1 April the Resident invested him with full ruling powers. In his speech on the occasion the new-style ruler expressed his loyalty to the central government.

Further to Martand Singh's position as constitutional ruler, the centre urged him to institute political reforms and forestall any attempt by Gulab Singh to destabilize the new order.[84] On 2 April 1946 the Maharaja formed a committee to draw up a constitution for Rewa. When the committee presented its report some 14 months later, the ruler's *ilaqadari* supporters persuaded him to include an upper house, where they held half the seats, to check the lower house elected on adult franchise. The Prime Minister was to enjoy a majority in the legislature and to advise the Maharaja; while the latter was to appoint a Chief Justice and other judges.

However, the transfer of power from Britain to India delayed the implementation of the constitution, and the government in Rewa only began preparing electoral rolls in late January 1948.

In spite of these reforms, groups loyal to the ex-ruler made trouble for his son as Maharaja.[85] Some criticized the landlord-dominated upper house, while others condemned the *ilaqadars'* treatment of their tenants. Socialists especially were tireless in abusing the new ruler. Pamphlets considered objectionable by the government were in circulation; and similar material attacking the Maharaja and the *ilaqadars* appeared in local newspapers. However, the landed were far more concerned for preserving their order in an increasingly democratic atmosphere than with local attacks which they could easily fob off.

Maharaja Martand Singh also endorsed the centre's policies relating to his father.[86] Having agreed to accede to the throne of Rewa on Gulab Singh's deposition, Martand Singh thereafter kept a distance from his father unusual in a Rajput family. The former Maharaja's view was that in collusion with the government his son instilled such fear in people that 'not a single bird of Rewa dares come near me'. Consequently, on his lightning visits to Rewa the ex-ruler publicly villified his son, with the result that on one occasion an excited mob injured the young Maharaja. Martand Singh interceded for his father when the centre arrested him in March 1948, persuading the States Ministry to intern him in Dehra Dun in consideration of his health; though he held out no hope to his father that he would be released to live and die in Rewa. Gulab Singh retaliated by calling his son his 'convictor and tormentor', and by dying intestate.

Martand Singh's submission to the central government notwithstanding, his regional loyalties lay just below the surface.[87] In March 1946 he cleared the decks by asking the centre to replace Smith, and on 1 May T.C.S. Jayaratnam ICS became Rewa's first Indian Chief Minister. In the uncertainty about the state's future before the transfer of power, on 7 August 1947 the Maharaja proclaimed Rewa's new constitution and by implication responsible government, and appointed Lal Yashwant Singh, the Thakur of Tala, as interim Prime Minister with a cabinet, in place of Jayaratnam whose appointment was about to lapse. It was notable that the Thakur's first act was to discharge all 'foreigners' in Rewa's civil service in the manner of the former ruler.

Disturbed at this display of regional independence, the Indian government asserted its authority over what it saw as a constituent of the new nation, and required the ruler to vacate the Chief Ministership in favour of a central nominee, Ramrao Deshmukh, latterly Indian High Commissioner in South Africa.[88] The cabinet resigned in anger, and compelled Martand Singh to protest to Delhi that the appointment of an outside Prime Minister retracted the self-government proclaimed in Rewa on 7 August and the regional sentiments expressed on that occasion.

While the centre's will prevailed, Deshmukh's Prime Ministership was marked by continuing tension between region and centre.[89] Lal Yashwant Singh did not resign until October and, though the Maharaja persuaded him and his cabinet to rejoin duty and work with Deshmukh, they refused to modify their written protest to the centre. Deshmukh blamed his predecessor for the tension:

I now know, I think, who is doing the bulk of the mischief, and why things were delayed.... It must be my predecessor, the Thakur Saheb of Tala. His Highness likes him.... (and) felt the greatest anxiety that his feelings would be hurt if he is asked to vacate the Prime Ministership.... He[i.e. Tala] was almost in tears with H.H., and said if H.H. had to suffer this indignity, why should H.H. make him P.M. for such a short time?[90]

Deshmukh also felt that the *ilaqadari* supporters of the Maharaja mistrusted him as an outsider, for contrary to their wishes he took no further action on the discharge of foreigners from the Rewa service.[91] Deshmukh, too, was unable to cope with Gulab Singh's sudden visitations to Rewa in 1948, and the resulting destabilization of the state's political life.

The centre's pursuit of the former ruler's tax liabilities could also not have pleased his son or regional loyalists.[92] The British Government of India initiated this search after it became clear in 1941 that Gulab Singh had appropriated state monies. Although the Income Tax Department initially exempted the Maharaja, the Finance Ministry took up the issue after his deposition. An Indian Finance Minister assessed Gulab Singh to income tax for the first time for the years 1947–9, though he was subsequently assessed from 1944 also. However, as the centre had frozen the ex-Maharaja's assets, the monies remained unpaid, and by 1948 the arrears totalled 7.67 lakhs. The centre realized part of the sum from the ex-ruler and part from Martand Singh, authorizing him to pay the amount from unfrozen accounts.

With Gulab Singh's death in 1950, the centre deemed his son the heir and liable to the taxation due on his late father's estate.[93] After paying arrears of 3.85 lakhs for 1948–52, Martand Singh was levied for a further seven lakhs. Despite his strong protests and the grant of extra time, he was constrained to pay the amount—a blow softened somewhat by the refund of a part of Gulab Singh's wealth— a dispute that was resolved only in 1953.

The recovery of this wealth was itself a source of friction between centre and region.[94] The British central government interested itself in the matter until 1946, but the incoming Indian government began to shift the responsibility for unlocking the assets to the region, taking the view that it was for the Rewa government to

decide ... what action if any, they could and should take to recover from Sir Gulab Singh the various shares, stocks, and bank credits ... which were the public property of the state.[95]

Following Gulab Singh's death Martand Singh claimed his father's fortune, a claim contested by the then Government of India who asserted their right to the monies. The dispute was only resolved in 1953 when the Maharaja and the centre agreed to divide the amount equally between them.

VII

CENTRE AND REGION IN THE ERA OF INDEPENDENCE, 1947–8

The above tensions were a mere shadow of the events that overtook Baghelkhand following India's Independence from Britain.[96] As we have seen, the centre declined to intervene in Rewa during the 1930s, but with Linlithgow's appointment as Crown Representative and Wylie's as Political Adviser, it adopted a confrontatory policy that culminated in the deposition of Gulab Singh. Under Wavell, with Corfield as head of the Political Department, central attitudes softened again; and though Corfield

supported fully his predecessor's tough stand on Rewa....[he] devoted this final and culminating phase of his career to seeing that the princes were given a fighting chance to maintain their patrimony.[97]

Corfield believed that the British government should help states who wished to join the new India and protect those who did not, advising them to hold out for independence. Martand Singh's appointment of Lal Yashwant Singh as Prime Minister with his cabinet in August 1947 would seem to reflect this view.

By then, however, Rewa was under central pressure to accede to the Indian State.[98] Much earlier in 1947 a princely conclave endorsed conditional union with India. However, when the Congress rejected those conditions, more influential states including Rewa met Prime Minister Jawaharlal Nehru to declare that they intended to join the Constituent Assembly. Congress leaders, for their part, reaffirmed their acceptance of the principle of monarchy. Thus, on 28 April representatives from Rewa took their seats in the Assembly together with representatives of the provinces and the larger princely states. By July more princes had joined the states supporting a united India.

Events moved rapidly in the same month, despite Corfield's last-minute efforts to support princely independence.[99] Once he had been sent to England on leave prior to retirement, V.P. Menon, Secretary to Vallabhbhai Patel at the States Ministry, opened negotiations with the princes for collaboration on deemed central subjects such as law and order. Mountbatten, the last Crown Representative, took matters much further by warning the princes that, though technically independent, they were part of India, and that it was in their interests to act accordingly. To this end he produced a draft Instrument of Accession, requesting the princes to cede central subjects to the Government of India.

Thus, when Martand Singh appointed Rewa's first Prime Minister and cabinet on the eve of Independence, he did so amidst the conflicting pressures of centre and region.[100] In order to counter regional demands, the Congress pressed the states to sign the Instrument of Accession. By 7 August Rewa had assented to the Standstill Agreement, holding further constitutional changes in abeyance until details were worked out. Yet as late as 14 August, Mountbatten was assuring the princes that 'the states will have complete freedom'. He also emphasized that the Instrument of Accession provided for the cession of limited powers to the centre,

without any financial liability. Further, that Instrument contains an explicit provision that in no other matter has the Central Government any authority to encroach on the internal economy or the sovereignty of the States.[101]

With this assurance Rewa appears to have tardily signed the Instrument, the States Ministry acknowledging the 'sacrifices made by Your Highness' as late as 22 August, the date of Gulab Singh's first visit to Rewa. The fact that Lal Yashwant Singh did not make way for Deshmukh till October adds to the impression that Rewa only reluctantly accepted central control.

Even so, if Rewa and other states believed that they could join the Indian Union as semi-autonomous regional entities, they were very much mistaken.[102] With the Instruments of Accession in hand, the centre mounted its second campaign against regional independence by merging small states with existing provinces or forming groups of states into single blocs. Although initially Martand Singh accepted central assurances that it would not touch 'viable' states, he foresaw that Rewa might disappear into such a grouping and so stalled moves in that direction—some believed under his father's influence.

However, the decision of the Rajput states in December 1947 to form a single province and the subsequent landslide of states into centrally sponsored unions or mergers forced Rewa's hand.[103] While holding out for favourable conditions, the Maharaja and his advisers were faced with either merging with Uttar Pradesh or the Central Provinces, or joining a union of the states of Baghelkhand and Bundelkhand. As the first option appeared unwieldy, the latter remained the only alternative despite the fact that the states of eastern central India were ill-matched. Apart from the traditional antipathy between Baghels and Bundelas, Rewa was approximately the same size as the Bundelkhand states put together. Alone of the states Rewa sent delegates to the Constituent Assembly; it alone was financially viable, surplus in food, and had a long history of administration and land settlement along British lines. However, as such it was also central to any reorganization of states in the area, and was in a strong bargaining position on that account.

Central pressure towards a union of the states of Baghelkhand and Bundelkhand gathered pace from January 1948, though regional emotions posed a daunting obstacle.[104] Gulab Singh made several dashes to Rewa to oppose the union, forcing the centre to silence him. V.P. Menon, the central representative in the discussions that ensued, found the attitude of the 'Rewa Ruler and people' doubtful, Martand Singh's *ilaqadari* advisers counselling a separate state. Other opinion was in favour: the Praja Mandal supported the union; while the petty princes of Baghelkhand and Bundelkhand welcomed it as offering the prospect of developing their backward states where the plight of people was appalling.

Menon's skilful diplomacy ultimately led Rewa into the proposed union.[105] In March 1948 Awadesh Pratap Singh, Narmada Prasad Singh, and others met Menon in Delhi to establish Rewa's conditions for joining the union. Later that month Menon went to Rewa, ready to concede points to the 'pronounced local patriotism' surrounding an 'inexperienced and young Maharaja'. According to one report, Menon

went to work on the young Ruler.... After much 'brain-washing', threats and cajolery, with the promise of a liberal privy purse of one million rupees and Rajpramukhship and some other concessions thrown in, Martand Singh was at last persuaded to join a union of states to be called Vindhya Pradesh.[106]

Far from making a complete sell-out to central pressure, Rewa obtained several important regional concessions:[107] there were to be separate ministers for Bundelkhand and Baghelkhand and a common chief minister, with the Rajpramukh as coordinator; and a special clause allowed Rewa to leave the union if she chose. On 13 March 1948 at Navgaon in Menon's presence the princes of the two regions signed a Covenant of Accession to the union, Martand Singh appending his signature later in the state capital.

Subsequent events exposed the defects of such a hurried and compulsive agreement.[108] Part of the problem lay with the colonial government. Despite last minute efforts to protect the princes, it 'did not have the foggiest idea what to do with them'. By contrast, Patel's agenda was clear: to bring the country together under a strong centre and create a manageable set of provinces or states comprising the new nation. As a result, states and regions that had existed for centuries under fluctuating central pressures disappeared overnight into mergers or unions, joining the nation on the centre's terms.

VIII

VINDHYA PRADESH, 1948–9: A CENTRAL MISCALCULATION

Spokesmen for the central government sought to impose their political vision on Vindhya Pradesh at its inauguration on 4 April 1948. In his message to the Rajpramukh Martand Singh on the occasion, Patel declared it an

immense pleasure to find that both the Rulers and people of Rewa and the Bundelkhand States had decided to pool their resources in order to bring to the full the glory of that ancient territory.... Let the units cease to think in terms of themselves: their guiding principle should be ... their new unified life under a common system.... All differences ... must be subordinated to the high purpose which I have set out.[109]

N.V. Gadgil, who administered the oath of office to the Rajpramukh on behalf of the central government, also underlined that it was time to forget sectional interests and 'look on everyone as Indian'.

Hasty central initiatives and continuing regional tensions led to the early demise of Vindhya Pradesh.[110] Due to a clash of parties, groups, and Congress factions, the Rajpramukh was unable to select a common Chief Minister to hold office until the provincial government could devise a constitution. The two-cabinet system also proved unworkable. The centre had thus to prepare a new agreement, the third such relating to their former states signed by the princes since 1 August 1947. Sensing further gains for Rewa, Martand Singh held out for permanent Rajpramukhship with an increased income, and a resolution of the question of royal property. Other rulers, too, wanted their privy purses enhanced.

Rewa indeed gained from the reshaping of Vindhya Pradesh.[111] In May 1948, when Patel authorized the Rajpramukh to select a Prime Minister for the revised union, Martand Singh chose Awadesh Pratap Singh. Without consulting the Rajpramukh, Singh selected his cabinet and drew up a constitution acceptable to Baghelkhand and Bundelkhand, and also to the centre. In return for abandoning the opt-out clause, Rewa was to select the Prime Minister who would form a cabinet representing both regions, the Deputy Prime Minister coming from Bundelkhand. Rewa was to be the interim capital, and Martand Singh was to be Rajpramukh for life with an enhanced allowance. The centre also agreed to discuss revised allowances for other former rulers. In June all princes signed a Supplementary Covenant, and the centre in turn guaranteed their 'privileges, dignities and interests'.

However, at the same time the revised constitution located Rewa and other former states firmly within the democratic nation by shifting power away from the Rajpramukh and the princes in favour of the Prime Minister and cabinet.[112] Singh's independent action and his work in devising the new constitution earned him central approval, but the ire of the Rajpramukh who realized that he had been edged out. Even though he tried to influence the selection of the cabinet, Patel upheld Singh's role as a democratic Prime Minister, with the Rajpramukh as a constitutional head:

I am glad to know that.... Your Highness has accepted the advice of the Prime Minister in regard to the formation of the ministry. As I explained to you, that is quite in accord with the constitutional position of the Rajpramukh ... [he] can only advise and warn in the matter of formation of ministries and other non-reserved subjects. If the Prime Minister or the Ministry still persist in their course of action, the Rajpramukh ... cannot press them further.[113]

However, despite central backing the second Vindhya Pradesh also failed.[114] The Congress ministers bickered with one another; and from within a faction-ridden Congress party members publicly critcized ministers and officials, and incited people against them. Socialists abused the Rajpramukh and condemned the *jagirdar*-dominated government, while the newly formed Kisan Sangh demanded the abolition of the *jagirdari* system. Critics protested against the retrenchment of public servants. The focal point of this agitation was the capital, but even in rural areas people longed for the 'good old days'. As early as February 1949 adverse reports from Vindhya Pradesh were reaching the central government.

The cabinet itself was a divided house.[115] Ministers attacked their Prime Minister Awadesh Pratap Singh, and tried to persuade the central Congress organization to dismiss him. Of the ministers, Narmada Prasad Singh attracted most criticism from inside and outside the cabinet, much of it related to alleged financial and other irregularities. In April 1949 the Minister for Industries, Rao Shiva Bahadur Singh of Churhat, was arrested in Delhi for taking a bribe when awarding a diamond mining licence to a Panna syndicate.

Loose financial accounting was one of the principal charges against the ministry.[116] The Government of Vindhya Pradesh abandoned the regular budget procedure introduced into Rewa before Gulab Singh was deposed, ministers bypassing their Finance Department which was unable to scrutinize proposals before they were included in items of expenditure. The cabinet also authorized payments to the Rajpramukh and Up-Rajpramukh without consulting the Finance Ministry or the States Ministry in Delhi; and took money from state reserves or borrowed from the Bank of Baghelkhand, making it impossible for the Finance Department to control expenditure. Further, Bundelkhand and Baghelkhand had separate Accounts Departments, adding to the confusion. The centre thus complained that the

general impression that one gets is one of complete lack of propriety, scrutiny or control in incurring expenditure.... The progress of expenditure is alarming, and will soon reduce the Union to a state of bankruptcy.... Innumerable financial favours have been shown, in cash or kind to individuals, Rulers and commercial concerns, in circumstances which give rise to grave suspicion, concerning ... the honesty of such transactions.[117]

Bureaucratic laxity went hand in hand with ministerial prodigality.[118] Even under Jayaratnam officials appealed constantly against his orders. Once the local administration took over, they grew restive at the delay in appointing a pay commission, and criticized controversial appointments, promotions, and removals from office. One official even signed his own travel allowance bills! Few of the uniting states had an efficient police force; and senior police officers did not know the boundaries of their districts or how many police stations they controlled. Central bureaucrats doubted whether treasury officers in Rewa were competent to run their department; while local observers remarked on the 'complete disorganization' in the secretariat where 'little work is being done'.

The ministry's severest critic was N.B. Bonarjee, the Regional Commissioner.[119] Appointed by the centre to develop an administration on the lines of the older provinces, Bonarjee regularly complained to the States Ministry in Delhi about non-performing officials and the nepotism and corruption of the ministers, whom he charged with making a mockery of cabinet meetings and fudging budget figures. In one report Bonarjee went close to casting the ministers as criminals:

We are not dealing with men of any political or any other form of morality, as I have found myself by bitter experience.... I bring to mind just a few instances of deception, irregularity, and disobedience.... I am dealing with men who can only appreciate the roughest and most severe treatment.[120]

Bonarjee's notes were reminiscent of Fisher's remarks on Gulab Singh. It was thus somewhat ironical that he charged the ministers with being more unpopular than the deposed ruler, and portrayed the people of Rewa as clamouring for his return.[121] Enraged by the Commissioner's constant carping and damning reports, the ministers filed strong complaints to Delhi and ceased to cooperate with him.

    With central control over India's provinces and regions largely in place, Patel dealt firmly with what had become an embarrassing situation.[122] On 15 April 1949, a year after Vindhya Pradesh was formed, he dismissed its second ministry and appointed Bonarjee to take charge on behalf of the central government. On 7 May he designated Bonarjee as interim Chief Minister, with Gulab Singh's supporter Brajendranath as Chief Secretary and Assistant Minister. A local man, S.N. Mehta, subsequently became Chief Minister pending more permanent central arrangements.

IX

THE INTEGRATION OF BAGHELKHAND AND VINDHYA PRADESH INTO THE INDIAN NATION, 1950–56

The final integration of Baghelkhand into the Indian State took place in stages. In a first phase, after again rejecting the division of Vindhya Pradesh among neighbouring provinces, on 1 January 1950 Patel declared Vindhya Pradesh a centrally administered 'Part C' State under a Chief Commissioner, inviting comparison with the actions of the British central government less than a decade earlier.[123]

    The central arrangements for Vindhya Pradesh extinguished any remnants of princely and regional power.[124] A fourth Covenant since 1947 required the princes to surrender 'full exclusive authority, jurisdiction and powers' relating to the governance of their former states to the central government. The centre overcame the princes' reluctance to sign by guaranteeing each a

privy purse ... free of all taxes....the privileges, dignities and titles enjoyed ... before 15 August 1947....full ownership of properties ... no enquiry ... no proceedings in any court....guarantees to permanent members of the public services; and no proceedings against any servant of any Covenanting State.[125]

Martand Singh was perhaps more disaffected than any former ruler. His privy purse remained at ten lakhs; and a Chief Commissioner now reported directly to the centre. There seemed no place for a regional Rajpramukh.

Central rule could not, however, continue indefinitely, and after a little more than two years the government shuffled its regional cards once more to restore democracy to the troubled state.[126] The decision revived the elected assembly and a ministry responsible to the legislature under a centrally appointed Lieutenant Governor. Following elections in 1952, when Congress defeated the Socialists and the pro-Hindu Jana Sangh, a Congress ministry took office on 2 April 1952 with Shambhu Nath Shukla of Rewa as Prime Minister and K. Santhanam of Andhra Pradesh as Lieutenant Governor. The official language of the state was Hindi.

Vindhya Pradesh was also dependent on the centre to bridge the gap between its revenue receipts and expenditure. Though the abolition of *ilaqadari* and other forms of landholding in 1952 and its allocation to former tenants in proprietary right, followed by a resettlement of land, increased the revenue intake, the payment of compensation to landholders proved a burden.[127] The state, moreover, gained nothing from the division of the assets of the deceased ex-ruler in 1953, the centre and Martand Singh agreeing to a half-share each of a sum that later totalled 14 crores.[128] In view of a shortfall in revenues, in 1955 the centre gave Vindhya Pradesh a subvention of Rs 124.5 lakhs to pay for development schemes and provide basic amenities in areas starved of capital.[129]

Despite administrative changes and the formation of a composite state, economic advance in Baghelkhand and Vindhya Pradesh remained tentative. For agriculture, a slowly expanding gross cropped area did not keep pace with the 25 per cent increase in population between 1951–61. Traditional farming methods continued to obstruct growth; and no year up to 1956 was wholly satisfactory for crops, such that the state had to import grain to make up the deficit. Industrial development remained at a low ebb, though work on a regional power grid had commenced by 1956.[130] From 1949 the Forest Department began the immense task of extending the Rewa forest model to the rest of Vindhya Pradesh which had no history of forest conservation. Limited progress in communications and transport were unable to breach Baghelkhand's age-old problem of isolation, or push development beyond a point.[131]

The region's growing population posed further problems for its development. Between 1941 and 1961 the population of Baghelkhand rose more steeply than in preceding decades due to improvements in health and literacy, control over famine, expanding communications, and immigration. Under these conditions, too, mortality rates fell, though in some areas young females continued to die in greater numbers from neglect in favour of their male siblings.[132] The rising population put additional pressure on the slowly increasing educational and health facilities of state and region; and as a result literacy levels remained low and people still died of disease. Ignorance, superstition, and indifference to hygiene continued to thwart efforts to inculcate modern attitudes to health.[133]

Thus, despite limited progress in various fields, the Vindhya Pradesh administration and its central sponsors could do little to reduce the poverty and social degradation that marked Baghelkhand and Bundelkhand alike. Apart from a small middle-class, the well-to-do landed, and the newly created peasant proprietors, the standard of living of most people remained at subsistence level.[134] These included those with leased or family plots that were too small to sustain them throughout the year, and the large numbers of landless.

Economic deprivation perpetuated the social and political inequalities of region and state:

The feudal outlook permeates every facet of local life. Anyone in a khaki dress is referred to as a sipahi. Titles such as Diwan, Kunwar and Seth abound as do impressive moustaches. In public transport poor peasants

are pushed off seats to make room for Thanedars, Advocates and
anybody with a claim to distinction. The feudal system is widely accepted
by the peasants.[135]

The efforts of administrators over the preceding century seem
to have come to nought: systemic backwardness continued to blight
Baghelkhand, as Vindhya Pradesh, in 1956.[136] A contemporary
observer characterized the belt from Orchha to Rewa as 'mediaeval, ... scratched here and there ... by the 20th century'. As ever,
social backwardness was intertwined with economic underdevelopment. In 1955 85 per cent of the region's population still depended on agriculture for a living, creating 'an economic and
social structure ... not conducive to industrialization'. Even where
development occurred, as in mining, it tended to feed an outside
market for raw materials. Apart from some employment in mining
activity, the large hill and forest population remained outside
development initiatives.

In 1956 Baghelkhand (and Vindhya Pradesh) found themselves
in the central melting pot again, when the Government of India
appointed a committee to investigate the boundaries of its states
and provinces. In its report, the committee advocated the formation of linguistic states in place of the existing multilingual units,
thus necessitating a redrawing of India's internal boundaries. In
central India, in place of the bilingual Madhya Pradesh, the committee proposed a Hindi-speaking state comprising the former
British districts in Mahakoshal and Chhattisgarh, together with
the old princely areas in Chhattisgarh, Madhya Bharat, and Vindhya
Pradesh. The former British districts in Nagpur and Vidarbha
were to join other Marathi-speaking areas of Bombay State to form
Maharashtra.

The central government accepted the report, triggering a debate in Baghelkhand on its inclusion in a composite Madhya
Pradesh.[137] Maharaja Martand Singh and his supporters, among
them former *ilaqadars*, opposed the scheme, but the centre brushed
aside regional sentiment on the grounds that there existed a
'remarkable consensus' on uniting the Hindi-speaking people of
central India. In April 1956 the Congress-dominated assembly of
Vindhya Pradesh debated the issue; and when a majority of members supported the centre's decision, the cabinet endorsed the
merger. Regional sentiment aside, it must have been clear to many

that only the resources of a composite state backed by the centre could redress the problems of Baghelkhand, which remained one of the most backward regions of the subcontinent.

Thus, on 1 November 1956, following a centuries' long dialogue between the region and various centralizing states, central initiatives prevailed over regional considerations. On that day a separate Baghelkhand disappeared to emerge as part of the Rewa Commissioner's Division of Madhya Pradesh, a state of the Indian Union.[138] And with this a new chapter in the region's history began.

Notes

1. CRR, CI, P, 45-P(S)/36, C. Corfield, 29 Nov. 1935; Bhargava, 'The Relations of British paramount power', PhD, p. 129.
2. Conversation with R.S. Misra.
3. CRR, CI, P, 45-P(S)/36, K.S. Fitze to B.J. Glancy, 22 Feb. 1936.
4. Ibid., FP, 45(5)-P, 1939, K.S. Fitze to B.J. Glancy, 29 Nov. 1939.
5. P, P branch, 82-P(S)-38, K.S. Fitze to B.J. Glancy, 6 Feb. 1938; CRR, CI, P, P branch, 30-P(S)/38, FR CIA 1/Feb. 1938; CRR, CI, 18-P(S)/ 42, Note of G.T. Fisher, 11 Feb. 1942.
6. RS, P, 1937–8, P office, 10 Dec. 1939; ibid., Conversation between Maharaja and Crown Representative, 11 Dec. 1939; ibid., Discussion of Maharaja with Mr Fitze, Resident in Central India, 11 Dec. 1939 (Linlithgow was present at this discussion); ibid., Conversation between Maharaja and Mr Fitze at Satna railway station, 13 Dec. 1939.
7. P, P branch, 3(7)-P(S)/40, G.T. Fisher, to F.V. Wylie, 31 Jan. 1941; RCE, vol. I, G.T. Fisher to CR, 23 Aug. 1941; CRR, CI, P, P branch, 18-P(S)/42, Conversation between Maharaja and G.T. Fisher, 14 Feb. 1942; CRR, CI, P, P branch, 18(4)-P(S)/42, G.T. Fisher to K.S. Fitze, 18 June 1942; CRR, CI, 18(7)-P(S)42, Robins' report, 1942, Bhargava, 'Relations of British paramount power', PhD, p. 102. Ravendra Sahib was a son of the Kishengarhi Maharani, who reportedly pushed her son's claims for a greater share of power in Rewa.
8. CRR, CI, P, P branch, 179-P(S)/4, G.T. Fisher to K.S. Fitze, 23 Aug. 1941; CRR, CI, P, P branch, 18-P(S)/42, K.S. Fitze, 8 Sept. 1941; ibid., K.S. Fitze to G.T. Fisher, 12 Nov. 1941; ibid., Statement of Gulab Singh, 11 Feb. 1942; RCE, vol. I, p. 187; Bhargava, 'Relations of British paramount power', PhD, pp. 129–30.
9. CRR, CI, P, P branch, 179-P(S)/41, G.T. Fisher to Maharaja Rewa,

17 Sept. 1941; ibid., K.S. Fitze to Maharaja Rewa, 18 Oct. 1941; ibid., K.S. Fitze, 25 Oct. 1941; ibid., J.C. Thompson, 7 Nov. 1941, ibid., H.D. Craik, 11 Nov. 1941; ibid., G.T. Fisher to K.S. Fitze, 29 Nov. 1941; *RCE*, vol. I, pp. 153–5.

10. CRR, CI, P, P branch, 179-P(S)/41, G.T. Fisher to PDept. 11 Dec. 1941.

11. Ibid., G.T. Fisher to K.S. Fitze, 23 Aug. 1941; ibid., L(inlithgow), 8 Sept. 1941; ibid., Linlithgow to SOS, 16 Dec. 1941; ibid., Polindia to Polad Camp, 17 Dec. 1941; ibid., illegible, 5 Jan. 1942; CRR, CI, P, P branch, 18-P(S)/42, H.S. Craik, 17 Jan. 1942; ibid., SOS to CR, 21 Jan. 1942; ibid., K.S. Fitze, 23 Jan. 1942; ibid., CR to SOS, 24 Jan. 1942; ibid., SOS to CR, 21 Feb. 1942.

12. M.S., P&R, 53-PR/47, Memorandum of C'wealth Relations Office, London, on the deposition of H.H. Maharajadhiraja, Sir Gulab Singh, Pol/1602/47; CRR, CI, P, P branch, 18-P(S)/42, H.S. Craik, 17 Jan. 1942; ibid., CR to SOS, 24 Jan. 1942.

13. Ibid.

14. CRR, CI, P, P branch, 18-P(S)/42, Maharaja's statement recorded by the Resident, 11 Feb. 1942; ibid., Polinda to Resident, 12 Feb. 1942; ibid., Resident to Polindia, 12 Feb. 1942; Bhargava; Relations of British paramount power', PhD, p. 132.

15. CRR, CI, P, P branch, 18-P(S)/42, Message to Maharaja Rewa delivered by Resident, 11 Feb. 1942; ibid., Resident to Polindia, 12 Feb. 1942; ibid., Polindia to Resident, 14 Feb. 1942; ibid., G.T. Fisher to Maharaja Rewa, 14 Feb. 1942; ibid., Maharaja Rewa to G.T. Fisher, 14 Feb. 1942; ibid., G.T. Fisher to B.N. Zutshi, 15 Feb. 1942; ibid., Polindia to L.W. Wooldridge 20 Feb. 1942; *ibid.*, K.S. Fitze to G.T. Fisher, 27 Feb. 1942; M/S, P&R, 53-PR/47, Memo of CRO, London, P.1602/47. The Maharaja was not permitted to come within a 100-mile limit of his state while under suspension.

16. CRR, CI, P, P branch, 18-P(S)/42, G.T. Fisher to K.S. Fitze, 24 Feb. 1942; ibid., G.T. Fisher to K.S. Fitze, 26 Apr. 1942; RS, 1943–44, P Dept, 114, 1943–4, Confdl, N.P. Singh to W.F. Campbell, 1 Apr. 1946.

17. Bhargava, 'Relations of British paramount power', PhD, pp. 133-4.

18. RCE vol. I, pp. 1–2; CRR, CI, P, P branch, 18(2)-P(S)/42, G.T. Fisher to Maharaja Rewa, 31 May 1942; ibid., Maharaja Rewa to PSec, 13 July 1942. Other members of the committee were as follows: Nawab Sir Saiyid Raza Ali Khan of Rampur; Rana Sir Rajendra Singh, Maharaj-Rana of Jhalawar; Sir S.S. Rangnekar (also spelt as Ragnekar), formerly of the Bombay High Court; J. De la Hay Gordon, formerly Resident in Mysore. Copland, *Princes of India.*, pp. 187–8, claims that permitting the Maharaja to plead his case before an independent commission under a regulation of 1920;

granting him full legal representation; and foregoing certain other charges, was part of a more sympathetic approach to the princes following their help in the war, somewhat repairing the damage caused by the debate on federation. There is no hint of this sympathy anywhere in the documents relating to the enquiry against Gulab Singh.

19. CRR, CI, 18(7)-P(S)/42, Robins' report, 1942; *RCE*, appx. IV, vol. I, A.N. Chaudhury, 13 July 1942, p. 24. I have made extensive use of the *Rewa Enquiry Report*, as this proved to be a substantially correct version of events, though it failed to stand up in the Court of Enquiry.

20. Ibid., p. 28.

21. CRR, CI, P, P branch, 18(2)-P(S)/42, Note by G.T. Fisher, 3 Apr. 1942; ibid., N. Sircar to H.D. Craik, 2 Aug. 1942; CRR, CI, P, P branch, 18(2)-P(S)/43, Note of S.A. Lal, 10 Mar. 1943; *RCE*, appx. IV, vol. II, Closing address of N.N. Sircar, 5 Oct. 1942; R.S. Misra to me, as related to him by Maharaja Gulab Singh, substantially endorsing the Crown's case against him in the enquiry. Uma Prasad came from a humble Brahman family, graduating by way of the ruler's Anandgarh *ilaqa* to become an ADC and part of the inner circle of the 'court'.

22. CRR, CI, P, P branch, 18(7)-P(S)/42, Robins' report, 1942; CRR, CI, P, P branch, 18(1)-P(S)/43, CR to SOS, 4 Feb. 1943; CRR, CI, P, P branch, 1892)-P(S)/43, Note of S.A. Lal, 10 Mar. 1943; M/S, P&R, 53-PR/47, Memo of CRO, London, P, 1602/47; *RCE*, vol. I, pp. 10, 35.
    Shanker Prasad, the son of a coppersmith, was employed by Narbada Patwa to take charge of his wife's two sons, Dadu Jagdish Prasad and Suraj Prasad, the former allegedly fathered by Gulab Singh. The Maharaja settled the Anandgarh *ilaqa* on Dadu in 1927, creating him Thakur of Anandgarh. Narbada Patwa had been an associate and playmate of Gulab Singh as the latter grew up. In 1935 he was made a *tazimi* sardar of Rewa State, but in 1939 was convicted of the murder of Shanker Prasad and sentenced to rigorous imprisonment for ten years. R.S. Misra confirmed that the Maharaja later confessed to having arranged the killing.

23. CRR, CI, P, P branch, 18(2)-P(S)/42, G.T. Fisher to H.D. Craik, 1 Aug. 1942; ibid., N.N. Sircar to H.D. Craik, 17 Sept. 1942; ibid., K.S. Fitze to G.E. Cuffe, 6 Oct. 1942; ibid., N.N. Sircar to H.D. Craik, 9 Oct. 1942; ibid., N.N. Sircar to K.S. Fitze, 19 Jan. 1943; *RCE*, Majority Report, pp. 14, 117–18.

24. CRR, CI, FP, 18(7)-P(S)/42, N. N. Sircar, 21 Oct. 1942.

25. CRR, CI, FP, 18(7)-P(S)/42, N.N. Sircar to H.D. Craik, 10 Sept. 1942; F, 3 Rewa/42, B.C. Awasthi, 27 Nov. 1942.

26. CRR, CI, P, P branch, 18(7)-P(S)/42, Robins' report, 1942; *RCE*, vol. I, pp. 8–9, 22–6, 28, 83, 150–1; *RCE*, appx. II, pp. 38, 44–53, 82. Harol was a State Army title.

27. CRR, CI, P, P branch, 18(1)-P(S)/43, Polad to PrSec Viceroy, 31 Jan. 1943; M/S, P&R, 53-PR/47, Memo of CRO, London, P. 1602/47; *RCE*, vol. I, p. 200.

28. CRR, CI, P, P branch, 18(2)-P(S)/42, H.D. Craik to N.N. Sircar, 13 Feb. 1943; M/S, P&R, 53-PR/47, Memo of CRO, London, P, 1602/47; *RCE, Majority Report*, pp. 117–24.

29. CRR, CI, P, P branch, 179–P(S)/41, H.D. Craik, 11 Nov. 1941; CRR, CI, P, P branch, 18-P(S)/42, H.D. Craik, 18 Aug. 1942; CRR, CI, P, P branch, 18(2)-P(S)/43, H.D. Craik, 30 Mar. 1943; M/S, P&R, 53-PR/47, Memo of CRO, London, P 1602/47; Wakefield, *Past Imperative*, p. 196.

30. CRR, CI, P, P branch, 18(1)-P(S)/43, K.S. Fitze, 3 Feb. 1943; CRR, CI, P, P branch, 18(2)-P(S)/43, K.S. Fitze, 29 Mar. 1943. The Maharaja's personal life did not become the subject of official complaints.

31. CRR, CI, P, P branch, 1892)-P(S)/43, K.S. Fitze, 1 Nov. 1943; CRR, CI, P, P branch, 18(4)-P(S)/42, Asst Sec, P Dept, Communique, 30 Nov. 1943; M/S, P&R, 53-PR/47, Memo of CRO, London, P, 1602/47. F.V. Wylie, the hard-line head of the Political Department, endorsed the proposals relating to Gulab Singh in what would appear to be a shift from the policy of non-interference followed earlier by the Government of India. (CRR, CI, P, P branch, 18(2)-P(S)/43, F.V. Wylie, 17 Nov. 1943)

32. M/S, P&R, 53-PR/47, Memo of CRO, London, P, 1602/47.

33. CRR, CI, P, P branch, 18(2)-P(S)/42, Maharaja Rewa to G.T. Fisher, 2 Mar. 1942; CRR, CI, P, P branch, 18(4)-P(S)/42, L.W. Wooldridge to G.T. Fisher, 21 Apr. 1942; RS, Judl, 1942–3, 79(4), 1942–43, E. de C. Rennick to L.W. Wooldridge, 30 May and 10 July 1942; RS, Judl, 1942–43, 79(c), 1942–45, Maharani, V.S. Gupte, 15 Aug. 1942; CRR, CI, P, P branch, 18(6)-P(S)/42, H.D. Craik, 27 Sept. 1942; ibid., W.F. Campbell to Maharaja Rewa, 30 Oct. 1942. The Maharani suffered from insomnia and loss of appetite, had reportedly 'lost all interest in everything', and was given to 'fits of crying'. She was also anxious that Martand Singh's marriage should not be delayed. Another charge against Kaushal Prasad was that he had stolen the *patta* of the Thakur of Burwa. Wooldridge's police failed to seize Prasad as he was returning to the palace by car in May 1942. As Wooldridge declined to arrest the offender inside the palace, it was left to his successor, Wakefield, to extern him from the state in 1944.

34. RS, P, 195-P/48, Order of Administrator, 25 Feb. 1942; CRR, CI, P, P branch, 18-P(S)/42, G.T. Fisher to Maharaja Rewa, 5/8 May

1942; RS, Private office, 1942, 50, 1941–42, Rev, A.R.S., 14 June
1942; RDO, B 8/32–3, Admin, 32–3, Bank, Order 39, L.W.
Wooldridge, 16 June 1942; CRR, CI, P, P branch, 18-P(S)/42, J.H.
Thompson, 2 July 1942; RDO, B 8/32–3, Admin, 32–3, Bank, Impl
Bank of India, Katni, to L.W. Wooldridge, 17 Aug. 1942; RS, Private
Office, 1942, 118, 43–4, Confdl, Shanker Singh, 22 Dec. 1942; CRR,
CI, P, P branch, 18-P(S)/42, Maharaja Rewa to Bank of India,
Bombay, 14 Jan. 1943; ibid., R.R. Newhill, 1 Mar. 1943; ibid., Res CI
to Polindia, 31 Mar. 1943; CRR, CI, P, P branch, 15(15)-P(S)/45,
Res CI to Maharaja Rewa, 2 Apr. 1945; ibid., India Office to L.
Griffin, 10 Sept. 1945; ibid., J.S.H. Shattock, 18 Oct. 1945.
35. CRR, CI, P, P branch, 18-P(S)/42, L.W. Wooldridge to G.T. Fisher,
4 Mar. 1942; RS, P, 1942–3, 117–II/42, P, List of agitators; CIA, P,
A, 40–A, 1942, N.R. Shukla, 14 and 30 Mar. 1942.
36. RS, 1936, Army HQ, 27, 1941–42, *Hitavada* (Nagpur), 25 Mar. 1942;
ibid., *Nagpur Times* (Nagpur) 31 July and 6 Aug. 1942; CRR, CI, P,
P branch, 18(6)-P(S)/42, L. W. Wooldridge to Polindia, 25 Sept.
1942; *Rewa Gazetteer*, pp. 50–1; Dubey, 'Establishment of democratic
political system', PhD, pp. 128–9. In September matters took an
unprecedented turn when a crowd of about 1000, students among
them, approached Rewa jail to release the student and other
leaders whom the administration had arrested. A feature of the
agitation was that younger, more militant members of the Congress
who replaced the arrested *ilaqadari* leaders were among those
leading the attempt on the jail.
37. CRR, CI, P, P branch, 18-P(S)/42, FR CIA, 1/May 1942; ibid., L.W.
Wooldridge to G.T. Fisher, 4 June 1942; VP. 1939–41, Comm & Ind,
Orders 54–6, Rewa Raj Gazette, 9 Aug. 1942; RS, P, 1942–3, 133/
42, P, L.W. Wooldridge, to L.C.F. Robins, 14 Aug. 1942; P, P branch,
9(8)-P(S)/42, FR CIA, 1/Sept., 2/Sept., 1/Nov. 1942; RS, Dak office, 1924–42, 76, 1934, Postal, L.W. Wooldridge, 12 Sept. 1942; VP,
1939–41, Comm & Ind, Orders, 54–6, Rewa Raj Gazette, 12 Sept.
1942; CRR, CI, P, P branch, 18(6)-P(S)/42, L.W. Wooldridge to
Polindia, 24 Sept. 1942; VP, 1940–1, Personal office, Rewa, 132, P,
Do W/500, 17 Oct. 1942; VP, 1943–4, Comm & Ind, Inds, 53/G,
1942–3, L.W. Wooldridge, 17 Mar. 1943.
38. CIA, War branch, 1572/1941, Maharaja Rewa to G.T. Fisher, 17
Sept. 1941; CRR, CI, P, P branch, 18-P(S), L.W. Wooldridge to Res
CI, 26 Feb. 1942; P, P branch, 9(8)-P(S)/42, FR CIA, 1/June 1942;
RS, P, 1942–3, 133/42, P, L.W. Wooldridge to L.C.F. Robins, 14 Aug.
1942; RS, Khasgi, 1941–2, 98, 1942–3, Confdl, Pawaidar Sangh to
L.W. Wooldridge, 9 Nov. 1942; P, P branch, 6(12)-P(S)/43, FR CIA,
1/Mar., 1/July 2/July 1943; Khan, *Glories of Bandhogarh*, p. 10. By
mid-July 1943 the administration had sent 162 recruits for technical

training and 9 for typist-clerk training, from Rewa.

39. CRR, CI, P, P branch, 18(2)-P(S)/43, F.V. Wylie, 17 Nov. 1943; M/
S, P&R, 53-PR/47, Memo of CRO, London, P, 1602/47; Wakefield,
Past Imperative, pp. 195, 199–200.

40. CRR, CI, P, P branch, 2(30)-P(S)/43, Illegible, 23 Nov. 1943;
Wakefield, *Past Imperative*, pp. 195, 198.

41. Ibid., p. 197.

42. P, P branch, 104-P(S)/44, memo of CM, June 1944; RS, 1943–4, P,
137-A, 1943–4, Admin, DO 39, 30 June 1944; RS, Khasgi, 1941–42,
25, Constit Reforms, Draft report, p. 13, nd; Wakefield, *Past Imperative*, p. 198. Ministers from outside Rewa included Brigadier Jai
Singh, a Sikh, who was to head the army; and Rao Kartar Nath from
CP who was IGP. Though Gulab Singh had presided at meetings of
the old council, Wylie rightly anticipated that as the Maharaja
would no longer control the proceedings, he would cease to attend the new council. He therefore directed Wakefield to preside.

43. RS, Army HQ, 1936, 4, State Cars, L.W. Wooldridge, 30 July 1942;
RS, H, 1933–42, Army, 117, 1943–4, CGStaff, 27 Feb. 1943; RS, P,
1944–5, 90, 1943, CM to H.A. N. Barlow, 8 Nov. 1944: Wakefield,
Past Imperative, p. 198.

44. CIA, Fin-C, 423-C, 1943, Note by Dr. H. Crookshank, nd; RS, Army
HQ, 1–36, Cab Office, 24, CM, 21, Dec. 1944; CIA, War branch,
139-W/1945, C.C.H. Smith to A.E. G. Davy, 13 Oct. 1945; CIA, 139-
B, 1945, Res CI to CSec, 11 Jan. 1946; *Rewa Directory*, pp. 8, 184, 187;
Rewa Gazetteer, p. 236; *Satna Gazetteer*, p. 123. Reforms continued on
into the Chief Ministership of Col. C.C.H. Smith, Wakefield's successor. Rewa's first Director of Agriculture tried to improve seed
and cattle; the Industrial Department issued a report on the state's
mineral resources; the Communications and Transport Department began a lorry service between Rewa and Katni; and key
bridges across the Chhoti Mahanadi (Markandeya) and the Son
(Kuldahaghat) began to take shape. In 1944 Darbar College became a degree college; and by 1945–6 the 150 educational institutions of 1937 had grown to 229. The Maharaja's Court became the
Rewa High Court in 1945.

45. P, P branch, 6(12)-P(S)/43, FR CIA, 1/Mar., 2/May 1943; RDO, B
15/45–6, S, Misc, 31–C, nd, Ram Kishore to Supt Customs, 1 Feb.
1944; CRR, CI, P, P branch, 6(3)-P(S)/45, FR CIA, 2/Feb. 1945;
Rewa Gazetteer, p. 159; *Satna Gazetteer*, p. 181; Wakefield, *Past Imperative*, p. 199.

46. CIA, War branch, 139-W, 1945, CM to H.A.N. Barlow, 24 May 1945;
Rewa Directory, p. 122.

47. P, P branch, 104-P(S)/44, E.B. Wakefield, to H.A.N. Barlow, 8 Aug.

1944; ibid., F.V. Wylie, 19 Aug. 1944; Wakefield, *Past Imperative*, pp. 200–1.

48. Ibid., p. 201.

49. RS, 1945–7, Local Admin, Confdl, 1945–6, 8/CG/46, CM to Maharaja Rewa, 15 Aug. 1944; P, P branch, 104-P(S)/44, F.V. Wylie, to W.F. Campbell, 23 Aug. 1944; ibid., E.B. Wakefield to H.A.N. Barlow, 26 Aug. 1944; ibid., CM to Res CI, 21 Oct. 1944; RDO, B 15/45–47, 172, Confdl, 1946, W.F. Campbell to C.C.H. Smith, 24 Oct. 1945; M/S, P&R, 53-PR/47, Memo of CRO, London, P, 1602/47; Wakefield, *Past Imperative*, pp. 201–5. When told by the Maharaja that Shiva Bahadur Singh of Churhat was 'a snake', Wakefield replied that 'Your Highness's subjects worship snakes'.

50. RS, 1945–7, Local Admin, Confdl, 1945–6, 8/CG/46, CM to Maharaja Rewa, 15 Aug. 1944; P, P branch, 104-P(S)/44, CM to Res CI, 21 Oct. 1944; CIA, War branch, 139–W/1945, C.C.H. Smith to A.E.G. Davy, 13 Oct. 1945; RDO, B 15/45–47, 172, Confdl, 1946, W.F. Campbell to C.C.H. Smith, 24 Oct. 1945.

51. Wakefield, *Past Imperative*, p. 205.

52. Ibid., pp. 205–6.

53. RDO, B 15/45–46, S, Misc Corresp, 31-C, nd, Maharaja Rewa to CM, Rewa, 27 Jan. 1945; RS, GAD, 1942–6, B 9, A branch, 132, 1943–4; Admin, 1 Feb 1945; CRR, CI, P, P branch, 15(15)-P(S)/45, Conversation between Maharaja Rewa and C.C.H. Smith, 11 Feb. 1945; CRR, CI, P, P branch, 6(3)-P(S)/45, FR CIA, 2/Mar. 1945; P, P branch, 15(3)-P(S)/45, CR to SOS, 17 Nov. 1945; P, P branch, 56-P(S)/45, W.F. Campbell to C.G. Herbert, 20 Dec. 1945; RDO, B 15/45–47, 172, Confdl, 1946, CM to A.E.G. Davy, 4 Feb. 1946.

54. CRR, CI, P, P branch, 18(2)-P(S)/43, K.S. Fitze, 25 Oct. 1943; CRR, CI, P, P branch 15(15)-P(S)/45, Interview of Maharaja Rewa by C.C.H. Smith, 11 Feb. 1945; ibid., India Office to L. Griffin, 10 Sept. 1945; ibid., J.H.S. Shattock to W.F. Campbell, 11 Sept. 1945; ibid;, W.F. Campbell to Maharaja Rewa, 22 Oct. 1945; RS, Private office, 1942, 18/49, Confdl, S. Singh to Pandit Shukla, 19 Jan. 1946.

55. CRR, CI, P, P branch, 15(15)-P(S)/45, Interview of Maharaja Rewa by C.C.H. Smith, 11 Feb. 1945.

56. CRR, CI, P, P branch, 18-P(S)/42, Maharaja Rewa to Mgr BOI, Bombay, 14 Jan. 1943; CRR, CI, P, P branch, 15(15)-P(S)/45, R.B. Chatterjee's report on the Bank of Baghelkhand, to CM Rewa, 9 Mar. 1945; CRR, CI, P, P branch, 6(3)-P(S)/45, FR CIA, 2/Mar. 1945; CRR, CI, P, P branch, 15(15)-P(S)/45, J.S.H. Shattock to W.F. Campbell, 10 Sept. 1945; ibid., Mgr BOB to CM Rewa, 2 Oct. 1945.

57. CIA, Fin C, 432-C, 1944, E.B. Wakefield to H.A.N. Barlow, 15 Sept. 1944; CIA, Fin C, 368-C, C.C.H. Smith to A.E.G. Davy, 8 Oct. 1945;

ibid., illegible, 19 Oct. 1945; RS, Priv Office, 1942, 18/49, Confdl, Appx B to Statement of Civil List, Rewa State, B.G. Paradker, 7 Mar. 1946. Interest on state monies recoverable from the Bank of Baghelkhand and the sale of food grains outside Rewa swelled the state's revenue returns. However, closing balances in 1945 and 1946 remained at Rs 61 lakhs, leading one official to state that Rewa's financial position was 'stationary'.

58. CRR, CI, P, P branch, 18-P(S)/42, ? to G.T. Fisher, 22 May 1942; ibid., G.T. Fisher to L.W. Wooldridge, 26 May 1942; ibid., G.T. Fisher to K.S. Fitze, 6 Aug. 1942; Wakefield, *Past Imperative*, p. 203.

59. RDO, B 15/45–47, 172, Confdl, 1946, CM Rewa to A.E.G. Davy, 4 Feb. 1946; and appended note, CM Rewa, 4 Feb. 1946; RS, 1943–4. P, 114, 1943–4, Confdl, N.P. Singh to W.F. Campbell, 1 Apr. 1946.

60. CRR, CI, P, P branch, 6(3)-P(S)-44, FR CIA, 2/May, 2/Nov. 1944; CRR, CI, P, P branch, 6(3)-P(S)/45,FR CIA, 1/Sept., 1/Oct. 1945; *Rewa Directory*, p. 109.

61. RS, 1936, Army Head, F Cab office, 24. Extract, *Bandhava*, July 1944; CRR, CI, P, P branch, 6(12)-P(S)/44, FR Rewa, 1/Oct. 1944; CRR, CI, P, P branch, 15(15)-P(S)/45, CM Rewa to Res CI, 29 May 1945; CIA, War branch, 139-W/1945, Maharaja Rewa to CM, 7/10 Sept. and 6 Oct. 1945; P, P branch, 15(3)-P(S)/45, L. Griffin to E. Jenkins, 13 Oct. 1945; ibid., C.C.H. Smith to A.E.G. Davy, 13 Dec. 1945.

62. CRR, CI, P, P branch, 6(12)-P(S)/44, FR Rewa, 1/Oct. 1944; CRR, CI, 6(3)-P(S)/45, FR Rewa, 2/Oct. 1945; P, P branch, 15(3)-P(S)/45, C.C.H. Smith to A.E.G. Davy, 21 Oct. 1945; ibid., V. Sundaram 13 Nov. 1945; P, P branch, 15(3)-P(S)/45, C.G. Herbert, 27 Nov. 1945, and SOS to CR, 27 Nov. 1945; CIA, P, A, 12-A/44, *Hindustan Times*, 10 Dec. 1945; P, P branch, 15(3)-P(S)/45, W.S. Campbell to C.G. Herbert, 15 Dec. 1945; Dubey, 'Establishment of democratic political system', PhD, p. 136.

63. *RCE*, vol. I, Maharaja Rewa to G.T. Fisher, 23 Aug. 1941, p. 188; CRR, CI, P, P branch, 18(4)-P(S)/42, W.F. Campbell to L. Griffin, 29 Mar. 1944; P, P branch, 56-P(S)/45, L. Griffin, 22 Aug. 1945; ibid., W.F. Campbell to L. Griffin, 17 Sept. 1945, and to Maharaja Rewa, 27 Sept. 1945; ibid., C.G. Herbert to Ramchandra, 15 Nov. 1945; P, P branch, 15(3)-P(S)/45, Maharaja Rewa to CM Rewa, 12 Dec. 1945; ibid., W.F. Campbell to C.G. Herbert, 15 Dec. 1945.

64. Bhargava, 'Relations of British paramount power', PhD, pp. 139, 141.

65. P, P branch, 15(3)-P(S)/45, C.C.H. Smith to Maharaja Rewa, 13 and 14 Dec. 1945; P, P branch, 56-P(S)/45, W.F. Campbell to C.G. Herbert, 20 Dec. 1945.

66. P, P branch, 15(3)-P(S)/45, SOS to CR, 27 Nov. 1945; ibid., W.F. Campbell to C.G. Herbert, 15 Dec. 1945; ibid., Res CI to PSec, 20 Dec. 1945; ibid., CR to SOS, 1 Jan. 1946; ibid., PSec to Commandant, CRPolice, 22 Jan. 1946; P, P branch, 54-P(S)/45, F.V. Wylie, 31 Jan. 1946; Allen and Dwivedi, *Lives of the Indian Princes*, p. 259.

67. CRR, CI, P, P branch, 15(15)-P(S)/45, R.B. Chatterjee report, Jan. 1946; *Rewa Raj Gazette*, C.C.H. Smith, 31 Jan. 1946. Chatterjee believed that the Maharaja should refund the following: cash withdrawals of 1.45 crores; loans of capital and interest, 63 lakhs; Rewa Coalfields shares and dividends, 19 lakhs; advance to *ilaqa* Pushprajgarh, 1.24 lakhs; deposits of state subjects 1.05 lakhs, totalling 2.30 crores of rupees. Other monies, including the shares of the Bank of Baghelkhand, the Rewa Electricity Supply, and Rewa Distillery companies, a deposit of 43 lakhs in the Bank of Bagehlkhand, 5,000 additional shares of the Rewa Coalfields, the 60 lakhs given to the Maharani before the Maharaja's suspension— also to be credited to the state—brought the total to over three crores. The ruler's detractors believed the sum owing to be closer to four crores.

68. *Rewa State Gazette*, C.C.H. Smith, 31 Jan. 1946; RDO, 15/45–47, Confdl, 280V, Dec. 45–Feb. 46, Procs of an extraordinary meeting of the State Council at Raj Nivas, 1 Feb. 1946. According to Allen and Dwivedi, *Lives of the Indian Princes*, p. 259, Corfield, then Political Adviser to Wavell, handled the deposition within the central government.

69. P, P branch, 15(3)-P(S)/47, CI to Polindia, 1 Feb. 1946; P, P branch, 15(3)-P(S)/45, W.F. Campbell to C.G. Herbert, 4 Feb. 1946, communicating the account of A.E.G. Davy; ibid., W.F. Campbell to C.G. Herbert, 23 Feb. 1946; RS, 1943–4, P, 114, 1943–4, Confdl, N.P. Singh to W.F. Campbell, 1 Apr. 1946.

70. CRR, CI, P, P branch, 33-P(S)/46, C.G. Herbert to PSec, IO (London), 4 Mar. 1946; P, P branch, 15(3)-P(S)/45, Polindia to Res CI, 16 Mar. 1946; ibid., L. Griffin, 1 May 1946. The former Maharaja was henceforth to be known as Sir Gulab Singh, G.C.I.E., K.C.S.I., ex-Maharaja of Rewa.

71. M/S, P&R, 29-PR/47, S.V. Patel to Gulab Singh, 23 Aug. 1947; and to PM Rewa, 23 Aug. 1947; *Sardar Patel's Correspondence, 1945–50*, ed., Durga Das, vol. V, Ahmedabad, 1973, p. 355, Martand Singh to V.P. Menon, 24 Aug. 1947; M/S, P&R, 29-PR/47, S, UP CID report, M.K. Sinha, 8 Sept 1947; CIA, Info Bureau, 1-IB/48, *Amrit Bazar Patrika*, Allahabad, 17 Mar. 1948; M/S,P, 10(88)-P/49, unsigned note, nd. R.M. Deshmukh, who became Prime Minister of Rewa for a brief period from October 1947, exclaimed of Gulab

Singh, 'While this restless soul is at Allahabad, he will not have, nor
will let anyone here have, peace'.

72. CIA, Info Bureau, 1-IB/48, *Amrit Bazar Patrika*, Allahabad, 21 Mar.
    1948; M/S, P, A, Group I, 266-P/48, S. Narayanaswamy, 3 Apr.
    1946; M/S, O, 195-P/48, 1948, S. Narayanaswamy, 16 Apr. 1948.
73. CIA, Info Bureau, 1-IB/48, *Amrit Bazar Patrika*, Allahabad, 18 Apr.
    1948.
74. CIA, Info Bureau, 1-IB/48, *Hindustan Times*, Delhi, 18 Apr. 1948;
    CIA, Info Bureau, 1-IB/48, *Amrit Bazar Patrika*, Allahabad, 19 Apr.
    1948; M/S, P branch, 653-P/48, 1948, unsigned note, nd; M/S, P,
    195-P/48, 1949, S. Narayanaswamy, 20 Apr. 1948. Visitors to Gulab
    Singh in Dehra Dun could meet him only in the presence of a
    policeman; and lights in his compound enabled the police guards
    to maintain security at night. The centre assigned the ex-ruler a
    small monthly allowance, supplemented by a contribution from
    the Government of Vindhya Pradesh.
75. M/S, P branch, 10(88)-P/49, 1949, Reply to question of D.S. Seth
    in parliament, 15 Dec. 1949; M/S, P branch, 17(61)-P/50, Gulab
    Singh to V.P. Menon, 2 Jan. 1950.
76. M/S, P branch (61)-P/50, 1950, *Hindustan Times*, Delhi, 14 Apr.
    1950; information supplied by R.S. Misra, Gulab Singh's Private
    Secretary, 1946–50. The Polish hospital refused the former Ma-
    haraja admission, and he was given oxygen in a private clinic. One
    hour later he was declared dead. Misra accompanied the body to
    Allahabad.
77. P, P branch, 343-P(S)/41, Major Handcock to G.T. Fisher, 15 Apr.
    1941. P, P branch, 15(13)-P(S)/41, FR CIA, 1/Apr. 1941; CRR, CI,
    P, P branch, 18(4)-P(S)/42, G.T. Fisher to K.S. Fitze, 22 Aug. 1942.
78. *RCE*, vol. I, Maharaja Rewa to G.T. Fisher, 23 Aug. 1941; CRR, CI,
    P, P branch, 18(4)-P(S)/41, K.S. Fitze to G.T. Fisher, 6 Apr. 1942;
    CRR, CI, P, P branch, 18(4)-P(S)/42, G.T. Fisher to Maharaja
    Bikaner, 17 Apr. 1942; CRR, CI, P, P branch, 18(6)-P(S)/42, L.W.
    Wooldridge to Polindia, 24 Oct. 1942; CRR, CI, P, P branch, 18(4)-
    P(S)/42, A. Napier to R.R. Burnett, 21 Mar. 1944; CRR, CI, P, P
    branch, 18(4)-P(S)/42, W.F. Campbell to L. Griffin, 29 Mar. 1944;
    CRR, CI, P, 174-P(S)/44, W. Owens to E.B. Wakefield, 5 July 1944;
    P, P branch, 56-P(S)/45, W.T. Webb to L. Griffin, 19 May 1945; ibid.,
    W.F. Campbell to L. Griffin, 3 Aug. 1945, and 17 Sept. 1945; P, P
    branch, 56-P(S)/45, U/sec, Ext Affairs, to Consul Genl for Egypt,
    14 Dec. 1945; ibid., Polindia to CI, 22 Dec. 1945.
79. CRR, CI, 174-P(S)/44, L. Griffin, 23 July 1944; ibid., Confdl report,
    W. Owens to E.B. Wakefield, 21 Oct. 1944; P, P branch, 56-P(S)/
    45, Notes of a talk with F.V. Wylie, W. Owens, 6 Feb. 1945.

80. P, P branch, 5(24)-P(S)/41, CIO, CPB, 18 Feb. 1941; CRR, CI, P, P branch, 18-P(S)/42, CI to Polindia, 26 Jan. 1942; ibid., G.T. Fisher to K.S. Fitze, 10 Mar. 1942; CRR, CI, P, P branch, 295-P(S)/42, H.D. Craik, 13 Feb. 1943; ibid., Maharaja Rewa to K.S. Fitze, 9 Mar. 1943; ibid., Maharaja Rewa to K.S. Fitze, 7 Apr. 1943; ibid., N.S. Arlington to K.S. Fitze, 20 Apr. 1943; ibid., W.F. Campbell to K.S. Fitze, 21 Apr. 1943; ibid., W.F. Campbell to K.S. Fitze, 17 July 1943; RS, P, 1942–3, 96, Wedding, 1942–3, L.W. Wooldridge, D Order, 18 July 1943.
81. Allen and Dwivedi, *Lives of the Indian Princes*, pp. 195–6.
82. P, P branch, 15(3)-P(S)/45, W. Owens to C.C.H. Smith, 16 Feb. 1946.
83. P, P branch, 15(3)-P(S)/45, CR to SOS, 15 Jan. 1946; ibid., W.F., Campbell to Martand Singh, 24 Jan. 1946; ibid., Martand Singh to W.F. Campbell, 30 Jan. 1946; ibid., A.E.G. Davy's account of the enthronement in W.F. Campbell to C.G. Herbert, 4 Feb. 1946; RS, P, 1945–6, 469, P, 45–6, Lord Wavell to Maharaja Rewa, 6 Mar. 1946; P, P branch, 15(3)-P(S)/45, Speeches of the Resident and Martand Singh at the Investiture, 1 Apr. 1946.
84. RS, PMO, 1946–47, 70/172, A/C, Admin, 1947, DO, Martand Singh, 8 Aug. 1947; CIA, Info Bureau, 1-IB/48, *Times of India*, Bombay, 30 Jan. 1948; *Rewa Gazetteer*, p. 52; N. Mansergh et al. (eds.), *India: the Transfer of Power, 1942–1947*, vol. XII, London, 1983, p. 769; Bhargava, 'Relations of British paramount power', PhD, p. 105; Dubey, 'Establishment of democratic political system', PhD, pp. 138–41. The well known barrister, Sir Hari Singh Gour, headed the committee. Other reforms ushered in by Martand Singh included an advisory council, a small *raj parishad*, elected municipal boards in main towns, and the abolition of school fees up to matriculation.
85. RS, PMO, 1946–47, 334/180, A/R, Admin, R branch, Praja Mandal to Rev Min, 4 July 1947; M/S, P&R, 29, PRO. S, 1947, L.Y. Singh to M/S Sec, 9 Dec. 1947; CIA, Info Bureau, 21-IB/48, *Bhaskar*, Rewa, 22 Dec. 1947, and 1 Mar. 1948; *Patel Correspondence*, vol. VII, R.M. Deshmukh to V. Patel, 19 Feb. 1948; CIA, Confdl, 22-Q/47(a), FR Rewa, 2/Feb. 1948; CIA, Info Bureau, 1-IB/48, *Leader*, Allahabad, 29 June 1948. To deal with opposition, the Rewa administration extended the life of the Rewa State Maintenance of Public Order Act, 1947.
86. M/S, P&R, 29-PR/47, S, UP CID Report, M.K. Sinha, 8 Sept. 1947; CIA, Info Bureau, 1-IB, 1948, *Amrit Bazar Patrika*, Allahabad, 18 Apr. 1948, and *Statesman*, Calcutta, 20 Apr. 1948; M/S, P, Group I, 167(1)-P/48. C.L. Saxena to M.J. Kirpalani, 28 Apr. 1948, encl Gulab Singh to Martand Singh, 27 Apr., 1948; ibid., C.L. Saxena, 11 May 1948; M/S, P, 17(134), P/50(S). N.M. Buch, 8 Dec. 1950.

87. CRR, CI, P, P branch, 68-P(S)/46, C.L. Corfield, 5 Mar. 1946; ibid., A.H. Layard, 24 Apr. 1946; RS, PMO, 1946–47, 70/172, A/C, Admin 1947, DO Martand Singh, 7 Aug. 1947; M/S, PR branch, 29-PRO, 1947, S, R.M. Deshmukh to V. Patel, 11 Nov. 1947; CIA, Info Bureau, 21-IB/48, *Bhaskar*, Rewa, 1 Dec. 1947; Bhargava, 'Relations of British paramount power', PhD, p. 105.

88. RS, GAD, 1942–6, B 9, 11, 1947, Admin, Martand Singh, 30 Oct. 1947; M/S, P&R, 29-PRO, 1947, S. Brajendranath to C.C. Desai, 10 Nov. 1947, encl Govt communique, Martand Singh, 1 Nov. 1947; ibid., R.M. Deshmukh to V. Patel, 11 Nov. 1947.

89. M/S, P&R, 29-PRO, 1947, S. Brajendranath to C.C. Desai, 10 Nov. 1947, encl Govt. communique, Martand Singh, 1 Nov. 1947; ibid., R.M. Deshmukh to V. Patel, 11 Nov. 1947.

90. Ibid.

91. CIA, Info Bureau, 21-IB/48, *Bhaskar*, Rewa, 1 Dec. 1947; *Patel Correspondence*, vol. VII, R.M. Deshmukh to V. Patel, 19 and 29 Feb. 1948, the latter enclosing R.M. Deshmukh to Martand Singh, 27 Feb. 1948; VPR, RCO, 19-Q, 1948, PM to RC, 5 Mar. 1948; CIA, Info Bureau, 1-IB/48, *Amrit Bazar Patrika*, Allahabad, 19 Apr. 1948.

92. CIA, Judl, 236-B, Res CI to PMin, RS, 19 Nov. 1941; ibid., IT Officer to Res CI, 23 Feb. 1944. (The exemption did not apply to taxes paid on behalf of the Rewa Coalfields Company); CRR, CI, P, P branch, 15(15)-P(S)/45, H.D. Chatterjee to A.E.G. Davy, 15 May 1946; CIA, Confdl, 16-Q/48, C.C. Desai to C.S. Venkatachar, 2 Dec. 1947; M/S, P, 195-P/48, 1948, S19, DO to CIT, Lucknow, 20 Mar. 1948; ibid., V.P. Menon to K.R.K. Menon, 20 Feb. 1950; M/S, P(B), 13(11)-PB/53, K.L. Mittal, 17 May 1952.

93. M/S, P, B, 13(11)-PB/53, K.L. Mittal, 17 May 1952; ibid., Dikshit Maneklal to C.S. Venkatachar, 30 Mar. 1953; ibid., K.L. Mittal, 1 May 1953.

94. M/S, P, Group III, 6(31)-P/49, B.G. Murdeshwar, 20 Sept. 1945; CRR, CI, P, P branch, 15(15)-P(S)/45, Rai Bahadur Chatterjee Report, 9 Jan. 1946; M/S, P, Group III, 6(31)-P/49, K. Sundaram, 24 Sept. 1946; M/S, P, 17(134)-P/50(S), N.M. Buch, 8 Dec. 1950; M/S, P, B, 17(107)-P/50, C. Ganesan, 23 Dec. 1951; M/S, P, B, 13(11)-PB/53, C. Ganesan, 22 Apr. 1953; M/S, P, B, 13(5)-PB/54, Articles of Agreement, President of India and Martand Singh, 3 May 1953. The two Dowager Maharanis were also signatories to this agreement.

95. M/S, P, B, 17(107)-P/50. C. Ganesan, 24 Dec. 1951.

96. Copland, *Princes of India*, pp. 198, 216, 276; M. Edwardes, *The Last Years of British India*, London, 1967, p. 201.

97. Copland, *Princes of India*, p. 216.

98. CIA, P, A, 8-A/47, 1947, *Hindustan Times*, New Delhi, 23 Apr. 1947; Copland, *Princes of India*, p. 242; Edwardes, *The Last Years*, p. 185; Bhargava, 'Relations of British paramount power', PhD, pp. 58–9. Bhopal had been a major sponsor of the conditional approach. The two representatives from Rewa at the Constituent Assembly were Yadavendra Singh, president of the Rewa Rajya Praja Mandal and the Rao of Churhat, Shiva Bahadur Singh.

99. Allen and Dwivedi, *Lives of the Indian Princes*, pp. 316–17, report Mountbatten's reply to Corfield at a meeting of political officers, when he tried to represent a 'princely' point of view: 'if there are any problems, ... they must be settled after independence, because there isn't time.... So you can leave here and tell the Rulers that the die is cast.' Edwardes, *The Last Years*, pp. 201–5; A Siddiqui, 'An assessment of the working of the former Vindhya Pradesh legislative assembly', PhD, APS Rewa, 1978, p. 11. By 25 August all princely states except Junagadh, Hyderabad, and Kashmir had acceded to the Indian Union.

100. CIA, Federal, 96-F(A)/48, Res CI to PM Rewa, 7 Aug. 1947; M/S, P, 8(103)-PR/47, C.C. Desai to Maharaja Rewa, 22 Aug. 1947; Edwardes, *The Last Years*, p. 205; Fitze, *Twilight*, p. 157; Dubey, 'Establishment of a democratic political system', PhD, p. 215.

101. Fitze, *Twilight*, p. 157.

102. CIA, Info Bureau, 1-IB/1948, *Amrita Bazar Patrika*, Allahabad, 31 Dec. 1947; M/S, 61-P, 1948, C.C. Desai, 2 Feb. 1948; ibid., V.P. Menon, 23 Mar. 1948; Bhargava, 'Relations of British paramount power', PhD, p. 106; D.R. Mankekar, *Accession to Extinction: The Story of the Indian Princes*, Delhi, 1974, p. 133; *Rewa Gazetteer*, p. 52, notes that Rewa had viability as a state in its own right as it was represented in the Constituent Assembly. It was also viable from a revenue point of view.

103. CIA, Confdl, 22-Q/47(a)FR CI States, 2/Dec. 1947,1/Jan. 1948, 2/Jan. 1948; M/S, 61-P. 1948, C.C. Desai, 2 and 6 Feb. 1948; ibid., V.P. Menon, 23 Mar. 1948; R.L. Handa, *History of Freedom Struggle in Indian Princely States*, Delhi, 1968, pp. 302–3; Mankekar, *Accession to Extinction*, p. 133.

104. CIA, Confdl, 22-Q/47(a), FR CI States, 1/Jan. and 2/Jan. 1948; *Patel Correspondence*, vol. VII, R.M. Deshmukh to V. Patel, 19 Feb. 1948; CIA, Info Bureau, 1-IB/48, *Amrit Bazar Patrika*, Allahabad, 6 Mar. 1948; M/S, 61-P, 1948, V.P. Menon, 23 Mar. 1948; *Rewa Gazetteer*, p. 53. *Ilaqadars*, some of whom were holding out for a separate Rewa State, did so because they were uncertain of their position in any merger or union.

105. M/S, 61-P, 1948, V.P. Menon, 23 Mar. 1948.

106. Mankekar, *Accession to Extinction*, p. 133. Menon reported that he negotiated with local leaders, while the Maharaja remained 'an interested but silent spectator'. Menon was horrified with the state of Rewa town, which he claimed lacked 'even the most elementary amenities of civilised existence'.

107. CIA, Info Bureau, 1-IB/48, *Hindustan Times*, Delhi, 17 Mar. 1948; M/S, 61–P, 1948, V.P. Menon, 23 Mar. 1948; *Rewa Gazetteer*, pp. 52–3.

108. Edwardes, *The Last Years*, pp. 199–206; Allen and Dwivedi, *Lives of the Indian Princes*, p. 325. The quotation is that of the Maharaja of Varanasi.

109. CIA, Info Bureau, 1-IB/48, *The Statesman*, Delhi, 6 Apr. 1948; ibid., *Times of India*, Bombay, 6 Apr. 1948.

110. CIA, Info Bureau, 1-IB/48, *Amrit Bazar Patrika*, Allahabad, 5 Apr. 1948; *Patel Correspondence*, vol. VII, Martand Singh to V. Patel, 7 Apr. 1948; M/S, 61-P, 1948, M.K. Kirpalani, 7 June 1948; ibid., Note by A.P. Singh, 13 June 1948.

111. CIA, Info Bureau, 1-IB/48, *Leader*, Allahabad, 21 May 1948; M/S, 61-P, 1948, M.K. Kirpalani, 7 June 1948; ibid., Note by A.P. Singh, 13 June 1948; CIA, Confdl-Q, 81-Q,48, S. Narayanaswamy to A.P. Singh, 17 June 1948; M/S, 61-P, 1948, M.K. Kirpalani, 22 June 1948.

112. M/S, 61-P, 1948, M.K. Kirpalani, 7 June 1948; ibid., M.K. Kirpalani, 22 June, 1948; ibid., V. Patel to Martand Singh, 23 June 1948; *Patel Correspondence*, vol. VII, Martand Singh to V. Patel, 27 June 1948.

113. Ibid., V. Patel to Martand Singh, 10 July 1948.

114. CIA, Info Bureau, 1-IB/48, *Leader*, Allahabad, 29 June 1948; M/S, P, 9(32)-P, 1949, C.B. Rao to M.K. Vellodi, 5 Feb. 1949; encl FR VP, 2/Jan. 1949; ibid., C.B. Rao to M.K. Vellodi, 5 Mar. 1949, encl FR VP, 2/Feb. 1949; ibid., CSec VP to Sec M/S, 7 Apr. 1949, encl FR VP, 2/Mar. 1949; *Patel Correspondence*, vol. VIII, A.P. Singh to V. Patel, 13 Apr. 1949. the new cabinet included Narmada Prasad Singh, Shiva Bahadur Singh of Churhat, Lal D.B. Singh of Khariha, S.N. Shukla, and L.Y Singh.

115. M/S, P, 9(32)-P, 1949, C.B. Rao to M.K. Vellodi, 5 Feb. 1949; ibid., CSec VP to Sec M/S, 7 Apr. 1949; *Patel Correspondence*, vol. VIII, A.P. Singh to V. Patel, 13 Apr. 1949; ibid., S.N. Mehta to V.P. Menon, 22 Aug. 1949; ibid., R.A. Kidwai to V. Patel, 12 Sept. 1949; ibid., V. Shanker to A.B. Chatterji, 30 Dec. 1949; Home. Judl, 40/29/54-Judl, S.S., 29 Jan. 1954.

116. RCR, 1948–49, 5, RCN, 1949, N.M. Buch to A.P. Singh, 18 Feb. 1949; ibid., N.B. Bonarjee to M.K. Vellodi, 11 Mar. 1949; *Patel Correspondence*, vol. VIII, A.P. Singh to V. Patel, 13 Apr. 1949; M/S, P, 9(32)-P/49. Brajendranath to M.K. Vellodi, 15 Apr. 1949, encl FR VP, 1/Apr. 1949; M/S, ISFEC branch, 16-ISFEC/1948, pt III, G. Swaminathan, Fin Review of VP, 16 Apr. 1949.

117. Ibid., Note by V. Dandekar, 13 Apr. 1949.
118. VPR, Mehmandari, 1949–50, Order, 120, 1946–7, T.C.S. Jayaratnam, 15 Jan. 1947; RDO, B 15/45–47, 84/2, 1946–47, Sec Subord Services Assn to HSec RS, 2 Mar. 1948; RCR, 1948, 7-RCN/1948, pt II, RC to PM, 25 Nov. 1948; RCR, 1948–9, 103-Q, 1949, N.B. Bonarjee to V. Prasad, 3 Apr. 1949; M/S, ISFEC branch, 16-ISFEC/1948, pt I, II, G. Swaminathan, Fin Review of VP, 16 Apr. 1949; VP, P, 1935–46, Asst Comptroller VP to U/S GAD, VP, 29 Sept. 1955; Dubey, 'Establishment of democratic political system', PhD, pp. 225–6.
119. VPR, RC, 1948, RCN/1948, N.B. Bonarjee to CSec, 21 Sept. 1948; ibid., N.B. Bonarjee to PM, 22 Oct. 1948; Patel Correspondence, vol. VIII, A.P. Singh to V. Patel, 13 Jan. 1949; RCR, 1948–9, N.B. Bonarjee to N.M. Buch, 15 Jan. 1949; RCR, 1948–9, 5 RCN, 1949, N.B. Bonarjee to N.M. Buch, 8 Mar. 1949; N.B. Bonarjee, Under Two Masters, Calcutta, 1970, p. 250.
120. RCR, 1948–9, 5, RCN, 1949, N.B. Bonarjee to M.K. Vellodi, 13 Mar. 1949.
121. Patel Correspondence, vol. VIII, A.P. Singh to V. Patel, 13 Jan. 1949; Bonarjee, Under Two Masters, p. 249.
122. RCR, 1948–49, RSN, 1949, PM VP to CSec VP, 14 Apr. 1949; ibid., RCR to Statesind, nd.; ibid., N.B. Bonarjee to M.K. Vellodi, 19 Apr. 1949; M/S, ISFEC branch, 16-ISFEC/1948, pt III, M. Bihari Lal to G. Swaminathan, 7 May 1949; M/S, Service, 30926-S/51, CSec to CM to U/S M/S, 3 Jan. 1951.
123. M/S, P, 9(32)-P/49. Brajendranath to M.K. Vellodi, 6 Aug. 1949; Patel Correspondence, vol. IX, V. Patel to J. Nehru, 28 Dec. 1949; Rewa Gazetteer, p. 54; Handa, History of Freedom Struggle, p. 304; Siddiqui, 'An assessment of the former VP assembly', PhD, p. 21. The so-called 'Tala group' led by Lal Yashwant Singh and comprising fellow ilaqadars strongly opposed the declaration of Vindhya Pradesh as a 'C class' state, and pressed unsuccessfully for 'B class' status which would have given local control over the administration.
124. M/S, P. 17(63)-P/50, M/S to all Rulers of VP, 8 Feb. 1950; Siddiqui, 'An assessment of the former VP assembly', PhD, p. 23; Handa, Histyory of Freedom Struggle, p. 303. At the same time the centre excised ten small Bundelkhand states from Vindhya Pradesh and added them to Madhya Bharat, the more successful union of princely areas to the west.
125. M/S, P, 17(63)-P/50, M/S to all Rulers of VP, 8 Feb. 1950.
126. VP Admin, 1952, p. 1; VP Admin, 1955, p. 84; Rewa Gazetteer, p. 54; Satna Gazetteer, p. 358; Siddiqui, 'An assessment of the former VP assembly', PhD, pp. 2, 23. The Vindhya Pradesh Legislative Assembly comprised 60 members.

127. *VP Admin, 1953*, pp. 3, 13; *VP Admin, 1955*, p. 12; *Satna Gazetteer*, pp. 248, 252.

128. See fn 94; R.S. Misra confirmed that the final total was about 14 crores, with Martand Singh receiving a share of about 7.5 crores. The amount was free of any dues, as the Bombay High Court declared that the monies were not taxable in India; and in England they were not subject to British death duties.

129. *VP Admin, 1955*, p. 12.

130. The government issued licenses for the construction of two cement plants in 1955. *VP Admin, 1955*, p. 63.

131. The administration built fair weather roads in trackless Shahdol, and linked Sidhi's *tahsil* towns with all weather roads. H, Judl, 40/3/54, Judl., K. Santhanam to President of India, 18 Jan. 1954; *M.P. Census, 1961, Sidhi Handbook*, p. lxix; Lal, 'Settlement geography', PhD, p. 128.

132. *Census of India, 1961*, vol. VIII, *Madhya Pradesh*, pp. 48–9; *M.P. Census, 1961, Shahdol Handbook*, p. lii; Lal, 'Settlement geography', PhD, p. 96; Dube, *Population of Rewa*, p. 23; Population increases in Baghelkhand ranged from 21.9 per cent in Rewa to 27.5 per cent in Shahdol.

133. By 1961 literacy levels in Shahdol were 14.6 per cent, Satna 15.6 per cent and in Rewa 19.7 per cent, Sidhi's remaining the lowest at 7.8 per cent. Modest improvements to the education system included the increased number of high schools, more rural schools, and institutions for backward communities. For health see *VP Admin, 1951*, p. 29; *Satna Gazetteer*, pp. 322–3, 331; *Rewa Gazetteer*, pp. 253, 257; Siddiqui, 'An assessment of the former VP assembly', PhD, p. 31.

134. Ibid.

135. Roy, *Planning the Environment*, p. 45.

136. *Project Report of Integrated Tribal Development Project, District Shahdol, MP, Govt. of Madhya Pradesh*, Bhopal, nd., pp. 43–4; *Sidhi Gazetteer*, p. 37; Sharma, 'Changing pattern of resources', PhD, 1992 pp. xiv–xv; Bonarjee, *Under Two Masters*, p. 247.

137. See earlier reports of the attitude of Martand Singh and his supporters to merger: M/S, P, 17(34)-P/50, S, V.K.B. Pillai to V.P. Menon, 2 Nov., 1 Nov., and 24 Nov. 1950. H, SRI, 8/25/56-SRI, Sec VP to HSec, 24 Apr. 1956; Bhattacharya, *Historical Geography*, pp. 57–8.

138. Rewa division comprised the former Bundelkhand States of Chattarpur, Panna, and Tikamgarh, in addition to the Rewa, Satna, Sidhi, and Shahdol districts of Baghelkhand.

Conclusion

ʘ₰ᕫ

In an attempt to understand the process of nationalizing the regions of India, this study has examined the case of Baghelkhand. As we have seen, the process of nation-building involved a dialogue between the region and centralizing or unifying powers and other external forces. This dialogue comprised two apparently conflicting parts: in one, the influence of central states together with immigration helped build regional uniqueness; in the other, these forces enlarged the power of central states vis-à-vis the regions, and created political, social and economic commonalities between the latter that proved stronger than regional separateness, both drawing the regions into the Indian state by the mid-twentieth century.

The outreach of centralizing states was a prominent feature of Baghelkhand's history from the first millennium BC up to 1956. Mostly based in northern India, these states intervened in the region in differing ways with profound consequences for it. Under the Mauryan State, for instance, Baghelkhand was traversed by national trade routes; Buddhists founded major sites from which to spread their faith; and northern immigrants established the first towns. The Guptas were even more insistent colonizers, conquering parts of the region, creating feudatory states, imposing taxes, and triggering the outreach of temple styles associated with their rule, though their power was then in decline. The Mughal State was perhaps the strongest nationalizing power of the mediaeval period. Emperor Akbar insisted on the personal submission of the

Baghel rulers; and when the Baghel State revolted against central pressure, he destroyed the key fort of Bandhavgarh and imposed direct rule on Baghelkhand, while forbearing to levy troops or impose taxes on the region.

Successive British central Governments of India were more successful in bending Baghelkhand to their will, and so nationalizing it to a greater extent than any previous central state. From early in the nineteenth century they compelled reluctant rulers to sign treaties that brought states like Rewa into central institutions of control, advice, ceremonial and degrees of precedence, together with graded rewards to rulers for complying with central expectations. Individual states also became part of composite entities such as the Central India Agency, through which these central policies were routed. At the same time requests by Rewa for central administrative assistance, and the presence, successively, of two minor rulers, gave the central government a commanding position in Rewa which was unusual for a princely state.

Though apparently at a disadvantage, the later rulers of Rewa turned central influence to regional gain in a series of moves that pushed the dialogue with the British centre somewhat in favour of Baghelkhand. Maharaja Raghuraj Singh used his ambivalent stance towards the revolt of 1857–8 to enlarge his state and win honours from the central government. Maharaja Venkatraman Singh defied Curzon over joining the Imperial Forces scheme, yet created a state army and also earned a commission in the British Indian Army. His heir, Gulab Singh, and his avowedly autonomous state held central interference at bay until 1942, though the Maharaja's policies led to his deposition by the Government of India in 1946.

This event set the terms for the dialogue between Baghelkhand and incoming Indian central governments from 1947, putting the final touches to the nationalization of the region. Through the Ministry of States, the Indian Government impelled the region into a union with the Bundelkhand states known as Vindhya Pradesh, in which with successive constitutional changes Maharaja Martand Singh of Rewa lost his traditional powers and his position as Rajpramukh of Vindhya Pradesh to a democratically elected Prime Minister. However, the Vindhya Pradesh experiment failed, and the centre included its two regions in the new Madhya Pradesh, together with the former Hindi-speaking British districts of the Central Provinces and the princely areas of Madhya Bharat and

Chhattisgarh. This fixed Baghelkhand within a constituent unit of the Indian State for at least the foreseeable future.

Migration was another key element in the dialogue between external forces and the region that helped to bring Baghelkhand into the wider national arena. Migration, mostly from the north, brought to the region agricultural practices, crop patterns, types of housing, styles of dress, folkways, and the religious beliefs and practices common to the areas from where the migrants had come. They also led to an intrusion of sculptural and architectural styles common to other parts of the country, though these could assume a regional character in execution.

In addition, the migrations—mostly those of the Rajputs—led to the formation of regional kingdoms covering smaller or larger parts of the region, and laying the basis for the dominant position of the Rajput community in Baghelkhand today. The most significant of these migrations was that of the Baghels whose rule gave the region a long history of continuous administration, besides making the state a player in national politics as it bent before successive Mughal governments. As noted above, British rule also placed Baghelkhand within a subcontinental context.

By proposing the idea of a long-term dialogue between centralizing states and the region as the key to nationalizing the Indian regions, this study suggests that knitting the regions into a national whole was not the work of the Indian National Congress and other political agencies alone. This work posits that ahead of what is called the Indian nationalist movement, a centuries-long process of interchange between unifying forces and the regions created a countrywide synthesis—more firm in some places than in others—on which political nationalism subsequently built its edifice.

It will be clear from this study that a region was not an immediate or ready-made entity awaiting connection with other similar areas to form a national whole. In prehistoric times Baghelkhand possessed little of its later identity, which only gradually came into focus as the result of external political currents, migration patterns, and cultural intrusions. The region was thus the product of a slow amalgam of distinctive social, political, and economic forces brought to bear on a territorial space—but forces that at the same time linked it with areas mostly in northern and central India.

In a different vein, two conflicting views of the state emerge from the discussion of the clash between the central government and Maharaja Gulab Singh. In one, information gathering and decision-making took place at various levels over a number of years before the central government deposed the Maharaja. While not ruling out subjective factors, this act reflected a view of the state which disapproved of certain acts and policies of a regional ruler, and proceeded to punish him for non-compliance with its decisions. Behind this lay the belief that a ruler had some responsibility for the welfare of his subjects. This outlook contrasted somewhat with Gulab Singh's view that the state and its revenues were his personal property, and that people's views and needs were of less importance. As noted above, this conflict also represented a clash between centralizing forces and those pressing for regional autonomy within the subcontinent.

It is noteworthy that the policies of the outgoing British Government of India and its incoming Indian successor both bent the region to the centre, and took a similar line with regard to Maharaja Gulab Singh. The British externment from Rewa of Gulab Singh and his return as nominal ruler several years later, together with the installation of centrally appointed civil administrations, were of a piece with the Ministry of States' externment and detention of Gulab Singh, its compelling Rewa into the Vindhya Pradesh Union, imposing central administrations on the area, and then sidelining Maharaja Martand Singh from direct participation in regional politics.

The work points up again the failure of Gulab Singh and other princes to understand the real issues at stake in the discussions on federalism in the 1930s. Unfitted by temperament or training to contemplate the surrender of power and wealth, Gulab Singh with many princes clung to autocracy, autonomy and British Paramountcy in the face of the deeper forces of nationalism that were to sweep away much of princely power by 1956. It is possible to see even the earlier deposition of Gulab Singh and his replacement by the more tractable Martand Singh as a step towards this end, removing royal autocracy and autonomy in favour of a more representative and integrated India.

In a related issue, the study seems to question the centre's action in pushing Baghelkhand into a hasty union of convenience with princely Bundelkhand from 1948–56. As Rewa enjoyed a revenue surplus and had an administrative history somewhat akin to the British-ruled provinces, there was a case for its continuance as a constituent unit of the new India. The fact that nobody knew quite what to do with Bundelkhand seems to be an insufficient reason for creating Vindhya Pradesh and using Rewa to prop up the Union—though the decision was also part of a wider scheme to transfer princely power to elected leaders, to tidy up the political landscape, and prevent the possible balkanization of the country. The tragedy of Vindhya Pradesh, and the emergence of small states in India in recent years, would seem to question the centre's hasty, if understandable, reaction to the problems of the years following 1947.

The study raises again the apparently intractable problem of economic and social backwardness or underdevelopment, which the efforts of regional and central governments from the 1830s on failed to resolve. Neither the developmental policies of Major Barr, Maharaja Gulab Singh, central administrators, or of any administration in Vindhya Pradesh were able to galvanize the economy and society of Baghelkhand into an onward growth cycle. Some of this was due to paucity of funds, especially with Gulab Singh's transfer of state monies to his private accounts; some to over-concentration on mining and forests; to the slow expansion of education and health-care; and until the early 1950s the concentration of landed wealth in the hands of a tiny nobility. The abolition of *jagirdari* and other tenures, the establishment of democratic government, and the flow of funds from the centre and from Madhya Pradesh has perhaps mitigated the problem of rural poverty, illiteracy, ill-health, and poor communications to some extent. However, these problems still hamper growth, such that projects in the public or private sectors remain mere points of capitalist development in a traditional social and economic sea, rather than part of a wider movement transforming regional society and economy. To blame British colonialism alone for this state of affairs is of little help.

Glossary

ᘓᘓᘔᘕᘔ

aam jungle	non-reserved forest
abkari	excise revenue from liquor
acharya	teacher, scholar
agama	non-Vedic Brahmanical text
aonla/anwala	fruit
arhar	lentil
Arya-dharma	righteous/noble religion
Aryavarta	north India
atavika	forest dweller
bania	trader
barahsinga	swamp deer
barat	wedding procession
bhajan-kirtan	devotional songs
bhaktiyoga	way of devotion
bhandar	store
bulbul	nightingale
chaddar	cotton sheet
chaitya	a design deriving from the window shape over the entrance of a chaitya hall
chaukidar	watchman
chaupal	village meeting place
chauth	one quarter
chela	disciple
chholi	blouse
chital	spotted deer

chowki	check post
dak	mail
dakshinapatha	southern route
dandiya nritya	stick dance
darbar	court, government
dargah	tomb of holy person
deorhi	(originally) entrance to a structure housing women; now female apartments
desa/desh	country, land
devi	goddess
dhamma	Prakrit form of *dharma*—religion
dhartia mata	earth mother
dhobi	washerman
dhoti	(literally) washed cloth; now, unstitched cloth length
dhrupad	early classical music composition
diwan	chief minister, administrative head
doab	(literally) two rivers, ie., country between the Ganga and the Yamuna
gaddi	seat, throne
gaghra	skirt
gana	member of Siva's band
garh	fort
garhi	fortress
gaur	bison
ghat	pass
golaki matha	round monastery or religious structure
gur	unrefined brown sugar
guru	preceptor
Harol	army title
harwaha	(literally) ploughman; now bonded labourer
harwahi	institution of bonded farm labour
ilaqa	territory, area, hence estate
ilaqadar	estate holder
izzat	respect
jagir	grant for service to the state
jagirdar	holder of a *jagir*
janapada	(literally) a settlement; generally an early state
juar	sorghum
kankali	skeleton

karinda	revenue officer
kavyam	poem
khanat	canvas wall forming an enclosure
kharif	autumn crop
khayal	a style of classical music composition
khillat	authorization of a ruler
khudkasht	self-cultivated farming land
kinkhab	embroidered cloth
kodon, kutki	lesser millets
koel	cuckoo
kothi	large dwelling
kshetra	sector, area
kumhar	potter
kund	tank
kunwar	a younger brother or descendant of a king
kurta	full-sleeved upper garment
lac	a resinous substance secreted by insects
lana	cave
langoti	loin cloth
lehanga	skirt
lingam	(literally) symbol; stylized phallus, representation of Siva
lohar	black-smith
machan	high platform used in hunting
mahajan	banker, moneylender
mahal	estate, proprietary holding
mahamandapa	great hall
maharajadhiraja	king of kings
mahua	tree valuable for its flower or fruit
makka	maize
mamla	a tenure; concerning land given in lieu of maintenance to younger member of the royal family
mandir	temple
mansab	military service grant
matrika	mother goddess
mela	fair
mochi	cobbler
mohalla	quarter of a town
mohur	seal, stamp

mrgaya shila	cave for hunting
muafi	revenue-free
muafidar	holder of a revenue-free grant
Muharram	Muslim month of mourning for the martyrdom of Hussain
mukhalingam	stylized phallus, with the image of .e.g. Siva carved on its side(s)
mukhtiyar-i-riyasat	chief revenue officer
muni	ascetic, versed in scriptures
muqqadam	legal representative of a state/estate
nadi	river
nai	barber
nala	small stream
nazarana	payment on entering a lease
nilgai	antelope
nilkanth	blue jay
nistar	a peasant's right to timber, grazing and produce in forests, village wastes
pagri bandhai	ceremonial tying of turban
parda	certain, veil
pargana	revenue subdivision
path	plateau
patta	documentary evidence of leased or granted land
pattala	administrative region
pawai	land grant
pind-daan	offering to ancestors
pitra-paksh	fortnight during which offerings to ancestors are made
pradakshinapatha	circumambulatory path
praja mandal	(State) subjects organisation
Prakrit	dialects of Sanskrit
rabi	spring crop
raj	government
raj guru	royal preceptor
raj parishad	state council
Rajpramukh	Governor of union of princely states
raj purohit	head priest
rajya	state
rashtra	country, nation

rishi	seer
rumal	handkerchief
sal	tree; *shorea robusta*
sambhar	largest Indian deer
sanad	certificate, testimonial
sandhya	evening ritual
sardar	noble of the court
sari	long cloth forming woman's garment
sarkar	Mughal revenue subdivision comprising a group of *mahals*
saropa	(literally) from head to foot; dress presented to honour a recipient
sarpech	head-dress
sati	literally, a woman true to her husband; act of immolation on husband's funeral pyre
sawar	horseman
seth	wealthy merchant
sewa	act of being present in the service of the king
shastra	body of religious legal literature
shikar(garh)	hunting (lodge)
sindur	vermilion
sir	inalienable land, ie., home farm
sloka	verse
suba	revenue subdivision comprising a number of *sarkars*
sutradhara	architect
tahsil	revenue unit
tahsildar	revenue official in a *tahsil*
tazimi sardar	a sardar granted *tazim* rights; i.e., rulers stand the receive them—an expression of regard. In receiving nobles without such rights, rulers would remain seated.
tapasyasthana	retreat
tazia	model of tombs of Hasan and Hussain carried in procession at Muharram
thagi	act of cheating, or of robbing and killing
thakur	a minor noble, lord
thekedar	contractor
tirtha	place of pilgrimage
tola	quarter of a village

torana	ceremonial gateway
ubari (dar)	a land grant wherein a subordinate paid the difference in revenue between an amount fixed by his lord and the income of his estate given by the lord; holder of this
unani	Arabic system of medicine based on Greek knowledge
Up-Rajpramukh	Deputy governor of a union of princely states
vakil	lawyer
vanijaka	connected with commerce
vanshawali	genealogy
varna	class
vibhasha	non-Sanskrit language, ie., language of a lower order
vyayamshala	gymnasium
watan jagir	hereditary *jagir* of a raja
yuvraj	heir apparent
zat	status, rank
zenana	ladies' enclosure

Bibliography

CRESO

Entries in the Bibliography are grouped in several categories. Unpublished material is listed under the location; published material is listed under the headings:

Government of Great Britain
Government of India (census reports, other material)
Government of the Central Provinces and Berar
Government of Madhya Pradesh
Government of the United Provinces
Government of Uttar Pradesh
Government of Vindhya Pradesh
Rewa Darbar/Administration of Rewa State
Autobiographies, biographies, and memoirs
Articles (journal, anthologies, A.H. Nizami)
Books
PhD theses

PRIMARY SOURCES
Unpublished Material

Private Papers

Madhya Pradesh Central Record Office, Nagpur
A selection of letters by Col. W.H. Sleeman

Government Records
National Archives of India

Records of the Foreign, Foreign Political, Foreign Secret, Political, and Home Departments; and of the Ministry of States

Records of the Central India Agency; and of the Baghelkhand Agency
The Crown Representative Records

The Madhya Pradesh Secretariat, Bhopal

Records of the Rewa Darbar Office/Rewa State
Records of Vindhya Pradesh

The Madhya Pradesh Central Record Office, Nagpur

Nagpur Residency Records, 1798–1843
Jubbulpore Divisional Records in Bundle Correspondence, 1818–59
Records prior to the Abolition of the East India Company, found in
　Jubbulpore Division, 1806–58

Institute of Forest Management, Jabalpur

Government of Madhya Pradesh, Forest Department, *Working Plan of the West Sidhi Forest Division, Rewa Circle, for the Years 1988–89 to 1997–98*, vol. I.

Working Plan for Mada, Waidhan, Jiyawan and Sarai Ranges of the East Sidhi Forest Division for the Years 1975–76 to 1989–90, vol. I.

Working Plan for Rewa Forest Division, Rewa Circle, M.P., 1982–83 to 1991–92, vol. I, pt. I.

Intensive Forest Management Plan for North Shahdol and Umaria Divisions, for 1984–85 to 1998–99, vol. I.

Working Scheme for West Sidhi Forest Division, Rewa Circle, from 1973–74 onwards, vol. I, pts I, II, 1973.

Working Plan for South Shahdol Forest Division, Shahdol Circle, M.P., for 1975–76 to 1989–90, vol. I.

PUBLISHED MATERIAL

Government of Great Britain

Imperial Gazetteer of India, vol. XXI, 1908.
Imperial Gazetteer, Central India, New Delhi, rpt, 1989.
Indian States Committee, vols I, II, III, IV, *Evidence*, London, 1929.
Mansergh, N., et al. (eds.), *India: the Transfer of Power, 1942–1947*, London, 1983.

Government of India

Census of India
Census of India, 1901, vol. XIX, *Central India*, pt I, *Report*.
―――, 1911, vol. XVII, *Central India, Report and Tables*.
Central India States Census, 1911, vol. IV, *Rewa State Census*, 1911, *Report*.
Rewa State Census, 1921, pt I, *Report*.

Census of India, 1931, vol. XII, *Central Provinces and Berar*, pt I, *Report.*
———, 1941, *Central India*, vol. II, *Rewa State Census*, 1941, *Report.*
———, 1961, *Madhya Pradesh, District Census Handbook, Satna, Sidhi, Rewa, and Shahdol Districts.*
———, *Madhya Pradesh*, pt VI, Village Survey Monograph, no. 11, 'Amwar, a village survey in Madhya Pradesh'.
———, 1971, *Madhya Pradesh, District Census Handbook, Rewa, Sidhi, Shahdol* Districts.

ARCHAEOLOGICAL SURVEY OF INDIA

Tour Reports

Beglar, J.D., *Report of Tours in the South-Eastern Provinces in 1874–75 and 1875–76*, vol. XIII, Calcutta, 1882.
Cunningham, A., *Report of a Tour in the Central Provinces in 1873–74, and 1874–75*, vol. IX, Calcutta, 1879.
———, *Reports of a Tour in Baghelkhand and Rewa in 1883–84, and of a Tour in Rewa, Baghelkhand, Malwa and Gwalior in 1884–85*, vol. XXI, pts I II, Delhi, rpt, 1969.
Garrick, W., *Report: Tour through Behar, Central India, Peshawar and Yusufzai, 1881–82*, vol. XIX, Delhi, rpt, 1969.

A.S.I;, Inscriptional material

Corpus Inscriptionum Indicarum, vol. II, pt II, H. Lüders, (ed.), *Bharhut Inscriptions*, Ootacamund, 1955.
———, vol. III, J.F. Fleet, (ed.), *Inscriptions of the early Gupta Kings and their Successors*, Varanasi, 1970.
———, vol. IV, pt I, V.V. Mirashi, (ed.), *Inscriptions of the Kalachuri-Chedi Era*, Ootacamund, 1955.

A.S.I., Memoirs

Banerji, R.D., *The Temple of Siva at Bhumara*, Memoir no. 16, Calcutta, 1924.
———, *The Haihayas of Tripuri*, Memoir no. 23, Poona, 1927.
Shastri, H., *The Baghela Dynasty of Rewa*, Memoir no. 21, Calcutta, 1926.

A.S.I. Epigraphia Indica

Banerji, R.D., 'The Rewah inscription of Malayasimha, the year 994', *EI*, vol. XIX pt 8, Oct. 1928.
Chakravarti, N.P., 'Brahmi inscriptions from Bandhogarh', *EI*, vol. XXXI, no. 23, 1955–6.
Desai, E.Z.A., 'A Persian–Sanskrit inscription of Karna Deva Vaghela of Gujarat', *EI* (Arabic and Persian supplement), 1975.

Mirashi, V.V., 'Rewah stone inscription of the time of Karna: the (Chedi) year 800', *EI*, vol. XXIV, no. 13, 1937–8.

Sircar, D.C., 'Bharhut inscriptions in the Allahabad museum', *EI*, vol. XXXIII, pt I, Jan. 1959.

———, 'Note on the Bhumara pillar inscription of Hastin', *EI*, vol. XXXIII, no. 32, 1959–60.

ASI, Review

Indian Archaeology: A Review, annual issues from 1961.

OTHER MATERIAL PUBLISHED BY THE GOVERNMENT OF INDIA

Aitchison, C.U., *A Collection of Treaties, Engagements and Sanads, Relating to India and Neighbouring Countries*, Calcutta, 1909.

Crofton, O.S., *List of Inscriptions on Tombs or Monuments in Rajputana and Central India*, Delhi, 1935.

Cunningham, A., *The Stupa of Bharhut: A Buddhist Monument Ornamented with Numerous Sculptures Illustrative of Buddhist Legend and History in the Third Century B.C.*, New Delhi, rpt, 1989.

Grierson, G.A. (ed.), *Linguistic Survey of India*, vols I, VI, Delhi, rpt, 1967–68.

Hughes, T.W.H., 'The southern coalfields of the Rewah Gondwana basin: Umaria, Korar, Johilla, Sohagpur, Kurasia, Koreagarh, Jhilmilli', *MGSI*, vol. XXI, pt III, Calcutta, 1895.

Luard, C.E. (ed.), *Chiefs and Leading Families in Central India in 1916*, Calcutta, 1916.

Report on Intensive Type Studies on Rural Labour in India, Rewa (1967–68), Delhi, 1975.

Report on the Political Administration of the Territories within the Central India Agency (title varies). Annual issues from 1866–7.

Basic material relating to Rewa District, collected by the office of the Director of the Anthropological Survey of India, Calcutta, under the Cultural Zone Survey report, 1959–62, District Rewa, M.P., 'Village Mahari', S.K. Biswas.

Government of the Central Provinces and Berar

Early European Travellers in the Nagpur Territories, Nagpur, 1930.

Government of Madhya Pradesh

Chakravarty, K.K., *Art of the Kalachuris*, Bhopal, 1991.

Misra, D.P., et al. (eds), *The History of Freedom Movement in Madhya Pradesh*, Nagpur, 1956.

Sinha, H.N., *Selections from the Nagpur Residency Records*, vol. III, *1812–17*, Nagpur, 1953.

The Tribes of Madhya Pradesh, 1961.

District Gazetteers

Rewa, 1980; *Satna*, 1994; *Shahdol*, 1994; *Sidhi*, 1994.

Government of the United Provinces

Banda: A Gazetteer, vol. XXI, Allahabad, 1929.

Government of Uttar Pradesh

Uttar Pradesh District Gazetteers, *Banda*, Allahabad, 1982.

U.P. State Archaeology Department

Misra, V.D., B.B. Misra, J.N. Pal, 'Recent explorations in the Adwa valley in the districts of Mirzapur (U.P.) and Sidhi and Rewa (M.P.), *Pragdhara*, no. 7, 1996–7.

Pal, J.N. 'Chalcolithic Vindhyas', *Pragdhara*, no. 5, 1994–5.

Tewari, R., and R.K. Srivastava, 'Excavations at Raja Nala ka Tila (1995–96), district Sonbhadra (U.P.): preliminary observations', *Pragdhara*, no. 7, 1996–7.

'Excavations at Raja Nala ka Tila (1996–97): district Sonbhadra (U.P.), preliminary observations, *Pragdhara*, no. 8, 1997–8.

GOVERNMENT OF VINDHYA PRADESH

Annual Administration Report, 1952–6.

REWA DARBAR/ADMINISTRATION OF REWA STATE

Barr, D.W.K., *Administration of the Rewah State*, Allahabad, 1886.

Report on the Administration of the Rewah State, 1905–17, 1923–27.

Rewah State Gazetteer, vol. IV, *Text and Tables*, Lucknow, 1907

Notes and Orders on the Introduction of Regular Survey and Settlement, Lucknow, 1922.

Zutshi, B.N., *Report on the Administration of the Rewah State during the Minority of His Highness Maharaja Gulab Singh Bahadur, 1918–22*, Bombay, 1922.

Sinor, K.P., *Mineral Resources of the Rewa State, Central India*, Calcutta, 1923.

Bomford, H., *Final Settlement Report of Rewa State*, Lucknow, 1929.

Report of the Committee Appointed to Enquire into the Nature of the Pawai Tenures in Rewa State, Allahabad, 1934.

Report of the Path Enquiry Commission, Appointed to Enquire into the Condition of the Path in Rewa State, Satna, 1935.

Rewa Land Revenue and Tenancy Code, 1935, Allahabad, 1935

Memorandum of the Rewa State on the Instrument of Accession, Rewa, 1937.

The Rewa State Gazette, 31 Jan. 1946.

Saksena, K.M., *Rewa State Directory*, Allahabad, 1947.

Rewa Commission of Enquiry, vols I–III, with *Appendices* and *Correspondence*, nd.

AUTOBIOGRAPHIES, BIOGRAPHIES, AND MEMOIRS

Allen, C., and S. Dwivedi, *Lives of the Indian Princes*, London, 1984.

Bonarjee, N.B., *Under Two Masters*, Calcutta, 1970.

Burrows, C.B., *Representative Men of Central India*, Bombay, nd.

Burway, M.W., *Raja Sir Dinkur Rao*, np, 1907.

Bute, the Marchioness of (ed.), *The Private Journal of the Marquess of Hastings, K.G., Governor General and Commander in Chief in India*, Allahabad, 1907.

Corfield, C., *The Princely India I Knew: From Reading to Mountbatten*, Madras, 1975.

Daly, H., *Memoirs of Sir Henry Dermot Daly, G.C.B., C.I.E.*, London, 1905.

Fitze, K.S., *Twilight of the Maharajas*, London, 1956.

Forsyth, J., *The Highlands of Central India; Notes on their Forests and Wild Tribes, Natural History, and Sports*, New Delhi, rpt, 1975.

Gaekward, P., *The Palaces of India*, London, 1980.

Mitchell, J., *The Wheels of Ind*, London, 1934.

Montgomery Hyde, H., *Lord Reading: The Life of Rufus Isaacs, First Marquess of Reading*, London, 1967

Morrow, A., *Highness, the Maharajas of India*, London, 1986.

Playne S., *Indian States: A Biographical, Historical, and Administrative Survey*, London, 1921–2.

Rousselet, L., *India and its Native Princes: Travels in Central India and in the Presidencies of Bombay and Bengal*, London, 1878.

Ruling Princes and Chiefs of India, Bombay, 1930.

Sardar Patel Correspondence, vols V–IX, Ahmedabad, 1973.

Sen, S.P., *Dictionary of National Biography*, vol. IV, Calcutta, 1974.

Sharma, R., *Vaghela Vamsha Varnanam*, with Notes and Summary by C. Malaviya, np, nd.

Sinha, P.P., *Raja Birbal, Life and Times*, Patna 1980.

Wakefield, E.B., *Past Imperative: My Life in India, 1927–1947*, London, 1966.

Zutshi, B.N., *Rewa and its Ruler*, Bombay, 1923.

SECONDARY SOURCES

Articles in Journals

Agarwal, D.P., 'Dating Indian archaeology by the radio carbon clock', *JMPIP*, no. 8, 1970.

Agnihotri, P.D., 'Language and literature in ancient Madhya Pradesh', *JMPIP*, no. 8, 1970.

Ali, R., 'Saivite mathas in ancient India', *JMPIP*, no. 11, 1980.

———, 'Vritta samsthanaka temples of Central India', *JMPIP*, 1981.

————, 'The Baghelas: an appraisal', *PP*, vol. XII, nos. 1–2, 1984.

Allchin, B., 'Whither South Asian prehistory?', *ME*, vol. XXIII, no. I, 1998.

Azmi, R.J., 'Discovery of Lower Cambrian small shelly fossils and brachiopods from the Lower Vindhyans of Son Valley, central India', *JGSI*, vol. 52, no. 4, Oct. 1998.

Badam, G.L. et al., 'A preliminary study of Pleistocene fossils from the Middle Son valley, Madhya Pradesh', *ME*, vol. XIII, 1989.

K.D. Bajpai, 'Presidential Address', *JMPIP*, no. 10, 1976.

————, 'The Vindhyan region and Banabhatta', *PP*, vols IX–X, 1981–2.

Banerjee, I, 'A preliminary study of the Maikal plateau of Madhya Pradesh', *GRI*, vol. XXII, no. 4, Dec. 1960.

Banurji, C., 'The Kaimur range', *JASB*, vol. XLVI, pt I, no. I, 1877.

Bhattacharya, A.N. and L.N., Verma, 'Rural settlement forms in the Son valley', *IG*, vol. 2, no. 2, 1957.

Blandford, W.T., 'Zoological notes', *JASB*, vol. XXXVI, pt. II, 1867.

Chakrabarti D.K., and N. Lahiri, 'The iron age in India: The beginning and the consequences', *Puratattva*, no. 24, 1993–4.

Chakravarti, R., 'Merchants and other donors at ancient Bandhogarh', *SAS*, vol. 11, 1995.

Clark, J.D., and M.A.J. Williams, 'Prehistoric ecology, resource strategies and culture change in the Son valley, northern Madhya Pradesh, Central India', *ME*, vol. 15, 1990.

Dev, Sukh and M.N. Bose, 'On some conifer remains from Bansa, South Rewa Gondwana basin', *The Palaeobotanist*, abstract 59, vol. 21, no. 1, 1972.

Dube, R.S., 'Land use patterns and population in the Lohandwar village, district Rewa, Madhya Pradesh, India', *IGJ*, vol. XLIV, nos. 3–4, July–Dec. 1969.

Guha, S., 'Lower strata, older races, and aboriginal peoples: racial anthropology and mythical history past and present', *JAS*, vol. 57, no. 2, May 1998.

J.M., 'Notes from Rewa', *IF*, vol. IX, 1883.

Jha, K., 'A study of some mutiny letters of Sohagpur', *IHRSProcs*, vol. XXXIII, pt 2. 1958.

Jha, V.D., and A.K. Singh, 'Fresh light on the prehistory of Sidhi district', *JMPIP*, no. 11, 1980.

Krishnaswami, V.D. and K.V. Soundara Rajan, 'The lithic tool industries of the Singrauli basin', *AI*, no. 7, Jan. 1951.

Lal, B.B., 'Further copper hoards from the Gangetic basin and a review of the problem', *AI*, no. 7, Jan. 1951.

Lal, R.K., 'Place names in the Kalachuri records', *JMPIP*, no. 4, 1962.

Mahajan, M., 'Topographical features of the Kalachuris of Tripuri', *Studies of Indian Place Names*', vol. 17, 1997.

McCombie Young, T., 'A field study of lathyrism', *IJMR*, vol. 15, 1927.

Meister H.W., 'Construction and conception: mandapika shrines of central India', *E&W*. vol. 26, nos. 3–4 (Sept.–Oct.), 1979.

Misra, P.K., 'Deorkothar stupa: new light on early Buddhism', *Marg*, vol. 52, no. I, 2001.

——, 'Discovering the past', np., nd.

Misra, R.N., 'Gupta temple architecture in Madhya Pradesh', *PP*, vol. XIII, nos. 1–2, 1985–7.

Misra, S.D., 'Geographical regions of Vindhya Pradesh', *DG*, vol. IV, no. 2, July 1966.

Pal, J.N., 'Upper palaeolithic cultures of the mid-Son valley', *Puratattva*, no. 12, 1980–1.

Pargiter, F.E., 'Ancient Cedi, Matsya and Karusa', *JASB*, vol. XIV, pt I, no. 3, 1895.

Pearson, G.F., 'Manuscript reports on different parts of India', *CR*, vol. XXXVI, no. LXXII, Jan. 1861.

Richards, J.F., 'The Islamic frontier in the east: expansion into South Asia', *South Asia*, no. 4, 1974.

Roy, A.K., 'Myth, fable and guile: the art of survival in Shahdol', *India International Centre Quarterly*, vol. 19, nos. 1–2, Spring-Summer, 1992.

Seilacher, A., Bose, P., and F. Pflüger, 'Tripoblastic animals more than one billion years ago: trace fossil evidence from India', *Science*, vol. 282, no. 5386, 2 Oct. 1998.

Sharan, R., 'The geographical background of Kalachuri art', *JMPIP*, no. 5, 1967.

Singh, J., 'Rural settlement types and patterns in Baghelkhand, M.P.', *NGJI*, vol. XVII, pt 4, Dec. 1971.

Singh, K., 'The territorial basis of mediaeval town and village settlement in eastern Uttar Pradesh, India,' *Annals of the Association of American Geographers*, vol. 58, no. 2, June 1968.

Singh, Upinder, 'Sanchi, the history of the patronage of an ancient Buddhist establishment', *IESHR*, vol. 33, no. 1, 1996.

Sinha, P., 'Probability sampling in the context of the stone age of Satna district', *ME*, vol. XI, 1987.

Sinha, S., 'State formation and Rajput myth in tribal central India', *MI*, vol. 42, no. I, Jan.–Mar. 1962.

Stadtner, D.M., 'Nand Chand and a central Indian regional style'. *AA*, vol. XLIII, no. I, 1981.

——, 'Kalachuri art at Singhpur', *OA*, vol. XXVIII, no. 3, Autumn 1982.

——, 'The tradition of Krsna pillars in North India', *AA*, vol. XL, 1987.

West, W.D., Letter, 22 Mar. 1962, *Current Science*, no. 4, vol. XXXI, Apr. 1952.

Articles in Anthologies

Ali, Rahman, 'Kalachuri and other contemporary art of central India', K.K. Chakravarty, *Art of the Kalachuris*, Bhopal, 1991.

Bajpai, K.D., 'The Vindhyas, their cultural impact', K.D. Bajpai et al. (eds.), *The Glory that was Bundelkhand*, Mahendra Kumar 'Manav' Felicitation volume, New Delhi, 1993.

Bhattacharya, S., 'Central Indian tribes: a historical dimension', K. Suresh Singh (ed.), *The Tribal Situation in India*, Simla, rpt, 1986.

Blumenschine, R.J., and U.C. Chattopadhyaya, 'A preliminary report on the terminal pleistocene fauna of the middle Son valley', G.R. Sharma, and J.D. Clark, *Palaeoenvironments and Prehistory in the Middle Son Valley*, Allahabad, 1983.

Blumenschine, R.J., S.A. Brandt, and J.D. Clark, 'Excavations and analysis of paleolithic artefacts from Patpara, Madhya Pradesh', Sharma and Clark, *Palaeoenvironments and Prehistory*.

Brandt, S.A., J.D. Clark, J.A. Gutin, and B.B. Misra, 'Rock shelters with paintings on top of the Kaimur escarpment at Ghagharia, and an account of the excavation and analysis of the mesolithic occupation of the Ghagharia I shelter', Sharma and Clark, *Palaeoenvironments and Prehistory*.

Chakravarty, K.K., 'Mother goddesses and the classical style in Kalachuri art', Chakravarty, *Art of the Kalachuris*.

Clark, J.D., and G.R. Sharma, 'A discussion of preliminary results, and an assessment of future potential', Sharma and Clark, *Palaeoenvironments and Prehistory*.

Clark, J.D. and M.A.J. Williams, 'Paleoenvironments and prehistory in north central India; a preliminary report', J. Jacobson (ed.), *Studies in the Archaeology of India and Pakistan*, New Delhi, 1956.

Jacobson, J, 'Static sites and peripatetic people: a note on the archaeology of population mobility in eastern Malwa', L.S. Leshnik, and G.D. Sontheimer, (eds), *Pastoralists and Nomads in South Asia*, Wiesbaden, 1975.

Mirashi, V.V., 'The Pandav dynasty of Mekala', *Indica*, Indian Historical Research Institute, Commemoration volume, Bombay, 1953.

Misra, O.P., 'Sakti cult and the art of Kalachuris', Chakravarty, *Art of the Kalachuris*.

Misra, R.N., 'Saivite ascetics and their origin in Madhya Pradesh', *Puratan: Saivite Tradition in Indian Art*, vol. 6, 1989.

—————— 'Kalachuri art: determinant factors', Chakravarty, *Art of the Kalachuris*.

Misra, V.D., J.N. Pandey, and B.B. Misra, 'Lithic industries of Maihar, Satna, Madhya Pradesh, a preliminary study', V.D. Misra, *Some Aspects of Indian Archaeology*, Allahabad, 1977.

Misra, V.N. and M. Nagar, 'From tribe to caste: an ethno-archaeological approach', D. Nathan, *From Tribe to Caste*, Simla, 1997.

Ramusack, B., 'The civil disobedience movement and the Round Table Conferences: the princes' response', B.R. Nanda, *Essays in Modern Indian History*, New Delhi, 1980.

Ratnagar, S., 'Hunter-gatherer and early agriculturist: archaeological evidence for contact', Nathan, *From Tribe to Caste*.

Ray, H.P., 'Bharhut and Sanchi: nodal points in a commercial interchange', B.M. Pande and B.D. Chattopadhyaya, *Archaeology and History: Essays in Memory of Shri A. Ghose*, New Delhi, 1987.

Satsangi, P.P., 'On the occurrence of dicrodium flora in Sidhi district, M.P.,' B.S. Venkatchalam and H.K. Maheshwari, (eds.), *Indian Gondwana*, Memoir 21, no. 32, Sahni volume.

Sinha, P., 'Economic and subsistence activities at Baghor III (India): a microwear study', J.M. Kenoyer, (ed.), *Old Problems and New Perspectives in the Archaeology of South Asia* (Wisconsin, 1989).

Soundara Rajan, K.V., 'Megaliths and black and red ware', A.K. Narain, and P. Singh, (eds.), *Seminar Papers on the Problem of Megaliths in India*, Varanasi, 1969.

Sussman, C., Blumenschine, R.J., J.D. Clark, and B.B. Misra, 'Preliminary report on excavations at the mesolithic occupational site at the Baghor II locality', Sharma and Clark, *Palaeoenvironments and Prehistoric*.

Tiwari, S.K., 'Riksha, an ancient tribe of Vindhyanchal', P.K. Misra and S.K. Sullerey, (eds.). *Heritage of India, Past and Present: Essays in Honour of Professor R.K. Sharma*, Delhi, 1994.

Varma, R.K., 'Rock art of southern Uttar Pradesh with special reference to Mirzapur', K.K. Chakravarty, (ed.), *Rock Art of India: Painting and Engraving*, 1984.

———, 'Rock art of the Vindhyan region', *Fifteenth Congress of the Indo-Pacific Prehistory Association*, Thailand, Oct. 1995.

Articles by Professor A.H. Nizami, Rewa

A.H. Nizami, 'Baghelkhand during the great rebellion of 1857–58', *Princely Historian*, Commemoration volume of Maharajkumar Dr Raghubir Singh, 1944.

———, 'Baghela dynasty of Rewa: genealogical sources', *Proceedings of the Eighth Indian History Congress*, 1945.

———, 'The Baghela dynasty of Rewa: early history', *Thirteenth all-India Oriental Conference*, Nagpur, 1946.

———, 'The Baghela dynasty of Rewa (Virasimhadeva)', *Bharatiya Vidya*, vol. X, 1946.

———, 'The Baghela dynasty of Rewa', *Proceedings of the Ninth Indian History Congress*, Patna, 1946.

———, 'Muhammadan Kalpi, and its historical background', *Islamic Culture*, vol. XXVII, no. 3, July 1953.

————, 'Biramdeo Baghela, Mukaddam of Gahora', *JIH*, University of Travancore, Aug. 1954.

————, 'Baghelkhand during 1857', *Durbar College Magazine*, 1956–7.

————, 'Baghelkhand's contribution to the 1857 revolt', *Amrit Bazar Patrika*, 22 Aug. 1957.

————, 'The Baghela dynasty of Rewa', *J. Vikram University*, vol. II, no. 2, May 1958.

————, 'A missing link in the history of Madhya Pradesh: Malikzada dynasty of Kalpi (Bundelkhand)', *JMPIP*, no. I, 1959.

————, 'Baghelkhand during the great rebellion of 1857', *Madhya Pradesh Chronicle*, Jan. 1971.

————, 'Chanderi under the Delhi Sultans and the Parihar rulers of Unchada', *JMPIP*, no. 11, 1980.

————, 'Early British relations with Bundelkhand, Baghelkhand, 1802–1818', *JMPIP*, 1980–1.

————, 'Elephant-catching expedition of Sultan Mahmud Shah Khilji to Bandhogarh and Sarguja, 1440–1441', *JMPIP*, vol. XII, 198?

————, 'Survey of art and archaeology in the Vindhyan Region', *Vindhyika Souvenir*, Jabalpur, 1994.

————, 'Historiography in Rewa–Vindhya Pradesh: retrospect and prospect', Seminar paper, Shahdol, Feb. 1996.

————, 'Ancient Baghelkhand', unpublished article.

————, 'Rewa, past and present', *M.P. Medical conference souvenir*, Rewa, n.d.

———— 'Nine gems of the court of Maharaja Bhavasimha of Rewa', *J. Ganganath Jha Oriental Research Institute*, Allahabad, vol. VIII, no. 4, nd.

Books

Agrawal, V.S., *Studies in Indian Art*, Varanasi, 1965.

————, *Evolution of the Hindu Temple and Other Essays*, Varanasi, 1965.

Ahmad, N., *The Stone Age Cultures of the Upper Son Valley (Madhya Pradesh)*, New Delhi, 1984.

Ali, Rahman, *Art and Architecture of the Kalachuris*, Delhi, 1980.

Allchin, B., and F.R., *The Rise of Civilisation in India and Pakistan*, New Delhi, 1983.

————, *Origins of a Civilisation: The Prehistory and Early Archaeology of South Asia*, New Delhi, 1993.

Allchin, F.R., *The Archaeology of Early Historic South Asia: The Emergence of Cities and States*, Cambridge, 1995.

Ashton, S.R,, *British Policy towards the Indian States, 1905–1939*, London, nd.

A Comprehensive Survey of Prehistoric and Tribal Arts in Madhya Pradesh, India: A Preliminary Report, Faculty of Letters, Osaka University, 1981.

Bajpai, K.D., *Indian Numismatic Studies*, New Delhi, 1976.

————, *Cultural History of India*, vol. I, *Madhya Pradesh*, Delhi, 1985.

————, and S.K. Pandey, *Malhar, 1975–78*, University of Sagar, 1978.

Ball, V., *A Manual of the Geology of India*, pt III, *Economic Geology*, Calcutta, 1881.

Banerji, R.D., *The Age of the Imperial Guptas*, Varanasi, 1993.

Bhattacharya, P.K., *Historical Geography of Madhya Pradesh from Early Records*, Delhi, 1977.

Bose, N.S., *The History of the Candellas of Jejakabhukti*, Calcutta, 1956.

Brown, P,, *Indian Architecture (Buddhist and Hindu Periods)*, vol. I, Bombay, 1971.

Buch, M.N., *The Forests of Madhya Pradesh*, Bhopal, 1996.

Burn, R. (ed.), *Cambridge History of India*, vol. IV, *The Mughal Period*, New Delhi, 1963.

Chakrabarti, D.K., *The Early Use of Iron in India*, New Delhi, 1992.

————, *India: an Archaeological History: Palaeolithic Beginnings to Early Historic Foundations*, New Delhi, 1999.

Chattopadhyaya, B.D., *The Making of Early Mediaeval India*, New Delhi, 1997.

Chattopadhyaya, S., *Early History of North India*, Calcutta, 1976.

Chaudhuri, S.B., *Civil Rebellion in the Indian Mutinies, 1857–1859*, Calcutta, 1957.

Copland, I., *The Princes of India in the Endgame of Empire, 1919–1947*, Cambridge, 1997.

Crooke, W., *The Tribes and Castes of the North-Western Provinces and Oudh*, Calcutta, 1896.

Desai, A.H., *Prehistory and Protohistory of Eastern India*, Calcutta, 1960.

Devahuti, D., *Harsha: A Political Study*, Oxford, 1970.

Dikshit, R.K., *The Candellas of Jejakabhukti*, Delhi, 1977.

Dube, R.S., *Population of Rewa Plateau: A Geographical Analysis*, Kanpur, 1979.

Edwardes, M., *The Last Years of British India*, London, 1967.

Elwin, V., *The Baiga*, London 1939.

————, *Folk Tales of Mahakoshal*, Oxford, 1944.

————, *Myths of Middle India*, n.p., n.d.

———— , and S. Hiwale, *Folk-Songs of the Maikal Hills*, Madras, 1944.

Foote, R.B., *The Foote Collection of Indian Prehistoric and Protohistoric Antiquities: Notes on their Ages and Distribution*, Madras, 1916.

Gangulee, N., *The Making of Federal India*, London, 1936.

Ghosh, A., *Remains of the Bharhut Stupa in the Indian Museum*, Calcutta, 1978.

————, *An Encyclopaedia of Indian Archaeology*, vol. I, *Subjects*, Delhi, 1989.

Ghose, B., *British Policy Towards the Pathans and Pindaris in Central India, 1805–1818*, Calcutta, 1966.

Gordon, D.H., *The Pre-Historic Background of Indian Culture*, Bombay, 1960.

Griffiths, W.G., *The Kol Tribes of Central India*, Royal Asiatic Society of Bengal Monograph Series, vol. II, Calcutta, 1946.

Gurung, K.K. and R. Singh, *Mammals of the Indian Sub-Continent, and Where to Watch Them*, Oxford, 1996.

Halim, A., *History of the Lodhi Sultans of Agra and Delhi*, Delhi, 1974.

Handa, R.L., *History of Freedom Struggle in Indian Princely States*, Delhi, 1968.

Havell, E.B., *The History of Aryan Rule in India, from the Earliest Times to the Death of Akbar*, London, n. d.

Hilton, R., *The Indian Mutiny: A Centenary History*, London, 1957.

Huntington, S., *The Art of Ancient India, Buddhist, Hindu, Jain*, New York, 1999.

Indian Wildlife, Singapore, 1963.

Jayakar, P., *The Earth Mother*, Calcutta, 1989.

Jha, D.N., *The Revenue System in Post-Maurya and Gupta Times*, Calcutta, 1967.

Kant, S., *Political and Cultural History of Mid-North India*, New Delhi, 1987.

Karve, I,. *Kinship Organisation in India*, Poona, 1953.

Khan, A.A., *The Glories of Bandhogarh*, n. d.

Khan, Shamsun-ud Daula Shah Nawaz, *Maathir-ul Umara*, vol. I, New Delhi, 1987.

Khare, M.D., *Painted Rock Shelters*, Bhopal, 1981.

Kosambi, D.D., *The Culture and Civilisation of Ancient India*, London, 1965.

Kumar, V., *India under Lord Hardinge*, New Delhi, 1978.

Lahiri, N., *The Archaeology of Indian Trade Routes up to 200 B.C.: Resource Use, Resource Access and Lines of Communication*, Delhi, 1992.

Law, B.C., *Indological Studies*, pt, I, Calcutta, 1950.

Lorenzen, D.N., *The Kapalikas and Kalamukhas: Two Lost Saivite Sects*, Delhi, 1991.

Luniya, B.N., *Life and Culture in Mediaeval India*, Indore, 1978.

Majumdar, B.C., *The Aborigines of the Highlands of Central India*, Calcutta, 1927.

Majumdar, R.C., *History and Culture of the Indian People*, vol. V, *The Struggle for Empire*, Bombay, 1979.

———, *History and Culture of the Indian People*, vol. VII, *The Mughal Empire*, Bombay, 1974.

———, *History and Culture of the Indian People*,vol. X. pt II, *British Paramountcy and Indian Renaissance*, Bombay, 1981.

———, *The Sepoy Mutiny and the Revolt of 1857*, Calcutta, 1957.

Mankekar, D.R., *Accession to Extinction: the Story of the Indian Princes*, Delhi, 1974.

McCrindle, J.W., *Ancient India as Described by Ptolemy*, Faridabad, rpt, n. d.

Metcalfe, C.T., *The Rajpoot Tribes*, vol. I, New Delhi, rpt, 1982.

Misra, B., *Polity in the Agni Purana*, Calcutta, 1965.

Misra, D.K., *Son ka pani ka rang*, Bhopal, 1983.

Misra, O.P., *Mother Goddess in Central India*, Delhi, 1985.

Misra, R.N., *Sculptures of Dahala and Dakshin Kosala and their Background*, Delhi, 1987.

Misra, S.N., *Gupta Art and Architecture, with Special Reference to Madhya Pradesh*, Delhi, 1992.

Mitra, D., *Buddhist Monuments*, Calcutta, 1971.

Mittal, A.C., *An Early History of Orissa*, Varanasi, 1962.

Moore, R.J., *The Crisis of Indian Unity*, Delhi, 1974.

Mukherjee, R., *A History of Indian Civilisation*, vol. I, *Ancient and Classical Traditions*, Bombay, 1958.

Nandi, R.N., *Religious Institutions and Cults in the Deccan, c. 600 AD–1000 AD*, Delhi, 1973.

Neumayer, E., *Prehistoric Indian Rock Paintings*, Delhi, 1983.

Oppert, G., *The Original Inhabitants of Bharatvarsa, or India*, Delhi, rpt, 1971.

Pal, J.N., *Archaeology of South Uttar Pradesh: Ceramic Industries of the Northern Vindhyas*, Allahabad, 1986.

Parmar, S., *Folklore of Madhya Pradesh*, New Delhi, 1992.

Pathak, H., *Cultural History of the Gupta Period*, Delhi, 1978.

Pathak, V.S., *Saiva Cults in Northern India*, Varanasi, 1960.

Phadnis, U., *Towards the Integration of the Indian States, 1919–1947*, New Delhi, 1968.

Prinsep, H.T., *History of the Political and Military Transactions in India. During the Administration of the Marquess of Hastings, 1813–1823*, vol. I, London, 1825.

Punja, S., *Divine Ecstasy: The Story of Khajuraho*, New Delhi, 1992.

Qureshi, I.H., *Akbar, the Architect of the Mughal Empire*, Delhi, 1987.

Raizada, A., *Tribal Development in Madhya Pradesh: A Planning Perspective*, Delhi, 1984.

M.S. Randhawa et al., *Farmers of India*, vol. IV, *Madhya Pradesh, Rajasthan, Gujarat, Maharashtra*, New Delhi, 1968.

Rashid, A., *Society and Culture in Mediaeval India*, Calcutta, 1969.

Ray, H.C., *The Dynastic History of Northern India (Early Mediaeval Period)*, vol. I, Calcutta, 1931.

Raychaudhuri, H., *Political History of Ancient India*, Delhi, 1966.

Roy, A.K., et al. (eds), *Planning the Environment: Based on Research Conducted in Shahdol District*, Gandhigram, 1982.

Saletore, B.A., *The Wild Tribes in Indian History*, Lahore, 1935.

Sankalia, H.D., *The Ramayana in Historical Perspective*, New Delhi, 1982.

Sankalia, K., *Tiger: The Story of the Indian Tiger*, London, 1978.

Sharma, G.D. and J.D. Clark, (eds.), *Palaeoenvironments and Prehistory in the Middle Son Valley*, Allahabad, 1983.

Sharma G.R. and B.B. Misra, *Archaeology of the Vindhyas and the Ganga: Excavations at Chopani–Mando (Belan Valley), 1977–79*, Varanasi, 1980.

Sharma, R.C., *Bharhut Sculptures*, New Delhi, 1994.

Sharma, R.K., *The Kalachuris and their Times*, Delhi, 1980.

Shrimali, K.M., *Agrarian Structure in Central India and the Northern Deccan (c.A.D. 300–500): A Study of Vakataka Inscriptions*, Delhi, 1987.

Shukla, H.L., *Language, Ethnicity and History: Dimensions in Anthropological Linguistics*, Delhi, 1985.

———, *Tribal History: A New Interpretation*, Delhi, 1988.

Siddhantashree, *Saivism Through the Ages*, New Delhi, 1975.

Singh, R.L., *A Regional Geography*, Varanasi, 1971.

Soundara Rajan, K.V., *Glimpses of Indian Culture–Architecture, Art and Religion*, New Delhi, 1981.

Srivastava, V.K., *Habitat and Economy in the Upper Son Basin*, Gorakhpur, 1975.

Stokes, E., *The Peasant Armed: The Indian Revolt of 1857* (ed. C. Bayly), Oxford, 1986.

Subbarao, B., *The Personality of India: Pre- and Proto-historic Foundations of India and Pakistan*, Baroda, 1958.

Thakur, U., *Mints and Mining in India*, Varanasi, 1972.

Thapar, R., *A History of India*, vol. I, Penguin, 1966.

The Harsa-Carita of Bana, transl. E.B. Cowell, and F.W. Thomas, Delhi, 1961.

Varadachari, V., *A History of Samskrta Literature*, Allahabad, 1952.

Varma, R.K., *Rewa Through the Ages*, Allahabad, 1991.

Walia, J.M., *Mughal Empire in India*, New Delhi, nd.

Williams, J.G., *The Art of Gupta India: Empire and Province*, New Delhi, 1983.

PHD THESES

Awadesh Pratap Singh University, Rewa

Baghel, B.S., 'Rewa ke Baghel rajya ka parrashtra sambandh: ek adhayan (1360–1359)', 1991.

Baghel, R.S., 'Ethno-ecological studies on tribals, with special reference to the Gond ethnic system', 1992.

Bhargava, A., 'The Relations of British paramount power with Rewa from 1858–1947', 1981.

Chacko, S.T., 'A cultural study of Bharhut sculptures', 1985.

Chauhan J.S., 'Spatial pattern of literacy amongst tribes in the Baghelkhand plateau region', 1990.

George, K.S., 'Impact of industrialization on the social conditions of Singrauli, the energy capital of India', 1992.

Gupta, V.P., 'Tribal economy in Baghelkhand', 1974.

Lal, J., 'Baghelkhand: a study in settlement geography', 1982.

Misra, O.P., 'Comparative study of floristic components of Bundelkhand and Baghelkhand regions', 1982.

Misra, S.C., 'Ethnobiology of tribals in Sidhi district', 1986.

Siddiqui, A., 'An assessment of the working of the former Vindhya Pradesh legislative assembly', 1978.

Rani Ahilyabai Holkar University, Indore

Agarwal, D.C., 'Agricultural efficiency in Vindhya Pradesh: a study of the impact of three five-year plans on agricultural industry', 1968.

Rani Durgawati University, Jabalpur

Dubey, A.K., 'A study of the movement for the establishment of a democratic political system in the princely states of Vindhya Pradesh', 1991.

Sir Hari Singh Gour University, Sagar

Dwivedi, S., 'Evaluation of land resource and land use in the Rewa plateau, M.P.', 1988.

Jain, S.K., 'Environment and nutritional deficiency diseases of Baghelkhand plateau', 1992.

Mishra, V., 'Economic development of forest resources of Baghelkhand region', 1966.

Sharma, S.K, 'Changing pattern of resources in the Baghelkhand plateau', 1992.

Tiwari, P.D., 'Agriculture and nutritional level in Rewa plateau', 1982.

Index

ॐ